High-Technology Crime

High-Technology Crime

Investigating Cases
Involving Computers

Kenneth S. Rosenblatt

KSK Publications
San Jose

This book includes the names of numerous products, to the benefit of the makers of those products. Rather than cluttering each page with trademark symbols, we simply name the products in an editorial fashion, without intent to infringe any trademarks involved.

KSK Publications, P.O. Box 934, San Jose, California 95108–0934.
© 1995 by Kenneth Rosenblatt. All rights reserved.
Printed in the United States of America.

Second Printing, October 1996. Minor changes have been made to correct errors and reflect recent developments.

ISBN: 0–9648171–0–1

Library of Congress Catalog Card Number: 95-78740.

Appendix C-1 was previously published in a slightly different form in *The Computer Lawyer* (Volume 8, No. 1, January 1991) (Prentice Hall Law & Business).

To Katy and Sarah, who waited for me

Contents

Using This Book

Chapter 1.   Introduction

Chapter 2.   Principles of High-Technology Crime
                Investigation

Chapter 3.   Investigating Theft of Components

Chapter 4.   Investigating Computer Intrusion

Chapter 5.   Investigating Theft of Information

Chapter 7.   Computers and the Fourth Amendment

Chapter 8.   Federal Privacy Laws

Chapter 9.   Drafting Search Warrants in Cases Involving Computers

Appendix A.   Checklists

Using This Book

The appendices

Readers unfamiliar with computers should begin by reading Appendix D, which offers an introduction to computer technology. Investigators regularly assigned to handle high-technology crime cases should also read Appendix D to become familiar with terms used within the high-technology industry.

This book recognizes that investigators do not have time to review dozens of pages of material in the middle of an investigation. Thus, Appendix A includes checklists of questions to ask and things to do during a high-technology crime investigation.

Appendix B contains sample language which investigators and prosecutors may find useful in drafting search warrants. Chapters 4 and 5 contain additional information about drafting search warrants in computer intrusion and information theft cases, respectively.

Finally, Appendix C includes an article discussing how to protect trade secrets from disclosure during a criminal prosecution, along with a sample protective order to be used for that purpose.

The floppy disk

The disk included with this book contains the following materials:

- A table of contents (*htcdisk.toc*) listing the files on the disk, and describing their contents.

- A duplicate copy of Appendix A, so that you can print checklists to take with you on interviews or when serving search warrants.

- The only copy of Appendix B, consisting of form and sample affidavits and warrants. The forms are fill-in-the-blanks documents which you can use to draft your own warrant for a particular type of investigation. Form warrants have the letters FRM in the file name. Sample warrants (SMP) are warrants which were used, with minor modifications, in actual investigations.

- The sample protective order included in Appendix C.

- Depending upon when you bought this book, your disk may contain a README file. The README file contains errata, along with new information which the author discovered after it was too late to change the text. Please read any README file immediately.

The information on the floppy disk is stored in an ASCII format and should be readable by all computers. Contact the publisher if you are unable to use the disk.

Do not blindly insert the language on the disk into a search warrant, affidavit, or protective order. Customize the information on the disk for your own situation, and be sure that the law in your jurisdiction does not require a different approach.

Restrictions on copying and distributing the information on the floppy disk

A book about investigating high-technology crime would be incomplete without copyright protection. However, copyright law runs a poor second to good faith and reasonableness in ensuring that information stays protected. Therefore, consider the following statement to be both a "legal notice" and "plea":

> You are granted a license to use the floppy disk as follows: you may print the checklists from the floppy disk for your own use, for the use of other persons employed by your organization, or, *for a single investigation*, for the use of others involved in that investigation to use in assisting you with that investigation. You are encouraged to use the information on the floppy disk to prepare your own search warrants. You may keep a copy of the contents of the disk on both your office and home computers, *and* on all computers used by your organization.
>
> However, except as provided above, you are not authorized to copy or distribute the contents of the disk. This means that you should not post it on the Internet, send it to your friends, copy it for your

students, etc.—let them buy their own copy of this book, which explains how to use this information.

Use this book cautiously

High-technology crime investigation is comparatively new, and there are no clear legal signposts. Investigators working in this area are unusually vulnerable to legal assault, including lawsuits based on alleged damage to equipment and data, invasion of privacy, and violation of civil rights. Readers, particularly those working for public agencies, should enter this area only after consulting with a private attorney or prosecutor.

The author is not your lawyer, and is not providing you with legal advice. This book seeks to illuminate certain legally uncertain areas to help you obtain advice from *your* lawyer.

Similarly, the author is not your resident computer expert. There is always a risk that a procedure recommended in this book may fail, resulting in damage to data, or conceivably, hardware. One law enforcement expert put it best when he urged the author to speak only in vague generalities: "Bill Gates is making changes faster than we are."

In other words, the applicable law and technology are so complex and unpredictable, and change so rapidly, that it is impossible to guarantee the advice provided here. Therefore, the publisher and the author disclaim any liability from damages, direct or indirect, attributable to the suggestions provided within this book.

Readers who object to this approach may obtain a prompt refund (including reimbursement of the costs of shipping at book rate) by returning this book within 30 days after receiving it.

This book is not the only true way

We do not live in an ideal world. Frequently, time or monetary constraints will make it impossible to follow the suggestions contained in this book. This does not mean that you should avoid investigating cases involving computers, or that your failure to follow a particular suggestion means that you have negligently lost evidence, failed to protect a defendant's rights, or otherwise failed to perform your job properly. The suggestions in this book are not rigid rules—they are only suggestions.

Similarly, the author urges courts to refrain from using this book to impose a standard of conduct on public and private investigators and lawyers. To do so would presume, incorrectly, that the discipline of high-technology crime investigation is sufficiently mature that its practitioners can agree on a particular standard of conduct. This book offers only one view, and a conservative one at that, of how to investigate high-technology crime—we are a long way from creating a specialty with established standards.

Errors and omissions

By putting pen (or printer) to paper, you can simultaneously influence the next edition of this book and save the author from embarrassment. As discussed above, law and technology change rapidly. Even in the unlikely event that the author has made no errors and omissions, developments since publication may invalidate some of the suggestions made here.

Perhaps you have developed a better procedure, or noticed a flaw in a procedure recommended in this edition. You may have discovered unpublished or published court decisions that change the legal landscape. Your comments concerning errors and omissions will be important to improving this book, and will be greatly appreciated.

Finally, this book is not the last word on this subject, but merely an attempt to provide organization and procedures to a new discipline. You are encouraged to suggest additional topics you would like to see included in future editions.

Acknowledgments

The community of high-technology crime investigators consists of a small and close-knit group of dedicated professionals. Members of that fraternity have contributed many of the facts, insights, and techniques presented in this book. Whether by reviewing portions of the manuscript, answering countless telephone calls, or simply lecturing at conferences where I sat in the audience, my colleagues have provided invaluable assistance.

Jerry P. Coleman, Assistant District Attorney and Head Attorney of the Special Prosecutions Unit of the San Francisco District Attorney's Office, has been especially generous with his time and expertise. I could not have written this book without him.

Donald G. Ingraham, Assistant District Attorney, High-Tech Crime Team, Alameda County District Attorney's Office, has been particularly helpful in developing and clarifying my analysis of various legal issues. His encouragement and acumen have been invaluable.

Don Greenwood, Manager, Security—Worldwide Operations, Sun Microsystems, Inc., has helped me better appreciate the "corporate" side of high-technology crime investigation.

Within my own agency, Investigator John C. Smith and Deputy District Attorneys Mark B. Hames and Michael T. Adams reviewed portions of the manuscript. I am particularly grateful to Deputy District Attorney Mike R. Galli, who contributed considerable expertise and time to this project.

I am also greatly indebted to the other professionals who reviewed portions of the manuscript or otherwise contributed to this book, including Richard Bernes; Kenneth C. Citarella, Deputy Chief, Economic Crimes Bureau, Westchester County District Attorney's Office; Sgt. Curt Codey, Fremont Police Department; William J. Cook, a partner in the law firm of Willian, Brinks, Hofer, Gilson & Lione; Fred B. Cotton, Manager—Training Services, SEARCH, Inc.; Dorothy A. Darrow, Senior Software Engineer, Teknekron Software

Systems; Kevin L. Fairchild, President and Director of Investigations, Cyte-M; Sgt. Patrick McGuire, San Jose Police Department; Sgt. Jim McMahon, San Jose Police Department; Joseph M. Pujals, CISSP; Jeremy Rosenblatt, Director, Complex Systems Group, ViewStar Corporation; Larry St. Regis, Operations Manager, Sunnyvale Department of Public Safety; Howard A. Schmidt, Vice-President, International Association of Computer Investigative Specialists; Fred Smith, Esq.; and William R. Spernow, Computer Crime Specialist, National White Collar Crime Center.

Of course, in this increasingly bureaucratic world, it is necessary to state that none of the organizations employing these professionals has reviewed the manuscript or endorsed its contents.

Along those lines, it also bears mentioning that I am solely responsible for any errors or omissions in the book, particularly where I strayed from the counsel of my peers.

Finally, I thank Barbara Kendrick, Janet Mowery, and Jennifer Thuillier (cover design) for helping me transform a collection of words into a book.

1

Introduction

1.00 Introduction

Each year, another several million people discover computer technology. Unfortunately, some of them are criminals. Computer intruders leave only electronic fingerprints. Thieves steal industrial secrets without leaving their homes.

The problem is greater than a few exotic crimes. As we approach the 21st century, investigators must obtain and evaluate evidence stored within computers in a wide variety of cases.

Narcotics and prostitution rings use computers to store records. Conspirators communicate via electronic mail. Evidence of fraud often exists only as data stored within computers. As new technology transforms the information superhighway from promise to reality, computer technology will become even more pervasive than it is today.

The purpose of this book is to help you investigate crimes involving computer technology. Besides teaching you how to investigate various computer-related crimes, this book will assist you in obtaining evidence stored within computers, whether the case involves a homicide or an insurance fraud.

1.01 High-technology crime defined

This book uses the term *high-technology crime* to identify two types of crime associated with high technology. First, the term includes new crimes created by society's widespread use of computers. For example, the crime of breaking and entering into computers flourished after businesses began connecting computers to sophisticated telecommunications networks.

High-technology crime also includes traditional crimes so transformed by computer technology that investigators handling such cases must be familiar with computers and the high-technology industry. For example, the traditional crime of inventory theft has been transformed by the item most commonly stolen in Silicon Valley and other high-technology manufacturing areas: the integrated circuit, or *chip*.

Chips are the size of your thumbnail, worth as much as $500, and are fungible (one looks much like the other, like pennies). Techniques for investigating pilfering do not work for this high-technology crime: you can understand why by imagining a workplace where staplers and paper clips are worth $500 each. Investigators must have a working knowledge of computers *and* understand the market for computer components to investigate component theft.

1.02   Why worry about high-technology crime?

High-technology crime is responsible for huge losses to industry, and victims are seeking law enforcement assistance as those losses increase. As of this writing, robberies of chips from high-technology companies in Silicon Valley are occurring *approximately every three weeks*, and losses from robberies and burglaries now exceed $30 million each year. During one stretch, robbers struck 30 companies in the Silicon Valley in three months.[1]

There are many other vulnerable high-technology manufacturing regions in the United States, including areas of northern and southern California, Texas, Massachusetts, Colorado, Arizona, Oregon, and New Mexico.

Intrusion into computer systems also continues to be a serious problem, as Fortune 500 companies spend large sums each year chasing intruders out of their computer systems. Aside from damage caused by vandals, disgruntled ex-employees, and extortionists, hundreds of companies of all sizes fall victim to *PBX attacks*.

---

1.   "High-Tech Heists Get Hot," *San Jose Mercury News*, April 14, 1995.

Groups of intruders penetrate and use corporate telephone systems (called PBXs) to make long-distance telephone calls. The victim's first hint of trouble is when its monthly phone bill is six inches high and arrives in a box. Losses from group attacks often top $50,000, and telephone companies insist upon payment in full from their unlucky customers. Industry estimates place annual losses from PBX attacks *alone* at over $500 million.

Finally, every business is a potential victim of information theft, from industrial secrets to customer lists. According to a 1988 study, *38%* of 150 high-technology companies surveyed nationally reported that they had been victims of information theft within the previous five years.[2]

1.10   Investigating high-technology crime

Chapter 2 discusses basic principles common to investigating high-technology crime. Chapters 3–5 examine the most common high-technology crimes:

- theft of components;

- computer intrusion; and

- theft of information.

These three chapters provide readers, *including those with no technical background or competence*, with the necessary technical information to investigate those crimes, along with a procedure for doing so. Appendix A includes checklists for those investigations.

1.20   Obtaining evidence stored within computers

The second part of this book examines a growing challenge facing every law enforcement agency in the United States: safely and legally obtaining evidence stored within computers.

---

2. Lois Mock and Dennis Rosenblum, *A Study of Trade Secret Theft in High Technology Industries*, prepared for the National Institute of Justice (Washington, D.C.: Department of Justice, 1988).

As noted at the beginning of this chapter, investigators must obtain and evaluate evidence stored in computers in a wide variety of cases, including narcotics, fraud, and vice. Unfortunately, computers and data are vulnerable to poor handling and sabotage.

There are many accounts of investigators breaking computers while executing search warrants. Taxpayers pay for such mistakes because police departments are liable for negligent destruction of computers seized during a search warrant.[3] With untrained investigators seizing computers worth thousands of dollars, and containing data worth much more, the need for training is clear.

Equally important is ensuring that investigators do not overlook valuable evidence stored within the computer. Chapter 6 teaches both novices and "power users" techniques used by computer experts in locating, searching, seizing, and analyzing computer evidence.

However, obtaining evidence from a computer without damaging equipment or losing data is just one part of the problem. There are also substantial legal hurdles to searching and seizing computer evidence.

Few courts have applied the Fourth Amendment to searches for computer evidence, which means that the law in this area remains unclear. Drafting search warrants to seize computer evidence is difficult because traditional concepts of search and seizure law do not fit easily with computer technology.

For example, many police departments assume that adding the word "computers" to their standard search warrant allows them to seize every computer, modem, and printer in sight, and to keep them indefinitely. That view is incorrect, and criminal defense lawyers are beginning to notice the gap between the law and current law enforcement practice.

The problem is not confined to the Fourth Amendment. Congress has confused matters by adding complex new laws intended to protect privacy in the Information Age. Most investigators and lawyers are unaware of those laws.

For example, a federal court recently ordered the United States Secret Service to pay $50,000 in damages, $195,000 in attorneys' fees, and $57,000 in costs for violating the Privacy Protection Act

---

3. *See* Chapter 6, note 1.

(42 U.S.C. 2000aa) when it seized computers used to publish a computer game newsletter. The Secret Service agent had not known about this federal law, which prohibits the use of search warrants to seize certain information from persons intending to publish that information to the public.

Some of those federal laws also apply to private parties. The Department of Justice has warned computer owners that the Electronic Communications Privacy Act (ECPA) (18 U.S.C. 2510 *et seq.*) *may* prohibit them from monitoring their own computers to capture commands sent by an intruder. The Department worries that courts may consider such monitoring to be an illegal "interception" of a protected electronic communication. Another part of the ECPA restricts seizures of E-mail (electronic mail).

These federal laws are more than complex—they are hopelessly unclear. For example, courts currently disagree on whether a violation of the ECPA will result in suppression of the evidence, or "merely" a civil suit against the unfortunate law enforcement official or private party. There is even one scenario in which the ECPA and the Privacy Protection Act are in direct conflict. To make it more interesting, Congress keeps revising the ECPA (most recently in 1994).

As more investigators begin searching computers, more criminal defendants will file motions to suppress evidence, and more businesses and individuals will file lawsuits seeking damages for allegedly illegal searches. Chapters 7–9 discuss the legal obstacles to searching and seizing computer evidence and suggest how readers can draft search warrants to surmount those obstacles.

1.30   This book is written for a wide audience

This book is written for:

- state and federal law enforcement investigators;

- corporate security investigators, including private investigators hired by victims; and

- lawyers involved in high-technology crime cases.

1.31 Law enforcement investigators

As with any new crime, law enforcement investigators must understand who commits the crime, how they commit it, and how officers can catch them. While this book covers that territory, it also tries to do more. Investigation of component theft, computer intrusion, and, in many cases, information theft, is like entering a new world. It is similar to transferring from narcotics to white-collar crime investigations—the environment changes.

Officers investigating high-technology crime need to understand the environment of the high-technology company and the new group of people they will encounter during their investigation: corporate lawyers, security managers, and the engineers whose ideas produce the money for everyone else. This book tries to give you a feeling for that new environment and suggests some strategies for adjusting your normal operating procedures accordingly.

Investigators assigned to the high-technology crime beat should read Appendix D, which describes terms used within the high-technology industry and identifies some of the major players in that industry.

1.32 Corporate security investigators

Unlike traditional police procedure manuals, this book is also aimed directly at corporate investigators.[4] They are usually the first investigators at the scene of a high-technology crime, and frequently conduct full-scale investigations before calling police. Most cases (probably well over 90%) are investigated entirely "in-house" and are never reported to law enforcement—corporations concerned about bad publicity tend to suffer their losses in silence.

This book will help you investigate the three most common high-technology crimes. In addition, it discusses federal privacy laws that

---

4. For purposes of this book, the term "corporate investigator" includes corporate security employees, private security services (e.g., Pinkerton), private investigation firms (e.g., Kroll and Associates), security divisions of large accounting firms (e.g., Deloitte & Touche), solo private investigators, and insurance company investigators.

restrict searches by corporate investigators for computer evidence. This book also provides guidelines for corporate investigators and law enforcement agencies concerning which high-technology crimes should be reported to, and accepted by, law enforcement agencies for further investigation.

Finally, on those occasions when your employer or client reports a crime to police, you can use this book as a checklist for gathering information which police or federal agents will request as part of their investigation.

1.33 Lawyers

Lawyers have an unusually large role to play in high-technology crime cases. First, there are more lawyers involved in these cases than in typical criminal cases. In addition to lawyers prosecuting and defending the accused, corporate victims of high-technology crime are usually represented by their own lawyers. Those lawyers may be employees of the corporation or members of outside law firms regularly retained by the corporation to handle its legal work. This book refers to all such lawyers as *corporate counsel*.

Second, lawyers often investigate high-technology crimes, particularly thefts of information. Corporate counsel frequently direct in-house investigations. Prosecutors often help investigators grapple with legal issues posed by the intersection of the Fourth Amendment and computer technology. (Prosecuting agencies frequently use their own attorneys and investigators to handle these cases). Defense lawyers must attempt to reconstruct the alleged high-technology crime.

Finally, lawyers need to understand how to investigate these cases because the meaning of the evidence, and the way in which it was gathered, are often pivotal issues at trial.

For example, identifying a computer intruder requires analysis of computer-generated evidence, such as computer logs, traps and traces, and pen registers. Tracing stolen components from the victim to the thief requires lawyers to interpret identification codes and computerized inventory records.

You need to understand how evidence in high-technology crime cases is created, and how to interpret it. In addition, you need to understand how that evidence was gathered. An investigator's mistake during the search of a computer may affect not only the legality of the search, but also the type and quality of the evidence obtained.

1.40   What this book does not cover

1.41   Embezzlement via computer

This book does not cover the classic "computer crime"—the electronic diversion of funds from normal accounting channels to the criminal's pocket. These are the crimes which often make headlines, primarily because thieves can steal millions of dollars in just a few minutes.

Such electronic "cooking of the books" is similar to the old-fashioned crime of embezzlement, although more efficient and harder to detect. However, this crime, like component theft, is far removed from its traditional counterpart because it requires specialized knowledge of computer technology to investigate. It has spawned a group of specialists called "electronic data processing auditors," also known as "EDP auditors."

This book does not cover computer embezzlement cases because EDP auditors usually conduct such investigations instead of law enforcement and corporate security officials. Even where the victim is willing to overcome its embarrassment and request prosecution, the investigation conducted by law enforcement is usually brief because these cases are often open and shut. Once auditors have followed the trail of money to the suspect, prosecutors need only show large amounts of money flowing from the company to the suspect without authorization. Demonstrating the computer technology and record-keeping which point to the suspect is anticlimactic once the jury is convinced that the suspect received the money without permission.[5]

---

5. This subject is discussed in detail in Parker, Donn, et al., *Computer Crime: Criminal Justice Resource Manual* (Washington, D.C.: Department of Justice, 1989).

1.42   Viruses

This book also does not cover high-technology crimes which are usually impossible to solve. For example, the popular press has dramatized the "computer virus." Viruses are computer programs which, when run by an unwitting user, replicate themselves onto the victim's computer. Most viruses include instructions which cause the victim's computer to operate in an unexpected manner. Many viruses damage or destroy data; others display funny or obscene messages. Some viruses are both amusing and destructive.

Although viruses are a serious problem, they are also untraceable. There is, as yet, no way to "fingerprint" a virus to determine its creator. You cannot prove that a particular person inserted that virus into the victim's computer, or onto a floppy disk that an unwitting employee used when operating that computer. (Although a real fingerprint on the floppy disk might help your case, it only proves that the suspect touched the disk.)

Unless you find a copy of the virus at the defendant's office or residence, you have no case. In the event that you identify a suspect, use Chapters 6–9 as a guide to obtaining a search warrant and locating a copy of the virus.

1.43   Software piracy

Software piracy refers to the illegal copying of software, both by individuals for their own use and by counterfeiters for resale. Counterfeiters generally seek to pass off their copies as originals by duplicating the packaging of the victim's product. Law enforcement investigators usually do not investigate individual acts of copying for personal use. Such small-scale copying is rarely reported to police.

Counterfeiting software is the latest version of a very old crime. Thieves have been bootlegging records, cassette tapes, and videotapes for years, and other material (e.g., Rembrandt's paintings) for centuries. Although this form of software piracy can cause huge losses to victims, its investigation is straightforward (although often exhausting).

The investigation begins when victims notice bootlegged copies of their products circulating in the marketplace. They then attempt to trace the goods back to their source. Victims ultimately request an impound order from a federal judge or ask law enforcement officers to obtain a search warrant to seize the allegedly bootlegged product.

Lawyers or officers will execute the appropriate order and seize bootlegged software.[6] The only issues are whether: (1) the seized software is a copy of the original; and (2) the suspect had authorization to make or possess copies of that software. The investigation is limited to finding the bootlegged software, confirming that it is bootlegged, and arresting everyone involved.

Although the stakes are large, the cases are usually simple. Victims who report such crimes to law enforcement are usually experienced in this area. They will usually furnish an expert to accompany officers to identify bootlegged software.

1.50   Other books and materials you should own

Investigators assigned to handle high-technology crimes on a regular basis should consider acquiring the following books and materials:

- A complete dictionary of computer terms. A dictionary can be very useful when you are deciphering your notes of an interview with a computer operator or engineer.

- A subscription to *PC Magazine* or *BYTE*. Subscribing to these magazines is a good way to keep current with the technology and become familiar with the prominent, and less prominent, players in the industry.

- Arkin, Stanley S., et al., *Prevention and Prosecution of Computer and High Technology Crime* (New York: Matthew Bender, 1988).

---

6.   Note that a search warrant and affidavit must provide sufficient information to allow officers to identify items to be seized as likely counterfeit merchandise. The affiant must also inform the court of any facts which would assist officers executing the warrant in excluding irrelevant property. For example, if an officer is writing a warrant to seize counterfeit videotapes and knows that the suspect has marked those tapes only with an orange band, the affiant must limit the property description to "videotapes with an orange band." *See, e.g., United States v. Cook*, 657 F.2d 730 (5th Cir. 1981); *United States v. Klein*, 565 F.2d 183 (1st Cir. 1977).

The publisher is no longer issuing supplements for this book. However, the book contains some useful case citations and discusses a few of the issues covered in this book from a defense attorney's perspective.

- The following United States Department of Justice publications provide an overview of investigation and trial of high-technology crime cases:

    •• Department of Justice, General Litigation Section, *Federal Guidelines for Searching and Seizing Computers* (Washington, D.C., 1994).

    •• Department of Justice, *Computer Crime: Criminal Justice Resource Manual,* 2d ed. (Washington, D.C., 1989).

    •• Department of Justice, *Basic Considerations in Investigating and Proving Computer-Related Federal Crimes* (Washington, D.C., 1988).

    •• Department of Justice, *Expert Witness Manual* (Washington, D.C., 1980).

The Department of Justice publications are generally available by mail from the Department at a small charge, and are well worth the modest investment.

2

Principles of High-Technology Crime Investigation

2.00   Introduction

High-technology crime investigation presents unique challenges. The most obvious difficulty is that investigators must be familiar with computer technology and the high-technology industry.[1] A more subtle, but equally important, problem is that most victims of high-technology crime are corporations.

Corporate victims take an active role in these cases. They usually perform at least a preliminary investigation before deciding whether to refer a case to police, and they may investigate the entire case using corporate security personnel and private investigators. Police and corporate investigators must be able to work together.

Another problem is that while corporate victims are more active than most, they are also more vulnerable. Corporate managers have a fiduciary responsibility to their shareholders and employees to avoid some of the risks which accompany high-technology crime investigations.

Such risks include bad publicity, legal fees, the need to take valuable engineers away from their work to assist law enforcement, and the risk that company trade secrets will be disclosed during a criminal

---

1. One way to do this is to attend meetings held by corporate security officials in your area. You may wish to host meetings of law enforcement and corporate investigators. You may also contact the High Technology Crime Investigation Association (HTCIA), a nationwide organization of public and private investigators with almost a dozen chapters in high-technology areas (see page 239).

prosecution. Defense attorneys are aware of these weaknesses and do not hesitate to exploit them during an investigation and prosecution.

This chapter discusses problems you will face when investigating high-technology crime, and it is intended to help you:

- understand the criminal justice process;

- conduct an initial investigation to determine whether a crime has been committed;

- decide whether the case should be referred to (or accepted by) law enforcement; and

- establish ground rules for cooperation between law enforcement and the victim.

This chapter skims the surface of high-technology crime investigation. Later chapters provide step-by-step procedures for investigating the most common high-technology crimes: theft of high-technology components; computer intrusion; and theft of information.

2.10   The criminal justice process: an overview

A victim reports a crime by calling a law enforcement agency. About a half-dozen police departments in the United States have specialized units handling high-technology crime—for the rest, victims should ask for the "fraud bureau" or a similar department. Callers should insist on speaking with a detective because the patrol division is not equipped to respond to high-technology crimes.

Police will seek information from a corporate representative, typically the security manager, or, in information theft cases, the corporation's attorney. (Corporate attorneys are referred to as *corporate counsel*; the attorney in charge is known as the *general counsel*). Police will review any investigation already conducted by the victim and decide how best to proceed.

Law enforcement investigations have two parts. Police first identify a suspect, and then seek evidence demonstrating that the suspect is guilty. In high-technology crime investigations, police usually use a search warrant to obtain evidence from the suspect's residence and business.

Prosecutors are often involved in both phases of high-technology crime investigations. They give legal advice as needed and shape investigations to produce evidence that will convince a jury at trial. The prosecutor may actively participate in an investigation, and may use his or her own investigators. In some cases, the prosecutor's office will handle the entire investigation.

With a few exceptions, the first search warrant served in high-technology crime cases is also the last. Computer evidence is destroyed easily—a police raid usually prompts accomplices to destroy evidence at other locations. Thus, a law enforcement agency will decide whether to prosecute a case shortly before or after the first warrant is served. That evaluation usually occurs two to six months after the victim reports the case to police.[2]

The procedure for prosecution is similar in state and federal courts. Prosecutors proceed by complaint or indictment. In cases where the prosecutor proceeds by filing a complaint, the court schedules a preliminary hearing.

The preliminary hearing is a "mini-trial"—the prosecution puts on an abbreviated version of its case. The defense questions the prosecution's witnesses, and may present its own evidence. The prosecution advances to trial by proving that there is a reasonable suspicion that the defendant committed the crime. The prosecution almost always prevails at this hearing.

The prosecutor may sidestep the preliminary hearing in the federal system, and in most states, by seeking an indictment from a grand jury. The prosecutor obtains an indictment by convincing the grand jury that the defendant committed the crime.

A case proceeds from indictment directly to trial without a preliminary hearing. Grand jury sessions take much less time than preliminary hearings because the defense is not allowed to participate.

---

2. The victim never makes a charging decision—there are no private prosecutions in the United States. Police arrest suspects, and prosecutors decide whether to charge those suspects. Indeed, victims do not even make decisions to drop charges once they have been filed—only the prosecutor may do so. Prosecutors may use subpoenas to compel unwilling victims and witnesses to attend criminal proceedings.

---

*Why state prosecutors frequently use the preliminary
hearing instead of the grand jury*

Federal prosecutors use grand juries for most of their cases. However, the much larger volume of cases in local jurisdictions means that grand juries can handle only a fraction of the cases presented to the prosecutor by police.

Preliminary hearings offer certain advantages to prosecutors and victims:

- Prosecutors can use hearings as "rehearsals" for trial, while evaluating which witnesses are best suited to presenting complicated technical information to a jury.

- If a witness testifies at a preliminary hearing, but dies before trial, the prosecutor may introduce that witness's preliminary hearing testimony at trial. (That option is not available for testimony presented to the grand jury.)

- The victim's witnesses do not have to testify before charges are filed. Instead of calling witnesses before a grand jury, the prosecutor can file charges and wait to see whether the case will settle with a plea bargain.

After charges are filed, the defendant may request information from the prosecution and third parties (e.g., the victim) concerning the charges. This process is called *discovery.*

Discovery requests can be massive—a victim in a recent large information theft case was forced to produce over 10,000 documents to the defense. As in civil cases, battles over discovery can be fierce and lengthy. The victim may be forced to hire lawyers to respond to those discovery requests.

Fortunately for victims, defendants are not allowed to serve interrogatories or depose prosecution witnesses (except in Florida, where depositions are allowed). Although defense attorneys may contact victims and witnesses to seek statements, they may not compel unco-operative witnesses to talk to them.

Most high-technology cases do not go to trial because the evidence against the defendant is overwhelming. For example, a typical case may include evidence that a computer intruder was calling from John Doe's residence. The prosecutor will show that police executing a search warrant found portions of the victim's software on John Doe's computer and that John Doe quit working for the victim three months before the intrusion. John Doe usually has little to say to a jury in such cases.

In other cases, judges will persuade defendants to plead guilty by offering light sentences. Guilty defendants may prefer to plead early and save the considerable legal fees they would otherwise pay defense lawyers. Courts generally do not impose substantial jail sentences, except in the most extreme cases.

If the case goes to trial, defendants will usually demand a trial by jury because it is generally more difficult for prosecutors to persuade all twelve members of the jury to convict than to convince a judge that the defendant is guilty.

Victims can expect adverse publicity when defendants use the press to portray themselves as victims of an "anti-competitive" company seeking to destroy the defendant. Victims will probably have to supply many of the witnesses for the prosecution, with little control over the scheduling of their appearance in court.

However, in spite of the delay and frustration which accompany our criminal justice system, criminal prosecution often makes sense for victims. As discussed later in this chapter, victims often need police assistance to recover their property. Police will offer that assistance only with the understanding that the victim will cooperate in a subsequent prosecution.

Criminal prosecution also offers a substantial reward: the guilty verdict. The victim may use that verdict to win a civil suit against the defendant. The verdict also sends a powerful message to the world (and to the victim's employees in particular) that the victim will defend itself against criminals. That message is often a powerful deterrent to theft.

Finally, there is the satisfaction of punishing the predator and creating a slightly safer place for innovation and enterprise.

2.20   Initial investigation—the first few days

Speed is critical in investigating high-technology crime cases. Stolen chips are commonly bought and resold several times in the first few days following a theft. Source code stolen from the company mainframe can be duplicated and sent to other states or overseas within hours. In one case, police caught a suspect in the international area of the airport a few hours after the victim's frantic phone call. Companies must be prepared to act quickly.

2.21   Forming the investigative team

The first step should be taken before any crime occurs. Most companies have security staffs responsible for investigating thefts and intrusions.[3] Companies should also form separate crime teams with overall responsibility for directing investigations and interacting with law enforcement investigators.

Note the use of the word "team" instead of "committee." Companies must handle high-technology crime cases immediately and intensively. There is little time to draft reports or obtain a company-wide consensus.

The team should include members of the following departments:

- security;

- legal;

- human resources; and

- senior management.

Preferably the crime team should consist of only one person from each of these departments—a larger group may be too slow to respond to changing events (e.g., ongoing intrusions).

---

3. Security departments should designate computer experts within the company to be "on call" in the event of a computer intrusion.

Obviously, one of the representatives should be the security manager. The team must also include a company lawyer (preferably the general counsel) because high-technology crime usually creates legal problems for the company.

For example, an intrusion into a computer system raises issues concerning what measures the company may use to track the intruder without violating federal privacy laws. A theft of information may involve legal action against the thief or the thief's employer. Finally, if the case is prosecuted, the company will be forced to respond to requests for discovery from the defense.

A representative from human resources (also referred to in some companies as personnel or H.R.) is useful because many high-technology crimes are committed by employees. H.R. has important information about those employees that may help in identifying suspects, including records showing disciplinary problems or access to company components or trade secrets.

H.R. may also have evidence that a particular employee intends to compete with the victim, such as a refusal to sign a nondisclosure agreement. Finally, H.R. is important when the company is considering employing undercover employees to detect or investigate crime.

It is true that H.R. has the reputation of being less than eager to work "against" one of its employees, and in many cases this reputation is well founded. However, H.R. is more likely to cooperate if the department manager is on the crime team.

The team must include a member of senior management to ensure that all departments cooperate in the investigation and that the company speaks with one voice at critical moments in the case.

2.22 Determining what happened

Many high-technology crimes rely on disguised identity for their success. For example, most computer intruders use a stolen password.

Assume that the victim's computer logs indicate that John Doe, an employee of the victim, logged in at 2:00 A.M. and downloaded software without permission. Is John Doe the culprit, or did someone steal his log-on and password and use it to gain entry? Can you prove at trial that John Doe was not the intruder? If you confront John Doe prematurely and he is not the intruder, but an accomplice, have you just destroyed your investigation? Similar problems occur in component theft and information theft cases.

You must understand what happened before you can figure out who did it. A corollary to that rule is: *make sure that something actually happened.*

Each year companies report a few cases to law enforcement which end weeks later with the victim saying, "Oh, we found out that it was nothing—never mind." In a recent case, representatives of a prominent computer company called law enforcement in a panic, reporting that an intruder was attempting to dial into the company's network every 15 seconds. A trap and trace revealed that it was another computer owned by the victim which was (mistakenly) programmed to dial into that computer every 15 seconds (instead of, say, 15 hours) and download information.

In another case, a prominent semiconductor company reported a theft of the *tape-out* (a digital copy of the design of a chip) of a several hundred million dollar product. A month later, it learned that an employee had accidentally erased the tape.

Unfortunately, not only did the company lose credibility with law enforcement, but the mistake came back to haunt the prosecution in another case involving that victim. The jury in that case heard all about the victim's "mistake," which the defense used to argue that the victim had again wrongly jumped to conclusions.

Equally important is determining whether the "event" was really a crime or just a harmless breach of procedure. Companies have reported losses of components which engineers from another division had removed for testing. Companies have also found that computer security had been breached internally, by engineers poking holes in security programs. The engineers were not malicious—they were just tired of having to follow cumbersome rules to get their work done.

The moral of these stories is to avoid jumping to conclusions. High-technology crime can be extremely threatening—one stolen trade secret can ruin a company. Emotions run high, and the urge to respond to threats immediately is great. However, while speed is critical, so is accuracy.

2.23 Determining whether there was a significant loss

Although stealing pencils is technically a crime, nobody wastes time prosecuting people who steal office supplies. You must determine whether the crime is worth your time and attention.

Equally important, you must determine whether law enforcement will consider the case to be worth their time and attention. Public agencies are always strapped for cash. While high-technology crime sounds exotic and intriguing, the cold reality is that many agencies (particularly the United States Attorney's Office) require the loss to exceed certain dollar limits to qualify for prosecution. Many agencies will be looking for reasons to reject these cases, which require considerable time, money, and expertise to investigate and prosecute.

Be very careful when calculating the loss. Any figure quoted to law enforcement or an insurer will be examined by defense counsel down the road. If your initial estimate is too high, you will be accused of having inflated the loss to attract law enforcement attention (or to commit insurance fraud). If the estimate is too low, you will be stuck with that estimate.

When calculating the loss, consider the following. For component thefts, consider the expected net profit that the company would have made but for the theft.

For computer intrusions, include the amount of time and money required to:

- determine that there was an intrusion;

- monitor the intrusion;

- obtain trap and trace orders and pen registers necessary to locate the intruder; and

- repair damage.

Include the salaries of staff members who were required to devote their energies to confronting the intrusion.[4]

---

4. For example, California law allows victims to recover those costs from defendants as part of a restitution order in a criminal case. *See* California Penal Code Section 502(e)(1). Companies may be able to collect such amounts from their insurer.

For thefts of information, include the amount of lost market share (and profits) which would result if a competitor used that secret to create a competing product faster than would otherwise have been possible.

2.30 Deciding whether the victim should refer the case to law enforcement

When should victims refer cases to law enforcement for investigation and prosecution? In a few cases, reporting is virtually mandatory. Insurance companies often require companies to file a police report before paying benefits. And companies that sue the defendant civilly for theft may be uncomfortable at trial when asked, "If you thought [defendant] stole from you, why didn't you call the police?"

However, in most cases, victims must perform a cost-benefit analysis to determine whether to report cases to law enforcement. Generally, victims will weigh the extent of the loss, the probability of apprehending the criminal, the cost in employee time of assisting police in an investigation and prosecution, and the affect of publicity of the crime on the victim's stock price and its reputation among customers and vendors.

2.31 Advantages to the victim of reporting the crime to law enforcement

The law authorizes law enforcement investigators to perform certain acts, such as taping certain conversations, which would otherwise be illegal. Most important, police can use a search warrant to recover the victim's property (*see box on next page*).

Police also have access to useful information outside the reach of private parties that can be used to identify and locate suspects. For example, police have access to criminal history records. Police can also obtain assistance from agencies in other states.

Law enforcement can also protect victims from being sued by suspects. The general rule is that a private party is immune from lawsuits for reporting a suspected crime to the police, or following police instructions, so long as that party acts in good faith. A victim undertaking a private investigation risks being sued for defamation by an individual or business identified as a suspect.

A search warrant is usually the only way for victims to recover their property

Although civil lawyers can obtain a court order known as a *writ of possession* allowing them to search a private residence or business for stolen property, that procedure is extremely risky. If the victim fails to find its property, the suspect will probably recover significant damages from the victim in court. The one exception to this rule arises in copyright infringement cases, where a federal district court authorizes the victim to impound unauthorized copies of its merchandise.

2.32 Disadvantages to the victim of reporting the crime to law enforcement

The greatest disadvantage to reporting a crime is that the victim loses control over the case. Law enforcement officials decide the direction of the investigation from that date forward—the victim may find itself in the middle of a costly and time-consuming prosecution without its consent.

Victims should not report a case to law enforcement unless they are willing to cooperate in a subsequent prosecution. Police investigate cases with an eye toward prosecution. Only in unusual cases will police agree in advance to serve a search warrant to recover the victim's property, yet refrain from prosecution.

Recognize that there are two different organizations at work here: the investigating agency (i.e., the police) and the prosecutor. The prosecutor makes the final decision concerning whether a case is prosecuted, and must approve any arrangement the victim makes with police. Since prosecutors are usually involved in drafting search warrants in high-technology crime cases, they will insist on moving forward where the execution of the warrant reveals evidence justifying a prosecution.

Another disadvantage to reporting a crime is a potential loss of confidentiality. A police investigation is noisy. The potential for leaks within the company and harmful publicity increases exponentially when the police arrive. Furthermore, any information provided to the police may become public, particularly if the case is prosecuted.

Finally, criminals are often willing to pay restitution directly to victims to avoid criminal prosecution. Companies able to identify a suspect without assistance from law enforcement may lose an opportunity to receive restitution by reporting the crime.[5]

2.40　Choosing the appropriate law enforcement agency

If you decide to report the crime, you need to determine whether your case falls within state or federal jurisdiction. Only a few cases, such as copyright infringement or violations of export control laws, are handled exclusively by federal authorities (and even those cases usually also involve violations of state law).

Local agencies investigate and prosecute most high-technology crimes. However, if your case involves a violation of federal law, you should consider calling a federal agency.

Federal agencies are especially useful when your case:

- involves matters which require particular expertise lacking in your local agency; or

- requires law enforcement investigators to act in more than one state, or outside the United States.

However, it may not be worth your time to call federal agencies if local law enforcement can handle your case. First, most federal agencies will not investigate cases which do not involve large losses. Second, while there are notable exceptions, many federal agencies move more slowly than local law enforcement. Federal agencies may take several weeks, or even months, to prepare search warrants, and

---

5.　Note that it is a violation of canons of professional responsibility for a lawyer to threaten to press criminal charges to obtain an advantage with respect to a civil grievance.

moving a case to an indictment or complaint can take more than a year. That delay will affect local authorities as well, who will hesitate to act while awaiting (perhaps forever) federal action.

Finally, in a few jurisdictions, federal agents and local law enforcement are fighting turf battles. Reporting your case to both federal and local law enforcement agencies can create unnecessary friction and delay.

If you decide to call a federal agency, you should know that while the federal government has jurisdiction over all federal crimes, some federal law enforcement agencies specialize in certain high-technology crimes. For example, if you are investigating a computer intrusion, you should call not only the FBI but the Secret Service as well. Any crime involving a bank or credit bureau is also within the domain of the Secret Service.

If your case involves export of components or technology outside the United States, call the Customs Service. Customs devotes significant resources to this area, and their performance has been impressive.

You should also call the FBI in any case involving movement of stolen components and/or information across state lines.

If you call more than one federal agency, or call both local and federal agencies, keep the following thoughts in mind. Tell everyone involved which agencies you have talked to about your case. There is nothing more frustrating for law enforcement than to find out weeks down the line that another agency is investigating the same case. Local law enforcement officers in particular are likely to resent, and remember, your conduct.

Make sure that everybody talks to each other, and quickly. As mentioned above, there are a few jurisdictions where the "feds" and the "locals" do not get along. There may well be more jurisdictions where different federal agencies do not talk to each other regularly. It is your job to monitor the progress of any investigation. If there is more than one jurisdiction involved, you should make sure they are talking to each other, and to you.

Even if your crime can be punished under federal law, always call your local agency. Your local agency is more likely to respond quickly and to treat you as a valued citizen in your community. Remember, corporate victims pay taxes which support the local police department. Although you should never throw your weight around (not only is it unethical, but it also breeds resentment and can be used against you at trial), your presence in the community will work to your advantage.

Even if the case seems more appropriate for federal action, your local agency will appreciate the opportunity to call federal authorities and solidify any relationship it may have with a particular federal agency. Furthermore, in some jurisdictions, local and federal agencies investigate cases jointly. You can only benefit from increased law enforcement resources.

2.50   Preparing to present your case to a law enforcement agency

As discussed below, law enforcement agencies do not place a high priority on investigating high-technology crime. Therefore, corporate investigators and corporate counsel must make it as easy as possible for law enforcement agencies to accept and investigate the case.

You should:

1.   Prepare a presentation for law enforcement.

Law enforcement agencies are woefully understaffed, and high-technology crime is a very low priority. Agencies are more likely to accept your case if you convince them that you are committed to a successful investigation and prosecution. A simple, but well prepared, presentation of the facts goes a long way toward persuading law enforcement to help you. (Leave your transparencies and overhead projector back at the office.)

2.   If your case is important to you, bring someone important.

The victim's security manager should attend the meeting. If the company's crown jewels have been stolen, it is appropriate for a vice-president or other high-ranking corporate officer to attend. However, resist the temptation to equate importance with numbers—limit your party to no more than three people.

3. Make sure of your facts before you begin.

Everything you say during any contact with law enforcement is "on the record." Defense attorneys may eventually question participants at the meeting about what the victim's representatives said about the case during the presentation.

4. Present the facts in a clear, organized, and nontechnical manner.

Investigators are impressed by victims who have done their homework and who can describe their problem concisely. Know your audience—your presentation will vary depending upon whether you are talking to experienced high-technology crime investigators or rookie detectives.

Remember that while investigators may be technologically ignorant, ignorance is different from stupidity. Talking down to investigators is not only unfair, but is also counterproductive. Good detectives enjoy learning; your job is to provide them with information about the crime which excites them about your case.

Explain technical information clearly and simply. If you have a network intrusion case, prepare a diagram of the network so that investigators can follow the path of the intruder. If you have an information theft case, consider using a customer support engineer to explain the technology; he or she will be experienced in explaining technical concepts to nontechnical people.

5. Calculate the loss before you make your presentation.

Be prepared to provide a carefully considered estimate of the loss. Explain that the figure is only an estimate and that it may later prove unreliable.

6. Gather and deliver relevant physical evidence.

Bring any relevant evidence to the meeting. For example, if your company has created logs of a computer intrusion, bring them. If chips have been stolen, bring samples for police to inspect. Chapter 5 discusses precautions you should take in information theft cases to protect trade secrets from disclosure.

7.   Be ready to explain the law.

If you are dealing with an agency which is unfamiliar with the high-technology crime committed in your case, make sure that someone on your side of the table can identify the laws which have been violated.

*8.   Describe any investigation conducted before the victim
      reported the crime.*

Investigators do not like to stumble into an ongoing investigation. If the victim has conducted a preliminary investigation, describe that investigation so that the investigators are confident that they will not waste time "reinventing the wheel."

9.   Emphasize the "real-world" impact of the crime.

Police are used to dealing with victims of violent crime. Corporate victims may appear less sympathetic, particularly where the victim can attempt to recover damages by suing the criminal. Too many cases are refused by law enforcement agencies as "civil cases."

Explain why your victim is a "real" victim. If the victim had to spend money to recover from a computer intrusion, explain the loss in dollar terms. If stolen information jeopardizes every job in a 5,000 employee company, do not hesitate to say so.

A corporate victim is usually an important citizen in the community. While you should not be overbearing, do not hesitate to emphasize that fact.

*10. Determine before you present the case whether the victim will
      cooperate in an investigation and prosecution.*

Make sure that the victim is ready to commit to cooperating in the prosecution of the case. In the event that the victim has not decided whether to make that commitment (e.g., because events are happening so quickly that the corporation has not had time to reach a decision on that issue), communicate that fact to law enforcement before you begin your presentation.

11. Discuss what assistance the victim is willing to provide to law enforcement.

As discussed later in this chapter, victims often offer assistance to law enforcement. Keeping the ethical and tactical problems discussed later in this chapter in mind, be ready to discuss what the victim can do to assist. Such assistance may range from providing employees as expert witnesses, to lending equipment to law enforcement agencies investigating and prosecuting the case.

2.60 Deciding whether a law enforcement agency should accept the case

Most law enforcement agencies are geared toward rapid turnover of cases involving violent crime. Caseloads are extremely high, and taxpayers and politicians evaluate agencies largely on their ability to arrest and convict large numbers of violent criminals.

High-technology crime does not fit well within this system. Most cases require painstaking and expensive investigation. Even the most dedicated and highly trained police detective cannot handle more than two or three dozen such cases in a year.

Even worse, since so few police departments have experience with these cases, police commanders will not understand that they are time-consuming. Many officers are assigned high-technology crime caseloads as an "extra duty" on top of a full caseload of bad checks, thefts, and other frauds.

Many high-technology crime cases are never solved. When offenders are apprehended, many are given very light sentences. Assume that you are the chief of a police department in a large city—is it worth spending a month of an officer's time on a computer intrusion when the criminal, if caught at all, may get off with probation?

High-technology crime investigation and prosecution is still in its infancy. There are only a handful of high-technology crime investigative units in the United States, and police departments maintaining such units rotate officers every few years. The result is that most units are staffed with officers who are still learning how to investigate high-technology crime. Of course, police departments without such units are in even worse shape.

Therefore, law enforcement agencies must choose their cases carefully. Since one bad case can waste months of effort, your primary task as a police officer or federal agent is to separate the winners from the losers as fast as possible.

As a law enforcement investigator, how do you decide which cases to accept? Although later chapters discuss this issue in more detail for particular crimes, there are three rules that apply to all cases.

First, you should perform your own initial investigation. Many victims come to law enforcement with suspicions, but little evidence.

Second, beware of any case where the victim has delayed reporting the crime. Victims delay reporting crimes for various reasons. Many prefer to investigate crimes themselves, and inform law enforcement only after a lengthy internal investigation identifies a suspect. Others require approval from multiple layers of bureaucracy before reporting the crime.

Whatever the reason for the delay, time kills high-technology crime cases. You must decide whether it is still possible to prove that the suspect committed the crime.

In a very small number of cases, the victim may be reporting the crime at a late date, not so much to prompt an investigation as to satisfy an insurance company or obtain leverage over a competitor in a civil dispute (typically an ex-employee). You should be concerned if the victim has no adequate explanation for a long delay in reporting the crime.

Finally, you should reject cases where you believe that the victim will not cooperate in the investigation and prosecution of the case. This last rule requires an explanation.

2.61 Corporate victims in high-technology cases present special problems

Victims play an important role in high-technology crime cases because they control access to much of the information law enforcement needs to investigate and prosecute the case. For example, in a computer intrusion case, the investigator needs to understand the victim's computer system to know what happened. Most cases require the victim's employees to testify as witnesses. If the victim chooses not to cooperate, or stops cooperating, the case is usually finished.

Defense attorneys frequently harass victims. They serve subpoenas requiring victims to produce hundreds, or even thousands, of documents at company expense. Defense attorneys may try to obtain, and threaten to reveal, the victim's trade secrets as part of discovery. Victims may spend thousands of dollars in legal fees producing documents and fighting subpoenas.

Meanwhile, engineers hired to produce a product instead spend much of their time meeting with lawyers and testifying in court. Victims occasionally decide that they would rather withdraw their cooperation than spend more time and money on the case.

The law enforcement investigator needs to evaluate the victim's ability and inclination to cooperate *before* accepting a crime report for investigation. While it is hard enough for an investigator to evaluate an individual victim, it is much more difficult when the victim is a corporation.

As discussed below, corporate victims present three problems for law enforcement:

- Corporations have multiple decisionmakers.

- Corporate victims have a different agenda from most victims; that agenda makes them more likely to withdraw from a case well after the investigation or prosecution has begun.

- Actions taken by corporate victims to protect their interests may hinder investigation and prosecution.

These problems require law enforcement investigators to exercise special care in determining whether victims will stay the course. The next part of this chapter discusses strategies which investigators can use to create a productive relationship with the victim.

2.61–a   *Corporate victims make decisions as a group*

Corporate decisionmakers in high-technology crime cases generally include the highest ranking local official, a lawyer representing the company, a representative of the department experiencing the problem, and the security manager. Other players may include the board of directors and venture capitalists who have invested money in the company.

Group decisionmaking creates two problems for the law enforcement investigator. First, it takes longer for a group to make decisions. Second, it may be difficult for the investigator to communicate with the decisionmakers.

There is very little you can do about the first problem except to stress the urgency of the situation. You should encourage the victim to hold meetings of its crime team as early and often as possible.

You can, and must, address the second problem early. Recognize that a corporate victim will usually assign someone to be a contact person, or liaison, with law enforcement. That person is usually a member of the security department. *Also recognize that in cases involving large losses, the liaison may not be a major player in the decisionmaking process.*

Unfortunately, many security managers wield little influence within their companies. The high-technology industry is still a relatively new industry, and does not have a tradition of protecting its assets. Although most security managers are highly qualified, senior executives often consider the security department to be an unproductive part of the company with little value.

In major cases, someone else in the corporation usually calls the shots, typically the general counsel or the president. Therefore, the law enforcement investigator *must* have a direct line of communication with that decisionmaker. If necessary, sit down with the security manager and draw an organization chart of the company to understand who will make the final decisions concerning the company's conduct in the prosecution.

You do not have to talk to that decisionmaker often. You are better off dealing on a daily basis with someone who is closer to the investigation, such as the security manager. However, you need to be able to reach the decisionmaker to obtain assistance if other parts of the corporation prove uncooperative down the line.

In addition, you must meet with that decisionmaker and discuss the case before beginning an investigation or prosecution. *One rule of thumb for major cases: you should always meet with the highest local official of the victim and obtain that person's commitment that his or her organization will cooperate throughout the investigation and prosecution.*

You are less likely to be abandoned by your victim once the person in charge has made a personal commitment to cooperate in an investigation and prosecution. If you are unable to communicate with the decisionmaker concerning a major case, you should seriously consider declining that case.

In any event, do not forget the security manager. Although the company may underrate the importance of the security manager, you should not make the same mistake. A good security manager is your ally within the corporation. You should make an effort to include that manager in your investigation. Security managers are often retired law enforcement officers, and they generally favor criminal prosecution.

Security managers can mobilize internal security to obtain information from within the company. In addition, the manager is your voice on the victim's crime team. If and when senior management debates whether continued cooperation with law enforcement is a good idea, a security manager with a stake in the prosecution may save your case.

2.61–b   *Corporate victims have a different agenda*

You must gauge your victim's motive in calling police. In order for law enforcement and the victim to work well together, each must understand the expectations and motives of the other.

Corporate victims are generally guided by four motives:

* anger;

* fear of further damage from ongoing criminal activity, and the desire to recoup losses;

* fear of further damage as a result of cooperating in the criminal justice process; and

* desire to deter future criminal activity.

2.61–b(1)   Recognizing and addressing corporate objectives

1. Anger.

A major reason for calling police is to punish someone. Unfortunately, anger fades. While it may propel a corporate victim toward police, any desire for vengeance usually disappears by the time the case is ready for trial.

This is particularly true when it comes time for sentencing. Corporations rarely send representatives to sentencing hearings, and often submit recommendations for lenient sentences when the crime involves a former employee. Occasionally victims will offer to recommend leniency in return for restitution. In one case, the victim agreed to urge leniency in exchange for a restitution payment of $5,000 (it spent much more than $5,000 investigating the case).

2. Fear of further damage, and the desire to recoup losses.

Another motivation for calling police is fear of further loss. For example, the victim may be afraid that a computer intruder will continue to wreak havoc unless stopped by police. The motive is similar in component theft cases: victims want to recoup their losses by recovering their stolen property. Remember that the corporate manager has a responsibility to both shareholders and employees to protect the corporation from further harm.

Unfortunately, the victim's interest in preventing further damage and recouping losses diminishes at a certain point. Victims fear further loss until police catch the criminal. Victims who have recovered their stolen property may not need further assistance.

The interests of law enforcement and the victim in pursuing a case may conflict after police serve a search warrant. Victims are often less interested in cooperating after the intruder has been apprehended or the property recovered.

This observation is not intended to be an attack on victims. Corporations are in business to make money. A victim may be unable to justify spending tens of thousands of dollars to help prosecutors secure a conviction after the danger to the victim has passed. As a law enforcement investigator, you must ensure that the victim who has been demanding immediate action for weeks understands that the investigation will not stop simply because you catch the criminal.

Law enforcement investigators and victims must establish ground rules for the investigation. The best approach is to agree that the victim may withdraw at any time before law enforcement executes a search warrant. The idea is that victims should be encouraged to call police without having to agree to support a major prosecution. However, law enforcement investigators should not have to put in the time and effort required to prepare and serve a search warrant unless the victim agrees to cooperate in a prosecution.

Emphasize to victims that preparing and serving search warrants in high-technology cases is a major undertaking. In one information theft case, the warrant took several weeks to prepare, numbered 61 pages, and was served at eight locations by 38 police officers (which was about half the number needed). Once those sorts of resources have been committed to a case, law enforcement will not allow the victim to walk away.

3. Fear of further damage resulting from a prosecution.

As discussed above, defense attorneys frequently target victims for harassment to persuade them to back away from the case. The best way to deal with this problem is to make sure the victim understands the potential costs of an investigation up front.

Insist on discussing those costs with your victim *before* you begin your investigation. You need to inform the victim that:

- The criminal justice system moves very slowly. The victim should not expect a conviction for at least a year.

- Any civil suit that the victim files against defendants will be *stayed* (postponed) until after the criminal case, although a court in a trade secret case may grant a preliminary injunction.

- The victim will lose engineering time and run up legal fees while the case is awaiting trial.

- The victim will probably suffer bad publicity. That publicity may be limited to revealing a breach of security, or it may publicize defense allegations that the victim itself has done something wrong (or is "anti-competitive"). If the case is especially large, such publicity could have an impact on the victim's stock price. Defense contractors should be particularly careful—an investigation into poor security could attract the attention of Department of Defense auditors.

- If sensitive information is involved, defense counsel may seek to discover it. There is no ironclad guarantee that such information will remain secret. The prosecutor should discuss mechanisms available to protect such information during the case (e.g., protective orders). Those mechanisms are discussed in Appendix C.

- The victim loses control over the case after referring it to law enforcement. Public investigators and prosecutors will decide whether, and when, the government will file a case against one or more defendants. Law enforcement will expect the victim to cooperate and make witnesses available. The victim may be asked to pay travel expenses for those witnesses.

- Any plea bargaining will be conducted solely by prosecutors, and the victim should not undercut any sentencing recommendation without discussing it with prosecutors first. (Victims have the right to recommend any sentence, but it is quite a shock as a prosecutor to learn about a recommendation for the first time at the sentencing hearing.)

At the end of that conversation, your victim will have a much better understanding of the risks involved in pursuing the case. Although some victims will decide not to refer their cases to law enforcement, those who do are less likely to abandon their case after you have spent your agency's time and money.

4. Desire to deter future criminal activity.

Victims will endure the pressure of a prosecution if they have a realistic goal that they can achieve only if the defendant is found guilty. Note that most goals are satisfied well short of that point.

A victim obtains revenge when the suspect is arrested, booked, and roasted in the hot glare of publicity. The victim avoids further harm when the suspect is arrested. The victim may obtain restitution through a civil settlement in which the victim agrees (quietly) to stop cooperating with law enforcement.

The one motive with staying power is the desire to deter further attacks by others (usually employees). Savvy victims know that their employees watch what happens to colleagues who commit crimes. Although calling the police and causing the defendant to be arrested will deter some theft, securing a conviction has an even greater impact. A company that wants to send a message to its employees and potential predators may be more likely to continue cooperating with law enforcement.

2.61–b(2)   Evaluate your victim

You should always ask victims what they want out of an investigation and prosecution. Listen carefully to the answers, and decide whether the victim's motives are likely to remain the same throughout the investigation and prosecution. Observe even more carefully the victim's reaction to your explanation of the costs of investigation and prosecution.

If you have doubts about the victim's staying power, discuss the issue frankly. Victims will be grateful that you warned them ahead of time, and are much less likely to back out once you have obtained their fully informed (*ad nauseam*, if necessary) consent. If you still have serious doubts about the victim's ability or inclination to cooperate, reject the case.

2.61–c   Corporate victims may hinder the prosecution unintentionally

As discussed above, corporations often perform their own investigations. Those investigations may cause problems for law enforcement.

2.61–c(1)   The myth of the attorney-client privilege

As a law enforcement investigator, your first trip to the facilities of a corporate victim may be surprising. After you have checked through security, you will be met by an escort. That escort is likely to be a lawyer from the general counsel's office. In larger cases, your escort may be a representative of an outside law firm hired by the corporation.

Whenever you interview a company employee, that lawyer will be with you. The lawyer will have instructed the employee not to talk with you without the lawyer present. That means that you may never have a chance to talk with that employee alone. Congratulations— you have just gained a partner in a three-piece suit.

It gets worse. Your partner is not on your side, and he or she knows information that you do not. Not only will the lawyer be there when you interview the employee, but that lawyer may have already interviewed that employee before you arrived. And the lawyer will never tell you what the employee said during that interview. Although the lawyer will keep notes of the conversation, and even prepare a separate memorandum recording what was said during the interview, those notes will be hidden from law enforcement.

What is going on here? Many companies rely heavily on a legal doctrine known as the attorney-client privilege. The law provides that a conversation between an attorney and his or her client is "privileged," or secret, and ordinarily cannot be revealed. Corporations often use lawyers to interview employees to make sure that the corporation does not have to share what it discovers with anyone else.

This use of lawyers to hide information is not intended to be sinister. Lawyers are creatures of habit. In cases where the corporation may be in trouble, such as when a thousand gallons of sulfuric acid are found a half mile downstream from the factory, corporations have an interest in finding out what happened without having to share that information with authorities or victims who sue the company. The law provides a privilege to encourage the corporation to find out what happened. This may not be something to be proud of, but at least the corporation's behavior makes sense.

Unfortunately, this habit of using lawyers to shield information carries over into cases where the corporation is the victim. Of course, where the corporation is really a victim, there is little to hide. The only reason to use this device is to make sure that an opponent in a civil suit does not call the interviewer as a witness to confirm what the employee told the interviewer about the case.

How does this affect you? This practice causes three problems. First, you may not get the full story about what happened because someone else has conducted the initial interview. You will be getting a story that has been shaped, usually unconsciously, but once in a great while intentionally, by the lawyer. Furthermore, the employee may simply forget to give you details he gave the lawyer.

Second, you may get contradictory stories. Many lawyers do not know how to investigate high-technology crime, and some do not understand technology. This causes problems because many engineers are very literal people. If you ask the wrong question, you will get the wrong answer. It is very easy to end up with apparently contradictory answers.

Third, *the attorney-client privilege is probably a myth in criminal cases.* Although there is very little case law on this point, you should be aware that a court may "override" the privilege where necessary to allow effective questioning by the defense lawyer. A defense lawyer familiar with this area of the law can tie a corporation (and the prosecution) into knots by demanding details of previous interviews with witnesses.

How do you prevent the problems discussed above? If you are an employee of the victim, such as the security manager, you must raise this problem with general counsel when the investigation begins. If you are part of law enforcement, you must discuss this issue with the victim's lawyers at the initial interview.

Your message is simple: if the victim calls police, and a prosecutor eventually files charges, everything discussed during the corporate and law enforcement investigation will be disclosed to the defense.

> ### 2.61–d   *Rules for corporate counsel and investigators conducting an internal investigation*

Corporate counsel and investigators should consider adopting the following rules.

1. *Conduct your investigation as if everything that is said and done is "for the record."*

Act as if you are a police department, because you will be treated like one. Tell your employees that their comments will be disclosed to everyone, and that they must not guess or speculate.

2. Avoid writing down information unless it is absolutely necessary for your investigation.

The defense in criminal cases is entitled to written material only from victims during discovery. Unless a corporate investigator is called as a witness, the defense is unlikely to obtain the investigator's recollections. You do not want to increase your workload when the defense sends a subpoena to your company for every piece of paper relating to the case. Nor do you want to be accused of having destroyed written records of your investigation.

3. When conducting interviews, only one person should take notes.

Synthesize your rough notes into a report that *accurately* and *completely* states the witness's recollection. Have the witness review those notes for accuracy. You should destroy any rough notes (state law may prohibit law enforcement investigators from destroying *their* notes). Again, the key is to include in the interview report *all* of the information contained in your rough notes.

4. Corporate and law enforcement investigators should record the facts, not their impressions of what was said and done.

Although the "work product doctrine" may protect some of those impressions, it is more difficult to protect them if they are on the same page, or in the same sentence, as factual material. If you must record your impressions, do so in a separate document.

5. Do not plan strategy in front of a potential witness.

Companies often summon employee experts to consult with the crime team and evaluate whether the company can win a civil suit against the thief. Do not offer that expert as a witness in the criminal case unless you want the details of your witness's opinion of your civil case (and your plans) turned over to lawyers for the defendant.

*6. Everything you tell police will be disclosed to the defense and
the press.*

The police are not an extension of the corporation. What you tell
them is a matter of public record. As discussed in Chapter 5, this requires special care in information theft cases.

7. Do not take minutes at meetings of the crime team.

The victim is entitled to plan its strategy without a defense lawyer
looking over its shoulder. For example, if you are thinking of offering
a reward, you do not have to write that down. If you suspect employee
X, you do not have to record that opinion. *You should take notes to
record facts, not impressions or strategy.*

8. Do not use this advice to hide "exculpatory evidence."

Exculpatory evidence is evidence which points to a suspect's innocence. This warning cannot be emphasized enough. "Hiding the
ball" is not only unethical, but rarely works. When it backfires, the results are disastrous.

In one major information theft case, the victim failed to tell the
prosecutor that some of the "trade secrets" had been disclosed to the
public before the theft (making them worthless). The defense discovered that fact by accident during a lengthy preliminary hearing. The
victim's expert, who was not aware of the disclosure, had already testified for three days when this information came to light.

The disclosure contradicted the testimony already given by the
victim's expert, whom the company had advertised to the court and
the prosecutor as the most knowledgeable employee about the subject. The court allowed the defense to recall that expert, a key employee on a development team, to the witness stand for *an additional
thirty days of testimony.* The victim's product was delayed at a huge
cost. The defendants were later acquitted at trial, probably in large
part because the jury was allowed to hear about the incident.

Although the truth does not always emerge during the criminal
process, experience has taught prosecutors that undesirable facts
about the victim and weaknesses in the case usually come to light.

Investigators run down many blind alleys. Defense attorneys can make a lot of mileage out of mistakes; they can paint a picture that is a gross distortion of the truth. You need to make sure that the only information recorded is accurate information uncolored by the impressions of victim investigators and attorneys.

2.61–e *Rules for law enforcement investigators conducting an investigation within a corporation*

Law enforcement investigators should also follow certain rules when conducting an investigation.

1. Find out who has talked to whom, and what they talked about.

As discussed above, corporations usually conduct at least a preliminary investigation before calling police. You should ask for copies of all corporate investigative reports and any other documents generated regarding the case. You should try to discover all contacts between the victim's investigators and its employees.

If the corporation asserts an attorney-client privilege when you ask for information, it will do so with the defense later. Resolve such objections immediately, and establish ground rules for the remainder of the case.

2. Insist on interviewing employees alone.

This request will allow you to discover the corporation's attitude about who is in control of the case. Many corporations will resist the request out of concern that an employee may blurt something out which will be made public. Keep in mind that the corporation may have a legitimate concern when the answers to your questions could reveal sensitive business or technical information.

Corporations may also worry about being "frozen out" of the investigation. This is particularly a problem in information theft cases, where the company may file a civil suit against the criminal and his or her new employer. Anything the witness says may be used against the corporation in its civil case. The victim may suggest that it has an interest in having its representatives attend the interviews.

You should negotiate this issue with the following thoughts in mind. You need some time alone with the witness so that he or she has an opportunity to tell you information without fear of reprisal from the company. Although this scenario is rare, you need that time in every case to prevent the defense attorney from suggesting that the witness was intimidated into parroting the company line by the constant presence of corporate "spin doctors."

This does not mean that you should always exclude corporate counsel and investigators. You will often need a corporate representative to translate what the employee is telling you from "Engineer" into English.

Corporate investigators often ask questions which would not occur to the typical untrained investigator. It is very useful to be able to turn to corporate counsel during an interview and ask for more information on a point just raised by an employee. Find a comfortable middle ground that allows you to obtain the unbiased information you need while satisfying the corporation's need for access to its own employees.

3. *Insist on being present at all employee interviews.*

This is *not* negotiable. Once the corporation has invited you to investigate, it is your investigation. You control who is interviewed and the subject of those interviews.

Restrict corporate investigators acting out of your presence to asking questions designed to determine whether an employee is a potential witness. It is acceptable for a corporate investigator or lawyer to ask an engineer out of your presence if that engineer worked on the X45 project; it is not acceptable for that interviewer to ask whether a manual on ion implantation was circulated without a "confidential" stamp.

You must consider the victim's attitude toward your investigation when evaluating whether to accept a case for investigation and prosecution. If the victim is limiting your access to witnesses, and insisting on "preparing" witnesses in advance without your knowledge, you are going to have constant problems during the discovery phase and at trial. You may profit from declining the case and devoting your precious resources to other matters.

2.70   Corporate financial contributions

Among all of the problems which can arise between corporate victims and law enforcement, one of the most subtle is the issue of financial assistance.

Historically, taxpayers have insisted that law enforcement concentrate on street crime. Agencies therefore do not consider economic crime to be a high-priority item. High-technology crime in particular is very expensive to investigate and prosecute.

Thus, agencies concerned about their budgets occasionally seek financial assistance from victims. The rationale is that corporate victims often have civil remedies available to them, particularly in information theft cases. If the victim wants to "make it a federal case," it should contribute part of the costs.

Corporate victims are usually willing to pitch in. Frequently, the potential losses facing the victim dwarf the few thousand dollars requested by law enforcement. The victim would pay many of the costs, such as travel expenses and expert fees, in a civil case in any event.

In general, there is nothing wrong with the victim paying expenses for its own employees to travel to, and testify at, hearings in the criminal case. Nor is there any problem with victims supplying experts to the prosecution, other than claims that the expert is biased at trial. After all, the small merchant who is the victim of shoplifting usually makes his or her own way to trial, or sends an employee to talk about the price of the stolen hamburger. (When resolving issues involving corporations, it helps to ask yourself whether the same conduct by an individual victim would be considered acceptable.)

Corporations should also not be concerned about "lending" equipment to law enforcement to be used in the investigation and prosecution itself. If police need a workstation to analyze data obtained from a suspect's computer, the victim should not have any concern about supplying one for the duration of the case. (However, federal agencies may be prohibited by regulations from accepting loaned equipment.)

However, there are cases where the victim wants to do more. The victim may offer to pay travel expenses for law enforcement investigators. The victim may offer to pay for "independent" experts hired by the prosecution. The victim may even offer to donate the workstation to law enforcement permanently.

There are two problems which can arise in this area. First, there is the appearance that law enforcement is coercing victims to pay expenses. As discussed above, this is usually not a problem because such contributions are pocket change to most victims.

Second, there is the appearance that the victim is "buying" a prosecution. You should take the following steps to avoid this problem.

Law enforcement should not discuss victim contributions until it has decided to accept the case, and preferably, not until after charges have been filed. Any discussion concerning contributions should be memorialized in writing and made public at the outset of the case.

Law enforcement should refuse certain contributions. Investigators should generally bear their own travel expenses. The prosecution must pay the costs of independent experts, or risk the jury's considering those experts to be nothing more than employees of the victim. (There is nothing wrong with calling employees as experts—you simply need to ensure that non-employee experts are not also attacked as biased because the victim paid their fees.)

And, of course, you must not accept any "freebies" from the victim to your office. This means no donated computers or software, or any other gratuity. And give back that workstation after the case is over.

A recent case suggests the perils of victim contributions. The victim paid $10,850 directly to independent experts used by the prosecutor's office to execute a search warrant. The trial judge *recused* (disqualified) the entire prosecutor's office, finding that the payments created a conflict of interest. Although an appellate court overturned the decision, it noted that such payments, particularly if large, could justify recusal; one danger is that a court may find that the victim offered contributions to induce prosecutors to pursue the case.[6]

---

6. *See People v. Eubanks*, 42 Cal. App. 4th 1297, *review granted*, 907 P. 2d 1324 (the case is still pending). If challenged, prosecutors may cite the recent approval by a federal court of corporate victims bearing some of the expenses involved in investigations. *See IBM v. Brown et al.*, 857 F.Supp. 1384, 1388-89 (C.D. Cal. 1994).

2.80   What not to do during an investigation

The next three chapters in this book provide step-by-step directions on how to investigate the three most common high-technology crimes: theft of components, computer intrusions, and theft of information.

However, there are a few general rules which apply to all high-technology crime investigations (and for many other types of investigations involving corporations). These are rules about what *not* to do. They have been gathered from many investigators and prosecutors, and each rule has been learned the hard way:

1. Keep your investigation secret.

Rumor mills within companies are extremely efficient. You should conduct your investigation on a strictly need-to-know basis. Officers who call the company should not identify themselves as police officers, except to people who are supposed to know about the investigation. Officers visiting the company should not arrive in uniform. If possible, they should sign in with security by prior arrangement as someone other than an officer (e.g., as a vendor).

Company officials should think carefully before choosing to inform any employees of the existence of an investigation. In one case, the victim's management, believing that it had found the culprit, announced in a company-wide meeting that the corporation had discovered that its software had been taken by a group of ex-employees. The company had failed to identify an accomplice who was still an employee; that employee attended the meeting. Within two days, copies of the company's source code began appearing all over the country.

Company officials should rely on security and H.R. employees to identify allies of potential suspects. Exercise great caution in discussing the investigation with those employees.

2. Do not rely on senior management's version of what happened.

No, they are not lying to you. It is just that they may not know what really happened. Senior managers rarely have a complete understanding of what is happening in their company, even within their own departments. If you want to know whether certain engineers shared passwords to the company mainframe, you have to do more than talk to the manager of the department. You have to talk to the engineers themselves. Managers tell you how things are supposed to work; lower-level employees tell you how things really work.

You have to talk to everyone to find out what happened. The victim will probably have identified key employees for you to interview. Use that list as a starting point, but make sure you identify and interview every employee who may have knowledge about the case.

This can be awkward, since the person chosen by the corporation to be your "contact person" may be upset by your request to talk to other employees about the case. The victim may object to your disrupting the work of other employees. Nonetheless, you must insist. Be as tactful as possible.

3. Do not leave evidence behind.

Part of your job is to gather evidence. You should start with evidence located at the victim's premises. When an employee mentions a particular document or record, ask for it to be produced for your inspection. If it is relevant, take that document or record, and give a copy of it to the victim for its records.

Do not assume that your victim will preserve evidence. If you want to preserve a log of accesses to the victim's computer on a certain key date, you had better make a copy of that file.

Many high-technology companies have a policy of regularly destroying particular documents every few weeks, months, or years. Computer logs and backup tapes are usually destroyed (or overwritten) weekly, or even daily. Distribution lists for information are often destroyed after a few years, as are inventory records for components.

These "mandatory destruction" policies are necessary to avoid turning the victim company into a landfill. You must act quickly to preserve evidence.

4. Do not dawdle.

High-technology cases are few, but they require intense effort. The initial investigation cannot be handled part-time. Corporate and law enforcement investigators must clear their calendars whenever one of these cases appears on the horizon. Be prepared to work intensively for days or weeks until you have identified a suspect, drafted a search warrant, served that warrant, and analyzed the evidence obtained from the premises.

3

Investigating Theft of Components

Because that's where the money is.
—Willie Sutton, when asked why he robbed banks

3.00   Introduction

3.01   High-technology components—the most vulnerable commodity?

At this writing, gold is priced at about $400 per ounce. Platinum has sold for as much as $600 per ounce. Weapons grade plutonium is fetching far higher prices.

Yet a persuasive case can be made that smart thieves should instead target high-technology components, especially those components installed in personal computers.

Most components are unprotected. Many computer companies keep integrated circuits and other components in easily accessible areas of a warehouse.

Many components are expensive. The microprocessors which run our personal computers are sold at wholesale for anywhere from $150 to $500 each, and occasionally even more. Disk drives small enough to be concealed in a pocket often retail for $400 or more. One Silicon Valley company stores $50 million in chips at one site.

Most components are small. A single integrated circuit is typically the size of a thumbnail. An employee can steal $1 million worth of integrated circuits using a handtruck.

Most computer components are difficult to trace. Integrated circuits are *fungible* (they all look alike). As discussed in this chapter, police are often unable to identify stolen components with the certainty necessary to obtain a criminal conviction.

There is a large legitimate secondary market for components. Since most components are difficult to trace, it is easy for thieves to market their components as legitimate. Millions of dollars in chips change hands every week.

It should be no surprise that there have been more than 130 losses from component thefts reported in the *San Jose Mercury News* (the leading newspaper in the Silicon Valley) alone during the last five years. And most small losses are never reported to police, much less to newspapers.

Theft losses in the Silicon Valley are estimated at well over $30 million each year. Other high-technology centers in the United States and worldwide are also experiencing huge losses.

The remainder of this chapter consists of four parts:

- A guide to components. This chapter tells you how components are manufactured, bought, and sold. You will also learn how to identify and trace individual components, and how to warn the high-technology industry that someone may be selling your victim's stolen property.

- A profile of the component thief.

- Some of the more common methods of stealing components.

- A step-by-step guide to investigating component theft cases.

3.10   A guide to components

There are two types of computer components: (1) integrated circuits; and (2) everything else. In order to investigate component cases, you need to understand how components are bought and sold. Since the chip market is complicated, we will start by discussing thefts of entire personal computers (PCs), disk drives, and motherboards. We will then discuss chips in more detail.

This section discusses initial steps you should take to track down each component. A later section suggests a procedure for investigating component theft cases.

3.11 Basic computer components

Thefts of PCs, disk drives, and motherboards are the closest we come in this book to garden variety crime. Computers are put together much like automobiles, and, as with automobiles, certain components are commonly sold in stores.

3.11–a Personal computers

PCs may be stolen after assembly from a number of locations, including the manufacturer, distributor, retailer, and end-user. Fortunately, computers manufactured by larger companies are usually serialized. Unfortunately, thousands of computers made by smaller companies are not. Worse, serial numbers are often printed on decals which can be peeled off. Finally, the internal components of the computer are rarely labeled in such a way as to identify them as belonging to a particular computer. There is a thriving used-computer market throughout the United States, and finding an individual computer is usually a hopeless task.

Tracing a large number of stolen computers is more feasible, but still very difficult. Occasionally you will find large quantities of stolen computers sold through traditional fences. You should keep in touch with the burglary detail of your local police departments when investigating such cases. You may also find stolen PCs at computer swap meets, computer shows, and flea markets.

Apart from reporting component thefts to law enforcement, your best chance to recover stolen computers is to contact the manufacturer to determine if any warranty claims have been made for computers bearing the stolen serial numbers. If so, you can trace the source of the computer by contacting the dissatisfied customer.[1] You will also want to spread the word to potential buyers, as discussed in § 3.42.

---

1. New owners are encouraged by manufacturers to fill out and return "registration" cards enclosed with their computers. However, fences are unlikely to provide those cards, and may tell buyers that the computers were registered by the previous owner.

3.11–b Disk drives and circuit boards

Disk drives and motherboards[2] are stolen from the manufacturer, the distributor, and, most commonly, *original equipment manufacturers (OEMs)*. OEMs are companies which buy components and assemble complete products (i.e., computers). These products may be used in turn by other OEMs in their computers. For example, motherboard manufacturers buy chips, place them in circuit boards, and sell the *populated* motherboards to computer manufacturers.

Disk drives are serialized. Unfortunately, as with personal computers, many serial numbers are placed on decals which can be peeled off the drive. Again, tracing an individual drive is often impossible. Since drives are usually sold as part of a new computer, and are therefore rarely registered separately by customers, there is little hope of recovering a stolen one. If you are lucky, the thief will attempt to sell a large number of drives under suspicious circumstances.

Unless and until the property surfaces, your best course is to contact potential legitimate buyers with identifying information. For disk drives, describe:

* the manufacturer;

* the capacity (e.g., 540 megabytes); and

* the serial number.

Some motherboards are not individually serialized. However, many motherboards are sold to manufacturers under exclusive contracts. Therefore, the chance of noticing a motherboard being sold where it should not be is somewhat higher. Again, however, usually the best you can do is to get a good description of the product, inform the market about the theft, and wait for something to happen. For motherboards, describe:

* the manufacturer;

* the microprocessor included on the board;

---

2. The circuit board containing the CPU (the microprocessor) is a major component of the computer, and is frequently referred to as the *motherboard*.

- the speed (in MHz) of that microprocessor;

- the amount of memory on board;

- the type of bus (PCI, VESA [also known as VLB]); and

- the serial number.

Thieves are now stealing PCMCIA and flash memory components. These components are about the size of a credit card and are designed for portable computers. These components are commonly unserialized and difficult to trace.

Thieves occasionally steal other circuit boards, including sound cards and graphics cards.

3.12 Integrated circuits (chips)

3.12–a   How chips work

This section is of interest primarily to investigators employed by semiconductor companies; other readers may wish to turn to § 3.12–b.

A chip is a piece of silicon the size of your thumbnail which contains transistors and other electrical devices.[3] The most important electrical device is the transistor. The transistor is the heart of all computers, and is used to move current from one point to another whenever it is "activated" to do so.

At any moment, a transistor is either sending current (a "1"), or is not sending current (a "0"). A transistor is "turned on" by applying electricity to the transistor itself. The transistor is "turned off" when no electricity is applied. Hundreds of thousands, and even millions, of these transistors created within a wafer of silicon and other materials form the integrated circuit known as a *chip*.

Silicon is the material of choice for chips because it is a *semiconductor*, meaning that its tendency to conduct electricity can be affected dramatically by altering its environment.

---

3. Some companies are designing chips using *gallium arsenide* (a compound of gallium and arsenic). These chips, known as *GaAs*, can be faster than silicon chips. However, they are also more difficult and expensive to manufacture. The difference is not important to the high-technology crime investigator.

By painting portions of the silicon with various other materials (called *dopants*, as in *doping* the silicon), designers can create channels in which electrons will travel from one point to another when a certain voltage is applied to that channel. In other words, designers can create transistors within silicon.

A chip contains hundreds of thousands, or millions, of these transistors connected in logical patterns. When the user sends instructions and data to the microprocessor chip, the pattern of transistors on that chip will produce a predetermined result. Different combinations of instructions and data produce different results.

There are several types of chips, differentiated by the design of the transistor and the dopants used on the silicon. Thus, you may hear chips described as *MOS (metal oxide semiconductor)* chips, which include *CMOS* and *NMOS*. Other types of chips include *bipolar* chips, which use a different method of conducting electricity along the transistor. *BiCMOS* chips combine bipolar and CMOS technology. The differences between them are not important to the high-technology crime investigator.

3.12–b   How chips are manufactured

If you skipped the last section, all you need to know is that a chip is a piece of silicon the size of a thumbnail which contains hundreds of thousands, or even millions, of transistors.

Do not skip this section, however. You need to know how chips are manufactured because, unlike most components, a substantial number of them are stolen during the manufacturing process.

Chips are designed on computers, using *CAD (computer-aided design)* systems which display the parts of the integrated circuit (transistors, resistors, capacitors, etc.). Once the design is completed, a magnetic tape is made incorporating that design in digital form. The tape is then used to create a copy of the design on a glass *mask.*

Each chip is composed of many layers of silicon and other materials, and a different mask is created for each layer. Masks are used as part of a photolithographic process in which the pattern of the circuit is etched into layers of silicon and other materials.

The manufacturing process is called *fabrication*. The process starts with melting silicon into circular *wafers*. These wafers vary in size—the most common are about three to twelve inches in diameter. Each wafer is used as the base for many chips. The wafers are passed through a series of machines which create a number of identical chips on the wafer.

At this stage, each chip on the wafer is called a *die*. Each die is a working chip, although it would rapidly become contaminated if exposed to the elements.

After completion, the die on the wafer are tested. Some of those die will have defects, and are marked for later disposal. The wafer is then cut apart with a diamond saw, and separated into individual chips. (The defective die are thrown away.)

The next step is *assembly*, or *packaging*. Each die is encased in a plastic cover; gold pins extend from the package and are used to connect the chip with the circuit board in which it will be placed. The package for microprocessors may be much larger than the chip itself—some assembled chips are over an inch square.

After packaging, the completed chips are tested. Many chips fail this test and *should* be scrapped. (More on this below.) The good chips are marked with certain identifying information (also discussed below), and are then ready for sale.

The most important item to remember about packaging is that most of it is done overseas. Although American companies still fabricate chips, most chips are sent overseas for packaging to take advantage of cheap labor. The chips are then returned to the manufacturer for sale. Thus, many chips are stolen in places such as Thailand and Malaysia.

3.12–c   The most commonly stolen chips

Thieves generally steal two types of chips: memory chips (typically grouped together in *modules*) and microprocessors. Thieves steal memory chips because demand for them is high, and so many are manufactured that they are difficult to trace. Microprocessors are difficult to trace for the same reason and are generally more expensive than memory chips.

Counterfeiting and remarking

Criminals find defective chips (sometimes just thrown away overseas), or create counterfeit defective chips bearing a "famous maker's label." The buyer gets defective chips, and the "famous name" gets an undeserved reputation for shoddy goods. A variant on this scheme is to buy working chips and *remark* them as better performing, higher priced, chips.

You should refer counterfeiting and remarking cases involving importation into the United States to the United States Customs Service. Federal and state agencies may be able to prosecute thieves based on violations of trademark or counterfeiting statutes. Victims may wish to pursue civil suits against companies which engage in this practice.

3.12–d   *Identifying integrated circuits*

In order to prosecute a thief driving a stolen car, you must prove that the automobile was stolen from a victim. To do that, you must be able to describe the car in enough detail to prove that it is the car owned by the victim. Similarly, the first step in prosecuting a thief is to prove that the components found in his or her possession were stolen from your victim. You must be able to identify the components.

As discussed above, many components are identifiable by serial numbers and other performance-related attributes (e.g., hard disk size). Integrated circuits are a little more complicated.

Figure 3–1 displays some of the markings found on a typical integrated circuit. Item #1 is a logo identifying the manufacturer. If you run across a logo you have never seen before, almost any chip manufacturer or chip broker should be able to identify it. You can also call your local chapter of the Semiconductor Industry Association.[4]

---

4. Another option is to purchase *IC Master*, a yearly catalogue of all chips on the market, from Hearst Business Communications, 645 Stewart Avenue, Garden City, NY 11530; 516–227–1300.

Figure 3-1.

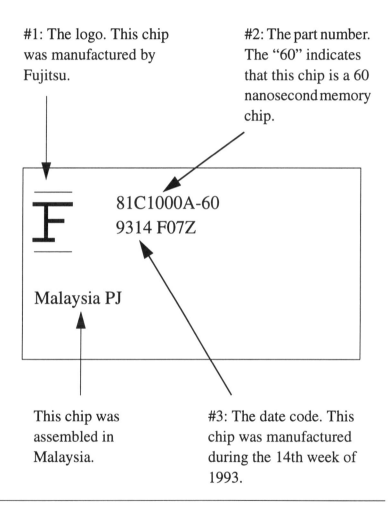

#1: The logo. This chip was manufactured by Fujitsu.

#2: The part number. The "60" indicates that this chip is a 60 nanosecond memory chip.

81C1000A-60
9314 F07Z

Malaysia PJ

This chip was assembled in Malaysia.

#3: The date code. This chip was manufactured during the 14th week of 1993.

Item #2, the string of letters and number which looks like a serial number, is not a serial number at all—it is a *part number*, or *ID code*. The part number is like a car model name and is placed on every chip of that type. The number will tell you the type of chip (e.g., a Pentium microprocessor), and something about its performance (e.g., that it is a 90 MHz Pentium microprocessor). The number may also include information about the *stepping* of the chip. Just like cars, chips are improved over time to fix problems or incorporate minor improvements. Each version of a chip is called a stepping. The part number may tell you which version of the chip you are holding.

Item #3 is the *date code*. This code indicates the year and the week in which the chip was manufactured. This code may be important to your case. If a group of chips is stolen from a chip manufacturer, then it is possible that each chip in that group will have the same date code. Finding chips with the same date code in the thief's possession may, in combination with other evidence, be enough to convince a jury that the chips belong to your victim.

A problem with relying upon date codes is that chips sold to OEMs often go through so many hands that your OEM victim may buy chips with a large number of different date codes. Even if the victim buys chips sorted by date code, it may well commingle (i.e., mix) those chips in inventory.

Nonetheless, a date code can be significant to your case. For example, some distributors and OEMs are assigned date codes by their suppliers, meaning that chips sold to that customer are marked with a unique date code placed only on those chips. In 1988, Panasonic assigned a special date code to some of its distributors. In one case, a fence was found with chips marked with that date code. The fence could not rely on the traditional defense that the prosecution could not prove that the chips in his possession were stolen from the victim.

Law enforcement investigators should inquire how the victim marked its stolen property. Some manufacturers are including serial numbers on magnetic media (i.e., on the hard drive itself), and Intel Corporation is marking Pentium chips with serial numbers which you can see by examining the chip with a microscope. Other chip makers may follow suit shortly.

3.20   The chip market

Computer makers must have a ready supply of chips. But the demand for chips fluctuates dramatically and unpredictably depending upon a number of factors, including customer demand, production capacity, and new technologies. Thus, the chip market is a boom and bust market.

When there are plenty of chips, the price drops, and computer makers easily obtain supplies for their use. But prices can rise dramatically during a shortage, and some computer makers unable to get chips face bankruptcy. Computer makers facing bankruptcy have been known to be less than fussy about the source of their product.

There is a separate and distinct market for each type of chip. Some chips, such as memory chips, are so common that they are treated like commodities. There has been serious discussion about establishing a DRAM memory chip market on the Pacific Stock Exchange, much like the market for crude oil or soybeans.

Other chips are distinct products which have specific applications and narrower markets. Certain microprocessors, such as Intel's Pentium chip, are made by only one company. That company supplies the market, and companies whose computers are built around that chip cannot substitute another microprocessor.

The most dramatic industry-wide shortage in recent history occurred in the DRAM memory market in the mid-1980s. It happened because American production had dropped steadily over the years due to foreign competition. When demand peaked, foreign manufacturers could not keep pace. Many computer companies had to reduce production because they were unable to obtain chips.

Large computer companies insulate themselves from this problem to some extent by signing long-term contracts directly with chip manufacturers. These companies pay a slight premium for a guaranteed supply of certain chips for a period of years. When a shortage occurs, chip manufacturers often place all customers on *allocation*. Preferred customers, who have signed long-term contracts, get their chips first. Thus, the smaller companies are hurt most by a shortage.

In addition to shortages caused by a lack of availability of chips, individual companies' demand for chips can vary based on the market for their products. Company A's computer sales may exceed expectations, prompting it to increase production and its demand for chips. This company may need to buy chips in a hurry. At the same time, Company B's product may not be selling well—Company B may be willing to sell chips. But with hundreds of different computer makers scattered around the country, how does Company A know that Company B has chips to sell?

Enter the *secondary market*, also called the *gray market*. The gray market consists of hundreds of *chip brokers*. These brokers buy and sell chips for a living. You can find a chip broker in any state in the country. Many brokers deal chips across the country and the world by telephone, fax machine, and on bulletin boards (as well as the Internet). It is a largely unregulated industry. These brokers often deal in other components, as well, such as disk drives, memory chips, and PCMCIA cards.

The small computer companies depend upon this secondary market for their existence. They usually need comparatively few chips. Large companies do not offer these companies good prices because they do not order in volume and are unable to commit to buying a large quantity of chips over several years. Small companies are more likely to be affected by shifts in demand for their product, and are less able to predict those fluctuations. They must be able to buy and sell chips in a hurry.

As you might expect, this flourishing gray market has an underside, the *black market*.[5] Black-market chip brokers will knowingly buy stolen property. Many more "dark-gray" brokers will buy stolen property at prices which scream "hot," without ever being certain that particular property is stolen.

The secondary market consists of brokers of all kinds. Some have offices in commercial buildings, others have tiny storefronts in strip shopping centers, and still others have an automobile, a pager, and boxes of inventory in their apartments.

Brokers sell thousands of parts a day, and it is not unusual for stolen parts to be sold by telephone and fax machine *several times within the first 72 hours after the theft*. The numerous sales mean that chips are usually "laundered" from the black market to the legitimate market extremely quickly.

---

5. The term "gray market" is often used to denote the black market. However, this does a disservice to the scores of legitimate brokers. It also makes them angry and uncooperative.

For example, a thief may sell stolen chips for 60% of the market price to a black-market dealer, who sells them over the telephone a few hours later to a gray-market dealer for 75%, who sells them to another broker for 80%, and so on, until the last "gray-white" dealer sells them to a legitimate broker for 97% of the market price. Law enforcement investigators and victims looking for suspicious transactions will have to trace the chain of purchases back to the suspicious "60%" sale from thief to broker.

In most states, chip brokers, unlike other secondhand dealers such as pawnbrokers, are not required to keep records of buyers and sellers. Thus, there is often no ready means of determining who sold "hot" chips to a broker.

This means that speed is essential in investigating component thefts. Every theft must be investigated immediately, and companies should report such thefts to police as soon as they discover them.

Police departments specializing in high-technology crime investigation should consider recruiting brokers as confidential informants. There are dozens of legitimate "white-market" chip brokers trying to earn a living in an intensely competitive field. Many of them are driven out of business because black- and dark-gray-market brokers buy chips from thieves for much lower prices than legitimate brokers must pay, and then undercut the resale prices offered by those legitimate brokers.

These legitimate brokers often know who is buying stolen property because they can see the prices being offered by their competitors. As discussed above, even legitimate brokers innocently buy property which has been laundered through black- and gray-market brokers. These brokers are an important source of information. You need to learn their business and cultivate contacts among them.

Using their information, you will meet black-market brokers and become familiar with local repeat purchasers of stolen property. Your goal is to cultivate a web of contacts which will allow you to trace property almost as soon as it hits the gray and black markets.

Another method which may be helpful is to scan newspapers for advertisements offering "CASH" for components (typically memory chips, hard drives, and motherboards). While many of these advertisers are legitimate, you may find that some of the advertisers are regular buyers of stolen property.

Note that confidentiality is just as critical here as in narcotics cases. Chip brokers depend upon mutual trust and reputation in their community for their livelihood. If you let word get out to the broker-age community that one of their own is a "snitch," you have just put your ally out of business. There is typically no reason to divulge the identity of a broker during a criminal prosecution—your broker merely serves to point the finger of suspicion at another broker who is offering property under suspicious circumstances.

3.30   Component thieves and their methods

Component theft has changed over the last ten years. In the 1970s, component theft was the province of the single entrepreneur. Individual employees would stuff handfuls of chips in their jacket pockets before leaving their shifts and sell them to whomever would buy—usually black-market chip brokers or scrap metal reclaimers (for the gold contained in chips and circuit boards).[6]

The face of the component thief has literally changed within the last five years. Although it is unpleasant to admit in our multicultural society, you must confront the fact that, at least in California, many component thieves are first- or second-generation Asian immigrants.[7]

---

6. This practice, called *reclamation theft*, is less lucrative than stealing chips. Nonetheless, a single 55-gallon drum of old or defective circuit boards can contain over a thousand dollars worth of gold.

7. Although recent statistics in this area are scarce, various media accounts of the problem note the prevalence of Asians among component thieves. *See* "Chip Theft: An Industry Under Siege," *San Jose Mercury News*, May 5, 1996 ("informal gangs, often rootless Vietnamese men, group together to steal chips"); "Computer Thieves Strike Yet Again," *San Jose Mercury News*, July 22, 1995 (police believe that most component robberies are linked to loose-knit Asian gangs); "Chip Heist Probe Nets 15," *San Francisco Examiner*, May 27, 1995 (arrest of fifteen members of suspected Asian crime "ring"); "High-Tech Heists Get Hot," *San Jose Mercury News*, April 14, 1995; "Your Chips or Your Life!," *Time*, May 2, 1994 (many robberies committed by gangs of Chinese or Vietnamese immigrants); Webster, "Chips Are a Thief's Best Friend," *New York Times Magazine*, September 18, 1994; "Congress Told of Jump in Asian Gangs," *San Jose Mercury News*, October 4, 1991.

Asian workers have come to dominate the low-level jobs at the high-technology companies where chips and other components are available. Most assemblers and testers in Silicon Valley are now Vietnamese and Chinese. Theft is an equal opportunity profession; you will find male and female thieves.

These employees are now far more mobile than in the past. OEMs and chip companies rely heavily on temporary manpower which can be laid off when recessions occur in the high-technology industry. As a result, employees can and do migrate to different companies frequently.

The current consensus in law enforcement is that part of the problem is caused by small groups of employees who move from company to company. These groups of employees steal chips from each company they work for, but rarely stay around long enough to get caught. Chips and other components are stolen from delivery trucks, shipping and receiving areas, production lines, and storage areas.

The newest mode of component theft is robbery. Groups of armed men were responsible for more than 130 robberies in California between 1990 and mid-1995. As of this writing, robberies are occurring about once every three weeks in Silicon Valley.[8]

These robberies are similar to traditional bank robberies. The robbers force all the employees into a room, take the chips, and leave. OEMs with large chip inventories are now "where the money is." Unlike banks, many of these crimes are inside jobs, with an employee letting the thieves in through "locked" warehouse doors.

Poor security is also responsible. In the smallest companies, the only protection may be a lock on the warehouse door. Security guards are usually unarmed, and smaller companies often do not hire guards at all.

Losses in Silicon Valley from burglaries and robberies have risen to as high as $30 million annually. The average theft is about $150,000, although million-dollar losses are no longer unusual. (Robberies typically net less than $50,000, due to time constraints.)

---

8. Indeed, robbers struck companies *thirty times* during the first three months of 1995. "High-Tech Heists Get Hot," *San Jose Mercury News*, April 14, 1995; and April 8, 1995. *See* "Chip Heist Probe Nets 15," *San Francisco Examiner*, May 27, 1995 (nearly 50 computer robberies reported through first five months of 1995).

There is currently debate within the law enforcement community as to the connection between these employees and traditional Asian gang activity. The consensus at this moment appears to be that component theft is still disorganized, consisting of many small groups of individuals. These individuals may also belong to Asian gangs, but no concrete connections have been shown. However, this situation could change at any time. For example, in 1994, federal authorities indicted 16 Asians who had allegedly formed a nationwide group involved in chip theft and narcotics trafficking.[9]

Generally, chips and other components stolen in one geographic area end up in another. Chips stolen in Silicon Valley often end up in Los Angeles or the Southwest; they may also be sold in New York or even overseas (e.g., Hong Kong or Thailand). Thieves still sell their wares to black-market brokers, but they are now also creating their own outlets by setting up small quasi-legitimate computer stores. This may be to our advantage because stores are likely to hold stolen inventory longer than chip brokers.

Asian component thieves present several problems for law enforcement investigators. First, Asian component thieves are much more likely to use aliases successfully because they may use two names: (1) their birth name; and (2) the name they use in the United States.

Their birth name may be used among their associates or on duplicate identification material. Their "American name" consists of a first name, middle name, and surname, which they will use in different order depending upon their needs. Police should not rely upon criminal history records—suspects may be found (if at all) under different names which may be identical to those of innocent third parties.

Second, many Asian component thieves are simultaneously distrustful and contemptuous of law enforcement, and often will not talk to police. Worse, Asian witnesses often fear police (because police in their former countries were corrupt and brutal), and may be reluctant to cooperate with authorities. The result is that cases are unusually

---

9. *San Jose Mercury News*, August, 19, 1994. Authorities suspect that a rash of 30 robberies in the first few months of 1995 are attributable to two to four gangs. *See* "High-Tech Heists Get Hot," *San Jose Mercury News*, April 14, 1995.

difficult to investigate, and recruiting Asian undercover officers and informants is extremely difficult.

Finally, Asian component thieves do not like negotiable instruments. They are more comfortable dealing with large amounts of cash. Purchasing chips with $50,000 to $100,000 in cash is common. Unfortunately, this means that traditional paper trails are not likely to exist.

3.40   A procedure for investigating component theft cases

Although theft of computer components is the easiest high-technology crime to understand, it is also the hardest to investigate and prove. Most commonly stolen components, such as integrated circuits, are virtually impossible to trace. Even if the component itself is unique, the industry usually does not keep track of components individually.

For example, assume that Xcorp, a computer manufacturer, purchases 1,500 individually serialized disk drives from Maxtor, a disk drive company. Unfortunately, Xcorp does not spend the time necessary to keep track of each drive by its serial number when it is stored in the warehouse. When Xcorp reports that it is missing 500 drives, there are no records identifying exactly which drives were once in inventory but are now missing. All Xcorp can tell you is that it had 15,000 drives in inventory in January, sold 5,000 since then, and has only 9,500 in its warehouse.

Even if you find an Xcorp employee trying to sell 100 (or even 500) Maxtor drives, how can you be sure that he is selling Xcorp's stolen drives rather than drives he may have purchased (or stolen) from another Maxtor distributor? Could the employee be running a legitimate parts or OEM business on the side? (A few engineers do exactly that.)

If you are a police officer, are you willing to arrest that employee without any other evidence of theft? You cannot prove that he took the drives from the factory—he may have received them from another dishonest employee. You cannot prove that the drives are stolen, since you cannot even prove they belong to Xcorp.

The answer becomes clear: you have no case. Add less than perfect inventory records suggesting that the culprit may be normal shrinkage or mistake, and the defense attorney will soon threaten you with a false arrest or malicious prosecution lawsuit.

Thus, most component cases are non-starters. The rest of this chapter discusses procedures that law enforcement and corporate investigators should follow in identifying, reporting, and investigating those cases which are likely to end with recovery of property and, perhaps, a conviction.

3.41   Evaluating your case

As you can see from the previous description of the component market, most reported thefts offer few avenues for investigation. The market is so volatile, fluid, and undocumented that, like residential burglaries, most cases are hopeless.

Just as some police departments are refusing to investigate routine burglaries, they should hesitate to investigate most reported chip thefts (with the exception of armed robberies) unless the victim has located the property or identified a suspect. Of course, this rule may prove to be toothless when a prominent company reports a theft of several hundred thousand dollars worth of inventory and demands immediate action from police and prosecutors.

3.42   Finding the property

The best way to locate the property is to let the market know that stolen goods may be circulating. Police may consider entering stolen property into the NCIC computer system.

Ask the victim to consider reporting the theft to prospective buyers, particularly if the components are unusual. Most brokers rely upon fax machines to send and receive bids and price lists. Victims may be persuaded to fax stolen property reports to prominent brokers in their area, along with the promise of a reward.

At some point, the stolen components may reenter the legitimate market—close ties with local legitimate brokers may increase the victim's chances of recovery, even if the victim has to buy its own product back. Buying back a portion of the property may lead to a thief who is holding the rest.

Encourage the victim to report theft to all interested trade associations. Suggest to victims too embarrassed to risk publicity that they at least ask their component distributor to watch for the property.

Do not sue the broker!

It is extremely bad form, and bad business, for a component owner to sue a broker who admits having innocently purchased stolen property for the tort of conversion (wrongful possession or use of property). Victims or their insurance carriers may be tempted to sue if the loss is large and the broker appears to be solvent.

This topic should be discussed with the victim before chip brokers are approached for assistance. Do not expect chip brokers to report having purchased stolen property, even unknowingly, unless the victim and its insurance carrier are willing to waive any legal action in writing.

3.43 Finding a suspect

First, determine whether the victim's security system has recorded the theft. You should review film from security cameras and logs from access control systems.[10] If the victim or law enforcement has identified local component fences, check the victim's phone logs for calls by employees to those criminals' telephone numbers.

The next step is to examine the victim's inventory records. As discussed at the end of this chapter, it is important for you to audit the victim's inventory records to ensure that you can prove that a theft

---

10. Remember that most robberies involve employees who open the door for the robbers. Consider who had access to security devices which were disabled. Do not overlook the possibility that the thieves hired the victim's security guards to turn a blind eye.

occurred. One of the purposes of such an audit is to narrow the number of people who could have committed the theft.

You should concentrate on those individuals who had access to the victim's inventory. Pay particular attention to those employees who have left the company suddenly, displayed evidence of recent wealth (e.g., the employee who buys a new car), or are suffering financial problems (e.g., compulsive gamblers).

Unfortunately, most companies must allow a large number of individuals to have access to their components. Given that most companies' recordkeeping is less than perfect, concentrating on employees who had the opportunity to steal is usually successful only in proving a loss of product, and does not help you identify a suspect.

After checking the victim's records, tap into the company rumor mill. Most component thefts are inside jobs by "entrepreneurial" employees. Occasionally, an honest employee will either observe the theft or hear rumors about the identity of the thief. In one case, a thief bragged about the theft *in advance* to an employee. After the theft, the co-worker reported the incident to management. Upon being confronted by police, the thief unexpectedly confessed and led police to almost $1 million in stolen chips.

Although the vast majority of cases are much harder to solve, do not underestimate the power of the internal rumor mill. Many employees resent thieves, whose activities damage the company's profitability to the detriment of employees' profit-sharing plans. In addition, rings of thieves may suffer from internal dissension; a disgruntled member may tip off management. In many cases, employees interviewed after the case was solved reported that they knew, or suspected, that the suspects were stealing from the company.

There are at least two ways to tap into this information source. First, although companies rarely do so, a victim may offer employees a reward for information leading to the apprehension and conviction of the thief. (The number of false reports prompted by a reward may be offset by the amount of property recovered.) Offering a reward for return of the property alone may also work, although it will often leave you without a suspect.

Second, management can use undercover agents, generally private investigators, to mingle with employees and attempt to identify the thieves or discover how the crime was committed. Employees who have stolen once often steal again, and may recruit additional employees to assist them in making a bigger "score." Although "hiring" undercover workers is controversial, it has worked in the past.

Police departments who become experienced in this area will eventually develop informants. Police departments should foster close communication between their gang task forces and their high-technology units—informants maintained by one unit may possess information needed by another.

3.43–a Stings

Police and federal agencies have broken several large theft rings by recruiting Asian informants and Asian police officers to pose as buyers or sellers of stolen chips. Law enforcement investigators use *stings* and *reverse-stings* to catch thieves.

The *sting* works by having an undercover operative buy stolen chips. These operations are difficult, however, because there is usually no way of proving that the chips sold to the operative were stolen from a particular company. If prosecutors cannot prove that the chips were stolen, they are unable to prove that any crime was committed. Thus, police rely heavily on reverse-stings.

A *reverse-sting* works by having an undercover operative pose as a seller of stolen chips. A local high-technology company furnishes the chips, usually worth between several hundred thousand and several million dollars.

The operative uses informants to arrange meetings with "buyers." Those meetings are taped (preferably videotaped), and police arrest the buyers during the "sale." Prosecutors then charge the buyers with conspiracy to receive stolen property and attempting to receive stolen property. (Some jurisdictions may not allow a charge of attempted receiving of stolen property if the chips offered to the fences were never stolen.)

This book does not provide a step-by-step guide to mounting undercover operations because they are practical only under limited circumstances. Very few police departments are fortunate enough to have a large high-technology company willing to risk $1 million in inventory, a supply of Asian informants or police officers, and the time and manpower necessary to undertake such operations. Furthermore, such stings can be very dangerous for the operatives involved. At least one Asian informant has been killed.

3.44 Recovering the components

Although stolen chips often disappear overseas or across the country, other components are occasionally resold locally. Assume that you have discovered the victim's property for sale, perhaps in a small gray-market outlet or through a crooked broker. There are two ways to recover it: (1) in an undercover buy; and/or (2) with a search warrant.

In an undercover buy, an agent of the police or the victim approaches the suspect and purchases the stolen property. The buyer may or may not be *wired* (fitted with a transmitter). An advantage to this approach is that suspects may admit that the property was stolen. Furthermore, a buy does not require a search warrant, making it particularly useful when time is of the essence or there is insufficient probable cause to support a warrant.

A disadvantage is that any such operation poses a risk to the buyer if the suspect is violent. Furthermore, many times such purchases are impossible because the suspect is not offering the components for sale—the buyer has no plausible explanation for knowing that the suspect has the components.

A search warrant is valuable because it gives police the right to seize the property from a specified location. A properly drafted search warrant will also allow the victim to help search for, and identify, its components. A search warrant may uncover other evidence, such as sales ledgers, phone books (with names of accomplices), and/or property stolen in other thefts.

A disadvantage is that a search warrant ends the investigation by tipping off the suspect. Unless the suspect is caught with the property under circumstances indicating that he or she had no business possessing it (e.g., a suspect who makes $20,000 per year holding $500,000 worth of chips precisely matching the description of those stolen), your case may end without a prosecution.

Most cases involving undercover buys also involve a search warrant. The buy is set up to sting the suspect. If there is sufficient probable cause before the buy to justify a warrant, the warrant will be executed at the conclusion of the buy to search for and seize property and other evidence. If there is not enough evidence for a warrant, but the buy is successful, the suspect will be detained until police can obtain a warrant to search the suspect's premises.

The search warrant requirement imposes discipline on an investigation because it requires the investigator to gather a number of key facts at the outset. In order to seize property, you must describe it. Therefore, the investigator must understand exactly what was stolen.

Identify components carefully

As discussed in Chapters 7–9, items to be seized must be described with particularity. The particularity requirement is important when seizing components from a dealer who normally stocks a large variety of different components. Seizing "integrated circuits" from a chip broker is like seizing "televisions" from Circuit City—the warrant will encompass hundreds of items unrelated to the probable cause justifying the warrant. The warrant should offer as detailed a description of the allegedly stolen components as possible.

The basis for a search warrant will usually consist of facts indicating that the suspect has no reason to possess those parts and is acting in a way consistent with knowledge that the parts are stolen. Appendix B includes a sample warrant designed for component theft cases, and the next section includes a list of questions directed toward obtaining probable cause.

3.44–a   A typical component theft investigation

The following scenario illustrates how investigators may use an undercover buy in conjunction with a search warrant.

Xcorp, a prominent disk drive manufacturer, has suffered constant losses of 540 MB drives from its warehouse during the past year. Xcorp keeps a list of serial numbers for all its drives.[11] The company ships 5,000 drives each month. Between 100 and 400 drives have been missing each time the company took inventory during the last two quarters. The drives are sold in computer stores for $400 each; their wholesale value is $300.

An employee of the victim has seen Xcorp drives at AB Computer, a small computer store with three employees located near Xcorp. AB Computer is not an authorized distributor of the drives and has never purchased drives from Xcorp before. AB is selling the drives for $225 each, $75 below wholesale cost.

Is there enough evidence to justify a search warrant? Perhaps, but AB may have purchased the drives legitimately on the gray market at a bargain-basement price from a failing computer manufacturer. Without further investigation, there is no hard evidence that AB Computer is guilty of knowingly receiving stolen property.

Police should be aware that publicity about the execution of a search warrant on a small business can badly damage that merchant. Since such merchants are also part of the high-technology community, their interests can be just as important as those of the large manufacturer who is missing a very small percentage of its inventory.

You need more information. The most important question is whether AB Computer is selling stolen drives. However, other information is also important. For example, how many of these drives are available? Does the store offer a warranty? Do they claim to be an authorized dealer? What reason does the store give for being able to sell the drives so cheaply? Can the store get more? A whole lot more? If the answer to the last question is yes, it is more likely that the store is dealing directly with the thief or thief's distributor, rather than snagging a one-time spectacular deal off of the gray market.

The way to get answers to these questions is to send a "customer" into the store to ask them. The customer should be well versed in the industry. The best choice is often a representative of the victim—it is

---

11. As discussed in the next section, police should not investigate any case where it is impossible to accurately identify the stolen property.

unlikely that even the most crooked and desperate fence will harm a potential customer.

Send the customer in with the victim's money and have him or her purchase one or more of the components.[12] It is best if the customer poses as a representative or employee of a very small OEM which is considering changing its source of supply. In addition to making the purchase, the customer asks the questions listed above and asks if AB Computer can provide the drives in volume.

The first step after the purchase is to check the drives against Xcorp's records to determine whether those drives are stolen. If they are not, and the victim's recordkeeping is accurate, this indicates that AB Computer purchased the drives from someone who originally purchased them from Xcorp.

At worst, Xcorp may be the victim of *dumping* by an authorized dealer. *Dumping* occurs when dealers seek to meet quotas by selling a number of drives at a loss to small merchants. Although this may violate the terms of a contract between Xcorp and its dealer, AB Computer is not at fault. It is not a police matter—the case should be dropped and Xcorp encouraged to pursue whatever civil remedies it may have against whomever sold the drives to AB Computer.

If the drives are stolen, it is still possible that AB Computer is an innocent third party (i.e., its source may appear to AB to be a legitimate operation). The answers to the other questions about the ability of AB to offer such a great price and the availability of more "bargains" will provide further clues concerning AB's culpability.

If AB Computer claims to be an authorized dealer, but is not, that suggests at a minimum that AB is perpetrating a fraud on consumers; consumers may be willing to pay more to buy from an authorized dealer because those merchants are often able to get defective components repaired or replaced easily.

---

12. Do not use police department funds—the victim should repurchase its own stolen property. Most purchases will cost only a few thousand dollars, which is pocket change to most corporate victims. Some police departments are so strapped for funds that they no longer investigate routine residential burglaries, much less repurchase stolen property. Suggest to the victim that its insurance company may fund a repurchase.

A telltale sign that something may be wrong is if the store tells the customer that he or she is getting a warranty from the store instead of the manufacturer. Fences use this dodge to discourage customers from contacting the manufacturer if the stolen component needs repair. If the manufacturer is presented with a broken component which, according to its records, should still be in its warehouse, the customer leads police right back to the store.

There are several reasons why the "customer" should ask how the merchant is able to purchase the component so cheaply. First, the question saves police time and embarrassment if either the manufacturer's records are wrong, and they actually sold the drive to AB Computer (or to an authorized dealer who sold it to AB), or if AB is an innocent third party who does not know that it bought a bargain from a thief.

Where the victim has made a mistake, asking the question may save the manufacturer from being sued by the merchant for malicious prosecution and defamation. If AB Computer is an innocent third party, there is a good chance that AB will lead police to the thief.

Second, a bona fide fence is not going to be surprised that a savvy customer recognizes a "bargain." Such a fence is going to have a ready-made story which will always be interesting to hear. (After it is proven false, that story will entertain the jury at trial and contribute to a conviction.) Thus, the risk of spooking the fence by that question is acceptably low.

Finally, the inquiry about availability in bulk has two purposes: (1) obtaining information about AB Computer's source; and (2) setting up a sting. If AB is able to obtain components in roughly the amount being stolen from Xcorp, then AB's source may well be the thief. Lesser quantities suggest that AB may be further down the chain.

If AB Computer appears crooked and agrees to obtain components in volume, it is time to set up a sting. Law enforcement investigators should prepare a search warrant similar to the one in Appendix B.

Note that this warrant allows police to search for the stolen property *and* AB's business records. Those records (or the lack thereof for the stolen property) can be valuable evidence in a prosecution against

AB. Those records may also lead law enforcement investigators to other stolen property.

The customer should be sent back in a few days or a week later to order components in volume. Depending on the circumstances, one or more "confidence-building" purchases may be made. If possible, the customer should require delivery within a very short period of time, pleading some sort of urgency.

Depending on the importance of the case and departmental resources, police may maintain surveillance on AB Computer and the site of the thefts. If everything works, the thief may be detected stealing components from Xcorp's factory to fill the order, or delivering the stolen components to AB.

However, it is often impractical to shadow the suspect and/or the store owner 24 hours a day. Delivery may occur somewhere other than the store. The thief may deliver goods stolen weeks before your surveillance, and steal more goods a few weeks later to replenish his or her stockpile.

Use pen registers to trace crooked employees

One way to identify the fence's supplier is to obtain pen registers on the fence's phone (see Chapters 4 and 8), and match the resulting phone numbers with the home or business phones associated with suspected employees. If the suspects are using pagers, prepare a second search warrant ordering the pager service to identify the owner of the pager (the pen register should pick up any secondary numbers dialed by the owner to deliver the page). Both warrants should order the recipients to refrain from notifying their customers until further order of the court.

In any event, police should serve the warrant when they believe that stolen property will be found on the premises. Attempts should be made to "turn" the crooked store owner against the thief. Further investigation may reveal that the store is only one link in a larger chain. Fast action may allow investigators to wire the store owner and use him or her against other links.

3.50   Facts to be gathered in the course of the investigation

There is no set timetable for component cases. Investigators are often forced to obtain a search warrant immediately in order to prevent the movement of stolen components. However, investigators should attempt to get as much information, as soon as possible, before seizing property or arresting suspects.

A thorough initial investigation may reveal fatal weaknesses in the case. Occasionally victims inflate or even fabricate losses. (At least one case has ended with a successful insurance fraud prosecution against the "victim" chip broker.) More often, the chips are simply "lost" within the company, as when engineers remove them for testing without adjusting inventory records. Finally, the prosecutor will demand a thorough investigation before initiating a criminal prosecution.

The next section discusses the information you should gather during your investigation.

3.51   Auditing the records

Your investigation is not complete until you can prove in court that the components held by the suspect are the components stolen from the victim. You must audit the victim's records to ensure that there is a match between the components lost and the components recovered.

In many cases, your evidence is circumstantial, such as where 50,000 Pentium chips were stolen from Xcorp on Tuesday, and 50,000 Pentium chips were found in an Xcorp employee's house on Friday. Very few employees have the independent means to purchase 50,000 Pentiums.

However, even in that case, you must prove that Xcorp is missing any chips at all. Without that proof, you cannot obtain a conviction. Furthermore, if all you can prove is that Xcorp is missing 10,000 chips, the prosecutor will have a problem explaining the discrepancy to a jury. If this employee should not have been able to procure

50,000 Pentiums, where did he get the 40,000 Pentiums? In addition, even if you obtain a conviction, the sentence and restitution imposed will depend upon exactly how many Pentiums the defendant stole.

Of course, it is easier if Xcorp's parts are individually serialized and Xcorp actually accounts for them by serial number. (This is not the case for most chips, of course.) But even with serialization, the prosecutor still has to prove that Xcorp did not sell those components to someone else, who then lawfully transferred them to the Xcorp employee.

The key is to construct a paper trail of inventory records establishing Xcorp's loss. You should take the following steps.

First, do not simply accept the victim's word on its losses. Require victims to substantiate those losses as soon as practicable. While law enforcement investigators may need to seek a search warrant to recover the stolen property before this task is completed, they should not initiate a criminal complaint or indictment without proof of loss. Corporate investigators should be equally insistent on this point to prevent later embarrassment to the victim.

Second, ask the victim to explain how it accounts for its components. Request the originals of all records pertaining to the allegedly stolen components. (Be prepared to make copies and return them to the victim so that it can run its business.)

Do this even after you have obtained components which appear to belong to the victim. Do not assume that a confession ends your problems. *A confession alone may not be enough to obtain a conviction unless you have independent proof that the stolen components belong to the victim.*

The *corpus delicti* rule prohibits prosecutors from admitting a defendant's out-of-court statements (i.e., admissions and confessions) into evidence unless and until the prosecution presents evidence that the offense was committed, including evidence that the victim is now missing its property.

Thus, even if your suspect confesses to stealing components from the victim, you must still show independently that the victim is missing components. That the suspect is selling components similar to those manufactured or stored by your victim is not evidence that he obtained *those particular components* from your victim.

You should request the following records:

1. *Records showing that the victim ordered the missing components from its supplier (assuming that the victim was buying those components, such as chips, to put into its own products).*

These records may include purchase orders or correspondence. These records may provide you with important information, such as the date codes for integrated circuits.

2. *Records showing that the victim received components (again assuming that the victim purchased those components elsewhere).*

These records should include invoices, packing slips, and any internal logs maintained by the victim.

3. *Records reflecting storage of components received by the victim.*

Many companies log their received goods into a cage or other secured room. An employee is assigned to log parts (and people) in and out of the area. These access logs may be critical to solving the case.

4. *Records reflecting use of the parts in production.*

Most companies account for how much inventory (i.e., how many components) they use in producing their product. If the company can prove that it received 1,000 chips from a supplier, used 500 of those chips in production, and has been missing 500 since Wednesday, you may have strong circumstantial evidence when on Friday you find 500 chips in the house of a production line employee.

5. *Records reflecting the number and serial numbers of components manufactured.*

Where the victim has lost its own finished product (e.g., the victim makes disk drives, and 100 of them are now missing), the first step is to prove that those drives were manufactured. There should be records indicating how many components were manufactured during a particular period (day, week, month, etc.) and the serialization (if any) of each part. There should be a log of serial numbers for all serialized products.

6. *Records reflecting storage of those manufactured components.*

Check access logs for any components which were stolen after manufacture.

7. *Records reflecting sale of components manufactured by the victim.*

It is very embarrassing to find that the victim's records indicate that the components you found in the "crook's" house were sold legitimately to the "crook" (or even to a third party). Save the victim a lawsuit by making sure that such records are checked to verify that the components were never sold. If the records reflect a sale which the victim is sure never happened, focus on individuals who could have altered those records.

8. *Copies of all documents submitted by the victim to any insurer in support of a claim.*

Corporate investigators should be especially aware of an occasional abuse by victims. Companies sometimes inform police that $10,000 worth of chips were stolen, while claiming $40,000 in losses to their insurance company.

Occasionally this is a case of outright fraud. More often the victim has experienced multiple losses in the past which it has not reported to police, and is now seeking to pin all of those losses on the one thief you apprehended.

Even if the victim is correct about the identity of the thief in each of those cases, you may not be able to substantiate those claims, and a defense attorney who is able to disprove one claim will try to cast doubt on all of them. Finally, you put both yourself and the victim in a better and more realistic position to obtain restitution by requiring the victim to substantiate all claimed losses at the outset.

If the victim refuses to provide details of an insurance claim, consider closing the case immediately.

As a last resort, consider calling the insurance company

Insurance carriers anticipate that their policyholders will cooperate with police. If the carrier learns that the victim is not cooperating with authorities, it may withhold payment until the victim cooperates. Law enforcement investigators should consider contacting the carrier only as a last resort where the victim's conduct appears suspicious.

Be prepared for less-than-stellar results from your requests for records. The "paper trail" in many cases is either nonexistent or very confused. Many companies do not keep careful records of what happens to their inventory (including manufactured components).[13] The problems can occur from the loading dock all the way through the sale of manufactured components.

The shipping and receiving departments make mistakes logging in inventory. Engineers often grab components held in inventory for use in production of larger components (e.g., chips used in computers) off of the line for special testing to see if quality control problems are being caused by shoddy goods from suppliers. Salespeople may grab manufactured components off the line as samples for potential customers. These "grabs" are often unrecorded, leaving open the possibility that the victim's missing components are still in the factory. Note that this possibility decreases in proportion to the value of the component.

Material handlers (warehousemen) misplace inventory. This problem is particularly prevalent in huge companies struggling to coordinate a number of warehouses and production centers. Computer inventory systems are vulnerable to breakdowns, erasures, and outright tampering.

---

13. This failure is understandable in some cases, particularly where the component is small and not serialized, like most integrated circuits. Smaller companies find it very expensive to institute strict inventory procedures. Inventory control is often not a high priority with most companies because it usually does not contribute visibly and directly to their bottom line.

Many companies have mandatory destruction policies for certain documents, including inventory records. *Secure all documents as soon as possible.* This is particularly important for computer inventory systems. When dealing with a computer system, request that the victim immediately secure backup tapes of all transactions which could affect the audit trail.

You must spend the necessary hours or days to understand and reconstruct the company's inventory in order to ensure that you can trace the components from the factory to the thief. You must be able to account for inconsistencies. You must convince a jury that the rest of your circumstantial evidence proves that some of the components found in the suspect's possession belong to your victim, even if you are unable to reconstruct an exact match between the suspect's components and the victim's record of losses.

Talk to the people in charge of maintaining and accounting for inventory. Do not accept the assurances of corporate counsel or senior management that their inventory procedures are bulletproof—they probably know less about inventory systems (including their own) than you will after your first few cases.

Obviously, since most cases are non-starters, you do not want to spend much time investigating the victim's inventory procedures at the outset. Your victim will also resist such requests if there is little chance of your finding the stolen property. Furthermore, some cases move so quickly that you must obtain a search warrant immediately.

A solution for law enforcement investigators is to request all pertinent records from your victim at the outset. Put the records in your case file pending further action (if any) on the case. If and when the case begins moving forward, press your victim to produce the rest of the records you requested but have not received.

In fast-moving cases where your preliminary investigation indicates that a theft has occurred, do what you must to get the victim's property back. However, *never* initiate a criminal prosecution until you have "walked the paper trail" yourself to make sure that it leads to a conviction.

4

Investigating Computer Intrusion

Bobby was a cowboy. Bobby was a cracksman, a burglar, casing mankind's extended electronic nervous system, rustling data and credit in the crowded matrix, monochrome nonspace where the only stars are dense concentrations of information, and high above it all burn corporate galaxies and the cold spiral arms of military systems.... But ... Bobby was losing his edge, slowing down. He was twenty-eight, Bobby, and that's old for a console cowboy.
—William Gibson, *Burning Chrome*

4.00   Introduction

4.01   Our society is vulnerable to computer intrusion

The electronic intruder has long been a fixture in science fiction novels. Unfortunately, life is imitating art, and our society has become increasingly vulnerable to computer intrusion.

Virtually every function performed in the modern office depends upon a computer. Computers control your telephones—when you make a long-distance call, your PBX (private branch exchange) handles it. The receptionist is rapidly becoming extinct, replaced by the computer "voice mail" system. When you need money on the road, you use an automated teller machine. And companies store most of their important information within their computers.

Each of those computers is vulnerable to intrusion. Intruders have caused cancer patients to receive overdoses of radiation at a prestigious hospital. Intruders have broken into NASA computers. East German spies have broken into NATO computers.

Less dramatically, intruders routinely dial into office telephone systems and use them to make long-distance phone calls. The victim discovers the intrusion when the company phone bill is six inches high and arrives in a box. Current law allows the phone company to stick the victim with the bill—the average loss is about $50,000.

Intruders constantly attack voice mail systems. Intruders have reportedly penetrated Pacific Bell's "Message Center" voice mail service. In a recent criminal case, a defense contractor discovered that its voice mail system was greeting customers with obscenities. After spending over $30,000, the company caught three juveniles who had taken over dozens of "mailboxes" on the system. Organized crime has also taken over mailboxes to arrange narcotics transactions.

Company computers are tempting targets. Disgruntled current and former employees dial into a company's computer system and erase or modify data, or download source code. Juveniles infiltrate those computers just for fun and occasionally damage programs and data. Industrial spies steal proprietary information.

Perhaps the most besieged computer systems belong to universities. Many intruders are college students intent on playing practical jokes, or in more serious cases, changing transcripts.

4.02 Companies must regard every computer intruder as a potentially serious threat because it is very difficult to determine which intruders are dangerous

To understand computer intrusion, consider residential burglary. The residential burglar gains entry without permission, and *may* commit other crimes while on the premises. For example, although most residential burglars enter to steal property, many juveniles commit burglary simply for the thrill of exploring a house belonging to someone else. In still other cases, burglars intend to commit rape.

When the homeowner hears an intruder downstairs, he or she does not know what the burglar has in mind, and must fear the worst. Our society punishes burglary harshly for that reason.

The computer intruder is very much like that residential burglar. The computer intruder gains entry without permission, and *may* use that entry to commit other crimes.

Most computer intruders are juveniles, committing the modern equivalent of trespassing on Farmer John's land. Some juveniles break into company telephone systems to steal free telephone time, a sort of "joyriding."

Other intruders, again mostly juveniles, intrude into computers to commit vandalism. This includes anything from planting obscene messages on voice mail systems, to planting viruses, to erasing data outright. Ex-employees also vandalize their former employers' computers.

Still other computer intruders are more sophisticated, and even more dangerous. A very small number of intruders are industrial spies. As companies store an increasing amount of technical information on computers, industrial spies find it easier to break into the company computer to "download" that information than to break into the company lab.

Like the homeowner who hears a sound on the stairs, companies must respond immediately to intrusions because it can be very difficult, if not impossible, to separate the juvenile burglar from the industrial spy.

4.03 Who are these people?

There are two types of intruders: those with a connection to the owner of the system, and random intruders. The former are generally easy to understand—disgruntled employees have always been a part of the business world. Whereas the disgruntled employee twenty years ago might have burned down a building or stolen the accounting records and ransomed them back to the employer, today's disgruntled employee sneaks into the computer and steals or destroys data.

Oddly enough, random intruders, while more frightening, are often less dangerous to companies than are ex-employees. A random intruder is more likely to be a juvenile interested in browsing through the system. An employee already knows what is there—he or she is more likely to have vengeance or theft in mind.

Employees are more persistent than most other intruders. An intruder may be merely curious about the victim's system—your victim was just "lucky" enough to have the first vulnerable system the intruder encountered that month. An employee wants something, and is therefore willing to return to a system after being detected and ejected. Indeed, employees are more likely to know several ways of returning to the computer (e.g., passwords of various co-workers).

Apart from industrial spies, most non-employee intruders are teenage boys,[1] and most of their activities are nothing more than a new form of juvenile delinquency. Juvenile intruders typically steal telephone access codes and credit card numbers. For example, police in a recent case realized that they might be dealing with a juvenile when the intruder used a stolen credit card number to buy baseball cards.

A word about hackers and crackers

Most newspapers and magazines refer to intruders as *hackers*. However, the term "hacker" has a long and respected history as a description of a gifted computer programmer who uses computers to perform mysterious and magical feats. To be a hacker is to be nothing more than an inventive computer user.

Although the media have been using hacker to refer to intruders for so long that the two words are becoming the same, there is another name for computer intruders that you should use instead: *cracker*.

A hacker includes anyone who breaks into computers. For the most part, "cracker" describes someone who intrudes with malice. The cracker wants to do more than explore—he or she wants to plunder or pillage information.

Regrettably, the media, reaching for symbolism, have occasionally painted these juveniles as the vanguard of a new social movement. Some of the more prominent crackers claim that their efforts are directed against an "establishment" which has tried to put constraints on the "free flow of information" (e.g., by charging money for

---

1. In recognition of this fact, this chapter will assume that your intruder is male.

telephone calls). Some sociologists have even trumpeted the creation of a new cracker "subculture."[2]

Of course, those claims are nonsense. Very few, if any, 14-year-old boys have a political or social agenda. Rather, they have an appetite for game-playing and exploration.

It is not surprising that one of the first computer games played on mainframe computers was called "Adventure"; it allowed players to explore a hidden maze of caverns containing treasure and monsters. "Dungeons and Dragons," another famous role-playing game, soon followed.

But even these games became boring after awhile, and corporate computers offered a more attractive vista for exploration.

> For many teens, the ... electronic bulletin boards became a kind of high-tech clubhouse and launching point for exploring a new digital universe. Computers linked by networks created a more compelling world than the most captivating session of Dungeons & Dragons, a role-playing game practiced by teenage science-fiction and fantasy fans. Maybe Mom and Dad wouldn't let their kid out after dark on a school night, but now he was free to travel anywhere in a far-flung cybernetic world, from the safety and comfort of his bedroom.[3]

The "high-tech clubhouse" is a far better model than "a form of social rebellion." As one commentator puts it:

> Are teenage hackers political terrorists? They are typically white, upper-middle-class adolescents who have taken over the home computer (bought, subsidized, or tolerated by parents in the hopes of cultivating computer literacy). Few are politically motivated although many express contempt for the "bureaucracies" that hamper their electronic journeys. Nearly all demand unfettered access to intricate and intriguing computer networks. In this, teenage

---

2. *See, e.g.*, Meyer and Thomas, *The Baudy World of the Byte Bandit: A Post Modernist Interpretation of the Computer Underground* (1990).

3. John Markoff, "Rebel with a Modem," *Image*, a Sunday supplement of the *San Francisco Examiner*, March 27, 1988.

hackers resemble an alienated shopping culture deprived of purchasing opportunities more than a terrorist network.[4]

Although the power of computer technology and our society's
dependence upon that technology magnify the consequences of
theft and vandalism, the problem is similar to problems confronted
by parents every day. Juveniles commit a substantial proportion of
all burglaries; breaking and entering into computer systems is not
much different.

4.10   How intruders break into computers

The simple answer is that intruders reach out and touch a computer
via the phone company. Although there are a variety of ways to break
into computer systems, the common denominator is the telephone.

Any computer connected to a telephone line is vulnerable to intruders. That is why the Department of Defense does not allow any
computer containing classified information to be connected to a telephone line. The teenagers breaking into NATO or NASA computers
do not gain access to classified information.

Most companies and universities need to connect their computers
to telephones. Companies must allow off-site employees to access the
computer. Employees dial into PBXs from home or on the road to
make long-distance and conference calls. Companies also transmit
data between computers at multiple offices. Universities need to
transmit data between computers on campus, and to other universities.

The newest danger is posed by the ultimate in connectivity: the *Internet*. The Internet is a worldwide computer network consisting of
millions of computers. An outgrowth of a network called ARPA built
by the Pentagon, nobody owns the Internet. It is open to everyone and
used by millions of people. The number of users is growing by more
than 10% each year.

Most universities are "on the Net," and many companies are connecting as well. The Internet is extremely useful to scholars seeking

4. Dennis Hayes, *Behind the Silicon Curtain: The Seductions of Work in a Lonely Era* (Boston: South End Press, 1989), at 93.

to communicate information, to companies seeking to obtain information from government databases, and to many people who simply want to participate in the latest forum for communication.

The Internet poses a danger because it provides access to millions of computers worldwide, and anyone can access any computer on it from any other location. An Internet user in Los Angeles can talk to, and intrude into, a computer connected to an Internet node in Stockholm. That user can do so without ringing up international long-distance charges—once you are connected to an Internet node, you can go anywhere.

Many companies are connecting to the Internet without being aware of its dangers. It is possible for a company to maintain computer security by constructing a "firewall," a system that prevents Internet users from directly entering the company computer. However, many companies are not building firewalls.

In sum, while the telephone allows computers to communicate worldwide, it also allows crackers to intrude into computers worldwide. All the intruder needs is a *modem*, a device that allows a computer to transmit and receive data over a phone line. Some modems cost less than one hundred dollars.

4.11 Computer security is not secure

Banks are generally able to protect their money with guards and vaults. Why are wealthy corporations and universities unable to stop a group of teenagers from waltzing into their computer systems and causing thousands of dollars in damage?

Banks can protect their assets because they are able to examine their customers. Customers with sidearms are stopped before they reach the teller windows. Customers without identification are unable to make withdrawals.

Computer owners generally lack this ability to examine their customers. The 14-year-old cracker appears the same as the 40-year-old software group manager. Computer security thus depends upon requiring all callers to provide information identifying them as authorized users.

Some security systems provide an exception to this rule—they screen potential users based on biological information. These systems require users to present their voices, retinal images, or fingerprints to prove that they are authorized users. Some systems require users to sign their names with special pens or type a message on a keyboard (each person has a distinctive "typing pattern").

These systems are reasonably secure. However, they are also expensive to own and operate, and are imprecise—sometimes they refuse to allow access to authorized users. Thus, very few computer owners purchase them.

Computer security systems usually require potential users to provide two pieces of information: (1) a "log-in" identifying the user; and (2) a password associated with that user. This is very similar to the system you encounter when you withdraw money from an ATM. Your card contains your log-in, and your PIN (personal identification number) is your password.

There are several problems with this system.[5] Careless computer owners often use identification known to everyone. For example, computer companies usually deliver minicomputers and mainframes with functioning security systems. Unfortunately, the passwords are set to a well-known "default" password. Companies and universities installing those computers occasionally fail to change those passwords.

Worse, upgrades to operating system software can change passwords back to "default" passwords without informing the owner. Thus, unwary computer owners can leave gaping holes in their defenses after performing routine maintenance.

Even if management secures the system by changing default passwords, any employee can compromise security by using an easily guessed password. Crackers often run "dictionary" programs to break into computers. These programs dial-up a computer and enter possible passwords from a software "dictionary." These dictionaries include the passwords most commonly used by computer users. Although many companies assign passwords to their employees which

---

5. Section 4.42–b, beginning on page 117, provides a more detailed description of some of the vulnerabilities crackers exploit when breaking into computers.

are combinations of letters and numbers forming "nonsense words" (and thus not found in dictionaries), many do not.

Although many companies prohibit the practice, employees share passwords with other employees. For example, many companies have teams of employees working on projects. If a team member's work is "locked" in an account, and that employee is sick for a week, the team may be delayed unless that employee gives his or her password to other members of the team. Peer pressure ensures that employees share passwords.

Over time, many employees learn the log-in and password of other employees in the company. Once all the employees know this information, there is no way of proving who accessed the company computer. All of the employees become security risks.

Of course, companies can solve this problem by changing employees' passwords every few months. But changing passwords is like flossing—everyone says it is a good idea, but few do it because it is too much trouble. Few companies want to persuade 500 employees to change their passwords every six months, or field 100 phone calls from employees on a Monday morning complaining that they have been locked out of the computer because of a scheduled password change.

Password systems are also vulnerable to *social engineering*, the art of deceiving someone who knows a password into providing it to someone who does not. Crackers pose as employees who have "forgotten" the password, and find gullible employees at a remote office who are willing to "give another employee a break."

Intruders are occasionally able to steal the passwords. Mainframe computers and minicomputers maintain "password files." These files contain the passwords assigned to authorized users. When a potential user dials into a computer, the computer compares the password offered by that user with the password assigned to the authorized user. As discussed later in this chapter, flaws in certain operating systems may allow intruders to steal the password files themselves and access computers at their leisure.

Intruders may also intercept passwords en route to the computer. An increasing amount of computer traffic is being conducted via microwave links, allowing employees to use portable computers and cellular phones to communicate with the company computer. Unfortunately, cellular links are usually not secure. An intruder with the right equipment can intercept information, including a password, as it is sent to the company computer.

Finally, some computer owners are more vulnerable than others for reasons of culture and economy. Banks are aware of their vulnerability to theft, and their responsibilities to customers and regulators. Their computer security against outside intruders is tight. In contrast, universities are committed to wide open computer systems that facilitate the type of sharing of information that is the norm in academia. This culture produces poor computer security and an environment where computer intruders flourish.

Cost is also an important issue for businesses. Small companies may have poor security because they find sophisticated computer security procedures, equipment, and software, as well as the specialists necessary to maintain them, too expensive.

Competition is the enemy of security. Tight security usually requires employees to use cumbersome procedures when using company computers. These procedures can lower productivity, employee morale, and profits. Some companies choose not to tighten security in the hope that higher profits will compensate for their increased risk of loss.

4.12 Crackers are like ants—one little opening is enough to invite a horde of attackers

You may wonder how crackers can afford to spend the time and effort required to discover a flaw in security. Crackers have two advantages: patience and cohesion.

Although crackers are impulsive, their computers are immune to tedium. Crackers write simple programs that instruct their computers to dial target computers and enter a password. If the first password does not work, the computer dials the same number and tries a different password.

Crackers allow their computers to run these programs for weeks at a time, 24 hours a day, "against" a single computer. (This is one reason crackers spend a lot of time obtaining and sharing stolen telephone access codes—they need to be able to use their computers to make free telephone calls around the clock.)

Crackers have cohesion—they talk to each other. When one person has gained access to a computer, everyone in that galaxy of crackers soon knows about it. Since we have a global communications network, crackers in Norway and Australia may learn about a successful intrusion by an English cracker hours after the feat.

This cohesiveness explains how companies can lose $50,000, or $500,000, in toll charges; all of the lucky cracker's friends use that company's PBX for a couple of weeks to make worldwide teleconference calls.

Crackers communicate on *bulletin boards*. (Another name for a bulletin board system is a *BBS*.) Bulletin boards serve as electronic communication forums. You can dial into one of these boards and communicate with users worldwide. The vast majority of these bulletin boards, including very large operations such as CompuServe, are legitimate and provide a valuable service.

However, there are also many "pirate" boards maintained by crackers. Those boards allow crackers to exchange information about vulnerable computers and stolen passwords. The boards are called "pirate" boards because they often offer illegal copies of software to users. If you want the latest release of WordPerfect at no cost, you dial into one of these boards, satisfy the operator that you are a crook, and download a copy.

You are often expected to upload an illegal, or *bootleg*, copy of another piece of software in exchange. (The latest term for such pirated software is *warez*.)

Think of the pirate bulletin board as the "water cooler" for the cracker community. If one cracker finds a "security hole," many more crackers will learn the news within hours or days.

If a cracker is too lazy to use a telephone, there is another avenue: buy a magazine. Yes, just as with any hobby, certain magazines, such as *2600*, cater to computer intruders. Think of a magazine for safecrackers ("Open Sesame," perhaps?), and you get the general idea. (Note that some of these magazines are sold in computer book stores.)

Under the guise of providing merely interesting information (such as how someone *could* break into computers), some of these magazines provide information to computer intruders. One magazine even had a "hack of the month," featuring a particular vulnerability found in one or more computer systems. The editor of one of those magazines has testified before Congress opposing efforts to punish computer intrusion.

Aspiring crackers with Internet access can participate in the *alt.2600* forum on Usenet. You might occasionally scan this and more mainstream newsgroups on Usenet (e.g., *comp.security.announce*; *comp.security.misc*; *comp.security.unix*) for information and rumors about the state of computer security worldwide. (You should probably resist the impulse to post messages on Usenet identifying your occupation—you will release your own E-mail address in the process.)

4.13 How crackers attack computer systems

Crackers often follow certain steps in breaking into computer systems. Those steps are described in Table 4–1 below.

Table 4–1: The cracker's progress

Objective	Method
Obtain the telephone number of the computer.	Obtain the number from other crackers, from the victim's trash *(dumpster diving)*, or by using a war dialer.
Gain access.	Obtain a password by using a dictionary program, stealing password files, intercepting passwords in transmission, social engineering, dumpster diving, or by asking another cracker.
Identify areas of interest within the computer system.	Scan directories.

Objective (cont.)	Method (cont.)
Install back doors before beginning activities to allow return to the computer if ejected.	Create new user accounts, change existing programs (such as loginout.exe) to allow access.
Examine any computers networked to the target computer.	Access networked computers.
Attempt to obtain "root" or "superuser" access.	Take advantage of known operating system holes which allow root access, such as manufacturers' default passwords which the owner has neglected to change. Access password files if not encrypted. If encrypted, run a dictionary program to guess the encryption password.
Destroy, alter, or copy data.	Enter appropriate commands. If desired, insert logic bomb which activates at a later date or on the occurrence of a specific event (such as deletion of the cracker's back doors).
Insert viruses.	Insert code containing the virus. That code may include a logic bomb.
Cover tracks.	Alter accounting logs.

The first step is for the cracker to find the victim's computer. Some crackers are "referred" to victims by colleagues or cracker magazines. Hardier souls have been known to steal printouts from the victim's dumpster and look for telephone numbers (and the names and "log-ons" of users). This practice is called *dumpster diving.*

Others find victims randomly by using software known as a *war dialer.* War dialers work by dialing a number and listening to what answers. If anything but a high pitched tone greets the call, the program hangs up. The high-pitched tone, signaling a computer on the other end, prompts the program to record that number for later use. The cracker will then attempt to break into the computer associated with that telephone number. Thus, crackers choose many victims at random.

Next, the cracker obtains access by discovering a user's log-on and password. As discussed above, crackers do this by using dictionary programs, intercepting passwords as they are transmitted to the computer, "social engineering" vulnerable employees of the victim, dumpster diving, and talking to other crackers. In some cases, crackers obtain password files which have not been adequately secured, and run dictionary programs against them.

Once "inside" the victim's computer, the cracker may begin by briefly exploring the terrain. The easiest way to do this is to scan the file directories. Names of directories and files may provide clues as to the type and location of information stored on the computer.

Careful crackers begin making contingency plans shortly after breaking into a system. There is the ever-present risk that the victim will change passwords, or that a system administrator will notice the cracker's unusual activity and boot him off the system.

Most crackers initially know only one way into the victim's system. The risk of detection makes it important to discover, or create, other ways of gaining access should the cracker be ejected.

One way to do this is to insert altered versions of the programs which control logging in and out of the computer. Another is to create an account under a new name and assign the phantom user a new password. If the cracker needs to reenter the system, he has a new account waiting for him. Crackers may attempt to hide their trap doors as hidden files.

Crackers often do not stop with the computer system they have entered. If the victim's computer is connected to other computers, crackers will use the victim's computer to explore those computers, as well. Once a cracker has penetrated a network, he is often able to access every computer on that network.

The ultimate achievement for a cracker is to gain control of the system. Mainframe and minicomputers are configured to allow users with different levels of authority. Ordinary users are restricted in what they can see and do on a computer system. However, system administrators' accounts are given *root* (also known as *superuser*) status, which allows them access to every file and function the computer has to offer.

An intruder with superuser status can change passwords, insert programs which download certain information, and hide his activities on the system. Such an intruder can literally take over the system and lock authorized users out by changing all of the passwords. A more subtle intruder can create programs that monitor the system, and obtain any interesting information (such as new passwords).

Crackers attempt to gain superuser status by taking advantage of known operating system flaws which allow users to obtain root access without permission. Another method of gaining access is to steal the system administrator's password. Most crackers are unsuccessful in obtaining superuser status, and confine their activities to those allowed ordinary users.

After gaining access to the system and exploring its domains, the cracker will start "playing." If the cracker is just curious, he will roam throughout the computer looking for interesting things. If he is bent on destroying or copying information, he will send the commands necessary to perform those functions. Crackers can also alter information as a form of vandalism (e.g., causing certain spreadsheet files to randomly reverse certain numbers) or commit theft (e.g., by adding his own name to the accounts-payable list).

The cracker may also use a few techniques to wreak havoc even after he has logged off the computer system. Among other nasty devices, the cracker's arsenal includes the *logic bomb*, the *virus*, and the *Trojan Horse*.

A *logic bomb* is a file which is triggered by an event, such as a date or a command entered into the computer. Logic bombs are fearsome weapons because they can be "detonated" even after the cracker has been ejected from the victim's computer. For example, assume that an intruder is extorting a company by threatening to destroy all of its records. Even if the company takes the drastic step of shutting down its computer and changing every password, it still may be vulnerable to a logic bomb.

The intruder may have left a logic bomb behind in the form of a program added to the software which controls the company's payroll system. When the company backs up all of the files and restores them to the "clean" computer, this new program is also restored.

The program is executed each time the company makes payroll and scans the account log for the intruder's name. On the 30th day of the month after the intruder's name no longer appears as an authorized user, the bomb "explodes" by ordering the operating system to delete or modify every file on the computer system. As discussed below, victims must check their computers very carefully after ejecting an intruder.

A *virus* is a computer program which replicates itself from one medium to another. When the *host* program containing the virus is run, the code making up the virus is also run; one of the instructions in that code is to copy the virus to the computer executing that code.

For example, if you run an infected program (the *host*) contained on a floppy disk, the program will instruct your computer to copy the *virus* onto your hard disk. The virus will be inserted into a program which is frequently run by your computer's operating system. The virus may contain a logic bomb which ultimately does the damage.

A *Trojan Horse* is a program which is other than what it seems. A virus maker may insert a few instructions into a bootlegged computer game, and hand out free copies. The altered and infected computer game is a *Trojan Horse*. Crackers often use Trojan Horses to insert programs into target computers. Those programs may replace the log-in program with a program that always allows the cracker access, thus creating a back door into the computer system.

Finally, sophisticated crackers attempt to cover their tracks. Most computer systems monitor activity for every authorized account on the system. At a minimum, the computer maintains a *log* file which records (or *logs*) when each account *logged on* and *logged off*. Thus, if you log on to CompuServe at 9:30 A.M., and log off at 10:02 A.M., the computer system at CompuServe records that information.

Computer owners use those logs for various purposes. Commercial providers of computer services, such as CompuServe, use those logs to bill users for using the computer system. System operators, or *sysops*, examine the logs in "real-time" to determine who is using that computer. If there is unusual activity on a particular account, the sysop can identify and communicate with that user. Some companies monitor employees' computer time to determine whether they are using system resources efficiently.

A cracker may alter those logs to erase all record of his access. If the accounting log would normally record the log-on and log-off of "Authorized User Dr. X," and the cracker has obtained Dr. X's password, the cracker will access the computer posing as Dr. X and insert a program into the log-on program which instructs the computer to erase all records of Dr. X's entry and exit.

That program will run after the cracker leaves the computer and will erase that portion of the log recording his entry. One clue that a cracker has done this is a gap in the accounting logs. A thirty-minute gap with no entries may be a clue that a cracker is at work. Unfortunately, some crackers take the extra step of having the log assign those blocks of time to other users.

In sum, a cracker is usually organized. He first seeks to gain entry, then to explore, next to prepare for discovery and expulsion, and finally to take over the computer system and examine, obtain, alter, or destroy data.

As discussed in the next section, each of those activities may constitute a separate violation of state or federal law. However, before examining that law, you should be aware of two types of crime associated with computer intrusion: PBX fraud and invasion of voice mail systems.

4.14   PBX fraud—the most costly computer crime?

To understand PBX fraud, you have to know something about the more generic crime of *toll fraud*. Toll fraud is the fraudulent theft of telephone service.

It started several decades ago with *blue boxes*, the tone generators that allowed thieves to make long-distance calls from pay phones for free. The thief would use the *blue box* to generate tones which would "fool" the telephone system into placing the call without charge.

What began as a student's free phone call home has spawned a multibillion-dollar racket involving both juveniles and adults. The widespread use of calling cards means that thieves are no longer limited to using pay telephones. Once they steal a calling card number, they can make long-distance calls on any telephone.

Thieves obtain those numbers by *shoulder surfing* (looking over a caller's shoulder while the caller enters the card number) at public facilities, such as airports. They sometimes use video cameras to record the numbers dialed, and review the tapes in slow motion. Thieves posing as telephone company representatives persuade consumers to disclose their calling card numbers.

Thieves do more than use these numbers for themselves: they sell them. Buyers include people who need to make many long-distance phone calls without being traced (e.g., narcotics traffickers). They also include entrepreneurs running *call-sell operations*, which allow customers to place phone calls for reduced fees. These thieves often take over public telephones, and sell time on those phones to drug dealers (who need untraceable calls) and immigrants (who want to call home). The calls are placed on stolen calling card numbers.

However, calling card fraud is not a perfect crime. Telephone companies can use their own computers to detect the theft of a card number. (For example, motorhome salesmen rarely place 300 calls a week to Colombia.) Phone companies such as MCI and Sprint are adept at cancelling cards quickly, even before victims complain about outrageous phone bills. Thus, thieves must constantly obtain new calling card numbers.

The latest wrinkle in toll fraud is PBX fraud. A *PBX (private branch exchange)* is the computer which operates the telephone system in most companies. If you dial "9" to get an outside line, you are using a PBX.

Some PBXs are maintained by a telephone company within its own computers, such as Pacific Bell's CENTREX service. Other PBXs are sold to companies by PBX manufacturers, including ROLM, AT&T, MCI, Northern Telecom, and others. It is those office-installed PBXs which are targets for fraud.

Crackers use various methods to break into PBXs. For example, many companies configure their PBXs to allow service technicians to fix problems over the telephone, but fail to change the default passwords guarding those service accounts. Crackers are often successful when they guess correctly that the password is the manufacturer's name, "SERVICE," or "MAINTENANCE." Crackers may also attack PBXs with war dialers and special computer programs.

Another common vulnerability is the *direct inward system access* (*DISA*) feature included in most PBX installations. DISA allows employees to dial into the PBX from outside the company, enter an authorization code, and make long-distance calls through the PBX. Crackers discover this code by guessing or social engineering, and use the PBX to make free calls.

A new feature causing trouble is PBX call forwarding. Executives on the road can program their PBXs to forward their phone calls to a designated remote location (e.g., their hotel room phone). Crackers can use this same feature to reprogram the PBX to route (their) incoming phone calls to other long-distance destinations.

Crackers sell PBX information to customers, such as organized crime and call-sell operations, or provide it to their friends. They may also post those stolen numbers on numerous "pirate" bulletin boards for other crackers to use.

The victim's PBX is usually swamped with long-distance phone calls within hours or days of the theft. The bills often top $50,000, and there are reports of companies and government agencies (including NASA and the DEA) losing over $1 million in a frighteningly short period of time. Industry estimates place losses from PBX attacks at over $1 billion *annually*.[6]

Telephone companies and PBX manufacturers have been successful in requiring victims to absorb those losses on the grounds that customers can configure their systems to reduce the risk of attack (e.g., by disabling the DISA feature, or restricting the service to domestic calls only).[7] The result is that thieves have shifted the risk of loss from

---

6. According to Pacific Bell, there were over 40,000 cases of PBX fraud in 1994, with an average loss of about $40,000, for a total loss of about $1.6 billion. Some industry estimates place the loss at over $2 billion.

7. Companies can avoid this risk of loss by using the PBX services provided by the telephone companies, contracting with the manufacturer to handle security for the PBX, or tightening security by properly configuring the PBX. Ironically, the very services touted by the PBX manufacturers, such as DISA, present some of the greatest risk to customers.

the telephone companies, which absorbed calling card losses, to the business community at large.[8]

The advantage to the thief of PBX fraud over telephone calling card theft is the time lag between the use of the PBX and the discovery of the fraud by the victim. Telephone companies monitor calling card calls as they occur, and can "shut down" a card within hours or days of the theft. PBX owners typically do not discover the attack until they receive their next phone bill in a box.

Crackers and call-sell operators can run up hundreds of thousands of dollars in a weekend. By the time the victim calls law enforcement, they have moved on to another PBX. This means that PBX frauds are almost impossible to investigate. Telephone companies recommend that customers simply shut down their PBX immediately upon detecting fraud.

Apart from using informants and undercover operations directed at suspected call-sell operators, most investigations of PBX fraud are a waste of time. If the victim insists, consider applying for a trap and trace as discussed below, but do not expect good results. Instead, consider examining the first few calls on the victim's huge phone bill.[9] Crackers may make their first free phone calls to their fellow crackers.

Law enforcement and corporate investigators should urge victims to obtain professional advice on securing their systems to prevent future attacks.[10]

4.15 Voice mail invasions

Intruders break into voice mail systems for several reasons. Juveniles enjoy changing messages and using mailboxes as their personal

---

8. The Federal Communications Commission is reportedly considering requiring telephone companies to share up to two-thirds of any loss resulting from PBX fraud.

9. If the victim continues to operate the PBX in the hope of catching the intruder, it should enable the station message detail recording (SMDR) feature, which provides information on the calls made through the PBX.

10. Pacific Bell publishes an excellent guide to securing PBXs and voice mail systems. The "Pacific Bell LockOn Handbook" is available from that company.

answering machines. Other intruders invade for profit—organized crime uses voice mailboxes as an untraceable method of communication. Call-sell operations use mailboxes to store stolen calling card and PBX numbers.

Breaking into voice mail systems is easy. When you are assigned a voice mailbox, you are also assigned, or allowed to choose, a passcode which you must dial to access that mailbox. Intruders break into voice mail systems by guessing that passcode, usually with the aid of computer programs. Intruders also break into unused mailboxes which have not been assigned passcodes (or have been assigned obvious passcodes, such as "1234").

Fortunately, it is not especially difficult to investigate voice mailbox intrusion once the victim becomes aware of the problem. The intruder will call the mailbox for messages, and a trap and trace should (eventually) pinpoint the intruder's location.

4.20 Laws punishing intrusion

Virtually every unauthorized intrusion violates a federal or state law. Table 4–2 provides a guide to the laws which may apply to your intruder's activities.

Table 4–2: Laws punishing unauthorized intrusion

Did your intruder:	Then look at:
Access a computer across state lines?	18 U.S.C. 1030 (Computer Fraud and Abuse Act) and state laws punishing computer intrusion.
Access a U.S. Government computer?	18 U.S.C. 1030 (Computer Fraud and Abuse Act) and state laws punishing computer intrusion.

Did your intruder (cont.):	Then look at (cont.):
Access another computer?	State laws punishing computer intrusion.
Add, alter, or destroy data?	State laws punishing computer intrusion resulting in addition, alteration, or destruction of data.
Copy information?	18 U.S.C. 1343 (wire fraud); 18 U.S.C. 2314 and 2315 (transportation and receipt of stolen property); 17 U.S.C. 506(a) and 18 U.S.C. 2319 (copyright infringement); state laws punishing intrusion accompanied by theft of information; state laws punishing theft of information.
Steal credit or financial information from a bank or credit agency?	The laws listed in the row above. Such thefts also violate 18 U.S.C. 1030 (Computer Fraud and Abuse Act) regardless of whether the computer was accessed across state lines.
Use or traffic in unauthorized access devices (passwords, access codes, credit card numbers, blue boxes), or possess more than 15 such devices?	If the use or trafficking facilitates or affects an *interstate* computer intrusion, consider 18 U.S.C. 1029. In all cases, consider state laws punishing possession or use of unauthorized access devices.
Export software or data outside the United States?	50 U.S.C. Appx. 2410.
Intercept electronic communications (e.g., by tapping a data line)?	18 U.S.C. 2510 (Electronic Communications Privacy Act).

4.21   Federal laws punishing intrusion

4.21–a   The Computer Fraud and Abuse Act

The Computer Fraud and Abuse Act[11] is the basic federal computer crime statute. The Act punishes anyone who:

- accesses a computer and obtains classified information;

- accesses and obtains credit or financial information from a bank, credit issuer, or consumer reporting agency;

- accesses a U.S. Government computer, or a computer partially used by the Government where the offense affects the Government's use of the computer;

- accesses a computer across state lines with the intent to commit fraud or theft, and obtains anything of value (excepting the use of that computer);

- accesses a computer across state lines, and

    •• intentionally and without authorization transmits a program, command, or information;

    •• with intent to damage a computer system, network, information, data, or program, or deny the use of same, or with reckless disregard of a substantial and unjustifiable risk that the transmission may cause such a result; *and*

    •• the transmission causes a loss of more than $1,000 during the course of a year, or actually or potentially interferes with a patient's medical care or treatment; or

- traffics in passwords, if that trafficking:

    •• affects interstate commerce (e.g., multistate bulletin board numbers); or

    •• involves the password to a computer owned or used by the U.S. Government.

---

11. *See* 18 U.S.C. 1030.

An unlawful "access" includes cases where the defendant was authorized to gain entry to the computer, but exceeded his or her authorization in obtaining or altering data.

In sum, whenever an intruder accesses a computer across state lines, that intrusion will probably violate federal law. However, the Act does not punish "joyriders" unless they recklessly risk damage, or denial of access, to computers or information.

4.21–b   Unlawful use of access devices

Section 1029 prohibits any of the following activities relating to access devices which affect interstate or foreign commerce:

- using or trafficking in *unauthorized access devices* with the intent to defraud, and obtaining by that conduct $1,000 or more in a year.

- possessing more than 15 unauthorized access devices with intent to defraud.

Unauthorized access devices include passwords, telephone access codes, and credit card numbers which have been stolen or obtained by fraud. Note that § 1029 requires prosecutors to prove that the activity affected interstate or foreign commerce. The key is to demonstrate that the intruder used the access codes to break into computers located across state lines or communicated the codes to bulletin boards with a nationwide clientele.

4.22   State laws punishing intrusion

Although intrusion is a "computer crime," you may be able to use more traditional state laws to punish offenders. Consider laws punishing persons who:

1.   Obtain free telephone service by fraud.

Telephone companies were battling toll fraud long before computer crime came to the attention of the public and legislators. Thus, many states, apart from their computer crime laws, have enacted laws punishing those who defraud the telephone company. Those laws typically cover use of blue boxes and stolen telephone access numbers.

Do not overlook these statutes when dealing with intruders—crackers in particular need to cheat the telephone company to finance their long-distance assaults on computer systems.

2.   *Obtain and/or use stolen access codes.*

Telephone companies were not the only early participants in the legislative arena. Like some forms of toll fraud, credit card fraud relies on the theft of access codes.

Look for laws in your jurisdiction punishing theft or misuse of access codes; the definition of access code will probably include telephone access codes (particularly since many telephone companies have introduced calling cards).

3.   *Steal data.*

As discussed in Chapter 5, many information thieves are finding it easier to break into the company computer via telephone lines than breaking into the company lab to steal information stored within computers. Copyright and theft laws may be used to punish certain computer intrusions.[12]

Finally, of course, you should consider the applicability of your state's "computer-crime" law to the intrusion. There are a wide variety of such laws, and each has its own quirks and problems. However, with few exceptions, each law is broad enough to prosecute any intruder.

When examining your state's law, consider: (1) what the intruder did; and (2) the intent with which he did it. In some states, the act of the intruder, and its consequences (i.e., the damage caused), determine the severity of the crime. In other states, just trespassing into the computer can be a serious felony if the intruder intended to steal or vandalize. Many states use both factors in determining punishment.

Generally, state computer crime laws punish anyone who, without authorization:

---

12. *See, e.g.,* New York Penal Code Section 156.30 (unlawful duplication of a computer program); 156.35 (knowing possession of any data copied in violation of 156.30).

- accesses a computer;

- uses a computer (i.e., steals computer time);

- denies or disrupts computer services (e.g., inserts a virus or worm which shuts down the computer system);

- alters, damages, or deletes data stored within the computer (which may include inserting a virus as well as committing vandalism);[13] and

- takes, copies, or makes use of data stored within the computer without authorization (this conduct may also violate information theft laws, as discussed in Chapter 5).

Some states do not punish all of the forms of computer assault listed above, or impose additional obstacles to prosecution. For example, as of this writing, New York does not punish an intruder for computer trespass unless the target computer was equipped with a security system designed to resist intrusion.[14]

A few states expand traditional protections. For example, California law punishes those who aid and abet an intruder.[15]

The penalty for intrusion often depends upon the intruder's intent. California makes every intrusion a felony if the intruder intended to devise or execute a scheme to defraud, deceive or extort, or obtain money, property, or data.[16] New York makes it a felony for an intruder to use, or cause to be used, a computer without authorization with the intent to commit, attempt to commit, or further the commission of *any* felony.[17] Thus, an intruder who takes over one mailbox on a voice

---

13. California specifically prohibits inserting a "computer contaminant" without permission. *See* California Penal Code Section 502(c)(10).

14. *See* New York Penal Code Section 156.05. However, intruders into unprotected systems may be punished if they: (1) intend to commit a felony; (2) knowingly obtain access to medical records, New York state records, or trade secrets; or (3) intentionally alter or destroy data. *See* New York Penal Code Sections 156.10, 156.20.

15. *See* California Penal Code Section 502(c)(7). Such state laws can be very useful in pursuing crackers who help confederates break into computer systems.

16. *See* California Penal Code Section 502(c)(1).

17. *See* New York Penal Code Section 156.10.

mail system to conduct narcotics trafficking can be charged with a felony.

In many states, the penalty for intrusion is tied to the damage caused by the intruder or to the value of the data the intruder obtains. For example, California makes trespassing without intent to commit theft an infraction if the loss to the victim does not exceed $250, a misdemeanor if the loss exceeds $250, and a felony if the loss exceeds $5,000.[18] This means that the victim should keep careful records of all expenses incurred in responding to the intrusion.

You should also be on the lookout for the occasional loophole in your state's law. In New Jersey, "the copying or altering of a computer program or computer software shall not constitute theft for the purposes of chapters 20 and 21 of Title 2c ... or any offense under this act if the computer program or computer software is of a retail value of $1,000 or less and is not copied for resale."[19] Apparently you can bootleg software in New Jersey with impunity (at least until you are hauled into federal court for violating federal copyright law).

California has an odd provision allowing employees to use their employers' computer systems for any purpose as long as they do not alter, delete, damage, or destroy hardware or data, and do not use more than $100 in computer time.[20]

Finally, remember that some states, most notably California and Illinois, allow forfeiture to the state of computers used to break into other computer systems. Indeed, Illinois allows forfeiture of computers used to commit non-computer crimes.[21]

4.30 How we catch intruders—an overview

We catch intruders the same way many of them gain entry—we use the telephone company. With an appropriate court order, which

---

18. *See* California Penal Code Section 502; *see also* New York Penal Code Sections 156.20, 156.25, 156.27; Illinois Compiled Statutes, Ch. 720, 5/16D-5.

19. New Jersey Code of Criminal Justice, Section 2C:20–33.

20. California Penal Code Section 502(h)(2).

21. Illinois Compiled Statutes, Ch. 720, 5/16D-6; California Penal Code Section 502.01.

may be a search warrant in some states, the phone company installs a *trap and trace* on the victim's phone number.

If the intruder is naive and is making a local call, one trace will lead you to him. If the intruder is smart and determined, you can spend six months chasing a trail through half a dozen computer systems and numerous long-distance services in several countries. Police are usually unable to catch a skilled intruder.

Once the intruder is located, the next step is to obtain another court order allowing the telephone company to install a *pen register* on the intruder's telephone. A pen register records all numbers dialed by that telephone. This makes sure that the intruder is not using call forwarding or some other scheme to make it appear as if the calls are being made from a particular number.

The final step is to obtain a search warrant to search the intruder's residence. The goal is to seize the intruder's computer, which usually contains evidence of the intrusion. The intruder's hard drive will contain any software stolen from the victim's computer, as well as programs designed to break into computers. In addition, the intruder has probably recorded the phone number for the victim's computer near his machine.

Investigators deliver the coup de grace by matching telephone company records against records maintained by the victim's computer. As discussed below, computers can keep track of the time of day when users log on and log off, and, in many cases can monitor the intruder's activities on the system.

If computer records show that the intruder called on January 4, 1994, at 4:05 P.M., and logged off that same day at 4:32 P.M., and the pen register installed on your suspect's telephone line shows that he called the computer at 4:05 P.M., and ended the call at 4:32 P.M., he is going to have a bad day in court.

The rest of this chapter provides a step-by-step guide to investigating computer intrusions.

4.40   Initial investigation

Your initial investigation of a computer intrusion has six goals, listed in order of importance.

- To understand how the intruder is entering the system.

- To obtain the information you need to justify a trap and trace of the phone line the intruder is using.

- To discover why the intruder has chosen the victim's computer. As discussed below, this information will help you judge whether the victim can afford to allow the intrusion to continue while you trace that intruder. Many investigations end when the victim feels compelled to eject the intruder to protect itself from damage or theft.

- To gather as much evidence of the intrusion as possible. This evidence will do more than demonstrate that an intrusion is occurring—it will convince a jury that the person you identified by the trap and trace is the intruder, *and* that the intruder committed various criminal acts while accessing the computer (i.e., he destroyed or downloaded data).

- To obtain information that may narrow your list of suspects, or at least confirm that the intruder is not a current employee.

- To document the damage to the victim caused by the intruder, including the time and effort spent by the victim in investigating the incident and determining the amount of damage to its computer. A court may require the defendant to compensate the victim for those losses.

4.41 Background information

Your first step is to gather information about the victim's computer system. You will need to include much of this information in your request for authorization to trap and trace.

You should obtain the following information from the person(s) in charge of the computer system.

4.41–a How the computer is used

Knowing how the computer is used will help you understand the intruder's motive and the threat posed by that intrusion to the computer owner. If the computer is a PBX, then the intruder wants to make free phone calls. If the computer controls the company voice mail system, then the intruder wants to take over one or more voice "mailboxes."

The potential for damage from an intrusion also depends upon the information stored within the computer. If the computer contains confidential information, you have a potential crisis. If the computer is merely a voice mail system, you have an annoyance.

4.41–b   How the computer is connected to the outside world

Ask for a list of all phone lines which can be used to access the computer, and the victim's reason for allowing such access. You need to know how authorized users dial into the computer in order to:

• understand how the intruder gained access;

• eliminate potential suspects; and

• identify all phone lines which should be "trapped" pursuant to a court order.

Many companies maintain more than one phone line which employees use to access the computer from outside the office. Some companies install additional lines to allow technicians employed by the manufacturer of the victim's computer to access the computer to fix problems remotely.

The telephone lines used by an intruder may tell you whether he has "inside knowledge" of the victim. If the intruder always uses the same number, you may conclude that the intruder does not know the phone numbers of the other dial-in ports. However, if the intruder uses various phone lines to dial into the computer system, then he is either a current or former employee, or an outsider who learned the other numbers by communicating with other crackers on a pirate bulletin board.

If the intruder is using the phone line reserved for technicians, that information may suggest something about the intruder's connection to the company. (It may also prompt you to check with the victim's computer company to see if the victim is misinterpreting unusual maintenance activity as an intrusion.)

Finally, when you request a trap and trace order, you need to list the telephone lines subject to the trap. You should list not only the number used by the intruder to dial in, but the other numbers as well. An intruder who knows the victim's computer system well may use more than one line to escape detection.

If the Internet is the source of the intrusion, ask for the name of the service provider handling the victim's access to the Internet. You will use that company to assist in tracking the intruder.

4.41–c   *Computer security measures in place before the intrusion*

As discussed in Chapter 2, you need to know what happened before you know who did it. Part of that task in intrusion investigations is understanding what security was in place, and how it failed.

Why worry about a security system that failed? You must demonstrate to a magistrate that the intruder has committed a crime in order to obtain a trap and trace order. The best way to make that showing is to prove that the intruder defeated security measures.

Furthermore, the intruder's method of obtaining access may provide valuable clues to the intruder's identity. If the only means of accessing the computer are internal (i.e., the computer is not connected to an outside phone line), then you know that the intruder is an employee. If the victim has never changed the password since the computer went "on-line" four years ago, then your field of suspects includes every employee who worked for your victim over the last four years. If the password was changed three days ago, you have far fewer suspects.

Victims occasionally have enough information to pinpoint an intruder, but fail to do so because they do not analyze the information at hand. Merely walking the victim through its own security system may solve the case.

Finally, if all goes well, you will need to present this information at trial. You are better off gathering this information at the outset than trying to reconstruct it later. You should ask the victim's representative to walk you through the procedure for accessing the computer.

Start by asking general questions about computer security:

1. *Does the system require a log-on identification?*

On most computer systems, each authorized user is assigned an account. The user must identify his or her account when accessing the computer. You should ask if that is the procedure used by the victim. You need this information to understand how the intrusion occurred. You may also need it to demonstrate that the owner intended the computer to be unavailable to the public.

2. *Does the system require users to enter a password?*

Ask whether there are restrictions on the type of password which users may use. Many employees use common names. Passwords which are at least six characters long, and are nonsense passwords composed of letters *and* numbers (and even symbols), are generally invulnerable to "dictionary" programs. If an intruder has successfully entered such a password, it is likely that the intruder is a current or former employee, knows an employee, or has obtained the password through social engineering of a gullible employee.

3. *How often is that password changed?*

Although passwords should be changed every three to six months, many computer owners never change passwords. Again, knowing the date on which the password was last changed may give you a clue about who knew that password.

4. *Does the computer allow different levels of access?*

Computer security systems allow owners to limit the access of certain users. For example, companies may use those systems to prevent personnel clerks from accessing proprietary engineering information. The level of access gained by your intruder may provide information about the source of your problem, particularly if the intruder is an ex-employee.

5. *How does the computer record when a user logs on and off the system?*

Accounting logs are critical to your investigation. As discussed earlier in this chapter, we convict intruders by demonstrating that the unauthorized access started and stopped at the same time that the intruder's telephone was connected to the victim's computer.

The time and duration of the intrusion will eliminate suspects. If John Doe's account was accessed at lunch, and John Doe was in a restaurant with friends, then John Doe is an innocent employee.

> 6. *Can the computer record the activities (e.g., the commands typed) by users?*

Most computer systems can be configured to keep detailed records of users' activities. Such monitoring may yield a list of the directories and files accessed by the user. *Keystroke monitoring* will record everything typed by that user from log-on to log-off.

A history of every command typed by the intruder is invaluable. You can use that history to determine the experience of the intruder (e.g., whether the intruder fumbled over commands). You can also use that information to determine whether the intruder was after specific information or was just browsing.

Once you have caught the intruder, that history can be used to prove that intruder's intent. Many state computer intrusion laws distinguish between "mere trespassing" and entry with intent to download, delete, or alter data. Juries may believe that an intruder was only curious unless they are shown a history proving that the intruder downloaded information.

Histories are also useful in determining the urgency of the situation. Besides determining where the intruder is browsing, a history can tell you whether the intruder is close to gaining control of the victim's computer system.

Although keystroke monitoring is desirable, there may be legal obstacles to its use. Although victims may usually monitor an intruder's activities, you should read Chapter 8 (§ 8.32) before suggesting such monitoring.

4.42 Questions about the intrusion

After learning about the victim's computer system and its computer security, your next step is to learn everything you can about the intrusion. You should ask the following questions:

- When did the intrusion begin?

- How many calls has the intruder made?

- Did anyone unsuccessfully attempt to access the computer within 30 days before the first intrusion?

Few intruders break into a computer on the first attempt. You are interested in whether the intruder made repeated (as in ten or more) attempts to enter the computer via the same route (e.g., a particular phone line or Internet address). Such repeated attempts, particular when they occur at fixed intervals, suggest a random intruder using a "dictionary" program.

If the intrusion was not preceded by unsuccessful attempts, your intruder may have inside information about the victim's system. Does that make your intruder a current or former employee? Maybe, but he could be a cracker who used any of the various methods discussed earlier (e.g., social engineering or interception of password information) to obtain a password.

- For each access:

  - •• What was the date and time of that call, and how long did the call last?

  - •• What phone line(s) is/are the intruder using?

  - •• What account(s) was/were accessed?

  - •• Who are the authorized users who have access to that account? (Some companies allocate accounts for particular workgroups which anyone in that group may access.)

You should interview authorized users to confirm that the access using their account was unauthorized. However, you should probably avoid this tactic if you have a large number of users who were authorized to use a particular account. Questioning all of them will alert the rest of the company to the intrusion and scare off any intruder who maintains contact with the victim's employees.

Before talking to authorized users whose accounts were used to gain access, determine whether the authorized user had a motive to do what the intruder did. Sometimes the obvious answer is correct, and your intruder *is* the authorized user.

An intruder examining personnel records may be an employee curious about a co-worker. An employee whose account is used to download proprietary information might be planning to take that information to a competitor. In such cases, ask the human resources department whether that employee has given notice.

Furthermore, even if the authorized user is innocent, that does not make him or her useless to your investigation. It is quite possible that the user divulged the password accidentally. Check to see whether the user was a victim of social engineering. Ask the user whether he or she displayed the password on scraps of paper taped to the terminal or left in an unlocked desk drawer.

As discussed earlier in this chapter, knowing how an intruder breached security may identify suspects. You will also need to eliminate any possibility that the authorized user was your intruder.

4.42–a   Ruling out the victim as the source of the problem

The anecdote in Chapter 2 about the victim whose "intruder" turned out to be its own computers is instructive. Make sure that the victim checks its data collection and maintenance software routines to verify that the unauthorized access is not actually one of its own computers obtaining data from the "penetrated" system.

4.42–b   Some of the well-known routes into poorly configured computer systems

As discussed above, the intruder may have used a simple war dialer to invade your victim's computer. However, it is more likely that your intruder exploited one of the well-traveled routes into unguarded, or sloppily configured, computer systems, including:[22]

---

22. The following discussion relies on Chapter 2 of William R. Cheswick and Steven M. Bellovin, *Firewalls and Internet Security: Repelling the Wily Hacker* (Reading, Massachusetts: Addison-Wesley, 1994). Although most readers are probably not qualified to track down the security breach, this brief tour may help you understand your victim's explanation of how the intruder entered the system.

- Bad passwords: Whether an intruder dials in or knocks on the door via the Internet, an easily guessed password is the equivalent of using a combination lock with only two numbers.

- Electronic mail: The *sendmail* program which handles electronic mail in most UNIX systems connected to the Internet has been called "a security nightmare."[23] Crackers can exploit flaws in this program to enter a computer via its mail system.

- TFTP and FTP: These programs allow users to transfer files between computers. Many computer systems, such as those owned by universities, maintain *anonymous FTP areas*. These areas allow outsiders to retrieve information from certain areas of the computer without authorization. They are used by universities and other computer owners to distribute material to the Internet community, such as scientific papers or software.

  Although such areas are useful, they pose security risks. Owners may inadvertently place password files in those areas, and lose them.[24] Crackers may use the anonymous FTP area to penetrate "the rest" of the computer. Finally, where the owner has allowed outsiders to place files in the anonymous FTP, crackers and others have obliged by storing stolen data, illegally copied programs, and pornography.

- Telnet: Telnet is used to call one computer from another. If crackers have compromised the "calling machine," they can record the passwords typed in by users using that computer to call the

---

23. Cheswick and Bellovin, *Firewalls and Internet Security*, at 30.

24. For example, in early 1994, a group of intruders stole password files for hundreds of computers connected to the Internet. The CERT (Computer Emergency Response Team) Advisory, July 13, 1994, warns owners of the flaw which made this raid possible.

   Computers running UNIX should be configured to ensure that password files are "owned" by the root (i.e., can be read only by persons with superuser status, as explained below), as opposed to the default configuration. Unless the owner changes the default configuration, many computers place the password file in the anonymous FTP area, where others can read or alter it. CERT suggests placing a phony password file in that area to throw crackers off the trail. *See* Cheswick and Bellovin, *Firewalls and Internet Security*, at 12.

victim's computer, thus intercepting those passwords for their own use.

- Network spoofing: This technique deceives the target computer into believing that it is being "called" by another computer on the network.

4.42–c. Records documenting which employees were at the victim's facility, and what they were doing

In a few cases, your trap and trace will lead straight back to the victim's facility. A clever employee may use a company phone to dial into the victim's computer.

These records may also provide evidence that an employee is doing something unusual (e.g., working late). While hard work is commendable, employees intending to steal proprietary information (or money) often stay late at the office to commit crimes unobserved.

4.42–d Determining what the intruder did

As discussed above, the intruder's activity will provide clues to his identity and motive. When discussing this issue with your victim, ask whether it has checked its computer for any new "files." As discussed earlier, crackers may have inserted phantom accounts to give them a "back door" into the victim's computer. Of course, victims must also be alert for any Trojan Horses, logic bombs, or viruses left behind by the intruder.

Any victimized computer owner should check its computers for such back doors, using outside expert assistance if necessary.

4.43 Collecting evidence of the intrusion

Identify evidence of the intrusion, and collect it immediately. Most evidence consists of records maintained by the victim's computer. Over the days or weeks of an intrusion, those records may be overwritten by new data. You must obtain that information before it is overwritten. You should also ask your victim to create a separate hidden area within the computer to store intrusion evidence as it is created. The safest course is to encrypt that information.

> *Do not use the victim's computer to discuss*
> *the investigation*
>
> Caution your victim not to use the computer to discuss the intrusion—crackers operating with superuser status may scan the victim's E-mail to determine the status of the investigation. Any information about the investigation which is stored on the computer must be encrypted. A victim who is technologically incapable of creating programs to track the intrusion which will be invisible to an intruder should hire an expert for the task.

Ask for the following information:

- all records of the unauthorized access;

- all records of system activity on the day (or within a few hours) of the access; and

- backup tapes of the above.

Make sure that you receive these records on an ongoing basis—you should collect evidence after each intrusion. When anyone gives you information, ask: "How do you know that?"

Your goal is to prompt people to point to physical evidence. If the victim's computer systems manager tells you that the intruder was looking at information about the X45 project, ask that manager to prove it to you. The manager will probably refer to certain evidence stored on the computer, which you will then collect.

Make an exact copy of the data in the form in which it existed in the computer (i.e., onto a backup tape). Make more than one copy if possible. You should also print out the data to have a hard copy record which you can display at trial.

4.44 Creating evidence of the intrusion

As discussed in Chapter 8 (§ 8.32), the law usually allows victims to use their computers to track an intruder's activity. You should discuss this issue with your victim at the beginning of your investigation. At a minimum, ensure that the computer is configured to "time-stamp" each log-in and log-off for each account.

4.45 Tracking damage

Advise your victim that its employees should keep a log of time they spend responding to the intrusion. This includes time spent verifying that the intruder did not damage the computer or leave any "trap doors" behind. That log can be used to:

- document an insurance claim;

- establish that the defendant caused sufficient damage to elevate the offense in some states to a higher degree; and

- form the basis for a claim for restitution as part of sentencing, or as part of a civil suit against the intruder.

4.50 Tracking down the intruder

4.51 The cat and mouse game—you can win the battle but lose the war

An intrusion investigation is often nerve-wracking. Computer intrusion is one of the few crimes where you must usually catch the intruder in the act, or not at all. Even worse, to catch that intruder in the act, you may put the victim at serious risk. You can end up catching the intruder only after he has ruined your victim. The next sections discuss this delicate balancing act.

4.52 It can be impossible to trace the intruder

As discussed above, intruders use telephone lines to invade computers, and we use the telephone company to trace them back. If the intruder calls from a local number straight into the computer, one trap and trace will suffice. You should be so lucky. What you will probably find is that the intruder has either dialed in directly from out-of-state and/or used one or more *cut-outs*.

A *cut-out* is another computer, or network of computers. If an intruder has access to the Internet, he will use one computer to legitimately gain access to another computer on the Internet, and then dial from that computer to the victim's computer. Virtually every university student with access to that facility's computer has access to the Internet.

Whether the intruder calls long distance, or uses a cut-out, or both, the result is the same: your first trap and trace will not reveal the location of the telephone used by the suspect.

4.52–a   Long-distance calls

When a call is placed from one calling area to another, it does not travel the entire distance on a single line. It is passed from telephone switch to telephone switch. When the call arrives at the switch in your area, that switch directs it to your telephone. Long-distance calls are carried from switch to switch on *trunk lines*.

If your intruder is calling long distance, the trap and trace will tell you only that a particular trunk line was used to route the call to your local switch—you must place a trap and trace on that trunk line to determine the location of your intruder. You may need to do several trap and traces to pinpoint a telephone in another state. Furthermore, a side effect of the breakup of AT&T is that there are hundreds of long-distance phone companies. You may have to deal with several different carriers to track your intruder.

This means that you have to wait for the intruder to call several times before you can locate him. Each time you trace the intruder back to another telephone switch, you will have to obtain another authorization for a trap and trace. This procedure takes time.

Once you move out-of-state, it may take quite a bit of time to arrange for a magistrate in a sister state (or a federal magistrate) to sign your court order authorizing a trap and trace. Time spent arranging those traps and traces is time that your victim's computer remains vulnerable to the intruder.[25]

---

25. If your case is important enough, you may wish to seek federal assistance as soon as you determine that your intruder is dialing in from out-of-state. A federal warrant is valid throughout the United States. A state warrant is generally valid only in the state of issuance.

If your intruder is calling long distance, you will have to negotiate with a number of different telephone companies. At this point, your local telephone company is your most important ally. It can act as an intermediary with long-distance carriers. *It is very important for law enforcement to establish a good working relationship with local "telcom" representatives.*

Consider ordering long-distance carriers to assist in tracing the call

Consider writing a clause in your trap and trace warrant ordering any and all long-distance carriers to render assistance as needed to carry out the command to trace the incoming call. Be forewarned, however, that it is unclear whether such a command is enforceable, particularly if it requires that long-distance carrier to act outside of the issuing state.

Another problem is that the long-distance carrier cannot be known until the first trap and trace is concluded. A reviewing court might balk at a court order directed at an unknown person which depends upon the officer's judgment (i.e., that the first trap and trace indicated that this particular carrier handled the call) to supply the probable cause, even though "judgment" in this context is really more akin to the result of a chemical test.

However, the warrant could be viewed as a single warrant to the local phone company, with a direction to all persons associated with that call to render assistance in carrying out the activity ordered by the warrant (i.e., tracing the call).

Unfortunately, many telephone companies are of two minds about cooperating with law enforcement. As victims of repeated assaults by crackers, their security teams are sympathetic to law enforcement. However, their lawyers and executives are not. To them, every user of the telephone network is a customer, regardless of that user's purpose or activities in using that network. The lawyers and executives are concerned, incredibly, with the company's potential liability to a cracker for invasion of privacy.

Thus, you may have the marketing arm of a telephone company pushing to sell CallerID, which allows anyone to trap and trace calls made to his or her number, while at the same time the company's lawyers are insisting on a search warrant before the company will perform a trap and trace to assist the victim of an intrusion. (Although the victim is also a customer, the victim is not going to sue the company.)

At the other extreme, friendly security teams may offer to install the trap before they receive a court order authorizing them to do so. They will then record the result, but wait to pass it along until you provide them with a court order. Although this procedure may violate the Electronic Communications Privacy Act, Congress does not appear to have required suppression of evidence resulting from such a violation.[26]

In any event, you should be cautious by making sure that you obtain trap and trace results identifying the source of a call made by the intruder only *after* you obtain the requisite court order or search warrant.

Once you discover that your intruder is calling long distance, you are at the mercy of out-of-state telephone companies. Note that large corporate victims may have more success with those companies than law enforcement. You should also contact the FBI and the Secret Service for assistance once your case crosses state lines.

In sum, with time and effort, you can trace a call back through several telephone switching stations and across many states. However, you still may not catch your intruder. Your intruder may use call forwarding, adding yet another trap and trace to your growing collection. Your intruder may call from different locations, or use different long-distance telephone companies.

Most ominously, your intruder may use a cellular phone with a fraudulent ID chip. Cellular phones use an identification code for billing calls. When you make a call, your telephone automatically communicates its identification code to a switching station. To reach

---

26. *See* 18 U.S.C. 3121(a); Chapter 8, § 8.34, beginning on page 361.

you, the switching station sends a signal that activates the phone with your identification code. That code is programmed into a single chip in your telephone.

There is currently a brisk black-market trade in phony ID chips. You can buy a cellular phone which will make free phone calls. But how do thieves know which numbers to use? Simple—they stand on the sidewalk and wait for you to drive by. With inexpensive equipment, they can intercept the identification codes sent by your phone.[27]

Needless to say, the telephone companies are not amused. They are also overwhelmed by the problem, as are federal law enforcement agencies. Even worse, clever crackers are beginning to realize that these calls are extremely difficult to trace. The phony ID codes are stolen from bona fide customers. A trap and trace therefore produces the name and number of the customer whose ID code has been stolen. A cracker with a phony ID chip is extremely difficult to trace.[28]

4.52–b   The Internet

The Internet poses similar problems. The good news is that the Internet is a network. Networks transmit information by sending it in "packets"—groups of data "packaged" in a particular format. A computer on the Internet packages data into a packet and sends it on its way. Part of the packet contains valuable information—the source and destination of the message.

Thus, any computer that receives a communication (including an intrusion) also receives information pinpointing the computer used to send that message. If your intruder is using the Internet to invade your

---

27. A cellular phone is constantly transmitting its identification information to a substation so that calls for the user may be routed to that telephone. (The substation needs to know where the telephone is in order to dial it.)

28. It is possible to trace the intruder by pinpointing the source of the signal sent by the suspect's phone to the cellular switching station. (According to newspaper reports, this is how police pinpointed O.J. Simpson's Ford Bronco during his "flight" from prosecution.) However, a mobile intruder will be impossible to separate from the hundreds of other cars with cellular phones in the area. (In O.J. Simpson's case, his friend was telling police which car they were seeking.) If your intruder is calling from a residence, you may be able to trace the signal back to that residence.

system, you can trace the intruder back to the computer he used to dial into your victim's computer (i.e., the last link in the chain; the intruder's computer is the first link).

The second piece of good news is that the trail left by an intruder using the Internet may not vanish after the intrusion. If the intruder used a commercial service to gain entry to the Internet, that service may maintain account records that will allow you to work backward to your intruder.

The Internet is new enough that many intruders still do not understand that they are leaving an electronic trail. Therefore, if your intruder is using the Internet, you may be able to use the service provider's records to trace him well after the intrusions have ceased.

Unfortunately, there is also bad news about Internet intruders. First, crackers can use a different route to your computer each time they call. Crackers may maintain hidden accounts on dozens of computers connected to the Internet (typically university computers). They can choose the accounts they will use to intrude into the victim's system. Your analysis of the traffic to the victim's computer may lead you on a wild goose chase.

The second piece of bad news is that crackers can use *anonymous servers*. A few sysops have configured their computers to mask the source information which would otherwise be included in every Internet transmission sent from their computer. Crackers use these servers to disguise the source of the intrusion.

The third piece of bad news is that tracing your intruder may produce too many suspects. For example, you may trace your intruder back to a major university, with its hundreds, or even thousands, of computer users who may be sharing log-on IDs and passwords.

If you conclude that your intruder is using the Internet to break into the victim's computer, you can attempt to trace that intruder by calling the service which the victim uses to access the Internet. The services' security personnel may assist you in tracking the intruder.

However, if your intruder is careful, it is likely that nothing short of a major federal investigation will find him. Fortunately, there are plenty of lazy intruders who do not cover their tracks.

4.53 The victim may not be able to wait while you trace the intruder

The most important part of your investigation is determining how much time you have left to catch the intruder. As you know, tracking an intruder takes time. Throughout the investigation, your victim must make a crucial decision—"fish or cut bait."

Once you know how an intruder has gained access, it is usually easy to kick him off the computer system. If the intruder has used an authorized account, you can change the password. If the intruder has taken advantage of a default password, you can change that password. Assuming that you remove any "back doors" planted by the intruder, you have eliminated your problem.

But jettisoning the intruder often prevents you from catching him. Unless he is clumsy enough to leave a trail through the Internet, the only way to catch him is to obtain a trap and trace, and wait for the next intrusion. Because one trap and trace is often not enough, you may have to make this decision repeatedly, without a clue as to whether the next trap and trace will be the last. If you eject the intruder before tracing him, he may never come back.

How should the victim weigh the risks and rewards of continuing the investigation? The most important factor is the motive of the intruder, which you can assess to a degree by monitoring his actions.

If the intruder is looking for sensitive information, it may be too risky to allow him to remain for even a moment after you have discovered the intrusion. *Eject any intruder who is about to obtain superuser status.* In other cases, perhaps where the intruder is taking over unused boxes in a voice mail system, it may be worthwhile to allow the intruder to play while you set your trap (see box on next page).

On the bright side, your most dangerous intruders—disgruntled employees—may be the easiest to find. Such employees are unlikely to use the Internet or call from out-of-state. However, if you have tried one or two trap and traces without success, the odds are good that your intruder is a cracker.

This fact cuts both ways. Crackers may be more interested in browsing than destruction, which means that you may have more time to track them down. Then again, you have less incentive to do

---

The virtual sandbox

Sophisticated victims with ample resources should consider creating a "virtual computer" for the intruder to play in. The victim can create programs which confine the intruder to certain portions of the machine where interesting information (planted by the victim) is stored. The intruder may never realize that he has been detected, and happily play away in his "sandbox" until you track him down.

---

so. If you eject them, and make sure that the victim has tightened its computer security, you may have solved the problem.

In many cases, it is better for a corporation to halt the investigation after learning that the intruder is calling from outside your state. Of course, there are exceptions, such as where the intruder can be traced through the Internet. If your company or university is constantly besieged by crackers, you may need to send a message that you will not tolerate further intrusions. (Prepare for a fresh influx of crackers provoked by that decision.) If a particular intruder keeps finding new ways into the computer system (e.g., by planting trap doors that are difficult to detect), you may have no choice but to track him down.

In cases where you have identified a suspect, but are unable to prove that he is intruding into the victim's computer system, you may need to continue your investigation to amass evidence. You may also have to continue your efforts when your suspect is an employee.[29]

4.54 Negotiating with your intruder

Occasionally intruders will communicate with their targets. They will make demands for money or continued access to the computer system.

---

29. In such cases, law enforcement should consider simply calling the intruder and telling him to cease and desist. Many ex-employees can be easily convinced that the FBI will show up on their doorstep if they persist.

Most intruders who seek money are current or former employees. You should treat those demands as you would any extortion attempt. Backup all data immediately. If possible, transfer operations to different computers.

Crackers sometimes offer to stop disrupting operations if given an account on the victim's computer system. *Never agree to provide an intruder with authorized access.*

The cracker may use his new account to damage the system. Conceivably, management could be liable to shareholders for any such damage based upon a breach of fiduciary duty. Worse, the cracker may use that account to dial into other computers without permission; the victim may be civilly liable to those new victims.[30]

4.55   Obtaining a trap and trace

Your next step is to obtain permission from a state or federal court to install a trap and trace, and later, a pen register. Although the next few sections summarize some of the legal requirements for obtaining those orders, you should also read the more detailed information contained in Chapter 8 (§ 8.50).

Your first step is to obtain a court order allowing installation of a trap and trace. To satisfy the Electronic Communications Privacy Act, the official must certify to the court under oath that "the information likely to be obtained by such installation and use is relevant to an ongoing criminal investigation."[31] The order allows installation for a period of no more than 60 days.

State law may require a more elaborate showing. In some states, such as California, you will need to obtain a search warrant.

A trap and trace order should direct the telephone company not to disclose the installation of the trap and trace to any person. The order should be filed under seal. The law enforcement official seeking the installation must reimburse the telephone company for the reasonable cost of that installation. Telephone companies will generally insist on

---

30. *See* William Cook, *Paying the Bill for Hostile Technology: PBX Fraud in 1991* (Chicago: United States Attorney's Office, Northern District of Illinois, 1991), at 7–8; Cheswick and Bellovin, *Firewalls and Internet Security*, at 52.

31. *See* 18 U.S.C. 3123(a).

prompt payment. (Appendix B includes sample trap and trace orders and search warrants.)

It is reasonable for the victim to pay the costs of a trap and trace. (Some phone companies request that the warrant recite that the victim will pay for the trap and trace.) The victim should request that the intruder repay those costs as part of restitution after conviction.

Your trap and trace will produce a record of every call made to the victim's computer. Since you made sure during your initial investigation that the victim's computer was configured to log all accesses, it is a simple matter to match the date and time of the intrusion with the date and time of the trap and trace.

Remember that no two clocks keep the same time. Computers use their own "clocks," referred to as *system clocks*. Invariably, the computer's system clock will be anywhere from a few seconds to a few minutes "off" from the telephone company computer's system clock.

4.60   Closing in on your intruder

The next step after you have used a trap and trace to locate your intruder is to confirm that your trap and trace *has* located your intruder. Crackers can use call forwarding. Crackers with access to university or corporate computers can break into another account and impersonate that user. Think of the results of the trap and trace as a midpoint, not an end, to your investigation.

If the location returned by your trap and trace is an institution (e.g., a company or a university), contact that institution and seek assistance. As discussed in Chapter 8 (§§ 8.32–b(1) and (2)), they may wish to monitor the account being used to access the victim's computer. The risk of spooking the intruder by contacting the institution is slight because it is unlikely that officials of that institution will notify your suspect. However, you should emphasize the need for secrecy.

If the source of the intrusion is a residence, you should obtain various records for that residence, such as utility bills, which identify the occupants. If your victim knows one of the occupants, you have probably found your intruder.

You should also consider checking whether your local school or police department is familiar with a juvenile living at that residence. In either case, however, you are *not* yet ready to seek a search warrant for that location.

4.61   Obtaining a pen register

Your next step is to install a pen register on the location identified by your trap and trace. A pen register records every number dialed by a particular telephone. You will use that pen register to confirm that the telephone revealed by your trap and trace is being used to call the victim's computer system.

Again, the law requires you to obtain a court order to install a pen register; some states require a search warrant. (Appendix B includes a sample order authorizing installation of a pen register, and a sample search warrant.)

The pen register should be installed for no more than 60 days. Be prepared to spend several hundred dollars (or even more) to install a pen register for the first 30 days.

You can use the results of your pen register to:

- confirm that a particular location is the source of the intrusion;

- identify other computers under assault by your intruder; and

- identify the intruder's confederates, caches of stolen data, and pirate bulletin boards he uses.

You can confirm the results of your trap and trace by matching the record of calls produced by the pen register against the victim's log of accesses. If your intruder is dialing from outside the state, remember to account for time zones.

Your pen register may identify other computers targeted by your intruder. It may also reveal that your intruder is using a war dialer. If the intruder is using a war dialer, the pen register will show dozens or hundreds of calls spaced every few seconds to various locations. Numbers listed repeatedly are probably associated with computers under assault by your intruder.

You should also examine numbers called by the intruder to identify confederates, data caches, and pirate bulletin boards. Crackers are like German U-boats during World War II. An individual cracker may spot a vulnerable target and communicate that information to scores of colleagues. Those crackers may elect to join the attack. A pen register will identify the calls to your intruder's confederates.

The pen register may also identify data caches. Although most crackers only browse through victims' computer systems, some steal data. Savvy crackers do not store stolen data in their own computers, for fear that police will find the data when executing a search warrant.

If your intruder is stealing data, you may find him downloading that data to his own computer and then uploading the data to another computer elsewhere. The pen register will reveal that location, which you will then obtain authorization to search.[32]

Your pen register may also record calls to bulletin boards used by crackers to communicate information. This may provide an easy way to identify pirate boards in your neighborhood. The pen register will identify the suspect boards, and the intruder's computer may contain evidence that he uploaded and downloaded bootlegged software to and from those boards. An intrusion investigation can easily develop into a copyright infringement case.[33]

It is often desirable to let the pen register run for as long as possible before raiding your intruder's location. (This usually can be justified only when your intruder is not constantly calling your victim's computer.) The more time the intruder has to make telephone calls, the more information you will obtain.

However, once you are confident that you have located your intruder, and have sufficient pen register data to prove beyond a reasonable doubt that your suspect is the intruder, you may wish to eject him

---

32. Special rules may apply if the intruder stores the data in a *remote computing service. See* Chapter 8, §§ 8.42, 8.45, 8.46.

33. *Caution: bulletin boards present complex legal issues which must be handled very carefully. Read Chapter 8 before searching or seizing a bulletin board.*

In addition, you should not impersonate your intruder on such a board without that intruder's permission (i.e., after you have "turned" him into an informant). The board sysop may be able to claim that the Fourth Amendment protected him from a police search, as his expectation of privacy only allowed authorized users (i.e., your intruder) to log on to the board. Indeed, it is unclear whether using an informant constitutes an unauthorized search, although that search should be no different from sending an informant to a meeting with a wire.

from the victim's computer system. Of course, in return for reducing the victim's risk of further damage, you incur the risk that the ejected intruder will erase from his computer all information documenting his intrusion.

4.70   The arrest

Once you have used a pen register to confirm that a particular telephone line is the source of your intrusion, you should prepare to search that location. Part of your pre–search warrant preparation should be to determine how to identify one or more of the people living (or working) at the location as your intruder.

Remember that the pen register simply identifies the telephone line being used; it does not tell you who is using it. You need to investigate the occupants of the residence or business to help identify your intruder. As discussed above, school or utility records may be helpful. Running license plates on cars parked in front of the residence is a good start.

When you are obtaining a description of the residence to include in the search warrant, drive by the residence and look at the telephone line. There are reports, perhaps more urban legend than fact, of crackers hooking their phone line to a neighbor's line and laughing as police swarm into the house next door. It takes only a few seconds to examine the phone lines on each side of your target from across the street while you are obtaining a premises description—the job you save may be yours.

4.71   Preparing the search warrant

Chapter 9 provides step-by-step instructions on drafting search warrants, and Appendix B includes warrants for computer intrusion cases.

In addition to the items listed in that sample warrant, you should include material specific to your case, such as:

- phone numbers for dial-in ports used by the intruder;

- passwords to the victim's computer system used by the intruder (your victim must change any passwords after revealing them in the affidavit because search warrants are eventually made public);

- the name and account number associated with the account used by the intruder;

- printouts containing information unique to the victim's computer system, such as welcoming banners, the name of the victim, and even the name of the victim's computer (if named by its location, such as "Building 4 computer," or by number, "Computer X452"). You are looking for information that would normally appear on the screen or screen printout of an authorized user;

- a description of software or data which you believe the intruder stole from the victim's computer system; and

- messages or commands sent by the intruder.

(The warrants in Appendix B also include other property to be searched for and/or seized.)

You are looking for anything that the victim's computer would have displayed to the intruder. Many intruders regularly "dump" the contents of their screen to disk or to their printer. That material is valuable evidence of the intrusion, and it may be found anywhere in the residence (including in the trash).

4.72 Executing the search warrant

The first decision you must make is when to serve the warrant. In intrusion cases, you are generally better off serving the warrant when your suspect is not at home. Suspects can erase information within seconds while you are still performing a knock-notice at the front door.

Chapter 6 discusses the proper procedure for searching for, and preserving, computer evidence. In addition to following those procedures, look for evidence of confederates, data caches, bulletin boards, passwords, magazines relating to cracking (e.g., *2600*), and computer manuals for mainframes and minicomputers (particularly those written for your victim's computer).

Keep an eye out for blue boxes, which are damning evidence that the owner is a cracker. (If there is more than one potential intruder in the residence or institution, you may wish to examine such equipment for fingerprints.) Telephone access codes and credit card numbers are also valuable evidence, both of new crimes, and, circumstantially, of the intruder's intent to defraud.

If you believe that your intruder is a cracker, examine all pads of paper near any telephone or modem which may contain access codes. Consider asking for authorization in your affidavit to seize blank pads of paper, as forensic analysis may show what the cracker wrote on the page of the pad which he tore off before you arrived.

Finally, you should look for evidence identifying the user of the computer. Computer manuals with the user's name inside, floppy disks labeled with a name, and even data on the computer itself can be valuable.[34]

The interview is very important in intrusion cases. When executing a search warrant, devote one officer to interviewing suspects and witnesses, and another to performing the search. *Miranda* warnings should be given in appropriate cases.

As discussed in Chapter 6, intruders may "booby-trap" their computers. Ask the intruder whether the system has been rigged. If he admits that the system is rigged, that admission can be used in court as evidence that he intended to hide evidence of illegal activities within the computer. If he denies it, and the computer is rigged, then that evasion is powerful evidence of guilt.

Explain to the intruder that you have all the evidence you need to link him to the intrusion, and that further denials will not help his cause. You may shock your suspect into revealing important information immediately.

Time is of the essence in intrusion cases because your suspect may have confederates. If you are going to use the suspect to help investigate his friends, secure his cooperation immediately. A long delay (more than a day) before your "turned" suspect returns "on line" may

---

34. When searching the computer, keep in mind that many application programs require the user to type a name as part of "registering" the program. That name is stored in the computer. Game programs often keep records identifying users who earned high scores.

warn confederates that he is no longer their ally. If you are going to serve your warrant when the suspect is not at home, determine his whereabouts in advance so that you can contact him quickly.

4.73 Executing search warrants where the suspect is a juvenile

Do not serve a warrant with weapons drawn in cases involving juveniles.[35] The media have had a field day because many law enforcement agencies have treated search warrants directed at teenagers like other search warrants. You will achieve better results and avoid hostile press if you handle these cases more gently. Most crackers are merely teenagers who are testing limits. Their parents are innocent third parties, and you are about to turn their world upside down.

If compassion for them is not enough, consider this: parents are your allies. If you treat them gently, they will make their teenager tell you everything. However, if you scare them to death with guns, trample their furniture, and take their child away in handcuffs, you will get no cooperation. Instead, you will prompt parents to hire a lawyer and urge their child to fight to the end. Although juveniles need a shock to their system to understand the consequences of their actions, be assured that taking them away to jail for the night is shock enough.

One tactic which may be useful when dealing with parents is to remind them that they may be liable for their juvenile's activities. Intruders are toying with very expensive computers and even more valuable data. Many states impose liability on parents for their children's crimes. The realization that their child may have placed them in danger of financial disaster may change parents' attitudes concerning the seriousness of the matter.

But what about the risk that a juvenile intruder will destroy information while you politely discuss the matter with his parents at the front door? Although it is safest to serve the warrant while the intruder is not at home, you will get much better results (and fewer complaints to your department) if you perform your search when the parents are at home.

---

35. Of course, there are unusual cases in which the juvenile poses a threat to officers, and officers must act accordingly.

Another alternative is to serve your warrant while the juvenile is in school, and call the parent(s) home from work to witness the search. You can then wait with the parent(s) for the juvenile's return.

Most parents are cooperative, and many will want to assist you in interviewing the juvenile. They will eliminate other possible suspects (e.g., "Dan is the only person who uses that computer, and Jack has never been interested in computers"). They may put pressure on the juvenile to disclose his friends and reveal data caches. They may also help you convince the juvenile to work undercover for law enforcement.

You should seize the computer used by the juvenile, even if other members of the family use that computer. Unfortunately, the best you can do is promise to make backup copies of the data as soon as possible; do not leave the computer behind. You should allow a responsible parent to download copies of files that belong to the parents before you leave the scene.

5

Investigating Theft of Information

[A diplomat] in Bangkok describes the charge that his country's companies are slow to transfer technology [to foreign business partners] as a "myth." [A businessman from that same country] claims that "the Thais think they can sit behind their desks and the technology will fall on them from the sky. If they want the technology they should have the guts to do what we did, which is go out and steal it."

—*Economist*, May 7–13, 1994

5.00   Introduction

Information is valuable. Government spies seek military and economic intelligence. Insider trading scandals make headlines on Wall Street. Cheating on exams is epidemic in American high schools, colleges, and even military academies.

Stealing information is a way to get a jump on the competition. It is often an easy way to obtain the results of a competitor's research and development efforts without investing millions of dollars. Thieves use stolen information to plan marketing strategies or calculate contract bids. Departing employees steal client records and use those *customer lists* to take business away from their former employers.

Information theft is often a high-technology crime. Thieves in high-technology areas target scientific and technical information. Employees download information from company computers, and industrial spies break into computers and steal information and software. Thieves often store stolen information on their own computers. If you are going to investigate cases involving computers, you will encounter information theft cases.

Corporate investigators must be able to investigate these cases because information theft is common. In a 1988 National Institute of Justice survey of high-technology companies, 38% of those companies reported that they had been victims of information theft within the previous five years.[1]

Law enforcement agencies must learn to investigate these cases because more companies are reporting thefts to police. Twenty years ago, companies were content to use a civil suit to put thieves out of business. Venture capitalists would usually not fund a company accused of theft.

Although the majority of victims still avoid the police, many corporate victims now see less value in filing a lawsuit and greater value in persuading law enforcement to intervene. This is because the civil lawsuit has lost much of its deterrent value.

Courts with clogged calendars now take much longer to resolve civil suits, allowing thieves to prolong lawsuits until they have used the stolen information to make millions of dollars. The arrival of global competition has encouraged foreign industrial spies to steal secrets to use at home; civil lawsuits are often useless against foreign companies.

The marketplace no longer interprets a lawsuit to mean that the defendant is a thief. Many companies have discovered that they can use even a frivolous lawsuit to delay or destroy competitors, and have transformed the lawsuit from a remedy into a weapon. In this new environment, venture capitalists no longer regard a lawsuit as evidence of wrongdoing, and lend money to companies sued for information theft.

The result is that corporate victims are turning to law enforcement for help. Criminal prosecution offers victims several advantages. Police can use search warrants to recover victims' property. In addition, a criminal investigation is still a "nuclear weapon" in the marketplace. It is one thing for Company A to sue Company B for theft; it is quite another when law enforcement officials accuse Company B of

---

1. Lois Mock and Dennis Rosenblum, *A Study of Trade Secret Theft in High Technology Industries*, prepared for the National Institute of Justice (Washington, D.C.: Department of Justice, 1988).

theft. The publicity accompanying the execution of a search warrant can ruin the target, even if no criminal charges are filed. Thus, both private and public investigators will receive an increasing number of complaints of information theft over the next decade.

5.01 The importance of evaluating cases at the outset

Information theft cases are extremely difficult and time consuming. A single case can take years of effort, and even the best looking case can fall apart in the courtroom. Worse, most of the cases presented to you as a law enforcement or corporate investigator will not be suitable for criminal prosecution for a variety of reasons discussed below.

Thus, this chapter starts with a lengthy discussion of how to decide which information theft cases *not* to investigate, at least for purposes of pursuing a criminal prosecution. (Investigating for purposes of filing a civil suit is discussed later in this chapter.)

When you evaluate each case with the goal of weeding out the losers early, you conserve your resources for cases you can win. It is especially important for you to look for problems at the outset because there are many pressures on investigators to pursue cases which may not lead to a conviction.

One source of pressure is the seriousness of the crime to the victim. Corporate victims place information theft at the top of their agenda. Unlike most crimes, information theft can threaten a company's existence, or at least its future prospects in the marketplace. When a corporate victim wants law enforcement assistance in an information theft case, it *demands* law enforcement assistance. And the victim will be reluctant to take "no" for an answer.

The victim's concerns will usually receive a hearing at the highest levels of law enforcement, as high-ranking corporate officials and corporate counsel find it natural and easy to contact a chief of police or district attorney directly. When a prominent corporate citizen and taxpayer demands action, that demand is going to attract attention. It may not be fair, but it is a fact of life.

This does not mean that corporate victims, police, and prosecutors railroad innocent people and companies. The overwhelming majority of corporate victims report information thefts in good faith and, like any victim, do what they can to persuade law enforcement to render assistance. *It is not a question of overlooking innocence.* The problem is that victims and law enforcement often overlook problems, technicalities if you will, which ultimately allow the guilty to escape conviction.

The problem is compounded by the fact that these cases usually look open-and-shut. They look like crimes which, but for their oddity and expense, law enforcement would ordinarily pursue vigorously. Usually the victim can show that it has spent millions of dollars developing what appears to be secret information. It can often show that a disgruntled employee left the company for a competitor. It may even be able to show that the competitor is about to release a similar product.

The victim will argue that law enforcement has only been asked to prosecute a simple theft of extremely valuable property. A chief of police or district attorney may feel uncomfortable rejecting a "clear-cut case of theft."

But "no" is often the only answer which makes sense. As discussed below, some "clear-cut cases of theft" are not even crimes. Others are difficult or impossible to prosecute for various reasons.

For example, some cases involve groups of departing employees accused of stealing information from their former employer. Where the victim sees clear-cut theft by the defecting group, the prosecutor sees five or more potential defendants, with little prospect of separating those who took secret information from those who did nothing more than change jobs.

Saying "no" at the beginning is extremely important because once started, information theft cases are difficult to stop. The pace of such cases is usually so fast that investigators often have no time before seeking a search warrant to undertake the painstaking investigation necessary to ensure that the allegedly secret information was not disclosed by the victim or others.

That investigation is sometimes never conducted. Once you serve a search warrant, the pressure to file charges quickly can be irresistible. It often takes dozens of police officers to serve a search warrant in an information theft case. The media will often cover the event.

Your victim will want to obtain an *injunction* (an order from a civil court preventing the thief from using the secret) and will ask law enforcement to file charges to make it easier for the victim to obtain that order. Finally, the public and the victim may not understand why a prosecutor who believed in the case enough to have taken a company apart cubicle by cubicle is now reluctant to file charges pending further investigation.

If you are a police officer or prosecutor, it will often be your job to stop this train before it pulls out of the station. This chapter will provide you with the tools to decide which cases are worth investigating and which are not. Equally important, this chapter will also teach you how to investigate those cases which deserve your attention.

The story is different for corporate investigators because the criminal justice system is not the only game in town. Victims usually file civil lawsuits against thieves to prevent them from using stolen information. Although a criminal court can put a thief in prison, only a civil court can issue an injunction.

Thus, corporate security and private investigators should investigate information theft even when criminal prosecution is not a realistic option. Because this book is aimed at helping all investigators handle high-technology crime cases, this chapter will discuss investigation of high-technology crime directed toward both civil litigation and criminal prosecution.

5.10   What is information theft?

A broad definition of information theft is the unauthorized taking or use of private information of commercial value with the knowledge that the owner considers that information to be secret. Such a taking or use is also referred to as a *misappropriation* of information.

Information must be private to qualify for protection. The stock price of IBM, for example, is not protected. Nor is information which has no commercial value, such as the contents of your personal diary.

The law also allows employees to retain what they have learned on the job, with the exception of certain information specifically identified by the employer as secret when given to the employee. (The alternative would require employees to stay in their jobs forever out of fear of being sued or prosecuted for using information "in their heads" at their next job.)

Terms of art: trade secret, proprietary, and confidential

What do you call information which is not public? Lawyers call such information *trade secret, proprietary,* and *confidential.* A *trade secret* is defined by state law, and its meaning can vary from state to state. The terms *proprietary* and *confidential* are usually interchangeable, although some use the term *proprietary* only to refer to particularly valuable information, and use *confidential* to refer to information which must be kept private because its release might invade the privacy of employees or management (e.g., personnel files). Information theft cases are commonly referred to in both the civil and criminal arenas as *trade secret cases.*

5.20   Who steals information?

5.21   Competitors

Although there are foreign government spies working in high-technology areas, the vast majority of information thieves are competitors. Those thieves include employees of the victim who plan to join or start a competing business. Some thieves are former employees practicing extortion by threatening to disclose secrets to competitors. Although foreign companies steal information, the majority of information theft cases are strictly domestic.

5.22   Information anarchists

This handful of engineers believes that information should be free, and that they should help achieve this goal by copying and distributing secret information to the world. Their most prominent coup was when a group calling itself the NuPrometheus League distributed portions of Apple Computer's newest operating system to *MacWorld* magazine in the late 1980s. Similarly, anarchists in late 1994 posted on the Internet what news organizations labeled the "software formula" for one of the most popular commercial encryption schemes for software.[2] Although information anarchists are interesting people, you are unlikely to encounter them in your career.

5.23 Pack rats

These collectors are simply curious about new technology. Some crackers fall into this category, as do many engineers and scientists.

Engineers usually keep projects they have completed for Company A long after they have moved to Company B, even if that means keeping Company A's proprietary information without permission. Some engineers use the less sensitive portions of those projects as samples of their work when they apply for another job. They do not intend to use the information to hurt their ex-employer, and would be offended by the very suggestion.

Thus, finding a storehouse of the victim's technical manuals in an ex-employee's home does not necessarily mean that he is an industrial spy. Absent a financial motive to keep your victim's information (e.g., a new job directly related to the stolen information), your suspect may be a pack rat.

5.30   How we catch information thieves

Some thieves are caught in the act. In one case, an employee acted suspiciously in the days before his departure. On the day he left, company officials checked their computer system and found that he had downloaded secret information. The police arrested him a few hours later at the airport boarding a flight to his native France. (The thief later brought a motion to suppress the evidence taken from his carry-on suitcase because he was "in the international area of the airport"; he lost.)

---

2. *San Jose Mercury News*, September 17, 1994, 10D (reprinted from the *New York Times*).

An employee in another case was caught using the employer's fax machine to send specifications to a competitor. He also mailed blueprints to that company. When police raided the competitor's facility, they found a package on the president's desk. Inside the package was a copy of various secret blueprints belonging to the victim, and a note from the thief to the president. It read: "Dear Bob, now pay me, [expletive deleted]."

Computer intruders occasionally linger too long in their victims' computers and are traced back to their homes and businesses. One former employee of a victim was apprehended after spending 17 hours over several weeks downloading the victim's source code for its new software product.

However, these cases are unusual, as information thieves are usually caught well after the theft. Information theft is usually detected in one of two ways. First, and most common, are cases in which an informant informs police of the crime. Some informants are employees of the competitor who are upset that the thief is using the victim's proprietary information to advance his or her career. Others are employees of the victim who have learned that their former colleague left with stolen information.

Second, there are cases in which a competitor gains an unexpected edge in the marketplace. Perhaps the competitor's new product is surprisingly similar to the victim's new design. Or the competitor has won a contract by bidding just a few percentage points lower than the victim, or has used similar language or methodology in its contract proposal. In many cases, the victim concludes that the competitor was able to obtain that advantage only by stealing certain information from the victim.

5.40 Screening cases for referral to law enforcement

As discussed above, information theft investigations are extremely difficult and time-consuming, and most cases are best handled in the civil litigation arena. This section is intended to help law enforcement and corporate investigators determine which cases should be referred to, and accepted by, law enforcement for criminal investigation.

5.41 Identifying cases which should not be handled within the criminal justice system

In this author's experience in the Silicon Valley, *over 90% of complaints of information theft are inappropriate for criminal prosecution.* Some thefts are not covered by criminal information theft laws. Others do not merit the expense to the taxpayers of a full-blown prosecution. And still others fall into the Bermuda Triangle of information theft: they look good on paper, but you will never be able to prove your case beyond a reasonable doubt in court.

The phrase "beyond a reasonable doubt" is important here. The burden of proof in a civil case is *by a preponderance of the evidence,* meaning that the jury decides which side's version of the facts is more likely to be correct. Many victims and their lawyers, used to fighting battles in civil court, do not fully appreciate how difficult it is to prove anything beyond a reasonable doubt. It is part of your job to remind them that prosecutors must explain often technical material to a jury of mostly high school graduates, and convince them, beyond a reasonable doubt, to send clean-cut looking engineers and businessmen to jail for stealing contract proposals and technical manuals.

You can identify cases which are inappropriate for criminal investigation and prosecution by following a few simple rules.[3]

5.41–a   Facts which indicate that your case is probably not suitable for criminal prosecution

You should reject cases in which:

---

3. Like many of the rules stated in this book, there are exceptions which prove them. These are merely guidelines to assist you in screening cases. They are not infallible, and there will be cases worthy of attention which violate them. Perhaps most important, none of these rules is intended to suggest that you cannot obtain a conviction in a particular case, or that the cause is unworthy. Rather, if you have limited time and resources, you should usually reject cases which do not satisfy the criteria stated in this chapter.

- the stolen information is not scientific or technical information;
- the victim has lost information which is something less than its "crown jewels";
- the stolen information is not likely to be discovered in the thief's possession;
- the theft occurred more than six months before the report to law enforcement; or
- the thief's conduct is not considered theft within the industry.

You should also be wary of any case in which:

- the suspect is part of a group of employees *raided* by a competitor (the term is defined below); or
- the suspect is a *licensee* (also defined below).

The next section discusses each of these rules in more detail.

5.41–b   Reasons to reject a case for criminal prosecution

1.   The information which has been stolen is not scientific or technical information.

As discussed in the next section on the law of information theft, some states do not punish thefts of "business information." However, even if the law in your jurisdiction allows you to prosecute thefts of business information, you should avoid doing so except in unusual cases.

One problem is that too much supposedly proprietary business information is not kept secret. The *Wall Street Journal* is full of tidbits which businessmen considered to be secret—until the *Journal* published the information. Financial data and marketing information are often leaked to the press, or simply filtered through a very efficient rumor mill at the company. Although customer lists may be secret, it can be very difficult to prove *beyond a reasonable doubt* that none of the other companies in the industry knew the identity of the firm's customers.

Another problem is that the small amount of business information which is secret is usually so stale as to be worthless. Most business information has a very short "half-life." Marketing information may be very important for three months, and then worthless. Remember that your ultimate audience is a jury; it is difficult to persuade them to send Mr. Doe to prison for stealing financial information which would have become general knowledge in three months anyway.

Scientific and technical information cases often do not present these problems. Jurors can understand the importance of Coca-Cola's formula. The more exotic the secret, the tougher it is for the defendant to argue that it was available to the public. Evidence that the defendant took the information instead of spending time and money reinventing it suggests that the information was valuable.

Nonetheless, there are occasional business information cases worth pursuing. Contract bid cases can be compelling if you can prove that the competitor possessed a copy of the victim's contract proposal and subsequently underbid the victim by a suspiciously small amount.

A handful of customer list cases may be worth investigating where the victim is a sympathetic figure (e.g., a sole proprietor) who jealously guarded that information, and who faces severe financial damage as a result of the theft.

2. *The victim has lost information which is something less than its crown jewels.*

Like all organizations strapped for funds, law enforcement agencies must set priorities. Most resources are devoted to investigating and prosecuting street crimes, such as murder, rape, and narcotics trafficking.

Information theft cases are nonviolent, complex, time-consuming, extremely expensive, and frequently unsuccessful. If law enforcement declines to investigate, victims can usually pursue civil remedies against the thief. Police cannot justify spending time and money prosecuting information theft cases unless the victim has lost critical information.

This does not mean that only large companies with extremely valuable assets need apply—some of the most rewarding cases involve start-up companies whose one critical piece of information has been stolen. Juries and prosecutors are likely to be attracted by cases where the victim company is about to go bankrupt because a thief has taken its one secret.

The test is the same for all victims: how important is the information to you? (When the victim says the information is extremely important, that is the time to test their resolve by explaining about the time and money victims must spend as part of their cooperation with law enforcement.)

3. *The stolen information is not likely to be discovered in the thief's possession.*

Apart from such information as the recipe for Mrs. Fields cookies or the formula for Coca-Cola, most secret information cannot be memorized easily. It is stored on paper or in electronic form. A thief intent on using that information steals or copies it in that form, and retains it in that form.

This means that a stolen trade secret usually does not vanish into thin air. It exists after the theft within a notebook, a floppy disk, a thief's computer, or a technical manual. Find a *tangible* object (something you can touch, including software) containing the secret in your suspect's possession, and you are well on your way to a conviction.

However, without that tangible object, you will have problems proving: (1) that any theft occurred; or (2) that any particular person committed a theft.

For example, suppose that a victim claims that a competitor has introduced a product which, you are assured, the competitor could not have created without using the victim's secret. Although the victim is not aware of any missing documents or software, you are urged to charge the competitor with theft.

Your first problem is that it is usually difficult to preclude the possibility, *beyond a reasonable doubt*, that "great minds think alike." Absent the presence of 1,500 lines of identical code in two similar software products, it can be impossible to show that the competitor did not develop the same idea independently of your victim.

It will also be difficult to prove the identity of the thief without showing that your suspect had a tangible object containing the victim's information. Even if a departing employee is the obvious source of stolen information, it may be difficult to prove beyond a reasonable doubt that the competitor did not have another spy on the victim's payroll who stole the information.

Nor, in many cases, is it easy to prove the identity of a receiver of that information. Technical projects are often group efforts in which many people can be responsible for incorporating the stolen information into the competitor's product. Thus, you need to place that tangible object in your suspect's possession, or at least within his or her control.[4]

Of course, most investigations begin without law enforcement's having recovered the stolen information. The point of this rule is that there must be some indication before you begin your investigation that: (1) a tangible object containing that information was stolen from the victim; and (2) that you stand a good chance of finding that object, or a copy of it, in the thief's possession. (This rule eliminates all "memorization" cases because you need a "paper trail" to show that your thief took the victim's information.)

As discussed later in this chapter, the victim must be very specific about what information was stolen, and what tangible objects contain that information. The victim must be able to explain how Object A could have moved from the victim's facility to the competitor's facility. If nothing else, following this rule will help you create a property list to use when drafting a warrant to search for evidence.

Moreover, the victim should provide some reason to believe that you will be able to find the tangible object. For example, the victim may have evidence that a key employee entrusted with the tangible object (or with access to it) unexpectedly quit and joined the competitor who produced that suspiciously similar product. Perhaps the

---

4. It is usually impractical to charge a corporation alone with theft of information. Judges cannot send corporations to jail, and the deterrent value of a fine usually does not justify a criminal prosecution. Prosecutors want to send a message to the community that individuals can be sent to prison for stealing information. Moreover, it is difficult to justify making the victim put its civil suit on hold while the prosecutor pursues the defendant corporation.

victim's records show that the employee never returned the tangible item. An informant may tell you that there are documents at the competitor's premises stamped "[VICTIM] CONFIDENTIAL." Look with a jaundiced eye at any case in which the victim offers nothing more than vague promises that police are "certain" to find incriminating material at the competitor's offices.

> *4. The theft occurred more than six months before the report to law enforcement.*

Time is an enemy in information theft cases. A competitor may be able to raise a reasonable doubt by claiming that it was able to duplicate the victim's efforts in the six months to a year since the alleged theft. Worse, as time passes, it becomes more likely that the thief has already used the information in any stolen tangible object and has discarded that object.

An exception to this rule may be when an informant "freshens" the case by showing that the thief is still using the secret information and still possesses tangible items containing the information. Without such "freshening," the likelihood of finding the stolen information at the suspect's office or residence diminishes to the point that any search warrant may be invalid as "stale."

This aspect of information theft cases poses problems for victims who prefer to conduct their own investigations before reporting thefts to law enforcement. They prefer to investigate before reporting because it allows them to decide whether the value of the stolen information warrants their spending time and money on a criminal investigation.

While this is a valid strategy for victims, delay may make a criminal investigation impossible. Law enforcement investigators are very reluctant to handle cases when someone else has already conducted a lengthy investigation.

Victims who believe that they may need law enforcement assistance (e.g., a search warrant to recover property) should touch base with law enforcement immediately after learning about the theft. Victims should first confirm with law enforcement that merely reporting a theft will not trigger an investigation or result in publicity. This should not be a problem, as most law enforcement agencies are too busy to handle information theft cases and will not intrude into your investigation.

One advantage to early reporting is that law enforcement investigators may be able to assist in your investigation (e.g., by checking automated records), and will not have to spend valuable time getting up to speed once you refer the case for a criminal investigation.

Do not make the victim a police agent

When the victim is performing its own investigation, corporate and law enforcement investigators should ensure that they do not make that victim a *police agent* for purposes of the Fourth Amendment. A victim becomes a police agent when:

- the victim performs a search which the government would need a search warrant to conduct;

- the victim performs that search to assist the government, as opposed to furthering its own interests (i.e., protecting its rights or property); and

- the government is aware of the victim's conduct and does not object to it.

See United States v. Jacobson, 466 U.S. 109 (1984); *Coolidge v. New Hampshire*, 403 U.S. 443, 487 (1971); *United States v. Reed*, 15 F.3d 928, 931 (9th Cir. 1994).

A victim acting to protect its property by assisting police to prevent or detect a crime does not become a police agent. This includes publicly regulated telephone and utility companies. *See United States v. Cleaveland*, 38 F.3d 1092 (9th Cir. 1994).

Police should indicate in their reports that they have chosen not to participate in, or direct, any private investigation.

5. *The industry does not condemn the thief's conduct.*

In a few cases the letter of the law does not match the customs of an industry. For example, most companies require employees to sign agreements requiring them to return all documents, no matter how inconsequential, when they leave the company. However, engineers in high technology companies routinely ignore this requirement, and few companies enforce their policies rigorously.

Pack rats are legion in Silicon Valley, and engineers do not have a rigid view of "ownership" of information. Although management may stamp most technical documents "proprietary," engineers often substitute their own judgment of what information is truly worthy of protection.

You will find it difficult to win an information theft case involving technical information unless the technical community agrees that any engineer would have realized that it was unacceptable to take that information.

Therefore, you should usually reject any case where your suspect engaged in conduct which, while technically theft, is widely accepted within your victim's industry, and where the victim has not suffered significant damage. The phrase "a jury of your peers" still means something, and juries are more than willing to ignore the law when faced with a conflict between law and custom.

In addition to rejecting cases which fail any of the tests listed above, there are two additional circumstances in which you should be wary of accepting a case:

6. *The suspect is part of a group of employees raided by a competitor.*

A *raid* refers to one company's hiring a group of employees from another company. Raids occur fairly frequently in high-technology companies, particularly where a group of employees *spins off* (leaves together) from their firm to open a competing operation. Officials of the new firm may then hire additional employees from their old employer. Occasionally, established companies raid employees from competitors.

A raided firm is often suspicious that the new firm is hiring its employees, not for their talent, but to obtain the firm's secret information.

This is particularly true when an established firm is branching out to a new area already being exploited by the raided firm.

Raiding cases pose several problems which usually make them poor candidates for criminal prosecution. The first problem is that there are too many suspects. The more employees raided by the new company, the harder it is to prove that any particular employee stole the victim's information.

It is possible that only one or two of the ten raided employees stole information as part of their transition to new employment. You will have difficulty in such cases proving that some employees are guilty and others are not.

The second problem is that there may be questions concerning ownership of the information. Many lawyers advise aspiring entrepreneurs to work on their plans for their new companies after working hours before leaving their current employer. When a substantial portion of a company moves on to greener pastures, it may be harder to rebut the defense that the stolen information was developed by the departing employees on their own time before they quit.

Finally, raiding cases are like divorces. A firm can explain the departure of one employee as an isolated decision unrelated to the work environment and prospects at the company. A half-dozen or more departures are harder to explain, as employers and employees alike interpret a mass exodus to be a vote of "no confidence" in the firm.

Management's feelings of betrayal are intensified by fear of competition against former colleagues and formidable talent. Emotions run high, and victims may exaggerate their claims of theft out of outrage and a desire for revenge.

7. The suspect is a licensee.

A *licensee* is someone who has been given permission to use information for a price. Many companies will *license* their technology to other companies in exchange for money or other technology (called a *technology exchange*). Companies draft elaborate *license agreements* which spell out what a party may, and may not, do with the licensed technology.

Occasionally a company will accuse a licensee of using the secret information in violation of the license agreement. In some cases, the company will notice that the licensee has continued to use the information after the agreement ended. In others, the licensee is alleged to have used the information to create a competing product.

Most licensee cases should be handled in civil courts. Like raiding cases, licensee disputes involve a business relationship gone sour. There are usually issues involving the terms and scope of the license, the parties' intent, and perhaps a claim by the accused that the owner of the technology violated (or *breached*) the agreement in such a way as to allow the licensee to do whatever it wanted with the technology.

It can be very difficult to prove beyond a reasonable doubt that someone who was trusted by the owner with the technology intended to steal it. Just as most contract disputes do not end up in criminal court, most licensee cases should be referred to the civil arena.

5.42 Criminal law and information theft—determining whether the theft is a crime in your jurisdiction

The criminal law has evolved over centuries to the point where a simple rule is usually true: if someone did something wrong, we can find a law prohibiting that conduct. This is often *not* the case with information theft.

Unfortunately, you need to understand the complex law of information theft to identify cases which cannot be prosecuted in your jurisdiction. You also need to know the law in order to focus your investigation on the facts you will need to prove your case in court.

This means that you must consult with your prosecutor before you begin your investigation. This quite lengthy section on the law of information theft should convince you that these cases require an attorney just to decide whether a crime has been committed.

Furthermore, as discussed in Chapter 2, victims seeking to protect their information can create legal problems that will affect the case after charges are filed. Prosecutors can help explain those issues to victims, and assist in protecting proprietary information from disclosure.

Equally important, search warrants in information theft cases are extremely complex (see Appendix B for an example). Law enforcement investigators should enlist their local prosecutors to draft those warrants.

The law may differ in your area

Most states have information theft laws, and many vary in small, but potentially significant, respects. Because this book cannot cover each law in depth, you must examine the law in your jurisdiction carefully. If you have access to a law library, you should look at Appendix B–5 of *Milgrim on Trade Secrets* (New York: Matthew Bender, 1995) for the text (and a brief analysis) of each state's criminal trade secret theft statute. The same work is contained as Volume 12B in that publisher's "Business Organizations" series.

5.42–a   State laws punishing information theft

This section begins with state law because most information theft cases are prosecuted by local authorities. Federal law (discussed in § 5.42–b) does not address theft of information specifically, and the most suitable federal statutes apply only in cases where the stolen information crossed state lines.

There are two sets of state laws governing information theft:

- general theft statutes, such as larceny, embezzlement, and receipt of stolen property; and

- special trade secret theft statutes.

Until the 1970s, there were no criminal laws directed specifically at the theft of information. However, states gradually realized that certain thefts of information were not covered by general theft statutes, and began enacting trade secret theft statutes.

Trade secret theft statutes define certain information as a trade secret and punish any theft of that information. Most states have enacted such special statutes. (In the civil arena, secret information is always referred to as a trade secret. Both criminal and civil information theft cases are often referred to as trade secret cases.)

When considering whether to investigate a report of information theft, you must determine whether the suspect's acts are punishable under general theft laws and/or trade secret theft laws. The chart on the next two pages and Table 5–1 on page 162 may be helpful.

Figure 5–1: Flow chart for state law enforcement officers

1. Did the thief wrongly take or misappropriate information?
   Yes: Proceed to #2 below.
   No: Proceed to #7. If no other statute applies, reject the case.

2. Was the information stolen in a tangible form (e.g., a document)?
   Yes: You may be able to use a general theft statute. Proceed to #3 below.
   No: Reject memorization cases unless there are truly exceptional circumstances. If you choose to continue, proceed to #5 below.

3. Did the thief take the tangible object containing the information, or just make a copy of it?
   Take: You may be able to use a general theft statute. Proceed to #4 below.
   Copy: Check to see whether your general theft statute punishes copying. If it does, proceed to #4 below. If not, try to use a special statute—proceed to #5 below.

4. Did the thief have permission to possess the information?
   Yes: Where the thief was entrusted with the information, and abused that trust, you should be able to use a general theft statute based on an embezzlement theory. Proceed to #5 below to determine whether a special statute also applies.
   No: Can you show an intent to permanently deprive?
      Yes: You should be able to use your general theft statute. Proceed to #5 below to determine whether a special statute also applies.
      No: You must use a special trade secret theft statute—proceed to #5 below.

5. Can you proceed under the special statute in your jurisdiction? Consider the following:
   a. Does your case involve non-scientific and non-technical information?

Yes: Determine whether such information qualifies as a trade secret under your state's special statute. If it does, proceed to (b) below; if it does not, proceed to #7 below.

No: Proceed to (b) below.

b.   Does your information meet the criteria for trade secret protection, to wit:

    1.   it provides an advantage over competitors;

    2.   it is not generally available to the public; and

    3.   the owner has taken reasonable measures to protect it.

    Yes: Proceed to (c) below.

    No: You will not be able to use your special statute. Proceed to #7 below.

c.   Did the thief intend to use (or sell) that information, or allow another to do so?

    Yes: You should be able to use your special statute. Proceed to #6 below.

    No: You will not be able to use your special statute. Proceed to #7 below.

6. Preemption: Does your case qualify for *both* the general theft and special trade secret theft statutes in your jurisdiction?

    Yes: Check the law of your jurisdiction to determine whether you must use the special statute instead of the general theft statute where both apply, or whether you can use either (or even both). Proceed to #7 below.

    No: Use whichever statute you can. Proceed to #7 below.

7. Consider other statutes (see box on next page):

    a.   burglary;

    b.   computer intrusion;

    c.   commercial bribery;

    d.   conspiracy; and

    e.   copyright infringement.

Trade secret statutes are not the only game in town

Remember that defendants who steal information may have violated other laws. Computer intruders who steal information may be prosecuted under laws punishing computer intrusion. Burglars may be prosecuted for burglary. Crooked employees who sell company secrets may be prosecuted for commercial bribery. Groups of defendants who steal secrets together may be prosecuted for conspiracy. These offenses do not require a completed theft and are often *much* easier to prosecute.

You need to consider four issues when examining the law in your jurisdiction:

- what information qualifies as property covered by your statute;

- what constitutes a theft of that information;

- what you must prove concerning the suspect's intent; and

- what measure(s) of value you can use to value the information.

Table 5–1 starting on page 162 summarizes the legal requirements for prosecuting cases under general theft and trade secret theft statutes.

5.42–a(1) General theft statutes

General theft statutes punish the taking, embezzling, or receiving of a physical object. If a defendant takes his neighbor's plow without permission, he has violated a general theft statute. As can be seen by applying the four-point test discussed above, general theft statutes often cannot be used to prosecute certain thefts of information.

5.42–a(1)(a) What information qualifies as property

General theft statutes protect only information which is contained in a tangible form.

General theft statutes protect tangible property. As noted earlier, a tangible item is an object you can touch, such as a document, a dollar bill, or an automobile. Such statutes do not protect intangibles. An intangible is something you cannot touch, such as an idea.

Although information is intangible, courts have decided that theft of a tangible item is also theft of the information contained within that item.[5] A theft of a manual containing the secret formula for Coca-Cola violates general theft laws because the idea is in a tangible form (i.e., it is written in the manual).

While information in a tangible form is protected by general theft statutes, other information is not. For example, a person does not violate general theft laws by eavesdropping on two executives discussing the formula for Coca-Cola.

5.42–a(1)(b)   *What constitutes a theft of that property*

Some general theft statutes may not punish the copying or memorization of information.

Information is different from other property because it can exist in two places at once. Assume that Coca-Cola's corporate headquarters includes a vault containing two items: a gold ingot and a manual containing the secret formula for making Coca-Cola. Assume also that John Doe breaks into the vault and steals the ingot.

Only John Doe has that ingot. However, if John Doe memorizes the secret formula instead, then both he and Coca-Cola possess that formula. The same is true if John Doe uses a copy machine to copy the manual before he leaves. Although John Doe has not deprived Coca-Cola of its tangible property (i.e., the manual), Coca-Cola has lost control over its formula.

Depending upon your jurisdiction, general theft statutes may not punish the copying or memorization of information from a tangible object.[6] This is so even though the thief has still harmed the victim.

---

5. *See United States v. Bottone*, 365 F.2d 389 (2d Cir. 1966); *United States v. Greenwald*, 479 F.2d 320 (6th Cir. 1973); *United States v. Lester*, 282 F.2d 750 (3d Cir. 1960); *United States v. Seagraves*, 265 F.2d 876 (3d Cir. 1959); *see also People v. Dolbeer*, 214 Cal. App. 2d 619, 623 (Cal. Ct. App. 1963).

6. For example, California courts have failed to resolve the issue. *See Williams v. Superior Court*, 81 Cal. App. 3d 880 (Cal. Ct. App. 1978); *People v. Dolbeer*, 214 Cal. App. 2d 619, 623 (Cal. Ct. App. 1963).

Table 5–1: Legal requirements under general theft statutes and trade secret theft statutes[a]

Legal issue	General theft statutes	Trade secret theft statutes
What information qualifies as property?	Information in a tangible form. The information must have value.	Information which: • provides a commercial advantage over competitors; • is not generally available to the public; and • the owner took reasonable measures to protect. Note: Most statutes require the information to be in a tangible form. Note: Many statutes restrict coverage to scientific or technical information.
What constitutes a theft of that property?	Unauthorized physical movement of the tangible object containing the information, or misuse of information entrusted to the defendant. Some state statutes may punish copying.	Unauthorized physical movement of the tangible object containing the information, as well as copying. Some statutes punish unauthorized use of the information. Some statutes punish memorization.

Legal issue (cont.)	General theft statutes (cont.)	Trade secret theft statutes (cont.)
What intent is required?	*For larceny*: Intent to permanently deprive the owner of the tangible object containing the information. Defendant's return, or intent to return, the tangible object may be a defense. *For embezzlement*: Intent to misuse tangible property entrusted to the defendant.	Intent to deprive or withhold control of the trade secret from the owner; or Intent to misappropriate the trade secret to defendant's use or use of another. Defendant's return, or intent to return, the information is not a defense.
How do you calculate the value of the information?	Fair market value.	Fair market value.

a.   Remember that state laws can vary subtly, and that tables like this one may not correlate exactly with the statute in your particular state.

This odd result occurs because courts traditionally have interpreted the law of theft to require *asportation*—the physical movement of property. Memorizing information does not require asportation of the document containing that information. The same is true of photography and photocopying.

If courts in your state require asportation, look for evidence that the thief moved the property without authorization before, and for the purpose of, copying or memorizing that information. Courts may find that such movement satisfies the asportation requirement. For example, an employee who takes a document home from work, copies it, and brings it back has satisfied the asportation requirement.

5.42–a(1)(c)   *What intent is required*

Be careful to choose the general theft statute which punishes the defendant's intent in your case.

General theft laws cover three types of offenses:

* larceny;

* embezzlement; and

* receipt of stolen property.

Each offense has a different intent requirement.

1. Larceny.

To prove larceny, you must show that the defendant took the tangible object containing information with the intent to *permanently deprive* the owner of that object and the information within it. Problems can arise when the defendant returns, or claims an intent to return, the tangible object (e.g., a manual).

Of course, returning a manual after having the opportunity to memorize or copy the information it contains does not help the victim. However, it is always possible that a court might accept a claimed intent to return property as a defense. Look for evidence that the suspect in your case attempted to use the information, and argue that using information is incompatible with an intent to return it.

Another problem arises when the defendant is charged with copying the information. Assuming that your general theft statute punishes copying, you still have to confront the problem that information can exist in more than one place. John Doe's copying of the Coca-Cola formula does not deprive Coca-Cola of the formula, but only of *control* over the formula.

Has Coca-Cola been permanently deprived of its information? Common sense says yes, because the value of having a secret is that nobody else knows it. However, it is always conceivable that a court may decide otherwise.

2. Embezzlement.

To prove embezzlement, you must show that the defendant was entrusted with tangible property and misused, or misappropriated, that property in such a way as to violate that trust. Prosecutors usually charge embezzlement when an employee quits, fails to return company property, and then uses that property in a manner not authorized by the former employer.

In some cases, simply failing to return the property may be enough to show misappropriation, such as when an employee joins a competitor without returning company property containing proprietary information. An embezzlement charge may also be appropriate when a licensee has used the technology in violation of the license agreement.

In embezzlement cases, you do not have to show that the defendant intended to permanently deprive the owner of property. In addition, there is no asportation requirement; intentionally using the tangible property in a way not authorized by the owner is a crime.

If your general theft statute punishes copying of information, then the unauthorized copying from a tangible object entrusted to the defendant is embezzlement. Remember, however, that an embezzlement charge can be used only when the victim provided the defendant with the tangible object. Prosecutors may not charge a burglar with embezzlement.

3. Receiving stolen property.

To prove that a defendant received stolen property, you must show that the defendant knew that the property was stolen. Laws penalizing receiving stolen property generally prohibit knowingly possessing, concealing, or withholding stolen property.

Although you do not have to prove that the defendant received the property with the intent to permanently deprive the owner of that property, you still must prove that the property was stolen by *someone*, by larceny or embezzlement (meaning that you must satisfy the tests listed above). If a court finds that no theft occurred, then the property was not stolen and the defendant cannot be convicted of receiving stolen property.

5.42–a(1)(d)   Calculating the value of information

You need to consider the value of the misappropriated information at the beginning of your investigation, because most states use the value of the stolen information to determine whether the offense is a felony or a misdemeanor. In addition, certain federal laws do not apply unless the information is worth at least $5,000. (And federal prosecutors may be reluctant to act unless the information exceeds a significantly higher amount set by individual offices.) The value of information is also relevant for sentencing in federal court.

---

*When it is difficult to place a value on
the stolen information*

If valuing the stolen information is a problem, consider charging the suspect with receiving stolen property, conspiracy, or bribery. For example, in California, theft is either a misdemeanor or a felony based on the value of the stolen property. However, the offenses of receiving stolen property, conspiracy, and bribery are always felonies regardless of the value of the property, except that a prosecutor or grand jury may reduce the charge of receiving stolen property to a misdemeanor. (And California victims may recover treble damages from a defendant convicted of receiving stolen property. *See* California Penal Code Section 496.1.)

The value of information contained in a tangible form is the value of the tangible item, *including* the value of the information within that item.[7] The problem is in valuing the information itself.

The classic definition of the value of property is fair market value: what a willing buyer would pay a willing seller in the open market.

---

7. *See United States v. Wilson*, 900 F.2d 1350 (9th Cir. 1990); *United States v. Bottone*, 365 F.2d 389 (2d Cir. 1966); *United States v. Greenwald*, 479 F.2d 320 (6th Cir. 1973); *United States v. Lester*, 282 F.2d 750 (3d Cir. 1960); *United States v. Seagraves*, 265 F.2d 876 (3d Cir. 1959).

Unfortunately, by definition there is no open market for secret information, and you must pursue alternative measures of value.

Federal law allows juries to consider any reasonable measure of value where there is no open market.[8] State courts in your jurisdiction may be more restrictive. Consider using one or more of the following measures of value.

1. Development costs.

It takes time and money to create information worth stealing. Consider valuing information by calculating the amount of resources the owner spent in creating it.

This measure of value is simple because the prosecutor is often able to prove substantial development costs without using expert witnesses. However, this theory also allows defense lawyers to bombard the victim with subpoenas seeking all documents reflecting the amount of time spent on the project, from time cards to personnel files.

Furthermore, the valuation is likely to be too conservative because information is usually worth more than its cost of development. Finally, courts may prevent prosecutors from using this measure of value because development costs do not always reflect the value of a product.[9]

2. What a competitor would have to spend to develop the information.

A variation on the owner's development cost theory is to calculate the time and resources a competitor would have to spend to duplicate the stolen information. Most civil information theft cases use this measure of value to calculate damages to the victim.

---

8. *See United States v. Wilson*, 900 F.2d 1350, 1356 (9th Cir.1990); *U.S. v. Di-Gilio*, 538 F.2d 972 (3d Cir. 1976); *United States v. Lester*, 282 F.2d 750, 754–55 (3d Cir. 1960).

9. Federal law appears to allow this measure of value. *See United States v. Stegora*, 849 F.2d 291 (8th Cir. 1988); *United States v. Drebin*, 557 F.2d 1316 (9th Cir. 1977).

Civil lawyers use the term *lead time*, defined as the time and money a competitor saved by stealing instead of reinventing the stolen information. A more sophisticated version of this measure involves calculating the revenues gained by the competitor resulting from its ability to bring its product to market earlier.

This measure is particularly attractive in customer list cases, where owners have created a list of customers after years in business. Although it is difficult to calculate the cost of developing the list, it is easier to prove that a departing employee forming a competing business would be forced to spend a great deal of time and money to compile that list.

3. Market value.

Although there is no open market for secret information, there is a market for a product which depends upon that secret for its success. If your secret information is incorporated into a product already selling in the marketplace, you can calculate the market value of the secret.

Sales of the owner's product are evidence of market value, although courts may allow a defendant to show that a victim's profits from that product are far lower than its sales. If the owner licenses the information, the price paid for that license is relevant evidence.[10]

Three other measures of market value may be helpful in information theft cases:

* gain to the competitor;

* revenues lost by the owner as a result of thieves incorporating the owner's information into competing products; and

* the *thieves' market* (defined below).

The easiest measure of value is the revenue for any competitor's product which incorporates stolen information. Another similar measure is to show that the competitor's entry into the marketplace cost the owner revenue.

This second measure often yields a more impressive damage figure because the owner will have been forced to reduce the price of the

---

10. *See United States v. Stegora*, 849 F.2d 291 (8th Cir. 1988).

legitimate product to compete with the competitor (the competitor has higher profit margins because it did not have to spend money to develop the secret information).

Finally, if the thief sold or licensed the product to someone else, the sales price to that third party (or *thieves' market* price) may be used as a measure of the value of the product.[11]

Once you have determined the market value of the product, you should determine what portion of the value of the product is attributable to the secret. In some cases, the secret is the *key to the vault*. Without it, the product could not exist. This is the case with Coca-Cola and Mrs. Fields cookies.

In other cases, the secret can be valued as a percentage of the market value of the product. If a sophisticated new transmission contributes 5% of the value of a best-selling automobile, a jury might agree that the secret is worth 5% of the profit made by the automobile manufacturer on that car.

5.42–a(2)   Special trade secret theft statutes

As discussed above, general theft statutes are often inadequate to punish certain types of information theft. Although many states enacted trade secret theft statutes to plug gaps left by those general theft laws, those statutes created new problems. You may wish to refer again to Table 5–1 on page 162 to compare general theft and trade secret theft statutes.

5.42–a(2)(a)   What information qualifies as property

A major difference between general theft laws and trade secret theft statutes is the information protected under those statutes.

1. Most states require that the information exist in a tangible form.

---

11. *See United States v. Oberhardt*, 887 F.2d 790 (7th Cir. 1989); *United States v. Bakken*, 734 F.2d 1273 (7th Cir. 1984); *United States v. Drebin*, 557 F.2d 1316 (9th Cir. 1977).

Most special trade secret statutes cover all information contained within a tangible form. However, a few states appear to cover information in any form.[12]

2. Many states limit protection to scientific or technical information.

Many trade secret theft statutes were enacted out of concern that high technology was particularly vulnerable to theft. Thus, many states, including New York, protect only scientific or technical information.[13] *In those states, if your information is not scientific or technical, you must use a general theft statute.* Thus, general business information, such as customer lists, contract bids, and marketing information, is not protected under many trade secret theft statutes.

3. The information must be a trade secret.

Trade secret theft statutes protect only information which meets the definition of a trade secret. Although in civil cases the Uniform Trade Secrets Act (the civil trade secret law in most states) provides a definition of a trade secret, that definition should not preempt, or replace, criminal trade secret theft laws.[14]

---

12. In California, for example, the original trade secret theft statute (Penal Code Section 499c) punished only theft of "articles" containing information. In 1983, the Legislature amended § 499c to penalize the theft or use of a trade secret, without mentioning the word "article." This change appears to allow California prosecutors to prosecute an employee or licensee who has memorized a trade secret wrongfully (or, more commonly, who uses it at a later date without permission) with violating § 499c.

13. *See* New York Penal Code Sections 155.00(6), 165.07; *see, generally, Milgrim on Trade Secrets*, Volume 3, Appendix B-5 (New York: Matthew Bender, 1995) (Vol. 12B of "Business Organizations" by the same publisher). After the first printing of this book, California amended the definition of a trade secret to conform with the definition set forth in the Uniform Trade Secrets Act. As of January 1997, the definition of a trade secret under California criminal law will specifically include nonscientific information. It is still unclear whether such information was protected under California law before 1997.

14. *See, e.g., People v. Gopal,* 171 Cal. App. 3d 524, 536, 537, n.14 (Cal. Ct. App. 1985).

Each state's law includes its own definition of a trade secret. However, while the wording of each statute may differ slightly, virtually all laws require prosecutors to prove that:

- the information provided an advantage over competitors;

- the information was not generally available to the public; *and*

- the owner took reasonable measures to protect that information.

As a practical matter, general theft statutes have similar requirements. Prosecutors may not charge someone with stealing something which has no value, and information which provides no advantage is worthless. Information generally available to the public is also worthless. And information which is left out for anyone to take may not have value.

However, some of the language of these special trade secret statutes as interpreted by the courts may make it impossible to prosecute certain cases which can be prosecuted under general theft statutes. We discuss each of the three elements of a trade secret in turn.

5.42–a(2)(a)(i)   The information must provide an advantage over competitors

Most statutes require that the information provide the owner with an advantage over competitors who do not know of, or use, the secret. The advantage must be a commercial advantage, as opposed to conferring an emotional or psychological benefit.[15]

Note also that the advantage is the advantage to the owner, not to the thief. John Doe may not argue that the stolen information was useless to him—if it provides an advantage to the owner over competitors, that advantage means that the information has value. (Indeed, information which is useless would lack "value," and even general theft laws could not be used to punish the theft of such information.)

It is unclear how much of an advantage is required to make information a trade secret. The plain language of most statutes simply requires "an advantage over competitors." This would appear to allow

---

15. *See, e.g., Religious Technology Center v. Wollersheim,* 796 F.2d 1076 (9th Cir. 1986); *see also People v. Serrata,* 62 Cal. App. 3d 9 (Cal. Ct. App. 1976).

prosecution where the advantage means that the information has "value," however slight. This interpretation is consistent with theft law generally.

However, a recent case from an intermediate California appellate court suggests that more may be required for special trade secret statutes. The court in *People v. Pribich*[16] suggested that prosecutors proving "competitive advantage" may have to show that "substantial competitive injury would likely result from disclosure."

Pribich presents several problems for prosecutors. First, there are definitional issues. What is a "substantial competitive injury"? Is it different for a big company than for a small one?

Second, *Pribich* may require the victim to show that it "actually faces competition." This might exclude cases where a departing employee steals information which will not be used until after that employee establishes a business.[17] It would also exclude cases where the owner did not use the secret, but earned a handsome profit by licensing that secret to others.

Finally, juries might be called upon to decide whether "substantial competitive injury would likely result from disclosure" in a case where disclosure has already occurred—to the thief. Defense attorneys might argue that juries must acquit if the People are unable to prove beyond a reasonable doubt that the theft caused substantial competitive injury to the owner. In many information theft cases, it is difficult to show damage to the owner until months, or years, after the theft.

Prosecutors should attempt to persuade other courts not to follow this poorly reasoned decision (see box on next page).

5.42–a(2)(a)(ii) The information must not have been generally available to the public

Obviously, information that is available to all is worthless and is not entitled to protection. The problem with the many statutes which

---

16. 21 Cal. App. 4th 1844 (Cal. Ct. App. 1994).

17. *But see Sinclair v. Aquarius Electric*, 42 Cal. App. 3d 216, 222 (Cal. Ct. App. 1974) (a landmark case in civil trade secret law).

Attacking the Pribich decision

Aside from distinguishing California law from your state's law, your threshold attack on *Pribich* should be that the court's language on competitive advantage is *dicta*. In addition, the court erred by analogizing California Penal Code § 499c to provisions of the Freedom of Information Act protecting information provided to federal agencies. FOIA requires companies seeking to protect information from disclosure to demonstrate that "substantial competitive injury would likely result from disclosure." *See Sharyland Water Supply Corp. v. Block*, 755 F.2d 397, 399 (5th Cir. 1985) (cited by the Court of Appeal). The California Court of Appeal found that test "somewhat analogous" to the "competitive advantage" requirement, and adopted it. *Pribich*, at 117.

But FOIA deals with a different issue. "FOIA is designed to promote the disclosure of information." *Sharyland, supra*, at 398. FOIA is intended to *balance* two countervailing rights: the right of the public to disclosure of government records and the property right of a trade secret owner to protect his or her property. In balancing those rights to promote disclosure of information, Congress elected to require the owner to demonstrate, not just that the information was "property," but that release of that information would likely cause substantial competitive injury.

The issue of whether release of that information serves the public interest simply does not arise in trade secret cases because there is no interest in favor of disclosure to a thief. Thus, FOIA is not "analogous" to "competitive advantage," and the "substantial competitive injury" test should not be imported into trade secret theft statutes.

---

include this requirement is that the language "not generally available to the public" requires prosecutors to prove a negative: that the information was *not* available. Later in this chapter, we suggest questions you should ask to meet this burden of proof.

A different problem arises when the information is available to the public in a less valuable form. Assume that John Doe steals a client list from his former employer. His defense is that the phone book contains each of the names in the client list. The prosecutor's response is that although the names are generally available to the public, the client list, *in its same form*, is not generally available to the public.

This same problem can arise in a more troublesome form with technical information, where the defense can point to published papers which generally define a solution to a problem without providing all of the details. The defense may argue that the defendant could have obtained that secret from public sources.

The only way to rebut this defense is to show that such an effort would have taken a non-trivial amount of time and money. The prosecutor can then argue that this substantial difference between rough data and polished solution means that the solution was "not generally available to the public."

5.42–a(2)(a)(iii) The owner must have taken reasonable measures to protect that information.

Most trade secret theft statutes require that the information be "not generally available to the public" and "secret." These terms are different. "Not generally available to the public" means that the information was not widely known. "Secret" refers to the measures taken by the owner to protect that information.

"Secrecy" is an interesting concept. Under traditional theft law, a thief may be prosecuted for stealing property even when the owner failed to protect that property. An accused burglar cannot evade conviction by claiming that the owner left his or her door unlocked.

However, information is intangible, and it is harder to say who "owns" it. Thus, unlike general theft laws, special trade secret statutes require the owner to put the world on notice that he or she claims exclusive control over certain information. The owner must demonstrate that he or she took reasonable measures to protect that information, such as providing physical security (fences, locks, guards), providing computer security, and labeling information as proprietary.

5.42–a(2)(b)   *What constitutes a theft of that property*

The main advantage of trade secret theft statutes over general theft statutes is that trade secret laws specifically punish the unauthorized copying of information. In addition, some statutes punish the unauthorized use of such information. Finally, as noted earlier in this chapter, some states (e.g., California) appear to punish memorization of a trade secret.[18]

5.42–a(2)(c)   *What intent is required*

Trade secret theft statutes are confusing on the issue of intent. Most offer a choice—prosecutors may prove that the defendant intended to:

- deprive or withhold control of the trade secret from the owner; *or*

- misappropriate the trade secret to the defendant's use or the use of another.

The problem is that it is not clear what either choice means. At first glance, the first choice appears to be very narrow, covering only those cases in which the defendant takes the information to make sure that the owner no longer has sole control over it.

However, *any* theft of information deprives the owner of control. When John Doe photocopies a manual containing the formula for Coca-Cola, he deprives Coca-Cola of control over the formula. Thus, there is a persuasive argument that the prosecution wins if it can prove that the defendant knew that he or she was taking trade secrets belonging to another. For example, a defendant who steals a computer containing a trade secret has the requisite intent if he or she knows that the computer contains that secret.

The problem with this interpretation is that it makes the second choice meaningless. In every case where the defendant misappropriates a trade secret to his or her use or the use of another, the defendant

---

18. In addition, California punishes giving or receiving a bribe to obtain a trade secret. *See, e.g.,* California Penal Code Section 499c(c).

has also intentionally deprived the owner of control of the secret. Courts do not like to eliminate language from a statute.

In other words, it is unclear what intent is required. *For purposes of investigating thefts of information, you should assume that you must show that the defendant intended to use the secret, or to extort the owner by threatening to disclose that secret.* This is particularly true because juries are likely to be sympathetic to someone who can show that he or she did not intend to use the information.

The problem is that the defendant will often claim to be a *pack rat*, someone who collects information out of curiosity. Therefore, you must determine as a part of your investigation whether the defendant used, or had a motive to use, the owner's information.

Finally, a piece of good news. Most trade secret theft statutes state that it is not a defense that the defendant returned, or intended to return, the trade secret.

5.42–a(2)(c)   How to calculate the value of information

The valuation of information is the same for general theft statutes and special trade secret theft statutes.[19]

5.42–b   Federal laws punishing information theft

Federal law does not include either a general theft statute or a trade secret theft statute. Except for a few special cases (e.g., theft of classified or defense information, or release of trade secrets data submitted by businesses to the government in compliance with federal law) federal prosecutors must rely on laws punishing mail fraud (18 U.S.C. 1341),[20] wire fraud (18 U.S.C. 1343),[21] interstate transportation of stolen goods (18 U.S.C. 2314),[22] and interstate receipt

---

19. *See* § 5.42–a(1)(d).

20. *See Carpenter v. United States*, 484 U.S. 19 (1987).

21. *See Carpenter v. United States*, 484 U.S. 19 (1987) (the case construed both mail and wire fraud statutes).

22. *See United States v. Bottone*, 365 F.2d 389 (2d Cir. 1966); *United States v. Greenwald*, 479 F.2d 320 (6th Cir. 1973); *United States v. Lester*, 282 F.2d 750 (3d Cir. 1960); *United States v. Seagraves*, 265 F.2d 876 (3d Cir. 1959).

Preemption

Where two statutes punish the same conduct, the doctrine of *pre-emption* may require prosecutors to use the statute which is more narrowly targeted at that conduct. This means that you may have to use a special trade secret theft statute in your jurisdiction even if it would be easier to prove a violation of a general theft statute.

For example, if a thief steals a technical manual containing scientific and technical information, and your state trade secret statute covers such information, you may have to use that statute instead of a general theft statute to prosecute the case.

Preemption can cause problems when the owner's failure to protect the information disqualifies it as a trade secret, even though that information is nonetheless valuable and would qualify for protection under the general theft law. However, you can still use other non-theft statutes (such as burglary, computer intrusion, bribery, and conspiracy) to prosecute the defendant.

---

of stolen goods (18 U.S.C. 2315) to punish activities connected with theft of information. Federal laws punishing copyright violations (18 U.S.C. 2319) and computer intrusions (18 U.S.C. 1030) may also apply.

In most cases, only the interstate transportation and receiving of stolen goods statutes will apply. Thus, federal agencies generally become involved only when information has crossed state or national borders.

As with general theft laws, federal statutes protect information contained in a tangible form (i.e., documents). However, federal law also covers copying and transmission of information. For example, both the wire fraud and interstate transportation of stolen goods statutes prohibit the transfer or transmission of property. Both the interstate transportation and interstate receipt of stolen goods statutes refer to stolen property as property which has been "stolen, *unlawfully converted*, or taken."

*A few federal courts may not consider software
to be property*

Software is a collection of 0s and 1s kept in a tangible form, either as magnetically charged particles on a floppy disk or as electrical impulses within a computer or in transmission. Thus, software should qualify for protection as tangible property, and the theft of a floppy disk containing software should be punishable as a theft.

However, the Tenth Circuit Court of Appeals decided in *United States v. Brown*, 925 F.2d 1301 (10th Cir. 1991), that the mere copying of software does not constitute the theft of property under 18 U.S.C. 2314 (interstate transportation of stolen property). Thus, in the Tenth Circuit, although an employee who steals a computer containing proprietary data and takes it to another state may be prosecuted for interstate transportation of stolen property, that same employee could not be prosecuted for simply copying that software onto his own floppy disk and taking that disk to another state. *Cf. United States v. Lyons*, 992 F.2d 1029 (10th Cir. 1993).

Brown was incorrectly decided and will probably not be followed by federal courts outside the Tenth Circuit (Colorado, Kansas, New Mexico, Oklahoma, Texas, and Wyoming). In addition, such copying may violate the Copyright Act. Finally, as of this writing, the Department of Justice is preparing to ask Congress to amend 18 U.S.C. 2314 to overturn *Brown*.

This broader language indicates that prosecutors may prosecute copying or transmission (e.g., by fax or E-mail) of information under federal law.[23]

---

23. *See Carpenter v. United States*, 484 U.S. 19 (1987); *United States v. Morrison*, 844 F.2d 1057, 1068–69 (4th Cir. 1988) (no First Amendment protection for transmission of stolen Defense Department information by fax machine); *United States v. Seidlitz*, 589 F.2d 152, 160 (4th Cir. 1978).

The valuation problem is less serious under federal law because, as discussed above, federal law allows prosecutors to choose from a wide range of measures of value.[24] The only concern is that the interstate transportation and receipt of stolen property statutes require proof that the property was worth more than $5,000.

5.43 Screening cases for investigations aimed at filing a civil lawsuit rather than a criminal prosecution

As we have seen, most information theft cases reported to law enforcement will not, or at least should not, be accepted for investigation. The victim's only choice in most cases is to file a civil lawsuit or drop the matter entirely.

A civil suit typically begins with a complaint and a request for a temporary injunction (also called a preliminary injunction). Such an injunction will prohibit the defendant from using the allegedly stolen information until the lawsuit is resolved, or from taking actions which might increase the risk of disclosure of the victim's secrets. For example, a court may enjoin Company A from hiring Company B employees upon finding that Company B employees have been taking trade secrets to their new jobs.

Victims who win their civil lawsuits can convert those injunctions into *permanent injunctions*, which permanently *enjoin* (i.e., prohibit) the thief from using or selling the victim's information. In practice, a victim who wins a temporary injunction wins the case because a lengthy delay usually makes the stolen information useless to the thief.

Ultimately, a victim who wins a civil suit can obtain both an injunction and damages against the defendant. A prevailing defendant does not collect damages, but may sue the victim for malicious prosecution if the case was frivolous.

There are many different variables to be considered in deciding whether to file a lawsuit, and most of them are outside the scope of this book. Obviously, victory in a lawsuit will damage a crooked competitor, and prevent that competitor from using the victim's technology.

---

24. *See* § 5.42–a(1)(d), beginning on page 166.

However, such lawsuits are extremely expensive and can damage the victim's image in the community. Publicity may affect the victim's stock price and make it difficult for a start-up company to raise capital. Another danger is that the victim's secret information may be disclosed to competitors during the litigation. Lawsuits can end with both sides exhausted and vulnerable to other competitors who have spent their time inventing instead of litigating.

Victims should be careful to incorporate checks and balances into their decisionmaking process. Managers of groups "ripped off" by the thief, as well as employees responsible for competing against the suspect company, will be eager to file a lawsuit. Victims should consider all of the costs, and risks, of litigation before proceeding, and a decision to litigate should be made at the highest levels of the company.

Another way of adding perspective to the decision is to hire outside counsel for the sole purpose of determining whether litigation is the best option. The problem is finding a law firm that will give that advice without attempting to serve its own interests by advocating litigation (or advising against litigation if the firm believes that a rival firm will be retained to handle the lawsuit).

Nonetheless, there is no harm in investigating the case to determine whether a lawsuit is appropriate. A thief with control of the victim's secret information can cause extensive damage. Even simply identifying the thief and the way in which the theft occurred may assist the victim in competing against that thief and in tightening security.

While some cases may never make it to civil court, most of the reasons for rejecting cases for criminal investigation do not apply where the object is to file a lawsuit and obtain an injunction. For example:

1. *The information which has been stolen is not scientific or technical.*

Most civil information theft cases involve non-scientific and non-technical information. Without exploring civil trade secret law in depth, suffice it to say that business information can qualify as a trade secret. Since the burden of proof is a mere *preponderance of the evidence* (meaning that the jury decides which side's version of the facts is more likely to be correct), it is much easier to prove in the civil arena that business information was secret and valuable.

2. *The victim has lost information which is something less than its crown jewels.*

Victims may choose to sue thieves for small stakes based on a cost-benefit analysis of the risks and rewards of civil litigation.

3. *The stolen information is not likely to be discovered in the thief's possession.*

Again, the difference between the preponderance of the evidence and beyond a reasonable doubt standards is critical here. Companies frequently allege that competitors' products were created using stolen information. If the jury believes that this is more likely the case than not, the victim wins even if the jury has a reasonable doubt on that issue. Of course, finding tangible evidence of theft is extremely valuable, but it is not essential.

4. *The theft occurred more than six months before the report to law enforcement.*

This rule still has force in a modified form: victims must act on their suspicions quickly, and file suit promptly after those suspicions are confirmed. A failure to act promptly may allow defendants to claim that they developed the information independently. Equally important, the party seeking an injunction must show that it will suffer *irreparable harm* (irreversible harm) if it does not receive that injunction. That claim is hard to make if the victim delayed its investigation.

5. *The industry does not condemn the thief's conduct.*

This rule also has force because of the victim's reputation in the industry. A victim who sues a competitor or an employee over an insignificant violation risks tarnishing its reputation.

6. *Raiding and licensing cases.*

These cases are suitable for civil action because victims can obtain an injunction against a group of employees using stolen information without identifying the persons criminally responsible for the theft of that information.

5.50   Investigation

Whether you are aiming toward criminal prosecution or civil litigation, your initial investigation as a law enforcement or corporate investigator has three goals:

- determine whether the stolen information was in fact secret and valuable;

- identify suspects; and

- for law enforcement investigators, prepare for, and execute, a search warrant to obtain evidence of the theft from the thief's home or office.

The "initial" investigation suggested in this chapter is quite detailed and lengthy. Many times you will not have time to perform that investigation before you must seek a search warrant to obtain critical evidence. A thief may be preparing to leave the country. An informant may report that a competitor is about to destroy the stolen documents. You may not have the luxury of scouring the victim's offices for information before serving a search warrant.

However, never lose sight of the fact that information theft cases are some of the most hotly contested and difficult cases in the universe of civil and criminal litigation. The future of your suspect's enterprise and career are usually at stake, not to mention his or her liberty. Many cases involve two corporations, each well financed, throwing the kitchen sink at each other. Once a search warrant is served, the war begins.

At one point or another, law enforcement and corporate investigators will need to complete the investigation detailed below. The circumstances of your case will dictate whether you do it now or later. *In any event, law enforcement investigators must complete this investigation before making an arrest or seeking a criminal complaint.*

5.51   Determining whether the stolen information was a trade secret

Information theft cases are difficult to investigate because the subject matter is foreign, the witnesses are atypical, and you must learn

---

Filing a civil suit usually discourages police from obtaining a search warrant

Information theft prosecutions usually turn on the type and quality of the evidence police find when executing a search warrant. Unfortunately, it is easy for thieves to destroy important evidence within hours after learning of an investigation.

Filing a civil suit eliminates the element of surprise essential to a successful criminal investigation of information theft. Police usually will not pursue such investigations after the victim has filed a civil suit, absent unusual circumstances suggesting that evidence of the crime has not been destroyed.

If the victim decides that it must file a suit immediately in order to stop a competitor from using its secrets, corporate investigators and lawyers should always call their law enforcement counterparts first. Local law enforcement agencies have occasionally prepared and served information theft search warrants within days (in one notable case, the very next day). It never hurts to give your local police or prosecuting agency a chance to help you. After all, everyone will know about the investigation once the victim files a lawsuit.

Of course, filing a civil suit is only the most obvious way to disclose an investigation. As discussed in Chapter 2, law enforcement and corporate investigators must be extremely discreet in conducting investigations until police are ready to seek a warrant. Unfortunately, this means that investigators may have to seek a warrant without first performing a thorough investigation.

---

information, which, if disclosed during the prosecution, could ruin the victim.

Most investigators, including this author, are not technically trained. However, this lack of training has its advantages. If all goes well, a prosecutor will eventually have to explain the importance of the secret information to a jury. And juries are not technically trained either.

You have not completed your investigation until you can understand the secret and explain it to a juror (or prosecutor) who knows nothing about your case. Your lack of training will force you to simplify the case to the point where a layman can understand it.

Interviewing engineers

Many engineers have their own way of describing and interpreting information. They are trained to be precise, and not to guess when they do not know the answer. Lawyers are just the opposite—they make their living exploring different shades of gray. Investigators are also trained to live with ambiguity. The intersection of these disciplines can lead to difficulties. Misunderstanding what an engineer is telling you can pin a witness, and the prosecution, to an incorrect set of facts.

Always determine an engineer's "degree of certainty" in what he or she is telling you. Engineers may say they do not know an answer, but can "speculate" about it. To lawyers and police officers, "speculate" means guess. To an engineer, "speculate" may mean that there is "only" a 98% probability that the information or opinion is correct.

Similarly, when engineers say they do not know the answer, make sure that they understand that they have some leeway to give what they consider to be the best answer, even if it may be wrong. Then ask them about their degree of certainty in the answer.

5.51–a Background information

Your first task is to learn something about the stolen information. These questions are more than a formality—law enforcement and corporate investigators will use the answers to determine whether the case is suitable for criminal prosecution. Law enforcement investigators will use the answers when preparing a search warrant affidavit.

1. What is the information?

Allow your victim to describe the information in general terms so as not to reveal the secret. Your goal is to understand the subject matter of the secret (e.g., the secret is the part of the source code which allows the user to perform sophisticated financial analysis of stock options).

Remember that cases involving non-scientific and non-technical information may not be suitable for criminal prosecution.

2. How is the information used?

Once you know how the information is used (e.g., in a product or service), you will be able to begin evaluating the value of that information and determine whether the sale of a product disclosed the information incorporated within that product.

For example, if the information was used to make a chip, you could begin calculating the value of that information by referring to the victim's sales figures for that chip during the previous year. You could also have an expert check marketing brochures and technical conference papers discussing that chip to ensure that the victim has not already revealed the secret.

3. What tangible items contain the information?

As discussed below, identifying every item containing the information will enable you to:

- know what to look for when executing your search warrant;

- identify suspects who had access to any of those tangible items; and

- determine whether the victim protected each of those items from disclosure.

Reject cases for criminal prosecution when there is no reason to believe that suspects stole tangible items.

4. Why is the information valuable?

Do competitors make similar products which they could improve by using the victim's information? If the victim has a monopoly on this product or service, does the victim have any reason to believe that others want to enter the market? Has the victim heard that anyone else has tried to duplicate the information?

High-technology industries are very loose with product plans. If a competitor is planning to introduce a new product, it is likely that word of that introduction has reached your victim.

Be careful at this stage of your investigation when placing a dollar value on the information. Victims tend to exaggerate the extent of their loss at the outset. If they choose, and you record, an unreasonably high value, the rest of their testimony may be open to attack. If they choose too low a value, you will be stuck with that low value for the rest of your case.

Be careful that you do not obtain an estimate of value from someone who is unqualified to give it. Valuing information is different from creating it, and the inventor may not be qualified to value the information. Although an independent expert is your best bet (more on them later in this chapter), consider asking the victim to consult with several sources from different parts of the company (e.g., marketing and research and development) before estimating value.

Finally, note that some victims will consider the value of their secret information to be a secret. Assume that a company has a monopoly in the market for a certain component. It does not publish its sales figures for fear that a competitor may realize that there is room in the market for two companies. That victim will not want you to reveal its sales figures. You should ask for only the roughest approximation of value and label it as such in any report that you prepare.

5. The history of the information.

When was the information developed? Where was it developed, and by whom? Was there a single inventor or, as is usually the case, a team of developers? Are all the inventors still with the company? Have any of those people left the company recently? Have any of them joined a competitor?

The answers to these questions will help you evaluate the victim's claim that competitors could not have discovered the information unless they stole it. If the inventor of the information has joined a competitor, you may have trouble proving that the inventor did anything more than use the information in his or her head. While you might be able to claim that such use was illegal, you will have trouble winning a civil or criminal trial unless you show that the inventor unlawfully took tangible items when leaving the victim.

The situation can be even more difficult if the theft occurs months or years after some or all of the original developers left the victim. You need to know whether the defense will be able to claim that one of those developers publicized the information (thus ending its secrecy) well before your thief stole from the victim.

Finally, you need to learn which of the victim's employees know the most about the stolen information. You will need these people to educate you about the information, and to testify at trial.

5.51–b   Determining whether the information meets the legal requirements for trade secret protection

You must be able to prove at trial that the information qualified as a trade secret. Whether you use a general theft statute, a criminal trade secret statute, or the Uniform Trade Secrets Act, you will need to prove that:

- the information provided the victim with an advantage over competitors who did not know the information;

- the information was not generally available to the public; and

- the owner took reasonable measures to protect that information.

You will devote most of your investigation to establishing those three elements.

5.51–b(1)   Advantage over competitors

There are different types of competitive advantage. The most common is technological progress. A superior industrial process will create a better product, for example. But better in what way? Does the process allow the victim's product to out-perform a competing product? Does the process allow the victim to produce a product which performs just as well as a competitor's product, at half the cost? You must understand why the information is valuable.

Note that a unique technology is not the same as an advanced technology. Some companies may still use hand-driven looms for weaving. While that technology is probably unique, it is also antiquated. Make sure that the victim's technology is actually better than that available in the industry. Experts familiar with the victim's industry should be able to provide a second opinion concerning claims of technological superiority.[25]

Beware of cases where the only advantage is *competitive intelligence*—where the information reveals the marketing or technical plans of the victim. It can be difficult to prove that such information was not known throughout the industry.

You also need to quantify the victim's advantage. In most cases, the secret information could be discovered by a competitor with time and effort. You should estimate how much time and effort would be required. When doing so, remember to include the profits which would be "lost" because the competitor did not have the stolen information and could not enter the marketplace early.

However, as with quantifying the value of information, you must be careful not to obtain inaccurate estimates from unqualified people. The process of discovering secret information by examining public information (e.g., by taking products apart to see how they work) is called *reverse engineering*. For example, automobile manufacturers practice reverse engineering when they take apart their competitors' vehicles.

Reverse engineering is a separate discipline within the engineering field, and many engineers are not qualified to render an opinion in this area. If you want an estimate concerning lead time (the amount of time and effort it takes to duplicate information) you should consult an expert in reverse engineering.

---

25. Be alert to the possibility that the victim's own employees are disappointed with the technology (e.g., "We may be the only company that uses this process, but Company X's own process is better"). Such communications, either in documents or on company E-mail, can be devastating.

However, you can obtain a "first cut" at that estimate by asking the victim for its costs to develop that information. Although the cost of developing information is different from the cost of duplicating it, the results are similar enough for you to determine whether the case should be investigated further.

5.51–b(1)(a)   Independent experts: should you hire one?

Some state and federal law enforcement agencies require victims to hire an independent expert to render an opinion concerning whether the stolen information qualifies as a trade secret. This approach is recommended for law enforcement agencies generally, although in an ideal world of unlimited budgets the agency would absorb those costs.

The independent expert is valuable for several reasons. The expert is not biased in favor of the victim. The expert is likely to be aware of all of the information available to other experts in the field. Finally, the expert makes a good witness because the defense will find it hard to claim that the expert is biased. (Of course, the defense has a much easier time if the victim pays for the expert.)

However, deciding whether to use an independent expert is not easy. Timing is your first problem. Information theft cases move extremely quickly. You will usually not have time to find, hire, and wait for results from an expert before executing a search warrant.

Finding a competent and truly independent expert can be difficult. Many experts, especially in academia, consult for a wide range of companies. They may have ties to your victim, or worse, your suspect. If you consult an expert before serving a search warrant, you may warn your suspect. Moreover, victims may have legitimate concerns about showing their secret information to a truly independent expert.

Finally, your independent expert may not know the field as well as your victim. Some "experts" are incompetent. Your expert may not realize that the "secret information" has been made public. Conversely, your expert may mistakenly conclude that your victim's information is public or worthless. The prosecution in a criminal case must report all exculpatory information to the defense—even an incorrect opinion by an independent expert that the information was not secret or valuable will end your case before it begins.

When seeking an expert, consider asking your victim for a list of candidates. Instruct (merely asking may not work) your victim not to contact those candidates. Call the candidates and ask for a list of other experts. Consult with the experts suggested by the majority of your original candidates. Do not take the selection process lightly. A bad independent expert can ruin a good case.

5.51–b(2)   Generally available to the public

Most information theft cases are fought over whether the information was already public. After all, most thieves do not steal worthless information, and any victim angry enough about the theft probably took reasonable measures to protect the information in the first place. Therefore, the defendant must turn to the "everyone knew it already" defense.

That defense is often successful. Indeed, occasionally it is even true. In one recent high-profile case, it was revealed that one part of the victim telephone company was selling another division's "secret" manual to the public for $11.95. In another case, one of the engineers in an overseas division responsible for developing a "secret manual" had written an article explaining large portions of that manual. Although a significant amount of the secret information remained private, the damage to the case was immense.

Only a small amount of information in our society is truly secret. This is particularly true in the high-technology field, where engineers move from company to company and the pace of technological development is rapid.

Having to prove that information was not generally available to the public can be very difficult, particularly because you are in the position of proving a negative. How do you know that some engineer still employed by the company did not publish an article in the Atlantis Journal of Technology? How do you know that other companies outside the United States have not developed and published the same information?

The best you can do is confirm that your victim has not done anything to release the secret information to the public. In addition, questions you will ask about the owner's security measures will also support your showing that the owner's information could not have been generally available to the public.

Consider asking the following questions to investigate whether the owner's information has been disclosed.

1. How do you know that nobody else knows what you know?

Although the answer to this question may focus on the victim's efforts to protect its secrets, you should also focus on the victim's knowledge of the industry as a whole. How does the victim know that other competitors are behind it? Why isn't the information obvious to all qualified professionals in the field? Did the company have to spend an enormous amount of time and effort to develop that information? Has anyone else attempted to create such information, and failed?

2. Where are the inventors of the information?

As discussed above, you need to know whether your information could have been spread to other companies by an inventor. You should also check to see whether the technology has been licensed to other companies. If it has been licensed, make sure that the license agreement prevents disclosure.

Reject cases where the technology has been widely distributed, even with non-disclosure agreements. The problem is that there is too great a chance that someone has disclosed the secret.

As a matter of law, the theft of a secret does not disclose that information to the public. However, widespread dissemination of information before the theft, even when accomplished by improper means, may make it difficult for you to convince a jury to convict your defendant. Juries may conclude that the victim suffered no additional harm from the defendant's theft or unauthorized use.

3. What has been published in this area of technology?

Scientists and engineers have egos like the rest of us. Many of them publish their discoveries in conference papers and magazines as a way of enhancing their careers. Companies often encourage such publication as a way of boosting their corporate image, or, more frequently, promoting a product incorporating the secret information.

Make sure that a thorough literature search is performed for your topic. You may have to hire someone to do this—a recent case disintegrated partly because an attorney for the victim told the prosecutor that the company had performed a literature search when it had not done so. (This was the same case in which the overseas engineer had published the article disclosing part of the secret.) Do not accept the victim's claim that nothing has been published about a subject.

You should also examine any materials distributed as part of the victim's marketing effort. Companies often try to sell their products by pointing to technical features "found nowhere else." Occasionally the descriptions are detailed enough to reveal secret information.

5.51–b(3)   Reasonable measures to protect the secret

How much secrecy is enough? The courts have provided a vague answer: it must be reasonable under the circumstances. In other words, more security is expected from a big and wealthy company than from a small start-up. The more valuable the secret, the more security is expected.

This issue is most difficult to handle when your victim is a large company. The more employees need to share information, the harder it is to protect that information. Three people running a start-up company can show that they protected their documents (e.g., by storing them in one fireproof safe). Three thousand people working in a large company will not be able to make that showing. They will have to show that they created procedures for protecting information, and followed those procedures most of the time.

You must perform a "security audit" of your victim in every case. This audit should cover:

- physical security (e.g., gates, guards, sealed rooms);

- computer security; and

- personnel policies regarding secret information, including procedures for distributing and maintaining documents.

Keep in mind that most companies will fail the security audit suggested here. However, courts and juries are generally willing to accept security measures which put the world, and employees, on notice that the victim intends to protect its information. Obviously, there is a security breach whenever a theft occurs; a defendant must show that security was so poor that the victim essentially gave the information away to competitors.

5.51–b(3)(a)   Physical security

Courts and juries are impressed by physical security. You should ask the following questions:

- Are company buildings fenced?

- Are "no trespassing" signs posted?

- Are company buildings locked during non-working hours?

- Are entrances and exits controlled by guards?

  •• Must employees sign in and out of the building?

  •• Must employees wear badges at all times?

  •• May guards search belongings? Do they regularly search belongings? (Many guards are told to search only when they suspect theft.)

  •• Must visitors sign in and out of the building?

  •• Must visitors be escorted at all times?

  •• Are visitors steered away from sensitive areas?

- Are areas containing sensitive information segregated from the rest of the company (e.g., in separate rooms for secret documents and laboratories)?

- Must employees have separate identity devices (e.g., card keys) to enter sensitive areas?

5.51–b(3)(b)   Computer security

In cases where the stolen information was stored on a computer, you should audit the victim's computer security. Although courts have yet to rule that a company forfeited trade secret protection because of sloppy computer security, you should ask the following questions:

- Does each user have a separate log-on?

- What password system is used?

    •• Are the passwords assigned by the company or by the user?

    •• Is the password file within the computer protected from outside access?

    •• Are the passwords changed regularly?

    •• Does the company prohibit employees from sharing passwords?

  5.51–b(3)(c) Personnel policies regarding proprietary information

The most important part of security is the identification of sensitive information and communication to employees that the information must be protected. You should ask the following questions:

1. Identification of secret information.

- Are documents containing secret information marked "proprietary" or "confidential"? ("Proprietary" is used below to refer to both designations.)

- Are color-coded covers used to make those distinctions clear to everyone?

- Are such documents marked "proprietary" on every page?

- Is there a policy governing which employees receive documents marked "proprietary"?

Note that identification always presents a Catch-22 situation which you may need to explain to a jury. If the victim marks every single mildly sensitive document "proprietary," the defense will claim at trial that the victim used the term so indiscriminately that nobody, including the thief, could be expected to have taken it seriously.

However, if the company misses marking a document containing secret information, the defense will claim that this omission "proves" that the information contained within the document was: (1) never a secret; and/or (2) once a secret, but disclosed to the public by virtue of being included within a document which was not marked "proprietary."

2. *Policies protecting that information.*

- What are the company's procedures governing disclosure of proprietary information?

- Has every employee, supplier, and customer furnished with this information signed a non-disclosure agreement?

- Is any particular employee responsible for reviewing releases of information to the public (e.g., data sheets, brochures) to ensure that those materials do not disclose trade secrets?

- Are employees allowed to take proprietary documents home?

It is a common practice in many high-technology companies to allow employees to take documents home. Most engineers work long hours and need proprietary documents at home. Engineers are often allowed to dial into the company computer from home.

Although this practice may seem outrageous at first glance, it makes sense in large companies because of the *sealed vault problem.* Once a company employs more than a handful of engineers, it is impossible to keep proprietary documents in one place. No more than a handful of engineers can work in a *sealed vault*, or a single room with controlled access. Companies must distribute documents to employees to allow them to work.

It is a simple, if tedious, matter for a determined employee to smuggle out such documents a page at a time. They may take them home in their pockets (nobody strip searches employees), fax them to a confederate, photograph them, or even mail them out of the company. If employees can obtain those documents anyway, it is not a huge leap to allow them to take them home.

The key to security is not so much physical protection of assets— it is convincing employees that their future depends upon protecting those assets.

3. *Communication of security policies to employees.*

Are employees told:

- That they have a duty not to disclose company information to competitors or the public?

- That documents marked "confidential" or "proprietary" may not be disclosed to the public without approval of senior management or security personnel?

- That they must not take secrets home without permission?

- That they must return company property (including tangible items containing secrets) upon leaving the company?

In addition, you should ask how they are told this information:

- Are employees told about their obligations during orientation interviews?

- Do employees sign employment agreements?

- Do they sign non-disclosure agreements? (Virtually every high-technology company requires new employees to sign a non-disclosure agreement. Check to make sure that the employee signed such an agreement covering the stolen information.)

- When employees leave the company, are they asked to attend exit interviews during which company officials review the employees' obligations with respect to company trade secrets?

- Are employees frequently provided with memoranda or other materials discussing security?

- Does the company use training videos discussing security?

- Are there signs posted urging secrecy? (Such signs make impressive courtroom exhibits.)

Perhaps the most powerful evidence that a company took reasonable measures is the attitude of its employees. If everyone you talk to looks horrified when you ask if employees were free to distribute documents marked "proprietary" to the public, they will do the same in front of a jury. If you get an equivocal response indicating that employees did not take those markings seriously, you need to know that fact before proceeding with your investigation.

You will need to talk to more than one employee to obtain information about the different ways your victim communicated its policies to employees. Possible witnesses include:

- Personnel department employees who conduct entrance and/or orientation interviews for new employees.

- Lawyers who conduct exit interviews.

- Security managers who draft policies on protecting information.

- MIS managers (managers in charge of computer operations), for issues relating to computer security.

- Engineers (particularly managers) in the department responsible for the secret information.

- Managers or employees of departments responsible for marking documents proprietary.

This last source of information deserves further comment. It is one thing to have policies, and quite another to implement those policies. If your secret information was stored within a document, you will need to ask questions about Document Control.

5.51–b(3)(c)(i) Document Control

Most secret information is recorded within documents. Your problem is that any company of decent size will have its secret information recorded within many documents, perhaps hundreds. You need to show that the victim maintained some control over its documents.

As discussed above, companies typically have policies concerning handling of documents containing sensitive information. Many documents are stamped "proprietary" or "confidential." Some documents may be issued individually to employees, and a record kept of that distribution. Others may be handed out with the understanding that they will be returned when the employee leaves the company.

Most large high-technology companies have a department called Document Control. This department is charged with ensuring that each document containing secret information is distributed to employees who need it, that a record is made of which employees received it, and that older versions are returned when revisions are distributed.

In some companies, Document Control is one central department; in others, each technical department or project group handles its own documents.

You should ask the following questions about Document Control, and make sure that you have the supporting documentation for any documents which you know to have been stolen:

- How do documents get to Document Control?

- Who decides whether those documents are marked proprietary?

- What records are kept concerning which documents have been marked proprietary and which have not?

- What records are kept of which documents have been distributed to which individual?

  - •• Does the individual receiving the document have to sign for it?

- What records are kept concerning which documents have been returned (e.g., when an employee has left)?

- Is there any monitoring procedure to ensure that documents are returned after they are superseded by new editions or when an employee leaves?

- Is there a policy on deregistration of documents? (Deregistration means declaring that certain older documents no longer contain sensitive information. Without such a policy, the company may be vulnerable to the argument that it marks all of its documents proprietary whether or not they contain secret information. Most companies do not have a deregistration policy.)

Remember that competition is the enemy of security. Most security measures slow down employees. Companies that protect security with zeal and diligence are likely to find employees leaving for more enjoyable workplaces.

Therefore, do not be disappointed if your victim did not maintain an armed camp. Although the answers to these questions will reveal weak spots, they are also likely to demonstrate that the victim cared enough about its property to put the world on notice that it intended to keep its valuable information secret.

5.52 Identifying suspects

Information theft cases are different from other cases because it is virtually impossible to detect the crime when it is taking place, and difficult afterward. A thief who copies a technical manual will escape detection until he or she uses it, or reveals that manual to others. Even an outright theft of a document may not be detected by many companies which do not keep careful track of their documents.

Therefore, information thefts are usually detected well after the actual act of theft. More important, there is usually some event which not only informs the victim that it has been victimized, but also points the finger of suspicion at an individual or company.

Thus, the appearance of a nearly identical product on the market alerts the victim to the theft, and identifies as a suspect every employee who joined that competitor. An informant will not only inform the victim of the theft, but will usually identify one or more suspects.

Information theft investigations often skip the "whodunit" phase and go straight to the "can we catch the thief with the goods" phase. Nonetheless, you need to gather evidence that the person or company under suspicion was in a position to steal or use the secret information. In some cases, you may need to conduct a full-blown investigation to determine the thief's identity.

5.52–a   Access

1.   Access to sensitive documents.

Determine which employees had access to the stolen information and to tangible items containing that information. Retrieve all records from Document Control relating to those tangible items. Most larger companies segregate information—you may be able to focus on a small group of employees who received certain documents. Of course, any failure by an employee to return sensitive documents upon departing the company is critical.

Note that occasionally employees obtain information which is not relevant to their job. For example, an employee transferred to a new project may obtain documents relating to his or her old project in order to steal information related to that project.

2.   Access to sensitive projects.

If the victim has identified an employee as a suspect, retrieve that employee's personnel file. Before looking at it, make a separate copy. If the victim cannot turn that copy over to police for safekeeping out of fear of violating privacy laws, make sure the copy is segregated from the original in a separate part of the company for safekeeping.

Personnel files will usually contain performance reviews and documents associated with the employee's departure. In a very large company, every project your suspect worked on may be listed within one or more performance reviews.

Exit interviews may also provide information about projects handled by the employee. Many companies require employees to sign documents acknowledging that the employee has been exposed to specific information and agrees not to disclose that information without permission. Determine whether your suspect questioned or refused to sign such a document.

5.52–b   Current employees

Some thefts are ongoing. The fact that something was stolen two months ago does not mean that the thief has left the company. For example, there have been two cases in Silicon Valley since 1988 which involved security guards caught examining material. Both guards had engineering degrees which they never mentioned when getting their low-paying jobs; one of them worked for another high-technology company which was, surprisingly, *not* involved.

Consider baiting such employees with secret information. If the employee is stealing material from desks and computers, consider using security cameras to monitor the suspect's activity.

5.52–c   Suspicious products

Some information theft cases begin without a suspect, but with a suspicious product. The victim notices that a competitor has produced a product which appears to rely on the victim's secret formula or process. Victims should purchase such products through discreet intermediaries and use reverse engineering to determine whether the competitor developed the product independently.

When examining software, look for identical code and identical *bugs* (errors). Although an honest competitor might use similar code, it would not copy mistakes.

5.52–d   Motive

Employees who have left to join competitors are obvious suspects. Personnel managers should check for a pattern of raiding, in which one company hires away a group of employees.

Some employees raise suspicion by refusing to disclose where they are going to work after leaving the company. Note, however, that there are legitimate reasons for departing employees to remain close-mouthed.

Some employees are joining start-ups and do not wish to disclose that the start-up intends to compete with the victim. Some employees want to avoid having their former firm bad-mouth them or call their new firm and harass them about not using any of the new employee's "proprietary information." Be suspicious, but be realistic too.

If you have a group of suspects, look for two types of employees: (1) poor performers, who may move to another company and use your victim's information to make themselves look like talented engineers;

and (2) disgruntled employees who believe that they can make more money on their own.

If you have identified a suspect, check the personnel file for that suspect's performance reviews to determine whether he or she may be angry at the company. Perhaps your suspect made a demand for a promotion, a salary increase, or a new assignment which was refused. If the suspect has left, check to see whether the victim made any efforts to keep the employee, or breathed a sigh of relief.

5.52–e   *Unusual activity before the theft*

If your suspect is a former employee, examine that suspect's activity close to his or her last day working for the victim. Most companies have procedures for ensuring that departing employees return all materials containing secret information. Departing employees are well aware of those procedures, and may salt away company documents and software during the days and weeks before their departure. Thus, in addition to checking to see if the exit procedures were followed, check for unusual activity before the employee's last day. For example, check computer logs for unusual activity by your suspect in the month before his or her departure.

Building logs will tell you if your suspect entered the company at odd hours. The hardworking employee who is working late may be stockpiling sensitive information unobserved. Ask security personnel if the employee's office looked suspiciously "cleaned out" before his or her last day on the job. Finally, if you have one or more suspects, check phone records to determine whether they called competitors or other suspects.

You should usually avoid talking about the suspect with other employees until after you have served a search warrant—some of those employees may be the suspect's friends. However, once it is safe to interview employees, ask them if they noticed anything unusual about the suspect's activities in the weeks before the suspect left the company. For example, employees from other divisions who begin asking technical questions of employees for no reason may be intent on theft.

5.52–f   *Suspicious activity after the theft*

Do not forget to ask about a suspect's contacts with the victim after departure. Former employees may realize after leaving that they did not steal all of the information they needed. They may call their employee friends with technical questions. They may sneak back into the building, with or without the help of current employees.

Evidence that the defendant sought information after leaving the company tends to negate a common defense in information cases— that the defendant simply cleaned out his or her office and inadvertently took secret information.

5.53 Search warrants

5.53–a   When to obtain a warrant

Law enforcement investigators should usually delay obtaining a search warrant for as long as possible to allow them time to investigate the case thoroughly. It is better to discover that the victim's secret information was excerpted in *IEEE Micro* or another publication *before* you send 30 police officers into XYZ Company to look for evidence.

Remember, too, that the public and the business community considers a search warrant to be the equivalent of a criminal complaint. You can easily put a company out of business by serving one, even if you never file charges. That kind of power demands prudence.

Generally, you should not serve a search warrant until you believe that you will find evidence sufficient to win a conviction at trial. The warrant should be used to seal your case—not as a fishing expedition.

Of course, there are times when you need to serve the warrant immediately, such as when the thief is about to flee the country. The most common case for expedited treatment is when you believe that the thief may dispose of the tangible items containing the secret.

5.53–b   Drafting the warrant

Chapter 9 provides step-by-step instructions on drafting search warrants. Appendix B includes sample affidavits and warrants for information theft cases, along with a model property description. That property description provides sample language and includes suggestions on when that language may be appropriate for your situation. You should review Chapter 9 and Appendix B before drafting your affidavit and warrant. The next sections discuss problems specific to drafting warrants in information theft cases.

5.53–b(1)   Do not disclose trade secrets in your affidavit

Search warrant affidavits are considered public documents, and your disclosure of the secret in the affidavit will make that information public. It is prudent to send a copy of your affidavit to the victim's counsel for review before presenting it to a magistrate.

Do not rely on the magistrate to seal your affidavit to protect trade secrets. First, you will have to rewrite your affidavit if the magistrate refuses. More important, the victim's right to protect that information may, in certain cases, be superseded by the rights of the public and the defendant to obtain it. A higher court may vacate the sealing order.

5.53–b(2)   Avoiding overbreadth

As discussed in Chapters 7 and 9, avoiding overbreadth is a serious challenge when drafting your search warrant. Your aim is to describe the property to be seized broadly enough to encompass all items relevant to your case. At the same time, your description must be narrow enough to avoid encompassing unrelated material which would make your warrant overbroad. The problem is particularly severe in information theft cases because it is difficult to describe information.

Here are two ways to avoid overbreadth in your warrant:

- use overlapping requests; and

- seek tangible items which can be described easily.

Overlapping requests are sets of requests which differ in breadth. One request seeks a broad set of items, and the other requests encompass a more narrowly defined portion, or subset, of those items.

For example, a search warrant might include two requests. The first request authorizes you to search and seize "any and all documents and records describing the victim's X45 diffusion process."

The second request authorizes you to search and seize "all technical manuals with the words "VICTIM" and "X45" in their title [where X45 is a product code name used only by the victim]."

Both requests encompass the victim's X45 technical manuals. However, the first request allows you to seize any of the target's manuals, memoranda, and engineering notes which discuss or incorporate the X45 process. The second request is limited to the victim's manuals. While the first request allows you to seize engineering notebooks containing information which the thief copied from the victim's X45 manual, the second request does not.

The advantage of using both requests together is that overbreadth is severable. In plain English, this means that a judicial ruling that a particular request in a warrant is overbroad does not invalidate the entire warrant. As noted in Chapter 9, courts will generally suppress only those items seized pursuant to overbroad requests.

Using our example, if a court finds that the first request for all documents and records describing the victim's X45 diffusion process is overbroad, you would lose only those documents which could not have been seized under another (narrower) request in your property description. This means that you could still use any of the victim's X45 manuals you found during the search because your narrower request covered those manuals.

So long as you do not abuse this tactic to the point where an annoyed court declares your warrant as a whole to be overbroad (your broad request should be plausibly narrow and made in good faith— asking to seize "all documents" without restriction is a very bad idea), you will increase your flexibility in describing the information in your property description.

The second tactic for avoiding overbreadth complements the first. The best way to avoid overbreadth is to describe, not so much the information itself, but every tangible item likely to contain that information. Thus, the second request in our example seeks tangible items, X45 manuals.

It is easier to describe a tangible item than it is to describe information. A request for X45 technical manuals is easier to understand, and narrower, than a request for documents describing the victim's X45 diffusion process. The latter request requires a judgment that a particular memorandum or analysis describes that process, while a request for X45 technical manuals merely requires an officer to examine the cover of any manuals found at the scene.

Thus, when writing your warrant, use broad requests seeking stolen information, and narrow requests seeking tangible items likely to contain that information.

5.53–b(3)   Describing items to be searched/seized

The sample property description for warrants in information theft cases included in Appendix B provides a menu of requests from which to choose depending upon the facts of your case. The following items are chosen from that menu. Remember that you must establish in your probable cause section that material encompassed by *each request* is likely to be evidence of a crime. The sample property description discusses facts which you should include in your probable cause section to justify searching and seizing certain property.

1.   Tangible items containing or referring to stolen information.

Your property description should include every tangible item belonging to the victim which you expect to find on the premises. Be very specific as to the appearance of each item. If you are looking for the victim's technical manuals on its X45 diffusion process, list those manuals by title. Do not worry if you describe the same tangible item in several different ways—there are no prizes for elegance when drafting a search warrant.

You can also sweep up virtually every piece of property belonging to the victim by asking for all documents marked with the victim's logo. Of course, such a description is quite broad and should be qualified.

Your description should explicitly exclude copyrighted documents and other documents intended for public distribution (based on their appearance) because the target could have bought technical manuals provided by your victim to the public. The request should exclude correspondence between the victim and the target, and any victim memoranda or announcements which do not refer to technical matters (e.g., a memo announcing a company picnic).

The request should also exclude all financial documents, such as checks, payroll slips, and W-2 forms (in the appropriate case, you will seek such documents with a separate request, backed by a justification in your affidavit for seizing those materials).

If you are afraid that the thief has altered a tangible object to obscure information which identifies that object as the victim's property, consider using language such as: "the property to be seized includes documents on which [victim's] legend or logo on the original or a copy of stationery or paper has been whited out, altered, or otherwise obscured."

To justify such requests, present evidence that the target had no right and no reason to possess any of the victim's documents. If your suspect is a former employee, attach a copy of the suspect's employment agreement—that agreement should include a clause requiring the employee to return all of the victim's property upon leaving the company.

2. *Evidence that the suspect was intending to produce a competing product.*

A thief usually steals technical information in order to create a competing product. Documents comparing a competitor's product under development with your victim's product can establish a motive for theft. Such documents may also refer to the stolen information.

3. *Development schedules and progress reports.*

High-technology companies usually create elaborate project schedules for teams of engineers working on a project. Those schedules are changed constantly because the creative process for complex technology is unpredictable. You are looking for clues that someone knew very early in the process exactly how little time it would take to complete a portion, or all, of the project.

You are looking for *abnormal certainty*. For example, if the schedule affords little time to complete a portion of the target's product, it may be evidence that the author knew that someone would need very little time because he or she was using the victim's secret information. Similarly, the lack of testing of a product may demonstrate that the thief was confident that the victim's technology would work.

4. *Connections between your suspect and others.*

Most thieves are incapable of using stolen information without help. If John Doe steals the formula for Coca-Cola, he is unlikely to start a soft-drink factory in his house. He will need capital and equipment to compete. He may contact venture capitalists. Instead of competing, he may prefer to sell this information to an established competitor. You can use a carefully drafted warrant to identify third parties connected with your suspect.

Request authority to search and/or seize communications between your suspects and others, both pre-dating and post-dating the theft, concerning:

- employment of the suspect, either as an employee or consultant, including the terms of such employment;

- anyone using, selling, licensing, manufacturing, designing, developing, marketing, transferring, providing, furnishing, sampling, or examining any information relating to the stolen information, or your victim's product incorporating that information;

- anyone planning to contact vendors or customers of your victim about a product similar to your victim's product.

It is not unusual for a company to recruit an employee from a competitor. However, offering the new recruit a large salary increase, unusually generous stock options, or a promotion to a managerial position not corresponding with that recruit's competence suggests that the hiring company knows that the employee is bringing more than his or her skills to the new job.

Many times an employee is simply using the stolen information to look good at his new job, and the competitor will be as angry and surprised by the theft as your victim. Other times, however, this request strikes gold.

For example, police in one case suspected a small start-up of arranging the theft of information from a larger company. While serving a search warrant at the start-up's offices, police discovered a fax showing that another company, the victim's largest competitor, was purchasing a license for the start-up's product. The discovery changed the complexion of the case.

> *You may want to call the competitor before you serve your search warrant*
>
> In many cases, the facts will suggest that the competitor is not a party to the theft of information from your victim. The competitor in such cases may be eager to cooperate to show its good faith and avoid being sued by the victim. If you are confident that the competitor is not involved, you may wish to suggest that the victim contact that company. In most cases, it is more appropriate for law enforcement investigators to serve a search warrant, but seek the competitor's assistance in obtaining the necessary information.

Finally, plans to contact suppliers or customers may demonstrate an intent to use stolen information to compete against the victim. Furthermore, your suspect may have submitted stolen technical data to a company manufacturing the thief's product.

5.53–c *Serving the warrant*

Information theft warrants are not only difficult to draft—they are also difficult to serve. Most of your problems occur when you are searching a business suspected of harboring your victim's secret information. Your problems include:

- finding sufficient manpower;

- getting into the premises to be searched;

- identifying the property to be searched and/or seized;

- dealing with defense lawyers;

- using experts to assist in serving the warrant;

- handling the media; and

- protecting secret information belonging to the victim, the suspect, and third parties.

The following sections discuss these problems.

5.53–c(1)   Manpower

It is difficult to serve a search warrant when your target is a business with dozens, or hundreds, of employees. You may have to search twenty individual offices, three common areas, and five computers to find evidence. Simultaneously, you may execute similar warrants at the homes of various suspects. It is common to take 30 or more police officers on a single raid, plus one or more computer experts to search hardware and software.

Organizing dozens of police officers to serve warrants at multiple sites simultaneously is a daunting task. (If you fail to serve the warrants simultaneously, the first employee to leave the building will warn confederates at other sites.) You must ensure that each officer has read and understood the warrant. You need to establish a procedure for identifying dozens of employees to allow you to interview suspects at the scene while allowing innocent bystanders to go home. (Occasionally you might find other employees of your victim moonlighting at the target company.)

A search of a business can easily span several days. Thus, you must arrange for additional officers to be available to relieve members of the raid team. Of course, those replacements must be briefed as well.

5.53–c(2)   Entering the premises

You may be unable to surprise your target. For example, your business may be located in a five-story building (or in an industrial "campus" with several buildings). That business will have a security guard in the lobby. That guard may resist letting anyone, including police, into the building without first contacting building security. Once contacted, building security will insist on contacting management. Even if you start breaking down doors, you will probably lose the element of surprise well before reaching the inner sanctum of your target.

If the target business is friendly, and your investigation is confined to a single employee, consider calling the company's security officer in advance. Such a call to the right person can make sure that you enter the premises quickly and discreetly, before the rumor mill can inform your suspect that police have arrived. It will also preserve your good relationship with the business community generally.

If your target is both large enough to have a guard in the lobby and is completely crooked, consider serving the warrant just after business hours, or even at night. The guard may not be able to reach any of your suspects easily. (This may not work well if the business is completely locked and you cannot find anyone with a key.) Remember to include a justification in your affidavit for nighttime service.[26]

5.53–c(3)   *Identifying the property to be searched/seized*

Even carefully briefed officers will be uncomfortable searching through file drawers of documents written in techno-speak. They may not know which documents are significant and which are not. Confronted with dozens of file cabinets full of paper, they may be tempted to seize every document in sight and sort everything out later.

There are several problems with erring on the side of seizing everything. First, such tactics may result in suppression of all of your evidence. A properly drafted search warrant can become an impermissibly overbroad warrant if officers ignore its limits and seize everything without justification.[27]

A more subtle problem is that you will end up with more information than you need. You will waste valuable time sorting the important from the irrelevant. You will also have to provide all of the material to the defense in discovery. You may spend much of your time after serving the warrant copying instead of investigating.

---

26. Serving a warrant just after closing time is often a good idea in any event. Most of the employees will be out of the building, requiring fewer people to handle field identification. It is easier to conduct a full-fledged search when the building is relatively empty.

27. *See United States v. Heldt*, 668 F.2d 1228 (D.C. Cir. 1981); *see also United States v. Wuagneux*, 683 F.2d 1343 (11th Cir. 1982); *but see United States v. Santarelli*, 778 F.2d 609, 616 (11th Cir. 1985) (seizure was justified because on-site search would have taken days); *United States v. Fawole*, 785 F.2d 1141 (4th Cir. 1986) (seizure of briefcase containing 150 items without first examining the items justified because an on-site examination would have been time-consuming). This issue is discussed in more detail in Chapter 7.

Emphasize to your officers that they should check every item against the property description and make sure that there is a match. When in doubt, the officer should consult with one officer who has responsibility for making close calls. Consider using a prosecutor who will not be assigned to the case for trial.[28]

Although this approach works well for seizing tangible items, it does not help officers who are looking for documents incorporating stolen information, such as the thief's engineering notebooks. Officers should use an expert to evaluate those documents.

5.53–c(4) *Using experts to assist in serving the warrant*

Since police officers are generally unable to identify scientific or technical information, it is often necessary to use experts at the premises. If your suspect has stolen the X45 diffusion manual and copied its contents into his own specification for a similar process, you need an expert on the scene to identify that specification as a document which is covered by your search warrant.

Employing an expert to identify property during a search warrant has been accepted by courts in California and Texas, and makes sense.[29] The expert's role is to inform police when property matching the description of the secret information has been located. The expert does not decide whether that property should be seized. Indeed, the expert should have little more discretion than a bloodhound.

The most obvious candidate for your expert is an employee of the victim. The victim's engineers are better suited to recognize their handiwork than any consultant. Using an employee also eliminates the need to quickly hire a consultant, brief him or her on the victim's trade secrets, and send that consultant to the scene. Finally, someone has to pay a consultant, while the victim's employee comes free of

---

28. Note that a recent Supreme Court decision holding that prosecutors do not receive absolute immunity for assisting in drafting and serving search warrants may make it difficult to find a willing prosecutor. Prosecutors should consider seeking indemnity (in writing) from their employers before proceeding.

29. *See Schalk v. State*, 767 S.W. 2d 441 (Tex. Ct. App. 1988); *People v. Superior Court (Moore)*, 104 Cal. App. 3d 1001 (Cal. Ct. App. 1980); *see also United States v. Tamura*, 694 F.2d 591 (9th Cir. 1982) (citing this procedure with approval).

charge.[30] Note that any consultant paid by the victim will appear to be just as biased as the victim's own employee.

Although you should usually use an employee, you will pay a price for doing so. A common defense tactic is to paint law enforcement as the dupes of the victim. Allowing the victim to accompany officers on the raid allows the defense to claim that the victim trumped up the charges solely to allow its expert to examine the defendant's trade secrets.

Second, that defense complaint does contain a kernel of truth: the target may have its own trade secrets, and the expert may be exposed to them in the course of the search. If you use an employee, take steps to ensure that the victim does not learn the target's trade secrets.

The best procedure is for the employee to remain outside the premises; police should bring suspicious documents outside for an expert opinion. However, this may not be feasible where there are large quantities of technical documents at the scene. If you allow the expert entry, never allow him or her to roam unescorted; police should carefully supervise any search by the expert.[31]

As discussed in Chapter 9, your affidavit should request permission for an expert to accompany police. Consider using the following language:

> I do not have sufficient technical expertise to identify the following articles which, based on the facts related in this affidavit, appear to belong to VICTIM:
>
> *[List all items listed in your property description which appear to belong to the victim and which a police officer will be unable to identify.]*
>
> The only persons having such knowledge are technical experts employed by VICTIM *[or your independent experts]*.

---

30. As discussed in Chapter 2, at page 45, victims should not provide prosecutors with funds to pay independent experts.

31. *See Bills v. Aseltine*, 52 F.3d 596 (6th Cir. 1995) (liability for allowing victim representative to conduct illegal search).

Your affiant seeks permission to use [*name VICTIM employees or consultants*] to search the locations described above for the property just enumerated and for any other property belonging to the victim. These individuals have told your affiant that they will be able to recognize those items. Your affiant is aware that such a procedure was approved in [*cases listed in footnote 29, as appropriate in your jurisdiction*].

I ask this court to order EXPERT(s) to accompany me to assist as stated above.

Remember to include the actual court order in your warrant, to wit:

This Court hereby authorizes and orders EXPERT(s) to assist police in locating and identifying property identified in this warrant, including but not limited to the items described in paragraphs __ and __ above.

You may need two types of experts: one to identify the victim's property; and the other to search computers at the scene. Chapter 6 discusses using computer experts.

5.53–c(5)   *Dealing with defense lawyers*

As noted above, it takes time to serve information theft warrants. Suspects often have time to call their corporate counsel, who in turn may call criminal defense lawyers. Those lawyers may ask to speak to police and attempt to persuade them to stop the search until they can get to the scene. They may also announce that they represent all of the employees and "forbid" police to talk to any of their "clients." They will want to observe the search. Finally, they may ask a judge for assistance.

The prosecutor handling the case should be available to respond to the scene to deal with defense attorneys. Law enforcement should not avoid talking to the attorneys (e.g., refusing to come to the phone to talk to them). Aside from being unfair, such tactics allow defense attorneys to complain to the judge that the police are biased.

Absent a court order, there is no obligation for police to halt execution of a warrant until the defense lawyer can arrive at the scene. You should rarely agree to halt a search for any reason.

As for talking to employees, there is a great deal of controversy and uncertainty concerning whether law enforcement can talk to employees of a corporation under investigation when the corporation's lawyers state that they represent those employees. However, any conversations you have with employees before lawyers arrive on the scene or inform you of their representation may be permissible. *Obtain legal advice from your local prosecutor concerning the rules in your jurisdiction before serving your warrant.*

You might make sure that the lawyers actually represent those employees. For example, you might ask those employees if they are represented by counsel. You might ask the defense lawyer to name every employee whom he or she claims to represent. Remember that even if an employee is represented, you may always, subject to *Miranda*, ask that employee questions unconnected with the case (e.g., do you want us to backup the computer before moving it?). In any case, proceed with caution.

Once defense lawyers have arrived on the scene, they will want to examine the warrant and the affidavit. In some jurisdictions, including California,[32] you have no obligation to provide them a copy during the search and need only file it with the court afterward.[33] You should not agree to halt your search while a defense lawyer reads the warrant—as discussed below, while that lawyer is reading, another may be racing to the courthouse or telephoning a judge in an effort to delay your search.

Lawyers may also attempt to monitor the search. Police and defense lawyers must walk a fine line here. No person, even a lawyer, is allowed to interfere with police carrying out a court order—i.e., serving a search warrant. *Do not hesitate to remove a lawyer who is making it difficult for your officers to search the premises.*

---

32. *See* California Penal Code Section 1535.

33. However, note the recommendation in Chapter 9, at page 421, that in many cases you should serve the affidavit with the warrant.

However, to avoid unpleasantness and allegations that you are being unfair, you may wish to allow lawyers to observe the search to determine whether officers appear to be keeping within the bounds of the search warrant. Note that "observe" is not the same as question, hover over, or harass.

Do not allow lawyers to talk to officers to determine why they are searching and seizing particular documents or places. Also do not allow lawyers to stand next to officers, or remain within earshot of their conversations. If the lawyer's presence is affecting your officers, you have the right to do something about it.

You should politely inform the lawyer that he or she may remain on the premises in a designated spot which allows a view of some of the proceedings but keeps the lawyer away from officers trying to perform their tasks. It is best to keep the lawyer in a separate room next to, but not in the middle of, the search.

If the lawyer balks, note that any person observing a search is a witness to that search. Should the lawyer want to claim later that police committed misconduct during that search, the prosecutor can call that lawyer as a witness. In some cases, being called as a witness can create a conflict of interest between lawyer and client, requiring the lawyer to withdraw from the case.

The interaction between police and defense lawyers should always be polite and respectful. There are some issues which can best be negotiated on the scene, such as how data and documents will be removed, stored, and copied (for use by both sides during the case). The better defense lawyers will understand that they are in a weak position at this point in the investigation, and will respect your need to conduct a search without harassment.

Finally, you should be aware that while one lawyer is talking to you at the scene, another may be attempting to obtain an order stopping your search.

Judges will generally defer to the jurist who signed your warrant. Therefore, make sure that the judge who authorized the search knows how to reach you at the scene, and vice-versa, should the defense attempt to seek judicial intervention. Such attempts are unlikely to be successful.

5.53–c(6)   Handling the media

Never tip the news media about your search warrant. As discussed in Chapter 9, news media are not allowed to enter the premises simply because police officers have a warrant.[34] Moreover, if the press obtains evidence and then refuses to turn it over to the defense, a court may dismiss your case.

In some jurisdictions, the media may check search warrant filings every day. If you anticipate a delay between obtaining judicial authorization and serving the warrant, ask the magistrate to seal the affidavit and warrant until after the search on the grounds that disclosure of that affidavit might jeopardize your investigation.

Should the media learn of your warrant, discourage them from arriving at the scene. If they do arrive, keep them away from your search. Do not show them the warrant or the affidavit. If they want to see a copy of the warrant, they can wait until after you file a return.

Instruct your officers not to talk to reporters. One person should be designated to handle media inquiries. The only safe statement is: "We are serving a search warrant at XYZ Corporation. We are looking for evidence relating to possible law violations." If asked whether charges will be filed, stress that you are conducting an investigation. Tell them that the prosecutor will review the results of the search warrant, along with other evidence, before reaching any conclusions concerning possible wrongdoing by anyone.

You want to keep a hands-off policy with respect to the press because your search may come up empty. The fewer words you say about the suspect, the fewer words you will have to retract later. Second, you could tell the defense (or other potential suspects) more about your case than you want them to know.

The only time it may be useful to vary from this policy is if the defense begins making false or misleading statements about your purpose in serving a warrant. At that point, a few well-chosen (*and true*) words about your evidence of the target company's wrongdoing

---

34. *See Ayeni v. Mottola*, 35 F.3d 680 (2d Cir. 1994) (allowing a lawsuit against a Secret Service agent who invited CBS to enter a residence during execution of a search warrant).

should be a sufficient warning to defense lawyers not to start a media slugfest that will damage their client's public image.

5.53–c(7) *Protecting information belonging to the victim, the suspect, and third parties*

Your search warrant allows you to seize secret information belonging to your victim. That information may be contained in documents which include secret information belonging to your suspect, or to an innocent third party (e.g., the suspect's new employer who is ignorant of the theft).

Once you seize that information, you must worry about protecting it from disclosure to three contestants:

* the suspect;

* the victim; and

* the news media.

5.53–c(7)(i) *The suspect*

The defense may demand copies of your victim's secrets as part of the discovery process. Without some sort of restriction, the defendant could disclose that information by making it public. Thus, law enforcement and/or the victim needs to obtain a *protective order* from a judge.

Such orders prohibit lawyers and others from disclosing information provided to them in discovery. These orders are common in civil information theft cases, which means that the victim's lawyers should be able to provide one for your case. Appendix C–2 includes a sample protective order for criminal cases.[35]

---

35. This book does not cover the various pre-trial and trial issues arising out of the need to protect information during a criminal prosecution. However, be advised that you should spend considerable time and energy thinking about how to keep your victim's secret information out of the hands of the public. You may find California's statutory scheme to be helpful (*see* California Evidence Code Sections 1061, 1062, and 1063). This topic is discussed in the materials included in Appendix C–1.

5.53–c(7)(ii)   The victim

Victims often want to inspect evidence seized from a competitor. The prosecutor and police must be willing to protect secret information belonging to companies other than your victim. The law is unclear concerning whether law enforcement may show such evidence to the victim. You should not allow your victim to examine any evidence which is likely to contain the suspect's trade secrets without a court order.[36]

In any event, the defense will almost certainly seek a protective order requiring officers to keep potential trade secrets belonging to the defense in a secure area and prohibiting officers from showing that information to individuals not directly connected with the case.

5.53–c(7)(iii)   The news media

Although the media have an interest in obtaining information disclosed in documents admitted into evidence or filed with the court without seal,[37] they have no right to obtain documents in the possession of law enforcement or provided to the defense in discovery.[38] You should never show the media any information seized pursuant to a search warrant without a court order.

5.54   Investigation after serving the search warrant

Do not arrest anyone when you execute your search warrant unless a suspect is a flight risk. Most thieves are businessmen or engineers who will post bail immediately. Furthermore, there is very little risk in

---

36. *See IBM v. Brown et al.*, 857 F.Supp. 1384, 1388 (C.D. Cal. 1994), for one court's view of those responsibilities in cases not involving trade secrets.

37. *See e.g. Press-Enterprise v. Superior Court*, 478 U.S. 1 (1986) (*Press-Enterprise II*) (preliminary examinations); *Waller v. Georgia*, 467 U.S. 39, 45 (1984) (suppression hearing); *In re Capital Cities*, 913 F.2d 89 (3rd Cir. 1990) (sidebar and chambers conferences); *In re Search Warrant (Gunn I)*, 855 F.2d 569 (8th Cir. 1988); *Certain Interested Individuals v. Pulitzer*, 895 F.2d 460 (8th Cir. 1989) (search warrant affidavits).

38. *See Seattle Times Co. v. Rhinehart*, 467 U.S. 20 (1984); *but see Public Citizen v. Liggett Group, Inc.*, 858 F.2d 775, 787–88 (1st Cir. 1988).

releasing an information thief. While a freed burglar can sell the victim's property, and a cracker can dial back into the victim's computer, a freed information thief is usually harmless. Thieves are unlikely to attempt to steal from the victim again. If they have information hidden away, the glare of publicity will make it very difficult for them to find a buyer.

Once you arrest the thief, the case begins, whether you are ready or not. You usually want to buy as much time as possible between the moment you seize evidence and the date you have to prove your case.

Follow a search warrant with a subpoena?

If allowed by your state's law, consider promptly serving the target with a grand jury subpoena, administrative subpoena, or, once charges have been filed, with a subpoena duces tecum for the same property you listed in your search warrant, supported by the affidavit you used to obtain the warrant. In the event that your warrant is declared insufficient for any reason, you may be able to convince a court that you would have obtained that information anyway as a result of your subpoena. You may prevail under the doctrine of independent discovery.

There is usually a great deal of confusion in the target company after police have served a search warrant. Be alert for disgruntled employees in the target company who may want to talk to police about the theft. If defense attorneys fail to round up all of the involved employees and convince them to accept legal representation, interview as many target company employees as possible.

You need to examine all of the evidence seized during the warrant and consider whether you can prove that potential defendants:

- possessed items incorporating your victim's secret information;

- knew that those items contained the victim's secret information; and

- used, or intended to use, that stolen information.

Look for evidence demonstrating that documents containing stolen information were possessed by a particular person (e.g., handwritten notations on the victim's documents). Check to see whether other documents found nearby contain indicia of ownership.

Look for any mention of your victim. Obviously, competitors will often mention your victim in company documents. You are looking for comparisons which demonstrate unusual knowledge of the victim's technology.

Look for altered copies of your victim's information which can be used to prove that the thief knew that the victim's information was secret. If the thief claims later that he or she believed that the victim's information was publicly available, it is very handy to have physical evidence to the contrary. A copy of your victim's manual with the logo whited out, or the cover ripped off, is powerful evidence.

Look for an exact copy of the information in the thief's handwritten specification. This tends to weaken a defense that the thief thought that the information was public—if the information was public, why did the thief bother copying it in his or her own hand instead of inserting pages from the victim's manual, with the victim's logo?

Finally, look for the payoff. Information theft is risky. If you have a suspect, look for a reward, whether it be in the form of cash, a check, a stock option, or a promotion.

Once you have seized all of your evidence, the most interesting part of your job begins. *You must immerse yourself in the industry.*

Your search warrant will usually yield hundreds or thousands of documents. Those documents will reveal much of the competitor's operation. It is like entering a new world. Your job is to understand that world well enough to know what is normal business activity and what is not.

Although you can and should rely on your victim, the defense may persuade a judge to prevent the victim's employees from looking at many of the documents you have seized. It is a good, but very expensive, idea to hire an independent expert to help you.

Whether or not you have help, remember the description of information theft cases offered at the beginning of this chapter: these cases are extremely expensive and time-consuming. This immersion is part of that time and expense. It is at once the most frustrating, and fun, part of your job.

When you examine each piece of paper, do not lose sight of the big picture. Somebody stole information for a purpose. Your victim can provide informed speculation as to what that purpose was—your job is to determine whether each and every page suggests that the victim is right. Think about whether the evidence before you fits with a world in which nobody stole information. If it does not, then you are on your way to a conviction.

6

Searching, Seizing, and Analyzing Computer Evidence

6.00 Introduction

6.01 The challenge of searching, seizing, and analyzing computer evidence

Seizing, preserving, and analyzing evidence stored on a computer is the greatest forensic challenge facing law enforcement in the 1990s. Although most forensic tests, such as fingerprinting and DNA testing, are performed by specially trained experts, the task of collecting and analyzing computer evidence is often assigned to untrained patrol officers and detectives. While most forensic tests are performed in the analyst's own laboratory, investigators are required to search and seize computers at unfamiliar and potentially hostile sites, such as drug labs, residences, "boiler rooms," small business offices, and warehouse-sized computer centers.

The first problem facing the investigator is that computer evidence can be difficult to find. Magnetic media can be manipulated to hide evidence in non-obvious places. Once located, computer evidence and the equipment containing it are astonishingly vulnerable. Computers can be "rigged" to destroy evidence at the push of a button (or even upon the *failure* to push a particular button). A power surge or interruption can destroy data. A suspect with a magnet can destroy evidence in seconds.

The stakes are very high. In addition to failing to secure important evidence, one mistake by an investigator can destroy equipment and data. A computer may store nothing more valuable than a teenager's computer game. Or it may store the irreplaceable records of a small business which could be forced into bankruptcy if those records are damaged.

When you consider that police departments are liable for property unreasonably destroyed in the execution of a search warrant, and possibly for consequential damages as well (e.g., the failure of a business whose records were destroyed), it is surprising that anyone tries to seize computers.[1]

Perhaps the most frustrating problem for investigators is that there are few uniform procedures for seizing, preserving, and analyzing computer evidence. One reason for this lack of standards is that certain procedures can produce different results depending upon the computer equipment involved.

For example, turning off the power on most PCs merely *powers down* the system (turns it off in an orderly fashion) and preserves evidence stored on the hard disk. Thus, many investigators are taught that when they encounter a computer, running or not, they should pull the plug out of the wall and take the machine back to the police station.

However, on certain larger computer systems, turning off the power without first taking other precautions may cause a *hard disk crash*, destroying data and tens of thousands of dollars worth of computer equipment. Even if the hard disk does not crash, the loss of power can damage the organization of the data on the disk, making it difficult or impossible to find certain data.

Another reason for the lack of standards is that technology marches on. Computer owners can buy software which curtails access to data stored in computers once the computer is turned off. Pulling the plug will make it difficult to access the computer again without a special password.

---

1. Police officers must execute search warrants so as to avoid unnecessary destruction of property; departments risk liability if they fail to teach officers proper procedures for searching and seizing computer evidence. *See, e.g. Ginter v. Stallcup*, 869 F.2d 384 (8th Cir. 1989); *Tarpley v. Green*, 684 F.2d 1 (D.C. Cir. 1982). Furthermore, even a perfectly reasonable search which destroys property may be a compensable "taking" under certain state constitutions. *See, e.g. McGovern v. City of Minneapolis* 480 N.W. 2d 121 (Minn. Ct. App. 1982); *Steele v. City of Houston*, 603 S.W. 2d 786 (Tex. Ct. App. 1986); *but see Customer Co. v. City of Sacramento*, 10 Cal. 4th 368 (Cal. 1995). However, it seems likely that only innocent third parties would be eligible for compensation. *See Steele, supra.*

For example, the best-selling Norton Utilities software allows users to create one or more *virtual encrypted disks*. Every file in the virtual disk is *encrypted*. Encryption scrambles files into gibberish which can be deciphered (*decrypted*) only by using a special password known to the user. Many encryption schemes are designed so that even the company which sells the program cannot decrypt a file without the password.

To open a virtual encrypted disk and decrypt the files in that disk, the user must input a password when accessing the disk. When the computer is turned off, the disk "closes," requiring the user to reenter the password to access those files. Worse, some programs allow the user to set a timer. If the disk is not accessed after a preset interval (e.g., five minutes), the disk "closes."

Police who turn off an operating computer with a virtual encrypted disk will find it difficult, if not impossible, to access the data contained within that disk. Officers who leave the computer unexamined while they interview their suspect may find that part or all of the hard drive is locked when they return to examine the computer. Thus, procedures must be reevaluated frequently in light of new technology.

Another problem is determining whether the evidence seized will be admissible in court. If you leave the hardware behind, are the copies you made of particular files admissible? If you seize the hardware and examine it, does that examination change the character of the disk so as to make certain evidence found on that disk inadmissible? How do you authenticate the evidence without operating the PC in court? Although there are seemingly reasonable answers to those questions, courts have yet to speak on many of these issues, or to approve any particular procedure.

Finally, even if you have seized the computer without damaging it or affecting the admissibility of the seized evidence, how do you examine that evidence quickly? Many computer users have thousands of files on their hard disks, not to mention dozens of unlabeled floppy disks scattered around their desks.

Unfortunately, not everyone is obliging enough to have a file labeled "cocaine.sls" in their WordPerfect directory. Worse, looking only at files may result in your overlooking valuable evidence located in unusual places on the hard disk.

Thorough analysis of a single PC can take a week or more. In "Operation Sun Devil," the Secret Service's 1990 assault on crackers, agents seized over 40 computers and 23,000 floppy disks. They spent over a year on analysis alone.

So what do you do when you determine that there is a computer at the search warrant site? Do you leave the computer and its valuable evidence out of fear of liability? Do you decide that the time you may spend searching through floppy disks is better spent pursuing other leads?

Maybe so. But more and more business records and narcotics ledgers are being kept on computer, and many investigations and prosecutions may soon be impossible without computer evidence.

This chapter offers suggestions on how to seize, preserve, and analyze computer evidence so as to:

- avoid civil liability to the extent possible;

- gather all available evidence using procedures which increase the likelihood of its admissibility; and

- analyze that evidence quickly and thoroughly.

6.02　Caveat emptor

Read these warnings *very* carefully before proceeding further:

1.　If you do not know how to operate a computer, this is not the place to learn.

Searching a computer is like driving a car; many of the skills cannot be learned from a book. Although this chapter will assist those with no computer experience in locating and preserving computer evidence, readers who do not know how to operate a computer will need an expert to assist them in examining and seizing a computer system.

2.　If you have not been trained in how to search and seize computer evidence, you should have an expert assist you.

Searching and seizing computers is extremely difficult, and you should seek help. In addition to "civilian" experts who are familiar with various computer systems, there are many law enforcement investigators throughout the country who are trained in this area. A later section in this chapter discusses how to find those experts.

The procedures recommended in this chapter for searching, seizing and analyzing computers and data are complex. Although there are many occasions where a careful investigator with computer experience can perform those tasks with only a minimal risk of losing important evidence, there is no way of knowing in advance whether your situation will demand expert assistance.

If you are a computer user and cannot find an expert, you should read this chapter thoroughly, and act with *extreme caution*. As discussed previously, if you have never used a computer, you should never make your suspect's computer your maiden voyage.

3. *When using a non–law enforcement computer expert, make it clear that you are in charge and that you will have the final word on how the two of you will search and seize computer evidence.*

Computer users, including experts, tend to be fiercely independent people who have their own "best" way of doing things. Those methods may not satisfy standards governing admissibility of evidence in court. They may even result in damage to the evidence if the owner has "rigged" the computer. (Many engineers do not assume that anyone would interfere with the normal function of a computer—that idea is foreign to their training and experience.)

Sit down with your expert in advance to plan strategy—make sure that your procedures are technically feasible and that your expert's procedures satisfy legal requirements.

4. *Most of the advice in this chapter pertains to personal computers running DOS or Windows only.*

In all but the most exceptional cases, you should decline to search or seize a mainframe or supercomputer. Merely moving such a computer costs thousands of dollars, and doing so may damage both the computer and the data. The risk of being sued is extremely high.

Minicomputers and networks are a somewhat different story. You can search and, with extreme difficulty, seize them, and parts of this chapter apply to larger computer systems. However, you *must* employ an expert, and most of your time will be spent standing around watching that expert conduct the search. Searching and moving minicomputers and networks is much more difficult and dangerous than searching PCs, and the increased risk of liability cautions against such searches except as part of the most critical investigations.

Finally, most of the techniques in this chapter for handling computers pertain to PCs running DOS or Windows. Some suspects will use PCs running IBM's OS/2, Microsoft's Windows NT, or even a variation of UNIX. Others will use Apple Macintoshes, and still others may use ancient Commodores and Ataris. While some of the advice in this chapter applies to those systems, you will still need an expert familiar with those systems to assist you.

5.　*Even good procedures can produce bad results.*

There is no guarantee that following any or all of the procedures outlined below will prevent damage to computers or data. Computers are fickle. Hard disks sometimes fail to work even when experts transport the computer carefully. "Rigged" computers can destroy data in seconds despite an expert's best efforts. Indeed, some of the software discussed in this chapter could have heretofore undetected *bugs* (errors), or operate in unexpected ways in unusual situations. The author has not been able to test every software program discussed in this chapter.

It is impossible to provide a list of rules which apply to every situation. Sophisticated computer users may be able to defeat the procedures suggested in this chapter. However, most criminals are not sophisticated computer users.

The theory behind this chapter is that investigators cannot do their job if they must avoid searching, seizing, and/or analyzing personal computers because of the remote risk that they will be defeated by a suspect's security measures or other problems. This chapter is aimed at providing a short list of procedures which, *most of the time*, will do the job.

However, it is critical that you understand that searching and seizing computers is an art, not a science—nobody who knows what he or she is doing approaches the task without considerable trepidation.

New technology can render the advice which follows less useful or even counterproductive. All this book can offer you is a better chance at recovering information quickly and safely.

6. *There is no single "right" way to search a computer.*

As we shall see below, you have to make a series of trade-offs as you conduct your search. Those trade-offs will depend upon the circumstances and your expertise. How you resolve those trade-offs will determine what steps you take to search and seize computer evidence. *Remember: obtaining some evidence is better than avoiding the computer and obtaining no evidence at all.*

6.10   Preparing to search for computer evidence

6.11   The tools of the trade

Ballistics and fingerprint experts use tools, and so should you. Just as a doctor does not use an operating room to remove a hangnail, your tool kit will vary depending upon the complexity of your search. The items listed below may help you in your search for computer evidence (this list is reprinted in Appendix A–6a):

- A real computer tool kit (computer tools such as screwdrivers for opening the case, disconnecting items properly, etc.). You can purchase one of these inexpensively at a computer supply store. You should also purchase an anti-static bracelet (also known as a grounding strap). Your kit should include a 1/4-inch nut driver (for the computer case) and a Torx (screwdriver); one expert also suggests a 7 mm nut driver (for removing certain circuit boards).

- Wire cutters, hammer, nail puller, sharp knife. These are used for prying items out of walls, for example.

- Flashlight

- Computer cables: parallel, serial, 9 pin, 25 pin, null modem, RS-232, 50-pin flat ribbon (for disk drives). It can be useful to have a spare cable around when you are seizing peripherals or trying to get them to function on-site.

- Extension cords and power strips. The suspect may have used all of the outlets in the room or office where the computer is stored.

- Blank disks

  •• Purchase both 5 1/4-inch and 3 1/2-inch disks, each in double- and high-density formats. Buy name-brand diskettes only (such as 3M, Sony, Maxell, Verbatim). Buy pre-formatted disks—they will save you time.

    NEVER use the suspect's machine to format a disk.

    NEVER bring along disks which have already been used for anything else. If you must bring "used" disks, you must use only those disks which you have personally "wiped" clean with Norton Utilities WipeInfo or other program. Merely formatting disks does not erase their data.

  •• You may also want to use some blank formatted diskettes to insert into diskette drives when you seize the computer.

  •• Some disks are available in different colors. For searches where viruses are a serious risk (i.e., any cracker's computer), you may wish to use color-coded disks, as follows:

    ••• Green: For factory software for use in analysis

    ••• Blue: For backup of the suspect's data

    ••• Red: For destructive programs, such as viruses, found on the suspect's machine

- Diskette labels, preprinted with the case number and the location of the site to be searched. Use these to label blank floppy disks at the scene. In addition, before arriving at the scene, label any disks you bring with you. Otherwise, you risk confusing your disks with the disks you have seized from the suspect.

- Write-protect labels (to put over the write-protect tab on 5 1/4-inch disks)

- Felt marking pens. The more indelible, the better. Do not use ballpoint pens to mark disk labels.

- Color-coded stick-on tags, preferably tags which can be tied onto things (like cables). If they have enough space so that you can write letters or numbers, so much the better. Avery color-coded file folder labels work well. Wire labels are also useful and can be purchased at electronics supply stores.

- Package of 1" x 4" self-adhesive labels. Use these to label evidence.

- Boxes of large and small paper clips

- Scissors

- Stapler (with box of staples)

- Box of rubber bands

- Cloth gloves (where fingerprints may be important; otherwise, rubber gloves are adequate). You may wish to consider always wearing gloves to avoid depositing body oil on floppy disks.

- Materials for storing what you will seize

  •• Large and small boxes. Large boxes can be purchased from moving companies (e.g., Ryder, U-Haul).

  •• Packing material, such as shredded paper or molded styrofoam, for packing in boxes around seized computer components. (One expert reports that styrofoam balls can "shed" particles which can clog a hard drive. An alternative is to use foam wrapping. Pink or blue foam wrapping generally signifies that the wrapping is anti-static.)

  •• Grocery bags and paper bags (for cables and small components). Avoid using plastic bags—they can store static electricity which can damage electronic components.

- Tape

  •• Masking tape (for taping cables to computers and securing floppy disk drives with a disk inside the drive)

  •• "Fragile evidence" tape

- Floppy disk container (can be purchased at computer stores). Purchase 3 1/2-inch and 5 1/4-inch disk containers—you can also use shoeboxes to store 5 1/4-inch disks.

- Sleeves for 5 1/4-inch disks

- Magnetometer, or less ideally, a compass (for detecting magnetic fields)

- A computer battery. Batteries run down every few years, and your computer's battery may fail while it is in storage pending trial. If the battery dies, you lose the CMOS information necessary to operate the computer and must spend time and effort finding that information. (As discussed later, you will also obtain CMOS information when you seize a computer.)

- Graph paper for mapping the search warrant site

- Tape recorder

- Camera. You may want a Polaroid camera in order to make sure you can confirm that your picture is good before you leave the scene, and a 35 mm camera with close-up lens for critical pictures which you expect to admit into evidence. A tripod is also a good purchase.

  •• Film

  •• Flash attachment, recently tested

- Camcorder (preferably with clock counter). The Hi-8 camcorders are best.

  •• Videotape

  •• Recently tested batteries

- Standard desk telephone. You can use your telephone to make calls from the scene. Using the suspect's phone erases that phone's "memory" of the last call(s) made by the suspect.

- Recently tested size AAA, AA, and 9-volt batteries.

- Portable computer system, including portable printer, laser printer labels, and paper. Although such a system is clearly a luxury item, it can be very useful in logging evidence or, if the computer has a large hard drive, backing up evidence.

• Software: The following is a suggested list of software you should consider including in your tool kit. Each software intended for the IBM PC should be available in both 3 1/2-inch and 5 1/4-inch versions. You are encouraged to write the author with suggestions for other software for the tool kit; those suggestions will be incorporated in future editions. The author has not used every software package referred to in this chapter.

A word of caution: always use licensed copies of software. It would be embarrassing for an investigator to have to admit in court that he used bootlegged software, in violation of federal law, to search for evidence of a crime.

•• Two copies of the latest version of MS-DOS (and PC-DOS), along with the following older versions (some may be impossible to find):

••• 3.3

••• 4.01

••• 5.0

••• 6.0, 6.1, 6.2

•• The latest Apple operating system boot disk (e.g., System 7.5), as well as Systems 5.0 and 6.0 (for examining older machines)

•• The latest version of Norton Utilities for IBM and Macintosh computers

•• Fastback Plus backup software, version 2.0 (the last version of that product which can be run from a floppy). You may not be able to find this software.

•• Software capable of making an image backup. You can choose from SAFEBACK backup software, available to law enforcement investigators from Sydex Corporation

(503-683-6033), and CPR Data Recovery Tools, distributed by Tech Assist, Inc. (813-539-7429).

•• The latest version of Laplink (including cable)

•• Various versions of "zip" programs, such as PkZip, PkArc, LHArc, GZip, and either Nico Mak Computing's WinZip or Canyon Software's Drag and Zip

•• Any ASCII editor program

•• A graphics viewer program[2]

•• You may wish to create a disk with a "clean" operating system (a boot disk) and other utility programs to assist you in securing, examining, and backing up computers found during the execution of a search warrant. You may consider including the following software (for which you must have a license) on that disk:

••• MS-DOS 5.0 system files (IO.SYS, MS-DOS.SYS, COMMAND.COM, AU-TOEXEC.BAT). You can transfer these files by choosing the "make a disk bootable" option in Norton Utilities. (MS-DOS 5.0 can be used on older machines; you may want a separate disk with the newer MS-DOS 6.22 system files.)

••• CHKDSK (MS-DOS)

••• DISKMON (Norton Utilities)

••• NDD.EXE (Norton Utilities)

••• SYSINFO.EXE (Norton Utilities)

••• DISKEDIT.EXE (Norton Utilities)

---

2. Two viewers now available are VPIC, from VPIC Inc., Box 162857, Altamonte Springs, FL 32716, 407-869-5233, and WinJPG, written by Norman and Ken Yee, 58 Chandler St. Boston, MA 02116, 617-423-2399, nyee@osiris.ee.tufts.edu or kenyee@ksr.com.

6.12 Determining what computers are located at the search scene

A surgeon does not walk into an operating theater without knowing something about his or her patient. You should follow that example by trying to avoid serving a search warrant "blind." Preparing to search a single PC is a lot different from preparing to search a network or minicomputer. Just as orthopedic surgeons are not qualified to perform brain surgery, computer experts also have areas of expertise.

You are not going to find an expert who is qualified to search all minicomputers or networks. Therefore, it is critical that you obtain as much information as possible about the computers located at the search site ahead of time.

In many cases you will have no information at all, as in the case of the computer cracker who could be using an IBM, Macintosh, Amiga, or Atari personal computer, among others, to perform the same tasks. However, many law enforcement investigations target businesses which own more than one PC, and often a network of PCs. Those businesses are more susceptible to intelligence work.

Many businesses lease their computer equipment. Vendors often take a security interest in that equipment, which is recorded with the Secretary of State in each state. Those records are available to the public. Filings by computer equipment vendors can provide you with a great deal of information. The vendor can often provide further details.

A warning is appropriate here: vendors' loyalty to their customers usually far outweighs their sense of obligation to assist a police investigation. Many, if not most, vendors fear that their reputations will be blackened if the computer industry learns that they cooperated in an investigation of one of their customers.

Thus, subterfuge may be preferred to openness when dealing with the suspect's vendor. At the very least, do not reveal the target of your investigation until you have secured the vendor's commitment to cooperate at its highest level (i.e., make sure that the vendor's CEO or legal counsel approve).

Of course, if the vendor is local, you could obtain a search warrant or other court order for those records, and include as part of that warrant an order prohibiting the vendor from revealing the search to the customer. Unfortunately, there is a risk that an employee of the vendor will nonetheless tip off the suspect. Remember that these vendors are not like banks or telephone companies, which are accustomed to relying upon law enforcement for assistance.

Another approach for experienced computer users, which is a lot more fun than plowing through public records, is the survey technique. Tear out one of the surveys included in *PC Week, PC Magazine* or *InfoWorld* magazines. Posing as a sales representative for an invented magazine of a similar name,[3] call the suspect and ask to speak to their *MIS* manager. MIS is an acronym standing for management information systems, and refers to employees in charge of corporate computer systems. (The term has recently been shortened to IS).

Promise the MIS manager a free subscription in return for answering a few questions. He or she may also be familiar with the survey form, so stick to it. By the end of your conversation, you should have a good picture of their computer system. Of course, you can always add a few custom questions of your own at the end. Be sure to serve the warrant within a month or two after your interview (or buy the suspect a subscription).

Given the risk that the suspect realizes that the survey is a ruse, this scheme should be your last course of action. You must gamble that the suspect does not know that these magazines do not conduct telephone surveys.

A variant on this scheme is for a youthful investigator to pose as a high school or college student assigned to write a paper on computer technology in the workplace. Tell the suspect that you are required to compare the technological approaches to workplace automation used by similar businesses in your area. Have a list of similar businesses ready in case your suspect is suspicious. If required to recite that list to the suspect, call those businesses and run through the same drill.

Other options include contacting the fire marshal to determine whether the suspect has filed evacuation plans for a computer center, or infiltrating an officer or informant as a temporary employee. If you are able to do so without tipping off the suspect, you may wish

---

3. It is prudent to invent a magazine with a similar name. Although computer magazines should be thrilled by the idea that they are so desirable that criminals will injure themselves in order to get a copy, they may be upset by the publicity and concerned that other potential subscribers will not answer their surveys.

to interview the suspect's clients, ex-employees, service vendors, janitors, or landlord.

If you have an informant or other infiltrator, ask the following questions:

- What types of computers are on the premises (mainframe, mini-computers, networks, PCs, dumb terminals, portables)? Depending upon the sophistication of your informant, you may have to settle for information concerning the size of the computers and whether they appear to be connected to one another.

- What brands of computers are present (IBM, Digital, Apple, etc.)?

- How many computers are on the premises?

- What operating systems are being used (e.g., UNIX, VMS, Novell, Windows NT, Windows, OS/2, DOS, Apple System 7.5, etc.).

- Does the system receive and send electronic mail?

- Are there any modems on the premises?

- What programs are run on the computer (e.g., word processing, databases, spreadsheets)?

- What software is on the shelves?

  - •• This information can indicate whether your suspect is a sophisticated computer user. Look for such programs as Symantec's Norton Utilities, Symantec's Disklock, Central Point's PC Tools, and MS-DOS (note the version).

- What passwords, if any, must the employees use to access the computer, and where are those passwords stored? Are there any other computer security systems in place, such as SecureID (discussed below), or "destruct" switches or procedures?

- Are there any scraps of paper on or near the computer which might contain passwords?

- What kind of backup system does the suspect use, and where are the backup tapes or disks stored? Are they stored off-site?

If the case is very important, you should consider searching curb-side garbage bins for clues. (Crackers call this *dumpster diving*.) Many firms do not shred their printouts; those printouts may identify the computers at the site. Under current federal law, you do not need a search warrant to search through trash which a suspect has "abandoned" at the curb. You may need a warrant to do so in certain states.

6.13   Obtaining other intelligence

If you are searching a *hostile business* (i.e., where your suspects run the company), you need to locate power sources and determine whether you wish to obtain a warrant to cut telephone service to the site. (Cutting electric service is usually not feasible because electric utilities are not willing to risk being sued for damages caused by a sudden loss of power. It may be an option for residences where you are certain that the occupant is a cracker ready to destroy data.)

If you are searching a *friendly business* (where management is not involved in criminal activity), and your suspect is in charge of the computer or has access to it, you need to make sure that management terminates the suspect's system privileges *and* dial-up access capabilities. In such cases, consider calling the company's security officer in advance. Such a call can make sure that you enter the premises quickly and discreetly, before the rumor mill can inform your suspect that police have arrived. It will also preserve your good relationship with the business community generally.

6.14   Finding computer experts

You need to find your expert *before* you serve your search warrant. Consider the following sources for computer experts.

1.   *Your agency.*

Many metropolitan police departments hire their own computer experts to manage the department's computers. Some of these experts are suited to accompany officers on a raid and to search and seize computer evidence. Others assume that they know more than they do, and are dangerous. Make sure that your expert understands the principles of searching and seizing computers discussed in this chapter. *Computer experience is no substitute for training in how to search and seize computer evidence.* Use trained investigators whenever possible.

2. Federal agencies.

Most federal agencies have in-house technical experts. Unfortunately, many of them are located in Washington, D.C.[4] Furthermore, state and local agencies may not be able to borrow one of those experts to assist in a purely local case. However, those agencies may be able to refer you to other experts in your community.

3. Other law enforcement agencies.

Do not be shy about calling for help. Pick the largest agency in your jurisdiction and ask for assistance.

4. High Technology Crime Investigation Association (HTCIA).

The high-technology crime investigation community is small and close-knit. Most investigators belong to the High Technology Crime Investigation Association, with chapters in southern California, Silicon Valley, northern California (Sacramento), Texas, Arizona, New Mexico, the Pacific Northwest, Chicago, and New York.

The advantage of calling HTCIA is that the organization includes law enforcement *and* corporate investigators. This means that you may be able to obtain assistance from an expert who works for a company familiar with the computer you will encounter at the scene.[5]

---

4. A list of such experts is included in Appendices C and D of *Federal Guidelines for Searching and Seizing Computers* (General Litigation Section of the Department of Justice 1994). The Federal Law Enforcement Training Center (FLETC) in Glynco, Georgia, trains federal agents in computer crime investigation, and is staffed by specialists. Note that the IRS scatters its Seized Computer Evidence Recovery Specialists (SCER) around the country. Almost every IRS district has at least one SCER Specialist, and many have two. *Id.*, at 63. The Secret Service also has a few specialists outside of Washington.

5. Companies who are vendors or suppliers to computer manufacturers are likely to employ the expert you need. These experts will not be hampered by a vendor-customer relationship with the suspect.

5. SEARCH Group, Inc.

The Department of Justice, Bureau of Justice Assistance, funds SEARCH, an organization devoted to assisting the criminal justice community on information technology issues. Part of its support includes training law enforcement agencies in all facets of searching and seizing computers and computer evidence.

Its staff experts are knowledgeable and helpful and may be able to refer you to experts in your area. If you are planning to search and seize computer evidence on a regular basis, you should make every effort to take one of its courses.[6]

6. *International Association of Computer Investigative Specialists (IACIS).*

This non-governmental organization is based in Oregon, and offers well-regarded 72-hour and two-week training courses on searching and seizing computer evidence. It offers a certification in "computer forensics."[7]

7. Universities.

Consider calling the computer science department of your local university. Academic experts may be of assistance in searching large computer systems. They can also give you the names of various professional societies, which in turn may be willing to inform their members that you need assistance.

8. Victims in earlier cases.

High-technology investigators should expand their Rolodexes with each case. Assuming that you achieved a satisfactory result in their

---

6. As of this writing, Mr. Fred B. Cotton is the resident expert. He can be reached at 916-392-2550. The author gratefully acknowledges the generosity of Mr. Cotton and Mr. William R. Spernow (who has since joined the National White Collar Crime Center) in providing him with SEARCH's extensive materials on searching and seizing computers, and reinforcing those materials with copious advice. The author has supplemented, *and at several points deviated from*, those materials in this chapter. Readers should not take this chapter as a substitute for a SEARCH training course.

7. The phone number for IACIS is 503-668-4071.

cases, former victims may be enthusiastic about helping you investigate your latest case. As discussed below, remember to perform a records check on any private party who volunteers to assist you.

9. *The victim in your present case.*

Victims are usually a ready source of technical expertise. However, they are often not the best choice because the defense can accuse law enforcement of employing a biased expert.

10. *Volunteers.*

The public has been persuaded by the media that high-technology crime is exotic and interesting. Thus, you may find engineers in your community offering to assist you on "your next case." Although these people can be very helpful, conduct a background check before accepting their assistance.

Be close-mouthed about your case when contacting a non–law enforcement expert. You do not know whether your prospective expert knows your suspect. Simply describe the computer system to your expert. Do not reveal the location or target of the search until shortly before you execute the warrant. Although it is almost always a waste of time, conduct a records check on the expert—it would be quite embarrassing to unwittingly use a convicted cracker as your expert.

Finally, as stated earlier in this chapter, when using a computer expert, make it clear that you are in charge and have the final word on how the two of you will search and seize computer evidence.

6.15   Logistics and budgeting

Executing a search warrant for computer evidence can be a lengthy and expensive operation, particularly when the target is a business. If you expect to seize large quantities of computer evidence, plan for the following problems.

6.15–a   *Manpower*

Search warrants in information theft and fraud cases can easily require 30 officers working for 24 hours or more. One of the largest such operations involved 146 officers used in a $250 million fraud case in Riverside County, California, in 1991. (They held the briefing in an auditorium.) That operation also required a helicopter and traffic control. Even smaller cases will require more than one officer.

Remember that officers get tired and often go "off shift" at inconvenient times. This means that you must budget for overtime and for replacement officers.

Do not forget to include those replacement officers in your pre-raid briefing, if feasible (most will be off-shift when the briefing begins and on-shift when needed). Although recording or videotaping the briefing for later viewing by those officers appears attractive, it risks inviting defense attorneys to explore that briefing at length during a motion to suppress evidence. Worse, turning over a tape of the briefing may provide suspects with additional information concerning your investigation.

If your operation is large, notify your public relations officer that you may need assistance in dealing with the media.

6.15–b   Provisions

Your officers will need food and drink after many hours at the site—plan how to deliver it. Forcefully remind officers to keep all food and drink away from computer equipment.

6.15–c   Equipment needed to process data

Backing up a network, workstation, or mainframe requires special equipment (such as optical disks and/or magnetic tapes). If you need special equipment to backup the computer system at the scene, or at the police station, budget for that equipment, and obtain (and test) it in advance of your search.

Include equipment you will need to analyze the data, and if necessary, make arrangements to use equipment belonging to friendly companies in your area. Budget for expenses incurred in making copies of seized documents and data for the defense, even if you will be reimbursed for those expenses later. Remember that indigent defendants will probably receive free copies.

6.15–d Movers

You need to hire a company with experience in moving computers, and ensure that it can respond to the scene at the appropriate time (e.g., at 2 A.M.).

6.15–e Storage space for seized evidence

If you are planning to seize a large volume of equipment, you may need to store some of it off-site. At a minimum, reserve space in your department for seized equipment *before* you execute the warrant, and, as discussed later in this chapter, make sure that the area is safe for computer storage.

6.16 The pre-raid briefing

The briefing before executing a search warrant to obtain computer evidence is very important. Although you may have expert assistance, you will also have law enforcement investigators on your team who have no familiarity with computers whatsoever.

The briefing is your only opportunity to make sure that their understandable ignorance does not interfere with your investigation. Explain to them the basic considerations of computer evidence handling. Tell them not to staple any diskettes they find to their property report (yes, it has happened, as has virtually every form of mistreatment to a floppy disk you can imagine). Show them a floppy disk, a software manual, and a sample computer password so that they know what to look for.

Explain that they should not just seize anything that looks vaguely related to a computer because such careless gathering may transform a narrowly crafted warrant into a general search forbidden by the Fourth Amendment. Impress upon officers who *are* computer users that only certain persons are allowed to touch the computers, both before and after those computers have been seized and transported back to the police station.

Finally, take the opportunity to test your equipment, such as camcorders and tape recorders.

6.20   Locating and safeguarding all computer evidence

6.21   When to serve your warrant

As discussed above, computer evidence is vulnerable to destruction. In some cases, you may wish to search when your suspect is away. In the case of a business, nighttime service might be in order, with an explanation to the magistrate as to why the presence of computer users might lead to the destruction of valuable evidence. The disadvantage of this technique is that you may need the assistance of the target to access larger computer systems.[8]

6.22   Securing the scene

6.22–a   Isolate the computers

Your first priority when serving a warrant is to secure the scene. Move everyone away from the computers within 30 seconds of entry, forcibly if necessary. This includes any locations where backup tapes may be stored.

If 30 seconds seems too short a period of time, remember that 30 seconds is about how long it takes for a PC user running Norton Utilities to: (1) initiate the utility program WipeInfo, which, if left unattended, destroys all data on the hard disk with no hope of recovery; and (2) turn off the monitor so that you do not notice that the computer is running that program. Sophisticated users may have their own "home-grown" programs which do the same thing. Even if you interrupt WipeInfo during the minutes it takes to obliterate many hard disks, whatever data has been erased may be unrecoverable.

On larger systems, 30 seconds may be enough to turn the system off, risking an unrecoverable hard disk crash. And an industrious engineer with a magnet can wipe out a closet full of backup tapes in a minute. In the hundred-million-dollar fraud case mentioned earlier in this chapter, the suspects had added a switch labeled "self-destruct" to the operating panel of the mainframe computer.

---

8. Note that Chapter 5, § 5.53–d, includes some suggestions on searching a hostile business.

Do not waste any time with pleasantries at the front door of a business if you believe there is any chance that employees operating a computer system know that you have arrived. Your "knock-notice" should be as brief as legally permissible.[9]

6.22–b   Isolate power and phone connections

Once you have moved everyone away from computers and magnetic media, isolate them from two other important utilities: electricity and telephones. Although pulling the plug on most PCs is usually harmless, and sometimes even recommended, cutting off the power may damage certain minicomputers and mainframes.[10]

Never let suspects near cords, cables, electrical outlets, or circuit breakers during the course of a search.[11] Similarly, make sure that you know the location of the power source to the building, and consider taking steps to secure that power source.

Telephones are another potential danger. Until you are sure that computers are not connected to telephone lines, do not allow suspects

---

9. A problem with even the briefest of knock-notices is that a suspect may need only a keystroke to initiate an erasure of the hard disk. Consider using a ruse to get suspects away from the computer (e.g., to the door). Consult your prosecutor concerning whether a ruse complies with the knock-notice requirement. Note that the Supreme Court has recently held that some sort of knock-notice is required by the Fourth Amendment. *See Wilson v. Arkansas* __ U.S. __, 115 S.Ct. 1914 (1995)

10. Minicomputers often require elaborate power-down procedures, and failure to follow them can be disastrous. For example, a sudden loss of power can destroy part of the logical structure of the hard drive. If you lose power, immediately check to see whether the computer system is being supplied with power by a *UPS*, an *uninterruptible power supply*. These components are designed to supply backup power when the main power fails. The catch is that many of them supply power for only a limited amount of time (e.g., two minutes). You may need to initiate a power-down sequence immediately while you attempt to restore power.

11. If you are planning to search a large computer center, be on the lookout for *halon gas* dispensers. Computers are extremely vulnerable to fire. Apart from melting, magnetic media are easily destroyed by smoke. Many computer centers are equipped with halon gas systems, which release the gas when a button is pressed. Such buttons are typically placed in glass-enclosed boxes.

Consider checking with the fire department to see whether the company has included halon dispensers in its fire safety plan.

to use the telephone. This means that you must prevent suspects from leaving the area.

Many computers are connected together in *wide area networks* (local area networks spanning more than one physical location). If you are not careful, an employee allowed to leave the building might call one of the other locations on the network and have that user send commands to erase data to the computers at the site. Furthermore, you may want to use the computer at the search site (the "on-site" computer) to obtain data from other computers connected with it.

Using computers at your site to search computers located off-site

If you intend to access computers located in the same jurisdiction as your site, you should include in your search warrant the court's authorization to search that additional location. But what about when the "connected" computer is located in another jurisdiction (e.g., your site is in Los Angeles, and the server is in Chicago)? This issue is discussed in more detail in Chapter 7, at page 315. The short answer is that it is unclear whether you need a judge in the foreign jurisdiction to issue a warrant, and you should obtain such a warrant whenever possible.

One of your first tasks is to determine whether the on-site computer is, or can be, connected to a telephone line. When examining PCs, look for modems. For larger computers, look for other devices connected to a telephone line. Many larger computers are placed next to *modem racks*; a modem rack is a series of modems, each connected to a different phone line.[12]

You want to know whether the computer is connected to a modem, even if that modem is not operating, because the modem is

---

12. If the computer is running a UNIX operating system, the "mount" command will tell you what external devices are being accessed by your computer, including devices located at other sites.

a clue that the suspect is communicating with others. You may learn that what you thought was a small narcotics outlet is actually part of a larger networked operation.

If a computer is connected to a modem, the computer probably contains telecommunications software. Examining that software may reveal a list of the suspect's "electronic pen pals"—potentially valuable evidence. It may also reveal that the suspect is using stolen telephone access codes. Finally, the suspect's computer may contain programs which automatically dial and log in to other systems. Those programs will contain the telephone number of those systems, along with the suspect's log-in ID and password.

If the computer is operating and is connected to a phone line, you must decide whether to disconnect that line. You should disconnect the line immediately to prevent a user at another site from erasing data stored within the on-site computer, unless you plan to: (1) physically search another site which you believe is connected telephonically to the on-site computer; or (2) search another computer electronically from the computer at your site.[13]

If you plan to physically or electronically search the other site, disconnecting the phone line may warn those individuals that something is wrong. The risk is lower if the computer is not being accessed at the time, but you never know when someone off-site will notice that their link to the on-site computer no longer functions. You may be willing to run the risk of sabotage via an off-site computer to buy more time for your search and subsequent investigation.

In addition, disconnecting the phone line prevents you from using that line to download information from computers networked to your on-site computer. This could be very important if you are not sure whether the information you are looking for is located within the on-site or off-site computer(s).

If you elect to disconnect, first determine what operation the on-site computer is performing. For example, if the on-site computer is

---

13. One caution is that phone lines may also serve as network "cables." Disconnecting those lines while the system is "up" can corrupt data or damage files on both the server(s) and the nodes. Let your expert be your guide here.

downloading or uploading data to or from an off-site computer, you will lose evidence if you disconnect the line.

You may wish to delay disconnecting until the computer has finished the current task. As discussed below, you should have a camcorder running when you search a computer, and you should use it to film whatever the on-site computer is doing from the time you arrive until you disconnect.[14]

If your on-site computer is a PC attached to a modem, simply unplug the modem from the phone line. (As discussed in Chapter 9, your warrant should include authorization to seize the modem as evidence.) If you are dealing with anything more complicated, have an expert handle it.

6.22–c   *Confirm that the computers are not erasing data while you search*

Turn on every monitor at the scene. If a suspect has started a program such as WipeInfo and turned off a monitor, turning it back on may help you save your evidence. (If you believe that sabotage has occurred, take this step before you start checking on telephone lines.)

If such a program is running, hit the "Pause" key on the upper right hand part of the keyboard. If the computer is a stand-alone PC, *pull the plug*, as described below, and take the machine back to a lab to recover data which was destroyed by the program. If you are dealing with a network, call your expert to your side immediately.

6.22–d   *Check for physical traps*

Your next step is to check for physical traps around the computer system. Some suspects protect their systems with remote power switches. These devices may perform a variety of functions, including

---

14. This is particularly useful when the suspect's computer is running a *war dialer* program. As discussed in Chapter 4, these programs randomly dial phone numbers and record which calls are greeted with a modem tone (signalling another computer system which can be penetrated). The program then downloads those "hot" numbers for later use. Some of these programs actually input passwords in the hope of guessing the correct password. A recording of such a program in action is powerful evidence.

the benign (switching off the power to the PC's speaker) to the malignant (switching off the power to the hard disk). If the computer is operating and you find a toggle switch, tape it in its current position to protect against accidentally turning off the power. You should trace that wire to determine the purpose of the toggle switch before backing up the system.

Look for degaussing rings (tape erasers). These are magnets which are used for erasing tapes, and are commonly found in large computer facilities. Move them to a safe location secure from suspects. In fact, you should look for any source of magnetism. The following news story explains why:

> Federal officers in the Midwest entered a suspected criminal business to seize computer and other records. This time the staff was actually helpful as the agents verified that the records they sought were on both computer hard disks and backup floppies. When the agents got the computer back to their own shop, all the data had become unreadable. It turned out the owner had told his staff to cooperate fully if the police ever came, but to flip a certain switch. The staff complied. The switch set up a strong electromagnetic field around all the exits, which effectively erased every disk the agents removed from the scene. Even one agent's favorite audio cassette, which he had tucked in his shirt pocket before the raid, got wiped clean.[15]

Although this story is almost certainly fictional (most magnetic fields are too weak to damage data on floppy disks), there are enough stories of magnetic destruction of evidence floating around that you should not forget to check doorways and other areas for magnetic fields. You might even consider checking loose magnetic media on a computer outside the search site before leaving the scene to ensure that you can read the data on that media.

The best way to detect magnetic fields is to use a magnetometer (in a pinch, use a compass). Walk around the site with your magnetometer and sweep any area where you plan to store evidence during your search. (Do not put your evidence on the copy machine while

---

15. *Bay Area Computer Currents*, September 10–September 23, 1991.

making copies of documents, and do not use the copy machine to copy labels on seized floppy disks.)

6.23   Finding computer evidence

After you have secured the site, you need to search for computer evidence that you did not notice when you arrived. First, look for computers which you do not ordinarily think of as computers: wristwatches, telephones, fax machines, copiers, and personal organizers (e.g., Casio's Boss, Sharp's Wizard, or the H-P Palmtops).

Many wristwatches include an address book feature. Casio makes a $30 watch, the Data Bank, which can store 20 addresses and phone numbers. If you have included the appropriate language in your search warrant, do not hesitate to take the watch off the suspect's wrist, examine it, and if appropriate, seize it.

Similarly, you should include in your warrant permission to examine telephones which include an auto-dialer feature. If the suspect's most recent phone calls are critical to you, consider the following technique.

Find an officer with a pager. Using the phone you have brought to the scene for this purpose (using the suspect's phone will make it impossible to check the last number dialed from that phone), call the officer's pager service. When it is time to input the number of the phone dialing the pager, hold the suspect's phone to your officer's phone, and press the redial key to recall the last number dialed. That number should appear on the pager shortly. Repeat the process for all stored numbers.

Fax machines can also provide a wealth of information. For example, you may be able to recover the destinations (or even contents) of the last few faxes sent. The fax machine may also include a key or command which will print logs of faxes sent and received over the previous several days or weeks. If proving the origin of a fax is important, send a fax from that machine to your office—the output will include the phone number for that fax machine.

Before examining a fax machine, read the manual. In addition, as discussed in Chapter 9, make sure that you included language in your search warrant authorizing you to search fax machines.

Password cards

Some security systems depend upon a *one-time password* (also known as a *dynamic password*), meaning a password which changes after each use. These schemes are secure because any password which is lost or stolen becomes obsolete immediately.

These systems typically depend upon an electronic "card" given to the user with a display (similar in appearance to a cheap calculator). Every ten seconds or so, a password is displayed on that screen. The "card" is synchronized with the server, so that the server will accept the password appearing on the card if the user enters that password when logging on.

Other password cards are simpler—they contain a password embedded on a magnetic strip. The password never changes. The user places that card into a reader connected to a terminal to access the computer.

If you believe that the computer is protected by such a system, look for such cards, particularly in desk drawers and wallets.

Finally, do not overlook the copier. In some cases, such as those involving theft of information, it may be critical to determine whether copies were made from a particular copier.

Forensic analysts can make that determination by matching the questioned documents with 20 or so copies of a blank page made on the suspect's machine. (They match the marks made by flaws in the copier belt; each machine's flaws are different. And you thought DNA testing was impressive?) If such evidence is important to your case, write your search warrant to allow you to make blank copies on all of the machines at the scene.

Your next step is to look for backup tapes and other loose magnetic media. Backup tapes are often found in a cupboard close to a computer. If the suspect is a substantial business, it will store backup tapes off-site as protection against fire, flood, and earthquake—you should look for paperwork revealing the location of those tapes, and obtain a new warrant for that location immediately.

Loose magnetic media can be found everywhere. Do not ignore floppy disks which appear to contain software purchased from a commercial vendor (e.g., copies of WordPerfect). A suspect can reuse those disks to store different, and important, information.[16]

Search for passwords. You may not know whether a file has been encrypted until you try to read it back at the police station. Some companies share passwords among groups of employees, so do not confine yourself to a single area. If a computer is on a desk, search the drawers for scraps of paper. Check the underside of desk calendars as well.

Also check the exterior of the computer. Maintenance vendor tags (e.g., "ACME Computer Maintenance") will reveal the vendor who services that computer. That vendor may know the target's passwords or other back doors into the computer system.

6.24 Securing and documenting the location of computer evidence

After you have discovered computer evidence at the site, you need to document where you found it. You need to perform this task before you move or otherwise examine that evidence. Although there are as many ways to do this as there are investigators, consider the following method.

Immediately after securing the scene, and before you begin searching, walk around the site with a camcorder.[17] Make sure to videotape the screens of all computer monitors, whether they are on or off. The tape will show what the scene looked like before you began

---

16. Seizing what appears to be commercial software can raise objections from suspects that you have seized the lifeblood of their business. In that case, call the manufacturer, explain the situation, and obtain permission to make the suspect a copy of the software to be returned when you give back the original disks. In a pinch, such a copy may be legal as falling within the "fair use" exception to the copyright laws. Consult with your prosecutor or agency's attorney.

17. Note the recommendation in Chapter 9 that you obtain specific authorization in your search warrant to videotape a search scene.

your search and will go a long way toward refuting any claims that you "tore the place apart." If there are bookshelves near the computer with computer manuals, include those in your videotape.

Take a picture of each computer screen immediately. Many computer users use *screen savers*—programs which replace what is on the screen with a pretty picture if the keyboard has not been used for a certain amount of time. Some of those programs will not "surrender" the screen until you input a password. (If you are dealing with a single computer, you may consider tapping the Shift key every minute or so until you are able to examine or backup the machine.)

You may use your camcorder, a Polaroid, or a 35 mm camera with a shutter speed of 1/30 second or less (do not use the high shutter speed). Take a picture of the books near the computer, particularly software manuals and any identifying marks on those manuals. Those marks may identify the user, and the manuals may indicate that user's sophistication.

Photographing monitors can be tricky

Video screens constantly redraw the image appearing on the screen at very high speed. This can cause the image to appear on videotape as if someone had misadjusted the vertical hold on a TV screen. You may be unable to avoid this effect. When using a still camera, do not use a flash because it can "white out" the image. Rehearse with your camcorder and other photographic equipment at the police station before you take your show on the road.

If a video record is extremely important, consider purchasing an NTSC adapter for about $150. The NTSC clips in between the monitor and monitor cable, and directs the incoming signal into a camcorder directly.

Draw a diagram of the site on graph paper. It may be helpful to divide your diagram into areas (e.g., rooms or cubicles) marked with letters. For example, the president's office is Room A, the secretary's cubicle is Room B, and so on. Different rooms should have different letters. You can also organize your diagram around landmarks, such as desks in an office. If searching multiple sites, use a three-character designation.

Use one *finder*. The remaining investigators will perform the search; the *finder* will follow behind and record the location of each item discovered. During the search, the finder should mark the location of each item of evidence on the diagram (e.g., 1, 2, etc.).

Keep a running evidence log. Place a label on each item seized bearing the letter identifying the part of the site where it was found, along with a unique number or letter identifying that piece of evidence. (For example, the first piece of evidence "found" by the finder in a particular office might be labeled "C1.") Record a description of that evidence along with its identifier on the evidence log. The log should note whether you seized the item.

When you mark a computer, place the label in such a place that it can be photographed along with the computer. Mark a floppy disk by placing a diskette label at the top of the disk. (However, do not obscure any labels placed by the suspect. The contents of those labels may be evidence—put your label on the back of the disk if necessary.)

In addition to marking the location of the disk and its evidence number, you should label it with the case name. Your evidence log should state the proximity of the disk to the computer and to other disks (e.g., if it was in a particular box, note that fact). Place any seized loose magnetic media in a proper container.

Investigators with sufficient resources should consider using a laptop computer and a database (or even a spreadsheet) program to log evidence at the scene, and a printer to create a written record of that log. The laptop can also be used to print labels. The IRS and IACIS (described above) offer software designed to create such logs.

6.30   Deciding which computer evidence to seize

6.31   Hardware

Your most important decision is whether to seize the computer(s) containing magnetic media. Do not seize the computer unless the quality of the evidence you expect to obtain is worth the problems you will encounter.[18]

Your first consideration is whether you can move the hardware safely. Given that you might be sued for any breakage, attempting to move a minicomputer or network is a major problem and should be attempted only when absolutely necessary. At the very least, you will have to arrange for a professional mover before you execute your search warrant.

Let the MIS manager hear you call the moving company

If the MIS manager is reluctant to divulge passwords necessary to access the computer, and your search warrant allows you to seize it, allow the manager to listen to your call to the moving company.

Some managers have trouble believing that you really intend to seize their valuable system. In addition, the manager's fear of breakage may persuade him or her that cooperation is better than trusting the computer to your "ignorant" methods.

Do not threaten breakage, explicitly or otherwise—this might be interpreted as coercion. Reassure the manager that you will (as you must) do everything you can to protect against breakage. And make sure that you exercise due care in moving that system.

Another issue is the identity of the target. It is a lot easier to seize one computer from a juvenile than it is to take a company's entire

---

18. Also consider whether you can seize the computer pursuant to a state or federal forfeiture law. Computers used by narcotics dealers and pedophiles may be forfeitable. Some states, including California and Illinois, allow forfeiture of computers used to commit a "computer crime," or used as repositories for data obtained through the commission of a "computer crime." *See* California Penal Code Section 502.01; Illinois Compiled Statutes, Ch. 720, 5/16D-6. Illinois also allows forfeiture of computers used to commit non-computer crimes. *Id.*

computer system. You must determine whether the seizure will put the target out of business. Are you willing to put a company out of business, and can you afford to? You should consider several factors.

The type of business affected is important. You will have little concern about shutting down an ongoing criminal enterprise, such as a prostitution ring which stores its customer information on computers.

However, shutting down an entire legitimate business because one of its employees has misused corporate computers to break into other computers is almost always a mistake. Bad publicity about businesses going bankrupt does not reassure the high-technology and business community that you are protecting their interests.

The difficult issue is posed by the seemingly legitimate business which is engaged in criminal activity. Even if you are inclined to shut the target down, you may find that doing so is too much trouble. The largest problem is the target's threat of a lawsuit for damages from the seizure, including lost business.

Although a search pursuant to a search warrant should insulate public agencies from suit, the threat of legal action, coupled with allegations that the search was performed negligently or without probable cause, may convince a city attorney or city council to return the equipment immediately. In the long term, police agencies which consistently seize every computer in sight may lose the support of their municipalities.

Furthermore, the suspect may also threaten to sue the victim. Although a victim who in *good faith* informs law enforcement of facts constituting good cause is probably immune from suits for damages arising out of a subsequent search, defendants may threaten to sue the victim anyway, alleging that the victim lied to police in order to initiate a search which would put the defendants out of business.[19] This scenario is particularly likely in information theft cases, where the victim and suspects are usually competitors.

In addition to threatening a lawsuit, the target will usually go to court within a few days of the search asking for return of its computer equipment. If the court denies the request because the equipment is evidence, the target will demand copies of all seized media.

---

19. *See, e.g., Forro Precision v. IBM*, 673 F.2d 1045, 1051–1056 (9th Cir. 1982).

That request for copies is likely to be granted, leaving you with two problems.[20]

First, you need to copy all of the media you seized. Although the court will probably order the target to bear the cost of copying, you will still waste time arranging for that copying.[21] In information theft cases, that includes ensuring that the copying service signs a protective order.

Second, the seized media may contain information which you would prefer not to release (e.g., narcotics ledgers) or information stolen from your victim (e.g., trade secrets). This leads to an interesting problem. You will not know which data should be withheld from the target until after you have examined all of the seized information. But you may not be able to examine the evidence for weeks or even months, and the target will demand copies immediately, claiming that it is on the brink of insolvency. The court will probably order you to accelerate your examination of the data, even though you would normally give higher priority to other parts of your investigation. Unless you have virtually unlimited manpower, such an order could cripple your investigation.

6.32 Loose media

You should seize all loose magnetic and optical media responsive to your search warrant, unless doing so would close a legitimate business. Many criminals conceal their incriminating information on

---

20. The target is not entitled to substitute equipment for the hardware you seized. If police impound a car, the owner is not entitled to a "substitute car." Although the same principle could apply to magnetic or optical media, the difference is that the media can be copied. Courts are likely to order police to make copies of seized data, at the defendant's expense.

21. *See Premises Known as ... Statler Towers v. United States*, 787 F.2d 796 (2nd Cir. 1986); *United States v. Freedman*, 688 F.2d 1364 (11th Cir. 1982); *United States v. Hoskins*, 639 F.Supp. 512 (W.D.N.Y. 1986) (where one party is indigent). Note that *Statler Towers* essentially invites the defense to use a request for free copies as grounds for litigating the propriety of the search warrant via a motion for return of property. The suspect will argue that the government should return property improperly seized, and that a hearing is necessary to determine whether the government's warrant was proper.

floppy disks. If there are only a handful of floppy disks at the scene, you may wish to examine the media on site (on your own laptop) instead of seizing it. If you do so, use an anti-virus program to scan each diskette before examining it.

6.33 Documentation

As discussed in Chapter 9, you should include authorization in your search warrant to seize all computer manuals describing the operation of computers and software. These manuals are important because they:

- indicate what software resides on the computer;

- help you operate that software;

- may contain handwritten passwords; and

- may contain the name of the suspect, identifying him (or another) as the person who used the computer and the software to produce incriminating evidence.

6.40 Seizing the computer

After deciding whether to seize a computer at the site, you must next decide whether to operate it at the site before you take it away. Again, in an ideal world you will make this decision before writing your search warrant.

If you are not seizing the computer, you must operate it at the site in order to obtain any evidence at all. Even if you are going to seize the computer, you may still want to operate it in order to verify that it works, look for security programs installed by the user, make a backup copy of the hard disk, or seek additional evidence.

In some cases you will have little choice. For example, the computer(s) may be too big to move. In that case, operating the computer is your only chance to obtain evidence.

In other cases, your decision will involve a trade-off. The costs and benefits of each trade-off depend upon many variables, including the type of computer system you find at the scene and your level of expertise. Do not forget this sad truth about searching computers: *whatever action you take will often result in the loss of some evidence. However, that same action may preserve other evidence which you would otherwise lose.*

In order to understand and evaluate those trade-offs, you must understand how computers store data, and how such data can be eliminated or preserved depending upon your actions. You must also understand how criminals familiar with computer technology can hide data and set traps for the unwary investigator.

The following section will discuss those subjects. A later section will discuss how to decide which strategy makes sense in light of your situation, and provide guidance on how to implement that strategy.

6.41   How computers store data

Some of the following information is explained in more detail in Appendix D. The next few sections present a somewhat simplified explanation of a more technical subject.

Data can be stored in various places in a computer, including within RAM (random access memory), floppy disks, and hard disks. The data in each repository can be eliminated easily by an unwary user.

RAM refers to memory chips located on the motherboard or on other circuit boards within the computer. It contains the information the user is working with at the moment (e.g., a document or spreadsheet). If the computer is on when you arrive, there is a good chance that some information about the suspect's activities is in RAM. Information stored in RAM disappears when the power is turned off.

Floppy disks are identical to hard disks for purposes of this chapter, with one obvious exception: unless the floppy disk is in the computer, searching the computer will not affect data stored on the floppy disk.

6.41–a   How hard disks and floppy drives are organized

Hard disks and floppy drives can be thought of as phonograph records. Data is recorded on *tracks* on the circular magnetics surface. Each track is divided into *sectors*.

Although the hard drive is divided into sectors, there are so many sectors that DOS often keeps track of files by dealing with groups of contiguous sectors (sectors next to each other on the disk) called *clusters*. Depending upon the size of the disk, a cluster can be made up of four or more sectors.

Data in a computer consists of 1's and 0's. Each 1 or 0 is a *bit*. Eight bits are organized into *bytes*, which in turn are grouped into multiple bit *words* (16 bit, 32 bit, etc.).

When you save your work on a computer, the computer stores the data in *files* on the hard disk. When the microprocessor asks for data, the hard disk retrieves the requested data from one or more clusters.

The clusters making up a file are not always stored next to each other on the disk. In order to cram more information on the hard disk, files are often broken up, and the bytes making up those files are scattered among several clusters all over the hard disk.

In order to keep track of the location of all of the data on the hard disk, DOS maintains a *file allocation table* (*FAT*). The computer consults this table and a directory to determine the location of every cluster containing data which is part of a file. When you ask for a file, DOS consults the FAT and the directory, and then goes out to the hard disk and collects each byte of data requested from the sectors contained in those clusters. DOS will not write the contents of a file to a cluster which the FAT shows is already occupied by another file.

6.41–b   Erasing a file does not erase the data contained in that file

Why do you care about this information? When a file is erased, the first thing DOS does is to change the FAT to eliminate the pointers which indicate which clusters contain the data making up that file. It also replaces the first character of the file name in the directory with a special character which reflects that change.

But DOS does not erase the actual data. That data is still there and can be retrieved by certain software utilities, most notably Norton Utilities (using the UnErase program).

However, your ability to recover data gradually disappears if anyone continues to use the computer. In the normal course of events,

DOS will write new data to the same clusters as the "erased" data; this is called *overwriting* the data. (Overwriting occurs because the FAT entry which marked the cluster as having been used has been changed to inform DOS that the space is unused.)

For example, this overwriting occurs automatically if you instruct the computer to save a file bearing the same name as the erased file. If you have been working on a file for, say, 30 minutes, and then save it, DOS will take the new data to be saved and write it over some or all of the data which constituted your old file. It is normally impossible to retrieve information which has been overwritten.[22]

Even if the computer owner works on different files, DOS will eventually overwrite the otherwise recoverable "erased" file with new data, making that data impossible to recover. One way this can happen is if the software you use to examine the computer writes to the disk. As discussed in the next few sections, this means that you must take precautions when operating a seized computer to avoid overwriting data.

6.41–c   Slack space

An important twist on the "overwrite problem" is that DOS can create nooks and crannies which contain "erased" data even after a file containing that data has been partially overwritten. These nooks and crannies exist in what is called *slack space*.

Normally, a user stores data on the hard disk by saving a file. As noted above, DOS keeps track of data by grouping sectors into clusters, and will reserve each cluster for the contents of a particular file. This is important because files do not fit neatly within sectors.

For example, assume that you save a file which is 2400 bytes long. A sector on a typical hard drive contains 512 bytes. Four sectors will hold 2048 bytes; five sectors will hold 2560 bytes.

---

22. There are two important exceptions to this rule. First, some programs, including Norton Utilities and a utility within Windows called Sentry, can be configured to prevent "permanent" erasure of files. These programs can save copies of otherwise "deleted" files in a special portion of the hard disk. Second, *slack space*, discussed in the next section, can contain information stored in files which were partially overwritten.

Writing the file to five sectors will leave extra space in the fifth sector. That extra space is called *slack space*. Since DOS will not write more than one file in each cluster, this slack space will not be filled with data from another file.[23]

Slack space is important for two reasons. First, a clever criminal can store data in slack space by using software such as Norton Utilities. The beauty of this method is that data stored in this way will not be revealed through normal use of the computer because the FAT will show only that a particular file resides in that cluster. (Of course, this assumes that the user prefers to hide that data rather than encrypt it, which is unlikely.)

More important, overwriting a file will not eliminate any of the data stored in slack space. Thus, overwriting a large file with a small file may still leave information from the larger file in slack space.

For example, consider the case of a suspect writing a letter setting forth the details of a conspiracy. The suspect writes a draft of a letter outlining the conspiracy and saves it to a file. The suspect later works on that letter, eliminates some of the incriminating details, and saves it under the same file name.

That "save" overwrote the earlier file, but since that new letter is smaller, bits of the old letter contained in sectors which were not used by DOS to store the new letter still exist. Some important evidence may exist in that slack space.

Slack space may affect your choice of strategy in two ways, both of which are discussed in more detail below. First, you may want to use special software which searches for information contained anywhere on the disk, including slack space.

Second, not all backup software is created equal. For the moment, suffice to say that you will have to make a special effort to obtain a backup copy of the magnetic media which includes the information in slack space.

---

23. This rule also means that slack space is often larger than a portion of one sector. Most hard drives group four sectors into each cluster. Taking our example of the 2400 byte file, that file would fit within two clusters of 2048 bytes each. The first cluster would have no slack space; the second file would have 1696 bytes of slack space. Indeed, it is also possible to hide data in sectors of the hard disk not assigned to a file. (This chapter also refers to those areas as slack space.)

6.41–d   Encryption

As we have seen, a suspect can hide files in slack space. However, it is far more effective to store the data where everyone can see it, but not read it. This technique is called *encryption*.

Encryption is simply the coding of data into information which cannot be read by people. DOS normally translates the bits and bytes contained in each file into English characters. Encryption ensures that the English characters produced by DOS are encoded into what appears to be gibberish. Decoding requires a special key, or password.

Do not despair if you find encrypted data—you may be able to read it using the right tools. Call your nearby state or federal law enforcement agency for assistance.

For example, one basic encryption scheme includes the password at the very "front," or *header*, of the encrypted file itself. That password is concealed because it, too, is encrypted. However, it is a simple matter for an expert to defeat that scheme.[24] Other encryption schemes can be broken by using standard cryptanalysis.

One company sells software which breaks encryption schemes used by applications such as WordPerfect, Microsoft Word, Professional Write, Q & A, Excel, Lotus 1-2-3, Quattro Pro, and DataPerfect.[25] The programs are a few hundred dollars apiece.

Moreover, businesses are discovering that encryption is a very dangerous tool. What happens if the only employee who knows the password becomes disgruntled, or even dies? The company can be held hostage. Many software vendors are now looking to design "back doors" into their encryption schemes to ensure that company files remain available to management. Therefore, consider calling the software vendor to determine whether the company can break its own encryption scheme.

---

24. The expert encrypts a blank document using another password. Using Norton's DiskEdit, the expert overwrites the header on the encrypted document with the header on the blank document with the known password. The encrypted document is now protected by the expert's password, which the expert uses to access that document.

25. Contact AccessData, 87 East 600 South, Orem, UT 84058, 801-224-6970. The programs break passwords within seconds.

Can you force a suspect to tell you the password?

Courts have yet to address whether the government may compel suspects to disclose passwords. The Fifth Amendment prohibits the government from compelling a person to produce "nontestimonial evidence," such as the location of stolen property. However, suspects can be forced to provide incriminating documents in their possession, such as tax returns. This includes materials in their *constructive possession* (i.e., materials over which they have control). For example, the Supreme Court has held that suspects can be required to give their consent to a foreign bank releasing their bank records. *See Doe v. United States*, 487 U.S. 201 (1988).

The theory behind compelling passwords is that it is similar to compelling production of any other information, such as documents. Prosecutors may argue that since the password exists, the suspect may be compelled to produce it (with the restriction that prosecutors may not inform the trier of fact that the defendant knew the password).

Defense attorneys opposed to production will argue that the password exists only within the suspect's mind. They will argue that it is more like a combination to a lock than a physical key to that lock. While the encrypted data may exist in physical form, the combination does not. *See Doe*, at 210 n. 9.

Prosecutors should counter that the password is merely a description of the physical configuration of the data and that any physical information, or a description thereof, may be compelled from a suspect. Prosecutors may argue that it is illogical to allow suspects to hide documentary evidence simply because the "key" is a mnemonic.

For now, the best that can be said is that this issue is undecided. Police and prosecutors should proceed with caution.

Note that this is a delicate problem—companies do not want their customers to believe that their data is insecure.

Of course, there are some encryption schemes which cannot be broken without a supercomputer, and some that may be simply unbreakable with current techniques. But you should always contact state and federal agencies when you encounter encrypted data—you never know when someone will discover a way to defeat a particular method of encryption.[26]

If you are stuck, look for passwords used by the suspect in other contexts. If the suspect uses a password to dial into a computer at work, try that password on his or her system at home. Other possibilities include:

- the names of the suspect's relatives, friends, and pets;

- the suspect's residential address and telephone number;

- the suspect's driver's license and social security numbers; and

- the suspect's PIN (personal identification number) for an ATM.

You might even use a "dictionary program" (discussed in Chapter 4) to discover the password.

Pay particular attention to any backup media. Suspects may encrypt their hard disks, but transfer or archive files in a decrypted form. Even after they have uploaded data to their computer, they may forget to wipe the floppy disks, leaving the "clear" data for you to find by using Norton's UnErase (discussed later in this chapter).

Finally, do not discard encrypted data just because you cannot read it. You may find the password or a confederate willing to disclose it.

Always seize and keep the data until the case is closed. A defendant who insists on the return of at least a copy of encrypted data *might* be required to prove that the data actually belongs to him or her. (How do we know? We can't read it!) This is particularly true in

---

26. And perhaps the NSA will share it with you. However, it never hurts to ask the FBI or the Secret Service whether they can help you. You might also call SEARCH or IACIS (see § 6.14 above) and ask for assistance.

computer intrusion cases, where some of the data may have been stolen from other computers.

More important, encryption is evidence of an attempt to hide something. Although the issue has not been decided in any published court decisions, a jury *might* be allowed to determine whether encryption itself, combined with the other facts of your case, is evidence of a consciousness of guilt.

Finally, if you have enough evidence to proceed to trial, a defendant who testifies at trial waives any Fifth Amendment privilege. The prosecutor may demand the password from the defendant on the witness stand. Although the defendant's reaction to the request should be reward enough, obtaining the password is even better, as prosecutors may set up the computer and allow the jury to look at the hidden data as part of an in-court demonstration.[27]

6.42 Choosing your strategy

You have a choice of strategies when deciding whether to operate a computer at the site:

- *Pull the plug.* Seize the computer for further analysis at your lab without operating it first.

- *Hardware check.* If the computer is running, insert a floppy disk containing a "clean" operating system (explained below), extract certain information about how the computer is configured, and then "pull the plug."

- *Backup.* If the computer is running, reboot with a clean operating system, backup the data onto clean media for later analysis at your lab, and then "pull the plug."

- *Search on-site.* Operate the computer to search for evidence at the site. You may, or may not, subsequently seize the computer.

---

27. Prosecutors may want to obtain the password and examine the data outside the presence of the jury beforehand in order to avoid embarrassment if the data is innocuous.

Table 6–1: Pros and cons of different strategies

Strategy	Consider this strategy when	Advantages	Disadvantages
Pull the plug	Investigators lack experience with computers, or do not want to operate the computer at the scene.	Avoids mistakes at the scene. Easiest for investigators to implement, and saves time.	Do *not* pull the plug on anything larger than a PC, as you may damage it. May be unable to reboot a PC because security programs have "locked" the disk.
Hardware check	Computer is on, and investigators are familiar with computers.	If the computer fails to work, shields against claim that investigators damaged it in transit.	Takes additional time, and requires expertise.
Backup	The computer is on, and the data is valuable.	May avoid civil liability if the computer is damaged in transit.	Very time-consuming, and risks destruction of evidence.
Search on-site	Investigators are not going to seize the computer. Investigators need to find evidence immediately.	The quickest way to obtain evidence in a fast-moving investigation.	Ensures destruction of some evidence (usually insignificant), and increases the risk of destroying critical evidence.

This section examines the theory behind each strategy, along with its advantages and disadvantages. Before beginning that analysis, however, it is important to note two points.

First, there is no foolproof strategy. Each strategy has its drawbacks. Second, each situation is different. Your choice of strategy will depend in part upon the facts of your case. In most cases, your best choice is to pull the plug, perhaps after checking the integrity of the hardware. This allows you to make a copy of the data in the quiet of your lab, upload the data onto a "clean" machine, and analyze that copy without fear of tainting the original evidence.

However, you might backup the data before seizing the computer if your suspect is an employee in an "innocent" business and that business needs the data on that machine for its operations. Of course, if all of the records you need are on a mainframe, you may need to camp out at the business for a week while you search that computer.

6.42–a   Pulling the plug

Pulling the plug concedes the field to the suspect in order to gain a later home-field advantage. The theory is that the search scene is often chaotic and can lead to your making mistakes which you would avoid by searching the computer at your lab. For example, you are far more likely to trigger a trap set by the suspect if you examine the computer on-site. Moreover, operating the computer requires additional time you may not want, or be able, to spend at the scene because you need to document each step you take in examining the computer.

6.42–a(1)   Advantages of pulling the plug

Pulling the plug provides an important degree of security at the site. By pulling the plug on a PC (*not* on a minicomputer or network), you ensure that you do not alter any data stored on magnetic media.

Once you begin operating the computer, the chances of your altering data increase, even if you only overwrite certain temporary files created by the suspect immediately before you executed the search warrant. As discussed later in this chapter, defense attorneys have less fertile ground to explore if you do nothing more than turn off the computer.

Pulling the plug saves time. Backing up a system at the scene can be a painstaking procedure. In complex investigations, it is often easier simply to pack up the computer and worry about its contents after you return to the station.

Finally, pulling the plug is most useful where the officers on the scene are not the experts who will search the computer back at the lab. *Many police departments will want to institute a pull the plug policy which all officers can understand and implement.*[28] Pulling the plug is also a good alternative to trying to find an expert when you are executing a warrant at 2 A.M. and have just found a computer with which you are unfamiliar.

Note that you will almost always pull the plug of a computer that is not running when you arrive on the scene. If you are going to operate that computer, you should do so at your computer lab.

6.42–a(2)   Disadvantages of pulling the plug

Pulling the plug may damage a minicomputer or network, and should be avoided unless absolutely necessary. If you are going to pull the plug on any computer other than a PC, you must obtain expert assistance.

Pulling the plug on any computer may eliminate potentially important evidence.[29] Even on single PCs, you will immediately lose all evidence stored in RAM, including whatever the suspect was working on when you arrived at the scene. You must also delay your

---

28. The National Institute of Justice, the research and training arm of the U.S. Department of Justice, has prepared a video with the assistance of the Baltimore County Police Department called "Crime Scene Computer." As of this writing, you can obtain that video by calling 800-841-3420. The video demonstrates pulling the plug on a personal computer. Although the approach suggested is outdated, the video may be useful in acquainting officers with general concepts involved in seizing computers.

29. This is particularly true for any system running UNIX. UNIX encourages the use of multiple windows, each of which contains a separate program. Pulling the plug will eliminate evidence appearing in several running applications. It will also prevent you from easily determining the location of relevant data. When you encounter a UNIX system (just type "ls-sail"—if you get a list of files, you are in a UNIX system), type "mount" to obtain a list of drives currently in use. At this point, if you do not know UNIX, find an expert immediately.

examination until you get the computer back to the lab, hampering your ability to quickly follow up leads suggested by data contained within that computer.

Finally, and most important, you risk losing your ability to search for information when you reboot the computer at your lab. Moving computers can damage them. If you move the computer without backing up the hard drive, and the move destroys the contents of the drive, you lose your evidence. You also make it more likely that the computer owner will sue you for negligence.

Another problem if the computer is on is that certain commercially available software programs, most notably Symantec's Disklock and the Diskreet program contained within Norton Utilities, can be configured to "close" disk drives automatically when the power is turned off. The programs are designed to eliminate your ability to access those drives without a password once the computer is turned off. Certain computers, such as many portables and some of IBM's ValuePoint computers, include security systems which are intended to prevent users from using the keyboard or mouse without a password.

Circumventing these security systems after they have "closed" is, at best, annoying and time-consuming. If you need to hire an expert, it is expensive. At worst, it may be impossible to access the protected data. Even though experts are always developing new ways to break security systems, you can never be sure that there will be a "fix" for the scheme you encounter. As these security programs become more common, the benefits of pulling the plug on an operating computer may be outweighed by the risk of losing evidence.

6.42–b   Hardware check

This strategy simply adds a few steps to the pull the plug procedure. If the computer is running, you run a few simple programs to determine whether the computer is functioning properly. You may also decide to retrieve certain information which will allow you to operate that computer if it is damaged in transit, or if its battery runs low while you are holding it as evidence pending trial. Finally, you may look for security programs, and if they are present, backup the computer on the spot before you pull the plug.

6.42–b(1)   Advantages of conducting a hardware check

Nothing is more frustrating than pulling the plug on a "powered up" computer at the scene, carefully transporting it back to your lab, and turning it on the next week to begin your analysis, only to discover that it does not work. Maybe you are greeted with a message that the operating system cannot access the hard drive. Maybe you see nothing at all.

Was the computer damaged in transit? Was there an intermittent problem with the hard disk which you only discovered once you unpacked the computer at your lab? Did the graphics card malfunction? Do you owe the computer owner a new computer?

Performing a hardware check at the scene goes a long way toward eliminating these infrequent, but truly depressing, moments in high-technology crime investigation. The hardware check typically consists of running Norton's SYSINFO and Disk Doctor programs, and DOS's CHKDSK command. Finally, checking the AUTOEXEC.BAT and CONFIG.SYS files may reveal the presence of security programs and traps.

6.42–b(2)   Disadvantages of conducting a hardware check

Investigators who know nothing about computers should hesitate before doing anything other than pulling the plug. If you do not know what you are doing, do nothing more than absolutely necessary. Investigators who understand the references to Norton and CHKDSK, are familiar with obtaining CMOS information, and are willing to spend a few extra minutes at the scene should perform at least part of the hardware check described later in this chapter before pulling the plug.

6.42–c   On-site backup

On-site backup means operating the computer to backup the data contained on the hard drive. It is an insurance policy for the data stored on the hard drive.

The theory here is that most of the computer evidence is stored on the hard drive when you execute your warrant, and that you should obtain a copy of it before any of the bad things described above can occur.

6.42–c(1) Advantages of on-site backup

The main advantage of on-site backup is that you immediately secure a copy of the evidence located on the hard drive. In the event of an accident, you will have an extra copy of the data for analysis. You will also be able to provide the computer owner with a copy of any destroyed data. Although there are no published cases on the duty of care owed to the owner of a computer by a police department seizing that computer, there is probably a significant risk of liability in the event that police destroy data.[30]

In cases where the data is valuable, you should consider backing up the system, preferably in the owner's presence. (Do not allow a suspect to do it for you under any circumstances.) On-site backup gives the owner (who may be a suspect, or a "friendly" employer of a suspect) an opportunity to suggest precautions you should take to safeguard the computer and its data. The owner will not be able to complain if an undisclosed trap or unusual feature causes damage.

Another advantage is that defense attorneys may have less ammunition to argue that your search was clumsy or vindictive if you attempted to backup the suspect's data.

Finally, the suspect may be intimidated by the computer literacy of the police who backup the computer. Suspects, particularly teenage crackers, occasionally decide to confess quickly in hopes of leniency after seeing a computer-literate police officer backup their system. Some suspects believe that a police officer competent enough to backup the computer will eventually find the incriminating evidence.

6.42–c(2) Disadvantages of on-site backup

As discussed above, it takes more time to backup a computer than it does to pull the plug. The chaos of the search scene may cause you

---

30. *See* footnote 1.

to make a mistake in backing up the computer (e.g., missing a second hard disk drive or disk volume) which would not occur at the lab.[31] You might also trigger traps which could destroy data.

In extreme cases, backing up the computer may create too much evidence. The prosecution, including police agencies, must provide the defense with an opportunity to inspect and copy all materials seized during the execution of a search warrant. Although some courts will require non-indigent defendants to pay for making copies of evidence seized, the prosecution must nonetheless keep track of all that evidence and coordinate any copying. The burden becomes even heavier if some data is proprietary.

In very large cases where experts can ensure that the suspect's equipment will be seized and stored properly, it may be preferable not to create thousands of megabytes of backup media which must be properly accounted for, stored, and produced for inspection. The better course may be to require the defense to specify which backups they wish created from the seized computer equipment. This procedure will result in fewer backup tapes.

6.42–d Searching the computer at the scene

The theory behind searching the computer for evidence is that the rewards outweigh the risks. A quick probe into the contents of the hard drive can provide immediate information vital to a fast-breaking investigation. Evidence which could be found in an immediate search may otherwise be lost if the machine is damaged in a subsequent seizure or the backup fails.

---

31. If you do not copy all of the information when you perform your backup, the defense may claim that evidence which does not appear on the backup was added to the suspect's hard drive after police seized it. Granted, it is unlikely that only non-incriminating material would be copied in the backup, or that a jury is going to believe that police planted evidence. And the fact that the backup did not copy all of the evidence on the hard drive does not make the hard drive inadmissible, any more than the failure of a photocopier to clearly copy pages of a narcotics ledger would prevent prosecutors from admitting the ledger.

Nonetheless, it is never a good idea to give a defense attorney an additional defense, however implausible.

6.42–d(1)   Advantages of searching the computer at the scene

There are only four situations in which you may wish to search the computer for evidence before pulling the plug or backing it up.

1.   You are leaving the computer and its data behind.

If you are not going to take any evidence with you and are willing to run the risk of erasing data belonging to the suspect, you may as well search the computer. You may find important evidence in a particular file, and the possibility of damaging or losing evidence is less critical because you were not planning to take any evidence with you anyway. (Of course, you still may be liable for any damage you cause.)

2.   There is critical evidence in RAM.

If the suspect is working on narcotics or bookmaking ledgers in WordPerfect, do take the time to print that file and download it to a floppy before proceeding to backup the system. You may even want to scroll through that file on the screen. (Note that Windows applications often display the last five files opened by the user.)

3.   The computer is connected to a network.

If the computer is connected to a network, you may wish to use it to search the contents of the server. Although backing up the server first is feasible, many servers have gigabytes of data. You will almost certainly want to search for particular files rather than collecting megabytes of data you cannot use but will have to copy for the defense. Let your expert be your guide.

4.   Some investigations are not worth the time and effort required to seize and/or backup the suspect's computer.

You may be able to wrap up an investigation in 15 minutes by searching for, and immediately copying, certain key files off of the suspect's computer. As discussed later in this chapter, seizing a computer properly takes time, as does transporting it to the station and storing it properly. Even backing up the data can take hours.

If you believe that the computer probably contains very little, if any, useful evidence, you may wish to risk losing data in return for time to complete other portions of your investigation. Remember that a computer is nothing more than a container of evidence. Some evidence is worth more time and effort than other evidence. So long as you do not deliberately damage the computer or erase data, there is nothing wrong with forgoing elaborate evidence-handling procedures in exchange for the opportunity to gather and analyze more important non-computer evidence.

6.42–d(2) Disadvantages of searching a computer at the scene

First, there is the remote possibility you will trigger a trap while examining the computer, and lose some "original" evidence off of the hard disk. If you did not make a backup, or the backup was defective, you have lost that evidence.

The main disadvantage to searching the computer is that you give up the best of all possible worlds: the opportunity to search the suspect's data on a separate lab machine without any risk of destroying evidence. As discussed later in this chapter, in an ideal world you will take the computer back to your lab, make a backup copy of the data, and upload *that* copy of the suspect's data onto a "clean," and more powerful, lab machine for analysis.[32] If something goes wrong, only the last copy of the suspect's data can be damaged; you still have a backup copy and the original hard drive.

Once you search the computer, you may change the original hard drive forever; it cannot be restored to its pre-search state. Although, as discussed later in this chapter, such alteration does not prevent you from using the relevant portions of that hard drive in evidence, altering evidence does create the potential for legal mischief where none existed previously.

Another problem is that your search may eliminate useful evidence in slack space. As you search the computer, you will probably

---

32. As noted in another section below, it may be necessary to use the suspect's computer for analysis (i.e., where the computer has special hardware which you cannot replicate in your lab machine). This step is always a last resort.

create temporary files, or save new ones, to slack space. You may overwrite useful evidence contained in that slack space. Although the overwhelming majority of cases will rise and fall on the documents and spreadsheets found in the suspect's current files, occasionally evidence in slack space is useful.

6.43   Implementing your strategy

Once again: you are always better off having an expert help you. None of these procedures is without risk. Reading this chapter will not make you an expert—you need to get hands on training by taking one of the courses mentioned on page 240.

6.43–a   Pulling the plug

This section assumes that you are working with a PC.[33] It also assumes that you have checked for physical traps which could be triggered by a loss of power.

Consider the following procedure.

1.   Exit all application programs.

If you are in Windows, exit by typing Alt-F4 until you are at the DOS prompt. (If prompted to "save" a file, select the "cancel" button, and use the "save as" command to save the file to a floppy with a slightly different name.) Remember that Windows allows more than

---

33. You should probably never attempt to pull the plug on a minicomputer or network, but if you must, make sure that your expert *uses extreme caution*. First, ask the owner for the appropriate steps to take in turning off the computer, and, if possible, call the manufacturer to ensure that those directions are correct. If the owner is completely uncooperative, look for a Rolodex near the computer, and find the suspect's vendor for the system. You may find the vendor willing to respond to the scene and shut the system down.

If after considering the *grave* risks, you decide to pull the plug on a minicomputer or network running UNIX, consider changing the password in *root* (to *POLICE* or something similar) so that you can access the computer when you plug it back in at your agency. You should also consult with an expert to determine whether it is necessary to isolate the minicomputer or server for about 20 to 30 minutes to ensure that the information in the *cache* (a buffer in which data is stored for future use) has been written to the hard drive.

one program to run at a time. You should consider "paging" through the various applications programs running in Windows before exiting the operating system. (Remember to photograph the screen first.)

If the computer is running DOS, terminate the program running on the screen (probably after examining what the suspect was doing when you arrived). If it is a commercial application, exit it as provided for by that program. If it is not, first try the Escape ("Esc") key.

If this does not work, try pushing the Control ("Ctrl") and Break ("Brk" or "Pause") keys simultaneously. If this does not work, push the Control and "C" keys simultaneously. Also try pressing "Alt-X" and "Ctrl-Q." If you are still unsuccessful, you may have to pull the plug out of the wall (see Step #3 below).

If you are dealing with an Apple computer, select SHUTDOWN from the top menu bar.

If you have encountered a computer being used as a bulletin board, check whether the menu on the screen provides you with the option of changing the SYSOP log-in password. If so, try to view the old password (which the suspect may have used to protect other programs or files). Then accept the option of choosing a new password. If you are unable to change the password, attempt to exit the bulletin board program normally before proceeding.

Note that federal privacy laws protect bulletin board systems. Read Chapter 8 carefully before searching or seizing a computer which is being used as a BBS.

2. *If you are examining a machine over five years old and have brought disk parking software, place the disk with that software in the floppy drive and run it.*

Disk parking repositions the hard disk so that the heads are away from the magnetic media and are less likely to be damaged if jarred. DISKMON.EXE, included in Norton Utilities, includes a park command. Hard drives on newer systems (since 1990 or so) have "self-parking" heads, so you need not be alarmed if you do not have such software.

3. *Pull the power cord out of the wall by the plug (or from the surge suppressor, as the case may be).*

Do not turn the computer off by using the on/off switch. Place masking or electrical tape over the power plug on the computer to remind officers not to use that computer once it has been seized.

4. *If the power to the monitor and the computer does not go out, check for external and internal battery units.*

Do not proceed until you confirm that the computer is powered down.

5. *Label each cable entering or exiting the computer.*

If a cable is not attached at both ends, label it accordingly. Attach a corresponding label for each port of the computer the cable is plugged into. If a port is unused, label it as such.

After you have labeled all of the cables and ports, take another photograph of the computer. Photograph the front *and* rear of the computer. If the wiring is complex, consider drawing a diagram. The more information you can get, the better—you may not try to set up this computer for analysis until days or weeks after the search, when your memory of the scene will have faded.

One training organization divides its students into two teams and has each "take down" a computer. When they are done, the teams are then (and *only* then) told that their next assignment is to reassemble the computer disassembled by the other team using that team's notes and labeling. The results are often amusing. You will not be amused if you take this task lightly.

Carefully unplug each cable you have labeled. If possible, keep the cable attached to its peripheral. You should consider taking a photograph after the computer has been disassembled.

6. *Place a blank, write-protected, bootable diskette in each floppy disk drive, and use masking tape to gently tape it into place.*

Place a separate piece of tape labeled "EVIDENCE, DO NOT TOUCH," on the front of the case. Again, this will discourage accidental usage.

Tell everyone involved that using the seized computer for any purpose could destroy your case even if no evidence is disturbed. (As explained later in this chapter, this is usually not the case, but you should not take unnecessary chances.)

7. *Cover the keyboard with cardboard, and tape that cardboard down with evidence tape.*

This precaution is intended to protect the keyboard during transport and to deter curious officers back at the station from operating the computer.[34]

8. *If you have seized loose peripherals, label them as not having been connected to anything.*

You do not want to waste time trying to connect something which was never connected, and a defense attorney can make you look careless for having tried to do so.

9. *Move the computer.*

For minicomputers and/or workstations, you should use a moving company experienced in transporting computers. In addition, you should look for a company with plenty of insurance, so that it is able to pay for any damage it causes to the computer. (You should contact such a company *before* serving your warrant.)

Make sure that the movers maintain the computer in the same position as it was sitting on the desktop. Keep computers which were on their sides on their sides and computers which were upended (i.e., in *tower* configurations) in that same position.

If you are seizing several systems, consider placing each computer in its own padded box; label the box with information about the system and the location from which it was seized. (If you are searching a residence, check the attic, basement, and garage; the suspect may have kept the original packing box for the computer system.)

---

34. Fingerprint powder can damage keyboards and magnetic media. After backing up media, officers might consider using superglue fuming to lift prints.

Use padding in your vehicle whenever possible. Do *not* leave the computer or any peripheral in the vehicle any longer than absolutely necessary, and never leave it exposed to the sun (heat can destroy magnetic media).[35]

10. Store the computer in a safe environment.

Keep the computer away from magnets, speakers (such as those in boom boxes), and radio equipment (e.g., police transmitting equipment, including microwave towers). Keep the computer in a temperature controlled room (i.e., a room with a thermostat, like an office, rather than a warehouse or storage shed). Keep it at least several feet away from heating or cooling ducts. Make sure the room is relatively free from cigarette smoke, dust, and insects. If you are comfortable in the room, the computer will usually be "comfortable" as well.

Do not place objects on top of the computer (except the monitor). Do not plug in the computer unless it is actually in use. Do not allow any liquids in the room, or at least within three yards of the computer.

Make sure the room is kept under lock and key at all times.

11. If you operate that computer again, it is good practice to turn the computer off, either at the surge suppressor or at the on/ off switch.

Remember that you literally pulled the plug to turn the power off. If you simply plug the machine back in, you will turn the machine on. Booting up the computer in this way could conceivably, in a poorly designed system, create a power surge that could damage equipment and data. (This is nitpicking, but it never hurts to do it the right way.)

The right way is to plug in the computer after it has been turned off, and then turn on the computer the way the user would—from the on/off switch or the surge suppressor.

---

35. There is some concern in the law enforcement community that police radios can damage data. Therefore, you should consider not transporting a computer in any vehicle with an operating police radio. Do not place CPUs close to radio units in the trunk of a police car, and avoid transmitting while transporting the computer.

12. *Before leaving the scene, try to talk to the owner of the*
    computer about the system.

Remember to give appropriate *Miranda* warnings, and note that asking the suspect about the computer system can produce incriminating answers.

Pulling the plug can leave you with a "dead" machine in your lab with no owner to talk to. Ask suspects at the scene for "cooperation," namely, passwords and other information about the computer. Suspects may give you that information out of concern that you may damage their computer inadvertently, or simply to obtain leniency.[36] If they do not help you access their computer, you *may* be able to use their refusal to cooperate as evidence (courts have not decided this issue).

6.43–b   Hardware check

You should use an expert to perform a hardware check. Some of the steps listed below are most appropriate when you have reason to believe that the computer owner has rigged the computer or taken other steps to hide data.

This checklist assumes that the computer is on when you arrive. If the computer is off, it is usually better to pull the plug and conduct a hardware check back at your lab.

In order to perform a hardware check, you should have a floppy disk loaded with the following programs:

- MS-DOS 5.0 system files (IO.SYS, MSDOS.SYS, COM-MAND.COM, AUTOEXEC.BAT, CONFIG.SYS). You can transfer these files by choosing the "make a disk bootable" option in Norton Utilities. If you are searching a newer machine, you should also have MS-DOS 6.22 system files on another disk. As discussed below, you may need different boot disks with different versions of DOS.

---

36. Police who improperly extract that information by threatening dire consequences to the suspect's computer or data may find all resulting evidence suppressed on due process grounds.

- CHKDSK (MS-DOS)

- The following programs from Norton Utilities:

  •• NDD.EXE

  •• DISKMON.EXE

  •• SYSINFO.EXE

  •• DISKEDIT.EXE (this is optional)

Write-protect the floppy to ensure that viruses on the computer do not infect your boot disk. Consider booking this disk into evidence. If a suspect claims that you inserted a virus (or planted evidence) while examining the computer, you will have the clean disk available.

Take the following steps after you have exited all application programs and inserted your write-protected floppy disk into the A: drive.[37]

1. *Type A:\COMMAND, and press Enter.*

The computer should check the A: drive, and report that it is running MS-DOS 5.0 (or MS-DOS 6.22, if you used that version of DOS). The purpose of this step is to evade a trap which depends upon the user's running an altered COMMAND.COM file. If you receive an error message: "Incorrect DOS version," try different versions of DOS until you find one which works. If you are still unsuccessful, consider pulling the plug, or continuing with this procedure despite the increased risk.[38]

---

37. If the suspect was at the keyboard, and has left you at the DOS prompt, consider typing F3. Typing F3 results in MS-DOS displaying the command previously typed. You should then type the [up arrow] key. DOS 6.2 includes the DOSKEY program, which, if loaded during boot-up (through inclusion in the AUTOEXEC.BAT file), will reveal previous commands when the up arrow key is typed. Since that key is used constantly, your suspect will not booby trap it. If your suspect was able to type at the keyboard for a few seconds before you arrived, typing [up arrow] may reveal recent DOS commands of interest (e.g., exiting a particular directory, erasing a file, etc.).

38. Although the "ver" command will report the version of DOS running on the computer, it is an obvious command to "rig" (the suspect already knows this information and therefore has no reason to use the command).

Note that using your own COMMAND.COM file does not "clear" the computer of other, and equally deadly, traps. Your decision whether to continue will usually depend upon your assessment of the computer owner. Very few computer users who have the sophistication to alter the operating system decide to do so instead of simply encrypting important files. However, some crackers do fall into this category, so beware.

If you do continue, keep an eye on the hard disk light. If it begins blinking for a prolonged period of time, and the program you are trying to execute appears not to be working, pull the plug out of the wall immediately.

The hard disk light illuminates when the computer is writing data to the hard disk. A program writing zeroes to the disk to wipe information from the disk will cause that light to flash. If that light is flashing, and the program you think that you are running does not appear to be doing anything, you may have triggered a trap which is busily overwriting the hard disk. Pulling the plug will stop that process.

2. *Type A:, and press Enter.*

This will put you in the A: drive, and allow you to run the programs on your floppy disk. If you receive an error message instead, give up on the hardware check, and pull the plug as described above.

3. *Type DIR A:, and press Enter.*

The computer should display a list of files on your floppy disk. Again, if you receive an error message instead, pull the plug as described above.

4. *Type SYSINFO, and press Enter.*

This will start Norton Utilities' System Information program (SYSINFO.EXE). If the program does not start, or reports errors, proceed to Step #6.

The first screen presented by SYSINFO will give you a system summary. Record the number of hard disks present, and their size. You might also record the type of BIOS (e.g., Phoenix, Award) and the date. Do not print any information from SYSINFO.

Page through the program (by selecting the "Next" button) until you reach the CMOS Values screen. Record all of the information displayed on the screen.

Should the computer's battery fail while it is in storage (batteries typically last several years), you will need the hard drive type (typically a number between 1 and 50) to reaccess the drive after you install a new battery. (Readers should take note, and record their CMOS information on their own computers. Norton Utilities includes a feature in the DISKTOOLS.EXE program which places that information on a disk.)

Next, page through to the Disk Summary screen. This information will confirm the number of hard drives installed in the computer.[39] Then page through to the Disk Characteristics Screen, and record the information under Physical Characteristics (this is another way to make sure that you can reaccess the drive if you lose CMOS information).

Your next step is to page through to the Partition Tables screen. Check to see if there is another partition in addition to the DOS partition (labeled BIGDOS). The owner may be running more than one operating system and may have partitioned the drive accordingly. You will check any additional partitions back at your lab.

More common is to "divide" the drive into one or more logical drives; you will already have discovered such partitions by examining the Disk Summary and Disk Characteristics screens.

Finally, if you are familiar with computers, select "View Config.sys" from the menu (you can page through, but you will run benchmarks that will waste your time and possibly cause problems). Do not change the CONFIG.SYS file.

Examine the CONFIG.SYS file for unusual drivers, such as DoubleSpace (a feature of later versions of DOS which increases the amount of data available on a hard drive by compressing that data),

---

39. There are two exceptions to this observation. If the owner is running a computer security program, any encrypted, or "closed" disks may not be "seen" by SYSINFO. Or, SYSINFO may report a drive as "encrypted." In addition, a clever criminal may disconnect a second drive from the controller and plug it in only when he or she needs to access the data on that disk. You will explore that possibility after the computer is safely in your lab.

Stacker (a different compression program), or security programs (look for lines with words such as "Diskreet" or "Disklock"). Note that you may find drivers for memory management programs (e.g., QEMM, NETROOM, 386MAX); these do not generally pose a concern.

Finding DoubleSpace or Stacker means that you may need to take certain steps back at your lab in order to read it (typically by configuring your lab machine the same way; note that some versions of Stacker may require a "Stacker card," which is placed in the computer). You do not need to take any action at the scene.

If you find a security program, you should attempt to backup all logical drives before pulling the plug. If the computer owner opened the protected logical drive before you arrived, you should be able to backup all of the files in that drive.

You may have to perform this backup "manually" because your commercial backup program could fail to recognize the protected drive, or, worse, "hang" (stop working) when trying to backup files. If your backup program hangs, you will be forced to reboot, thus "closing" the drive.

5. *Exit SYSINFO.*

You should still be in the A: drive.

6. *If SYSINFO did not run, check for logical drives the old-fashioned way.*

Type D:\, and hit Enter, and do the same for all the remaining letters in the alphabet, from E:\ through Z:\. You will see either a corresponding prompt (e.g., "D:\"), or the message "Invalid Drive Specification." The prompt means that data is stored in a logical drive; the error message means that there is no logical drive with that label.

7. *For each logical drive you find, type CHKDSK [that drive]:, and press Enter.*

The CHKDSK program returns a description of that logical drive, including the size of the logical drive, the amount of data in that logical drive, and most important, a list of any problems with that logical drive (e.g., lost chains, corrupted FAT tables, etc.).

Do not attempt to fix any problems you find, and do not run CHKDSK/F. You do not want to alter the contents of the hard drive in any way. You can make changes in the copy of the data you upload to your lab machine. Simply document the problem to avoid accusations later that you damaged the computer.

8. *For each logical drive you find, type NDD, and press Enter.*

This Norton Utilities program checks the hard disk for various problems. Again, do not fix the problems, but do note them. (You can skip the scan test. If you do run it, and it appears to be taking more than a few minutes, check to make sure that it is configured for "Daily Scan." The "Weekly Scan" takes much longer to complete.)

9. *You have completed the hardware check*

You are now ready to pull the plug, or backup the computer, as you choose.

Practice makes perfect

Do not wait until you serve your next search warrant to try these tips. Practice them now on your own computer.

In addition to acquiring valuable skills, you will be able to function more effectively as a witness. It is one thing to testify that you are confident that your actions did not damage data because you followed instructions in a book; it is quite another to testify that you tested each of the techniques described in this chapter and confirmed that they worked.

Verify for yourself that each of these techniques works.

At worst, you will catch mistakes in this chapter while there is nothing at stake. At best, you will develop into a more skilled investigator and become a more formidable witness at trial.

6.43–c   Backing up the computer

6.43–c(1)   Preparing to backup the computer

The first step in performing a backup is to perform the hardware check procedure just described. This provides some assurance that the computer is in working order and that you have found all of the files residing on the system.

Next, reboot the computer with a "clean" copy of DOS. (The exception is where you have found a security program which will "close" when the computer is rebooted. In such cases, you must backup using the suspect's operating system.)

You should then run a *write blocker* program. Such programs prevent the computer from writing to the hard drive. (The DISKMON program from Norton Utilities is one such program—it is one of the programs you should include on the floppy disk used for the hardware check.)

Rebooting is a good idea because many traps depend upon your being forced to use the operating system as configured by the suspect. If you can get control by successfully rebooting with a clean copy of DOS, you have in effect bypassed the suspect's configuration, and with it, many of his or her traps. After rebooting, you are ready to backup the computer.

To reboot, place diskettes with copies of DOS in every diskette drive and turn the computer back on. The computer *should* boot normally. When the computer requests the date and time, just punch the "Enter" key—do not enter a different date and time.

If the computer does not boot normally, you should pull the plug and take the machine to your lab for a more detailed inspection. Of course, if the computer owner is insisting that you backup the computer, you should not hesitate to demand passwords and other information necessary to reboot the computer with a clean copy of DOS.

6.43–c(2)   Choosing your backup method

Every computer expert has his or her own method of backing up a computer. Computer crime units backing up files at the lab to another machine may use Laplink or other programs designed to copy large volumes of data. Departments with additional resources may use programs to download data to large portable hard drives, both at the scene and at the lab.[40] Within the next few years, many departments will backup data using the new CD-ROM recorders, which transfer data onto a CD-ROM.

All of these approaches are fine for experts, and this chapter does not seek to convert any expert to a particular method. The following discussion of backup procedures is directed to the non-expert, who is interested in backing up the most evidence possible with the greatest efficiency and the least risk.

1. Getting it all versus getting almost all of it quickly and easily

There are two types of backup: (1) file-by-file; and (2) mirror image. A *file-by-file backup* copies each of the DOS files off of a hard disk, by the logical drive specified (e.g., if you want to backup C: and D:, you have to instruct the software to do so).

A *mirror image backup*, also known as an *image backup*, copies each bit and byte off the hard drive, even if a bit is not included within a file. An image backup makes a "mirror image" of the hard drive.

The popular commercial backup products offer only file-by-file backup. The reason is that most computer users backup their systems to protect their files; the remaining collection of partially erased programs and unwritten disk space is irrelevant to them.

Image backups offer a major advantage to the investigator: they preserve the data exactly as it appeared on the suspect's hard disk. Thus, an image backup will include the slack space overlooked by the file-by-file backup.

An image backup also eliminates fights over whether the backup is less than the "best evidence" of the contents of the hard drive, and precludes any claim that some of the data not copied by a file-by-file

---

40. Note that such drives require officers to install a circuit board in, or software on, the target computer. An exception is Colorado Systems' inexpensive Trakker drive. Iomega's Zip drive, just appearing on the market at this writing, may be another attractive option. Investigators should look into both of these alternatives.

Another option for sophisticated users is to connect the suspect's computer with your computer along a network (e.g., using Novell NetWare Lite) and transfer the files along your network.

backup contained exculpatory evidence. Although, as discussed later in this chapter, the prosecution easily wins these legal battles, it is convenient to preclude this complaint from the outset.

Despite the advantages of image backup, file-by-file backup is usually the better choice. Although no statistics are available, anecdotal evidence suggests that at least 95% of the cases where computer evidence is decisive are won based on the evidence in a particular file.

This is not surprising—most files are overwritten with a newer version of the same file. The newer version is just as likely to be incriminating as the bits and pieces of the older version now residing in slack space. (The notable exception is where there is some evidence that the suspect, alerted to your arrival, has attempted to damage or erase data on the hard disk.)

Moreover, the technology for image backups lags well behind file-by-file backup software. As of this writing (a critical caveat), there are very few programs available for making image backups. Two programs to choose from include SAFEBACK and CPR Data Recovery Tools.[41]

You can get the best of both worlds if you have seized the computer. Make a file-by-file backup initially. If your analysis of the data on your lab machine does not yield enough evidence to obtain a conviction, you have two options. First, you can make an image backup of the data on the seized computer and analyze that data. Second, with appropriate precautions, you can use software designed by such organizations as SEARCH and IACIS to search the slack space on the suspect's hard drive.

---

41. SAFEBACK is sold by Sydex Corporation (800-43-SYDEX) to law enforcement agencies and is probably the most popular image backup product available. Sydex is working on a new version of SAFEBACK, due out in late 1995 or early 1996, which is intended to make the product more usable.

Sydex also sells a number of other useful utilities. The company is also a valuable resource for assistance in reading unusual file formats on any media (including unusual disk sizes and formats), and for media recovery generally. Note that Sydex sells only to law enforcement agencies.

At least one prominent and well-regarded computer lab relies upon CPR Data Recovery Tools for image backups. This program is available from Tech Assist Inc. (813-539-7429). CPR Data Recovery Tools also includes a suite of sophisticated data recovery programs.

6.43–c(2)(i)   *Using a file-by-file backup instead of an image backup does not affect the admissibility of the backed up data*

Do not worry that obtaining something other than an "exact duplicate" of the hard drive somehow taints your evidence.

It is true that the "best evidence rule" requires lawyers to introduce the best possible copy of a document into evidence. If the original is available, then the lawyer must introduce the original.

However, the argument that a file-by-file backup is not the best evidence of the contents of the hard drive is easily defeated. For example, the most common exception to the best evidence rule allows you to introduce a duplicate of the original document. Thus, a copy made on a copier can be admitted in lieu of the original, absent some showing that the copy is not a true and correct copy.

When you attempt to introduce the contents of a file into evidence, you are not attempting to introduce the entire disk into evidence— only the contents of the file. Since a file-by-file backup faithfully copies the contents of the particular file, that backup is a duplicate original of the evidence which matters: the suspect's document or spreadsheet.

That some of the attributes or archive bits of the file were not copied, or, in the case of archive bits, were even changed by the backup program, does not affect the fact that the document or spreadsheet is a duplicate of the information on the hard disk. Therefore, the backup qualifies as a duplicate original under both federal and state evidence codes, and satisfies the best evidence rule.

To put this legal argument into plain English, using a file-by-file backup is like copying only one page out of a very large ledger and introducing that one page into evidence. The contents of that one page are not altered by the omission of the surrounding pages. The defendant's only complaint may be that the other pages contain evidence which would put that one page into a different context (i.e., *exculpatory evidence*, meaning evidence which points to innocence).

But such a complaint is not an evidentiary challenge to the admissibility of that one page—it is a constitutional challenge which is extraordinarily difficult to win, for several reasons.

First, this constitutional challenge arises only if the original hard disk is not seized *and* the computer is used for a significant amount of time after the backup (to allow overwriting of the allegedly exculpatory evidence). Otherwise, those portions of the drive which are allegedly exculpatory are still available for examination.

Furthermore, the challenge must still fail because computer users keep their data in files. The only material in slack space will be parts of files which had not yet been overwritten when the backup was made. Once your expert testifies that the only material which was not copied was fragments of erased files, file attributes, and archive bits, the court will find that the defense has not shown that such material was exculpatory.

Moreover, if the suspect kept backups, then those backups should contain the same exculpatory evidence as was allegedly overwritten (this point is another reason for seizing all media found at the search warrant site).[42] If no backups exist, then the suspect is placed in the unenviable position of claiming that he or she erased potentially exculpatory evidence which would negate the more recent evidence found on the backup.

6.43–c(3)   Making your backup

There are dozens of backup programs you can use to make a file-by-file backup. However, you should use only those programs which you can run from a floppy disk—installing a backup program on the suspect's hard drive may overwrite slack space. If you want to perform a quick file-by-file backup, this probably means using Laplink, or picking up a very old copy of Symantec's Fastback Plus (version 2.0 or earlier).[43] If you want to create a mirror image backup, consider using SAFEBACK or CPR Data Recovery Tools.

---

42. Such backups are also useful when the suspect "inserts" new evidence into hard drives which you left behind at the scene and then claims that the backup failed to copy particular files. The suspect may forget to make such changes to the backup media.

43. Fifth Generation, maker of Fastback Plus, was purchased in 1993 by Symantec, maker of Norton Utilities.

If you are absolutely stuck, consider using the suspect's own backup program if you are familiar with its operation. It is unlikely that suspects will alter commercial software to booby-trap their own programs. Any defense argument that the backup was unreliable can be answered by replying "it was good enough for the suspect." Note that the program may change information in slack space. Another last-ditch alternative is to use the DOS backup command, even though it has a very bad reputation.[44]

When running a commercial backup program, following the directions carefully. Pay close attention when setting the parameters for your backup. Use all error correction and verification options available, and, if the program does not do so automatically, instruct it to backup all files, including hidden files. (Certain backup programs will not copy hidden files unless you instruct them to do so.)[45] Do not turn off archive bits when making your backup.

Make sure that you are left alone for this step—if you are distracted, you may not notice until you have returned to the lab that you failed to backup all of the data at the scene. Although usually not practical, it is desirable to make two complete backups of each machine if time permits.

Before you begin backing up, consider running Norton's UnErase program to restore any "erased" files. You should direct the program to unerase any files you find *to a floppy disk*. (Type "Alt-F", followed by "T".) Unerasing them to the hard drive will change the suspect's directory and FAT table.

If you are backing up onto floppy disks, label those disks in advance with the case name, case number, and, where more than one

---

44. Depending on the version of DOS running on the suspect's computer, you may be able to use the "backup" or "msbackup" command to backup the system. Before doing so, however, make sure you have disabled any batch commands. Again, realize that using any program on the suspect's computer is risky because the suspect may have replaced the program you think you are using with a home-grown version.

45. DOS gives every file an attribute. One attribute is *hidden*, which means that a "dir" command will not reveal that the file exists (use "dir/A"). DOS was designed to "hide" certain files from view to prevent users from accidentally erasing system files necessary for the computer to function. Most backup programs will copy hidden files.

computer is on-site, the type and location of the computer being backed up. All floppy disks should be brand new and formatted.[46]

6.43–c(4)   After you backup

Check your backup before you leave the scene. If you have a laptop handy, try restoring a file to the hard disk on the laptop. If you are backing up with Laplink, compare some of the files on the host and target computers.

After you have finished the backup, put floppy disks away in a cool, dry environment.

6.43–d   Searching the computer on-site

If you decided to search the computer because incriminating information was displayed on the monitor when you arrived, photograph that screen immediately. Next, use the application program to copy the important file to a clean floppy. (Do not save the file to the hard disk—you will obliterate the date and time on which the suspect last saved the program to disk. Worse, if it is a newly created file, the computer may write the data onto a different portion of the hard disk, overwriting evidence in slack space.)

Print as much of the document or spreadsheet as you can. When examining the document, be very careful not to change any data. When exiting the application program, do not save the current file to disk, but once again save it to a floppy, and use a different extension for that file.

Once you have obtained evidence from the program running on the screen, and assuming that you choose to search the computer without backing up, consider first gaining control of the system by rebooting, as discussed above in the section on backing up a computer. Then search the computer using the techniques discussed in the analysis section below. (If nothing else, after you have exited the program running on the screen, run a write blocker such as DISKMON

---

46. You cannot "make do" with used disks unless you have used Norton's WipeInfo in advance to overwrite all data with zeros. Otherwise, you may mingle old data in slack space with the suspect's new data.

to make sure that any further examination does not overwrite data on the hard drive.)

Perhaps you will choose to search at the scene because the computer system is a network that you do not want to move. You will be using experts to search such systems. Remind them not to overlook data which may be stored in the workstation they are operating. Many users store data both on the server and on a personal directory within the workstation. Indeed, you should usually backup both the server and the workstation.

6.50 Analyzing computer evidence

The First Commandment of computer evidence handling is: *Thou shalt not use the suspect's computer to look at data, or for any other purpose. Use another computer to analyze a copy of the data instead.*

Even if the hard drive is completely *write-protected* (meaning that the computer is configured to prevent a "write" to the hard disk), a hard drive crash back at your lab could wipe out all the data, leaving you with only a backup. If there is any problem with the backup, you are in trouble.

The Second Commandment is less critical, but is still important: *The computer that you use to examine the suspect's data should either not be used for anything else or have a hard drive partition reserved solely for the suspect's data."*

In other words, do not use your agency's computer to analyze a suspect's data. Unless you partition the hard drive to provide a separate space for seized data *for each case* (or use a second hard drive), you risk accidentally overwriting the suspect's data or your department's data during the course of analysis. You may also prompt an implausible argument that data relating to other cases has "contaminated" the data seized from the suspect. Finally, as discussed in the next section, you could import a virus from the suspect's media.

The only way to comply with these "commandments" is to have a separate dedicated "lab" computer available, with either a very large hard disk which can be partitioned (and wiped each time data from a new case is examined), or even better, a Bernoulli or other removable hard drive system.

However, as an investigator, you know that there are always legitimate exceptions to rules. Your agency may not have funds for a separate computer. Perhaps you could make only a file-by-file backup of the computer, and need to search slack space on the suspect's hard drive. Or perhaps the suspect's computer includes special equipment needed to run the particular software which contains the relevant evidence.

In the event you must work without a net, you should make two backups of the suspect's hard drive (one of them an image backup if possible) before you begin any analysis not complying with the two "commandments" set forth above.

6.51 Preparing the operating theater

As with surgery, you must first prepare the patient. Set up the seized equipment on a table. Avoid fancy computer tables which have nooks for your monitor, keyboard, and CPU. It is a fact of life that any computer system you seize will not fit your computer furniture.

Your best computer furniture is a 6' x 3' table, about 26 inches tall, and sturdy enough to withstand nudges, bumps, and (in California and the Northwest) minor earthquakes. If you have a tower system, buy a CPU stand, and place the computer on the floor or the table.

Make sure that your table allows you 360-degree access to the computer. If you back the table against a wall, you will constantly have to pull that table away from the wall to connect a peripheral or fiddle with a cable.

Next, open the computer and look for the following items. First, check to see whether the hard drive has a paper label with CMOS information on it. Copy that information (such as the drive type) in case you lose your CMOS information before trial.

Second, make sure that there is only one hard drive. Computer owners seeking additional hard disk space occasionally place another hard drive in their computers. This capability offers opportunities to conceal evidence. For example, the suspect in one case had two drives in his computer. The second hard drive was disconnected—the suspect would simply reconnect the drive when he wanted to access his hidden information.

Finally, examine the circuit boards in the expansion slots of the computer. You may find another hard drive (some drives are in the form of a circuit board—these drives are called *hard cards*), a hardware compression board (e.g., Stacker), or some other device or peripheral. If you plan, as you should, to examine the suspect's data on a laboratory machine, you may discover that you need to equip your machine with additional "cards" in order to access the suspect's data and run the suspect's applications properly.

You are now ready to transfer the suspect's data to your laboratory machine. Returning to medical metaphors for a moment, your first guiding principle must be to do no harm.

When you load data onto any computer for examination, you risk introducing a virus into that computer. Crackers are much more likely to have such "organisms" than other computer users because many of them download software from bulletin boards. You should have, and use, a well-known anti-virus program before and after uploading any data.[47]

You should only upload data into a partition (or removable hard drive) which is reserved for that data and which has been wiped clean. (You may have to prove to a court that data from your last case did not "infect" data from your current case.)[48]

If you use a backup program to upload data, you should enable all verification options. This ensures that the data you analyze is the data you backed up in the first place.

If you are examining floppy disks, take the following measures. First, ensure that all disks are properly labeled and write-protected. If you find an interesting file while searching a floppy, print out a copy immediately. (One expert staples the printout to an envelope and stores the disk in that envelope.) Floppy disks can disappear unless

---

47. Consider such programs as McAfee Associates' Scan, Central Point's Anti-Virus, and Symantec's Norton AntiVirus. At this writing, these companies offer free updates via special bulletin boards. The conscientious and not very busy investigator should obtain updates about once every three months.

48. Consider using Norton Utilities' WipeInfo program to "wipe" the disk. The need to use "sanitized media" makes a removable hard drive an attractive option. However, such drives are expensive. They are also somewhat slower and smaller than standard fixed hard drives.

you are careful; it can also be hard to remember which disk contained which file unless you take careful notes.

Second, if you find evidence on any floppy disk, consider immediately copying that floppy to another floppy disk and storing that second disk in another location.[49] Third, remember to run Norton's UnErase on the floppy to detect erased files. Suspects who transfer files from one machine to another may forget to wipe the floppy disk.

Finally, when you are examining the suspect's machine, either on the scene or at the lab, consider the following procedures.

- Use an uninterruptible power supply (about $200) and a surge suppressor when operating any computer. This is particularly important in areas prone to electrical storms or brownouts. At a minimum, use a high-quality surge suppressor.[50]

- If you turn off the suspect's computer, wait ten seconds before turning it back on. This allows the voltage in the circuitry to return to zero and the hard drives to spin down completely.

- When examining the suspect's computer, run Norton's UnErase from a floppy and copy any files you find to another floppy.

- Use an anti-static wrist strap when working inside the case to avoid damaging components.

6.52 When you cannot reboot the computer

At some point in your travels in high technology, you will inevitably experience that sinking feeling which comes when you attempt to reboot that computer you seized, only to have nothing happen, or worse, be greeted with a demand for a password.

---

49. You may use DOS DISKCOPY or a third-party utility for that purpose. If you are required to return a copy of data stored on the floppy disk to the subject, you should consider obtaining a disk duplication program. One such program is Disk Duplicator from North Beach Labs, located in San Francisco (415-693-0570).

50. There are surge suppressors, and there are "real" surge suppressors. Your surge suppressor should be rated for 330 volts per the Underwriters' Laboratory 1449 standard (a higher number is less desirable). Most basic "power strips" will *not* meet this qualification. However, 330-volt units are available in computer stores for about $30 to $50. Anything cheaper than $20 is probably inadequate.

Remain calm.

Most of the problems at this stage can be fixed, or at least are not your fault. First and foremost, it is unlikely that you broke a personal computer simply by moving it. And even in the worst case, sophisticated media recovery equipment can often retrieve mangled data, and save your case.

If the suspect is running a security program which closed a hard disk, the odds are good that you can find an expert who can circumvent it. If you cannot, well, you are paid to be an investigator, not a computer expert.

Before calling for help, take the following steps. First, make sure that you have plugged in the computer. Next, make sure that you have turned on the monitor. Finally, make sure that you are booting from the correct floppy drive with a clean copy of DOS. If the computer has two floppy drives, place clean copies of DOS in each, and close the drive doors before rebooting.

If you receive a demand for a password, this means that the suspect is using a power-on password enabled within the CMOS setup. Check any documentation which you seized along with the computer for ways to change this configuration. For example, one model in IBM's ValuePoint line of computers is configured with a password system which can be disabled by resetting certain "DIP" switches on the motherboard.

Another approach is to try to interrupt the boot sequence to access the CMOS setup utility to disable the password. Many CMOS setup programs allow you to reassign the A: drive as the bootup drive. Again, check the computer manual for information on how to access the CMOS during bootup. One common way is to hit the "Esc" key or the "Delete" key while the computer is booting up. (One expert recommends disconnecting the hard drive—a resulting error message may drop you into the CMOS setup.)

If you are still stymied, you need an expert to proceed. Your options may range from a simple bit of technical advice from the expert or the computer's manufacturer, to extracting the hard drive for further analysis by specialists in a media recovery lab. The latter course may cost several hundred (or even thousand) dollars, but may be worth it if you believe that the computer is so well protected (or damaged) that nothing else but a "hard disk transplant" will do.[51]

6.53   Examining the evidence

6.53–a   *Examine the evidence yourself*

The Third Commandment of computer evidence handling is: *Thou shalt do it thyself.* While computer-friendly investigators or civilian computer wizards may search the computer faster, they usually will not know what to look for.

Investigators are specially trained to recognize relevant evidence. Your local computer wizard may not have a clue as to what is significant, and another investigator may not be familiar enough with your case to recognize the one bit of information which will secure a conviction. Although ideally you will search the computer with a computer-literate friend or computer specialist, you must participate in that search.

6.53–b   *Let your fingers do the walking*

If you want to begin your examination by looking for incriminating file names, you should consider using the "chkdsk/v" command to obtain a list of the files in the data you uploaded to your lab machine. This command will list every file which DOS finds in a particular logical drive, including hidden files. To copy that list to a floppy, type "chkdsk/v > a:\chklist.txt". This command will create the file chklist.txt on the floppy in A:. To print that list, type "chkdsk/v > prn" (this may take several minutes to print).

There are several programs available which allow you to search the contents of files stored on hard and floppy drives. Symantec sells Norton Commander, which offers good *viewers* (programs allowing you to "view" files created by a wide range of applications without

---

51. If the media is damaged, trained investigators may consider running media recovery software, such as Norton Utilities' Disk Doctor, *on an extra copy* of the data. Another sophisticated data recovery package is CPR Data Recovery Tools, distributed by Tech Assist, Inc. (813-539-7429).

running the application itself). However, Norton Commander over-writes slack space by writing information to the disk.

You can also use Central Point Software's PC Tools and XTree-Gold for Windows, along with Symantec's Norton Utilities, to view files. The tool kit in this chapter lists two graphics viewers for pictures.

Compressed files

You may see files which appear to encrypted, but are instead only compressed. A compressed file is a file which has been "shrunk" for easier storage. These files can be uncompressed using the same programs which compressed them.

The best clue that you are dealing with a compressed file is the file's extension (the three characters after the "."). If your file has a .zip or .arc extension, you are dealing with a compressed file. As discussed at the beginning of this chapter, your tool kit should include various versions of the PkZip, PkArc, and LHArc programs.

However, before spending the next few months reading every file, try a simpler way. There are a number of programs capable of search-ing data for text (e.g., "cocaine") and strings of numbers (e.g., credit card numbers) and revealing the results (along with the file names) on your monitor.

Perhaps the most useful programs are those which allow you to input key words and instruct the computer to retrieve files containing those words. ZyIndex (ZyLab) and Magellan (Lotus—sold, but no longer supported) offer this capability but require you to first index the hard drive (i.e., the hard drive on your lab machine after you have uploaded the suspect's data, *not* the suspect's hard drive). ZyIndex is the program of choice because Magellan does not read files created by the latest word processors.

An easy program to use for searching floppy drives is Norton's FileFind, included as part of Norton Utilities. (This program is also handy for searching hard drives.) Various groups are creating more sophisticated search programs for law enforcement, including programs designed to search slack space efficiently.[52]

6.53–c   Climb every mountain

Sooner or later you may have to start looking at files one at a time. You might start by printing a copy of the directory of the hard disk and a directory of files contained within each directory. This allows you to organize your search.

Depending upon your case, you will want to focus on word processing, spreadsheet, or database files. Run a copy of the application program used by the suspect and examine files with seemingly relevant names.

It is important for you to be systematic—take notes of where you have been and where you are going. If you find valuable files, consider printing them out *and* making an additional copy onto diskettes. Label those diskettes with a distinctive name, such as "[*Your case name*] Hot Files."

Good luck, and remember, at least searching a computer is more interesting than plowing through a warehouse full of file cabinets.

6.60   You can never be perfect

This chapter is full of rules. Although it is true that your failure to follow these rules can result in disastrous consequences, your mistakes will usually not come back to haunt you. Do what you can with the resources you have available, and realize that nobody is perfect.

---

52. Law enforcement investigators can call Mr. William Spernow at the National White Collar Crime Center, Training and Research Institute (304-291-2080) to inquire about obtaining a copy of his own program, DISKHUNT (part of The HUNT Utilities). The UnErase program included within Norton Utilities can also be used to search slack space.

7

Computers and the Fourth Amendment

7.00   Introduction

The law of search and seizure based on the Fourth Amendment usually boils down to a simple commandment: when in doubt, draft a search warrant and find a magistrate to sign it. This advice is usually easy to follow because search warrants often consist of little more than a description of a dwelling, a description of readily identifiable contraband, and facts justifying probable cause.

Unfortunately, the law is more complicated in cases involving computer technology. New technology has created Fourth Amendment issues that courts have yet to address. In addition, Congress has created new requirements for certain searches, such as those involving electronic communications between computer users. Some of those new laws apply to private parties as well as to law enforcement, and are punishable by criminal *and civil penalties*. Mistakes are easily made, and can be costly.

The next three chapters discuss legal issues relating to high-technology crime investigations. This chapter is aimed at law enforcement investigators and prosecutors, although private parties should read § 7.11b (discussing private parties). This chapter discusses basic search and seizure law arising out of the Fourth Amendment, and examines how that law applies to searches for computer evidence.

Chapter 8 is aimed at all readers, and examines federal laws which restrict law enforcement *and* private parties from searching for certain computer evidence, including electronic communications (e.g., E-mail) and information held by persons claiming to be publishers (e.g., bulletin boards). Readers are urged to become familiar with these laws.

Chapter 9 is written to help law enforcement investigators prepare search warrants authorizing the search and seizure of computer evidence. Appendix B of this book includes sample search warrant language and checklists.

Chapters 7, 8, and 9 contain the most "legal" writing in this book and include many footnotes citing pertinent cases. If you have a legal question, those case citations will provide your private lawyer or prosecutor with a place to start.[1]

7.10   A Review of the Ground Rules

7.11   When the Fourth Amendment requires a search warrant

7.11–a   Law enforcement

The right of the people to be secure in their persons, houses, papers, and effects, against unreasonable searches and seizures, shall not be violated, and no Warrants shall issue, but upon probable cause, supported by Oath or affirmation, and particularly describing the place to be searched, and the persons or things to be seized.

United States Constitution, Fourth Amendment

The Fourth Amendment prohibits the State from "unreasonably" searching areas in which individuals or entities have "an expectation of privacy." An expectation of privacy exists not only in "persons, houses, papers, and effects," but in just about every place you would

---

1. *Do not use this chapter as a substitute for consulting with your own attorney or local prosecutor before searching or seizing any computer evidence.* Even if it were possible to cover the entire law of search and seizure in one chapter, the suggestions provided here might not apply to your particular situation, or even your jurisdiction. Although federal law provides uniformity, states often add their own requirements. In addition, the United States Supreme Court and lower federal courts constantly reinterpret federal law.

What is a search warrant?

For readers who are not law enforcement investigators, a search warrant consists of two documents: a warrant and an affidavit. The warrant is a court order authorizing police to search a particular location for particular property, and to seize that property. The warrant lists the particular property to be searched and/or seized. The affidavit is signed under penalty of perjury by the "affiant," the police officer, and provides the magistrate with the facts offered by the officer to justify issuance of the warrant.

A police officer prepares and presents the affidavit and warrant to a judge. The judge signs the warrant, and the officer files a copy of both the warrant and the affidavit with the court. The officer then serves the warrant at the premises to be searched. The officer may also choose to leave the affidavit at the scene.

After executing the warrant, the officer files a "return" with the court within a certain time period describing the items seized. Any items seized are held by the officer in the name of the court; officers may not release those items without a court order.

---

search to find computer evidence, including residences, office buildings, storage lockers, and automobiles.

The general rule is that such searches are "reasonable" only when authorized by a search warrant. However, there are exceptions to this requirement, most notably where the owner gives consent to search. Courts will also excuse a failure to obtain a search warrant where there were "exigent circumstances" making it unreasonable to seek one.

Those exceptions are usually not available in cases involving computer evidence. You cannot count on receiving a consent to search a computer. Furthermore, the exigent circumstances rule allowing warrantless searches in emergencies is unhelpful because computers usually do not erase data without human assistance.

Courts have not found exigent circumstances on the grounds that a suspect might erase evidence contained within a computer before police could obtain a search warrant. Even if you must seize a computer to avert its destruction, you will usually have time to obtain a search warrant to examine its contents. Thus, you should plan to obtain a search warrant before searching for computer evidence.

7.11–b   Private parties

Searches by private parties who are not working for law enforcement are not covered by the Fourth Amendment. Thus, evidence seized by a private party in a manner which would otherwise violate the Fourth Amendment is still admissible in a criminal prosecution.

A private party becomes a police agent, and the Fourth Amendment applies, when:

- the private party performs a search which the government would need a search warrant to conduct;

- the private party performs that search to assist the government, as opposed to furthering its own interests (e.g., protecting its rights or property); and

- the government is aware of that party's conduct and does not object to it.

See United States v. Jacobson, 466 U.S. 109 (1984); *Coolidge v. New Hampshire*, 403 U.S. 443, 487 (1971); *United States v. Reed*, 15 F.3d 928, 931 (9th Cir. 1994).

A victim acting to protect its property by assisting police to prevent or detect a crime does not become a police agent. This includes publicly regulated telephone and utility companies. *See United States v. Cleaveland*, 38 F.3d 1092 (9th Cir. 1994) (electric utility investigating theft of service); *United States v. Goldstein*, 532 F.2d 1305 (9th Cir. 1976) (telephone company investigating toll fraud).

However, this does not give private parties immunity from state or federal laws, such as those punishing trespassing, burglary, or invasion of privacy. In other words, although the prosecutor will be able to use the evidence, the private party may face prosecution or have to pay civil damages to the suspect.

This distinction has practical consequences for employers. A heightened interest in privacy has sparked lawsuits by employees accusing employers of violating privacy rights. Employees have sued companies for reading E-mail, monitoring their work, and reading files stored on "personal" directories of corporate computers.

It is too early to tell whether courts will find that employees acquire privacy rights in their "personal spaces" within employer owned computer systems. Companies should therefore develop policies balancing employee morale with corporate access to computers used by employees. (Those policies should also cover non-computer items, such as desks, file cabinets, memoranda, and telephones.) Companies should develop and publicize policies establishing which areas are deemed accessible by the employer.

If a company wants unfettered access to employees' work spaces and computer files to assist in internal investigations, it should eliminate any expectation of privacy which employees might otherwise acquire in the absence of any expression of corporate ownership. (Of course, corporations intent on maximum access may create such a repressive atmosphere that valuable employees decide to leave.)

Finally, as discussed in Chapter 8, federal and state privacy laws may pose obstacles to prosecutors seeking to use evidence obtained by private parties, including employers.

7.12 Probable cause

In order to obtain a search warrant to search a particular location, you (a law enforcement investigator) must show "probable cause" that a crime has taken place, or is about to take place, and that evidence of that crime will be found at the location to be searched. A search warrant unsupported by probable cause will be found defective, and evidence gathered pursuant to that search warrant will be suppressed.

The good faith exception

There is an exception to the rule that evidence must be suppressed if the search warrant is defective. In *United States v. Leon*, 468 U.S. 897 (1984), the Supreme Court held that evidence seized pursuant to an invalid warrant may be admitted into evidence where the officer had a good faith and reasonable belief that the warrant was valid. This rule tends to save a warrant where the affidavit falls just short of demonstrating probable cause, or where the warrant contains a mere technical error (i.e., a typographical error). *See, e.g., United States v. Clark*, 31 F.3d 831 (9th Cir. 1994).

There is no precise definition of "probable cause." Like obscenity, you are supposed to know it when you see it. An oft-cited Supreme Court case provides the most current definition of the showing required to obtain a search warrant:

> The task of the issuing magistrate is simply to make a practical, common-sense decision whether, given all the circumstances set forth in the affidavit before him, including the "veracity" and "basis of knowledge" of persons supplying hearsay [second-hand] information, there is a fair probability that contraband or evidence of a crime will be found in a particular place.[2]

You do not have to show with absolute certainty that the evidence you seek is at the premises to be searched. You need only show that it would be reasonable to expect to find that evidence at that location.

In addition to demonstrating that it is reasonable to expect to find items at a particular location, you must state facts, as opposed to mere

---

2. *Illinois v. Gates*, 462 U.S. 213, 238 (1983) (material in brackets added). There are rare cases where a showing of probable cause by itself does not justify a search. Where extraordinary privacy interests are implicated, a court may weigh the need for the evidence against the privacy interests involved. *See United States v. Koyomejian*, 970 F.2d 536 (9th Cir. 1992), *citing Winston v. Lee*, 470 U.S. 753, 763 (1985) (warrant to perform surgery to extract a bullet). *See* Chapter 9, § 9.43, beginning at page 449 (officers may need to justify videotaping during a search warrant).

conclusions, indicating that the items you intend to seize are likely to be evidence of a crime. As discussed later in this chapter, this can be a challenge where you seek to seize items which appear to be innocuous (e.g., modems).

7.13 Particularity

The Fourth Amendment requires that search warrants "particularly describ[e] the place to be searched, and the persons or things to be seized." This requirement was included within the Fourth Amendment as a reaction to the use by the British of "writs of assistance."

Those writs allowed soldiers to engage in *general rummaging searches*, where soldiers would not specify what they were looking for in advance. Instead, they would examine everything at the premises and seize any evidence which they thought might assist them in their investigation.

The Framers of our Constitution were determined to ensure that searches be as unintrusive as possible. With that intent in mind, courts interpret the Fourth Amendment as:

- requiring warrants specific enough to ensure that police search and seize only that evidence relevant to the investigation; and

- preventing officers executing a warrant from searching or seizing property not listed in the warrant.

We review each of these requirements in turn.

7.13–a   *Warrants must be specific*

Courts use two tests in deciding whether a description of property to be searched for and seized is sufficiently particular. (A warrant which fails to meet either of these tests is referred to as an *overbroad* warrant.)

First, the description must be clear enough so that any police officer can identify which property is covered by the warrant. A description of property to be seized as "all evidence of a crime" would fail this test because it does not inform the officer of what is to be seized, and what is to be left behind.

Second, the description must include only that property which could be seized based upon the probable cause demonstrated by the affidavit. A warrant seeking financial records from a suspect's residence would generally fail this second test if it allowed search and seizure of "all papers" instead of, say, "periodic financial statements for account #034696203 dating from August 1, 1992, to the present." Since "all personal papers" could include personal correspondence, newspapers, diaries, and junk mail irrelevant to the investigation, the warrant would generally be considered overbroad.[3]

Courts apply these two tests flexibly, considering the type of property sought and the facts of each case. The outcome will turn on what you knew about the case, and whether you should have been more specific about what property was relevant to your investigation.[4]

Evidence seized pursuant to an overbroad warrant must be suppressed. However, if only portions of a warrant are insufficiently particular, then the remaining portions of that warrant remain valid.[5]

Thus, if a warrant with an overbroad description of business records also included authorization to search for and seize "amyl nitrate," and that part of the warrant was supported by probable cause, any amyl nitrate seized would be admissible. As discussed later in this chapter, investigators must draft descriptions of property, including computer evidence, as narrowly as possible.

7.13–b   Officers may seize only items covered by the warrant

Evidence seized pursuant to a sufficiently specific warrant may still be suppressed if officers negligently seize items not covered by

---

3. In addition, the affiant must inform the court of any facts which would assist those officers executing the warrant in excluding irrelevant property. For example, if an officer is writing a warrant to seize counterfeit videotapes and knows that the suspect has marked those tapes only with an orange band, the affiant must limit the property description to "videotapes with an orange band." *See, e.g., United States v. Cook,* 657 F.2d 730 (5th Cir. 1981); *United States v. Klein,* 565 F.2d 183 (1st Cir. 1977).

4. *See, e.g., United States v. Santarelli,* 778 F.2d 609 (11th Cir. 1985); *State v. Petrone,* 468 N.W. 2d 676 (Wis. 1991).

5. *See, e.g., United States v. Clark,* 31 F.3d 831 (9th Cir. 1994); *United States v. Gomez-Soto,* 723 F.2d 649 (9th Cir. 1984); *United States v. Cook,* 657 F.2d 730 (5th Cir. 1981).

that warrant.[6] Officers may not use a valid warrant as an excuse to make a wholesale seizure of any items which look incriminating. Nor may they seize whole file cabinets based on the discovery of a single document in one drawer.

Of course, courts recognize that officers may inadvertently seize irrelevant material, particularly in complex cases. Officers are not required to separate pages of ledgers or to rip pages out of books.[7] A court will not suppress evidence where irrelevant material was taken unless it finds that officers flagrantly disregarded the boundaries of the warrant.[8]

Careful planning can reduce the risk that a court will make such a finding. You should brief all members of the search team and supply them with copies of the warrant and affidavit. If possible, consider reviewing documents as they are seized to ensure that all officers remain within the boundaries of the warrant.[9]

While not required, these precautions may make a difference in high-technology cases. Courts will appreciate your effort to prepare officers to search for material which is difficult to identify, such as software.

7.13–c   The plain view doctrine

There is an exception to the rule preventing officers executing a search warrant from searching or seizing property not listed in that warrant. Known as the plain view doctrine, it allows officers to search and seize property where the "incriminating character" of that property is "immediately apparent."[10]

---

6. *See United States v. Heldt*, 668 F.2d 1228 (D.C. Cir. 1981); *see also United States v. Wuagneux*, 683 F.2d 1343 (11th Cir. 1982).

7. *See United States v. Schandl*, 947 F.2d 462 (11th Cir. 1991); *United States v. Beusch*, 596 F.2d 871 (9th Cir. 1979).

8. *See United States v. Mittleman*, 999 F.2d 440 (9th Cir. 1993).

9. *See, e.g., United States v. Dale*, 991 F.2d 819 (D.C. Cir. 1993); *United States v. Maxwell*, 920 F.2d 1028 (D.C. Cir. 1990); *United States v. Wuagneux*, 683 F.2d 1343 (11th Cir. 1982); *United States v. Heldt*, 668 F.2d 1228 (D.C. Cir. 1981).

10. *See Horton v. California*, 496 U.S. 128 (1990); *Arizona v. Hicks*, 480 U.S. 321 (1987).

The theory behind this exception is that it makes little sense to prevent officers from seizing contraband or other obviously incriminating material. To make police stop a search for bank records and seek another warrant to pick up a bindle of heroin not mentioned in the first warrant is pointless.

There are two restrictions on an officer's ability to seize items in plain view. First, if officers have recovered all property listed in the warrant, they may not continue their search to look for other incriminating evidence. Second, officers may not disturb property unrelated to property listed in the warrant in order to bring it into "plain view." If officers are executing a warrant authorizing them to seize cocaine, they may not turn over stereo equipment at the premises to check whether that equipment is stolen.[11]

This second restriction is an important limitation on searches in component theft investigations. As discussed in Chapter 3, most components are "fungible," meaning that each one looks like the other. Often the only identifying feature is a serial number or other numeric marking. Thus, as recommended in Chapter 9, if you have probable cause to believe that your suspect is a fence, you should include language allowing you to examine serial numbers on all components found on the premises.

7.20   Applying the Fourth Amendment to computers

7.21   The computer is no different from a wall safe

How do the ground rules discussed in the previous section apply to computers? *The most important thing to remember is that a computer is nothing more than a container, just like a file cabinet or a wall safe.*

Although you may end up seizing computers, from a legal standpoint you are usually not searching for them. You are searching for evidence which you expect to find at the premises; that evidence may

---

11. *See Arizona v. Hicks*, 480 U.S. 321 (1987). This rule also applies to instances in which officers enter without a warrant under exigent circumstances and examine property unrelated to their investigation.

be in the form of documents or data stored on a computer or on floppy disks.[12] When you consider the law of search and seizure as it relates to computers, think of the computer as a container.

There is no special expectation of privacy in information stored within a computer

The court in *Commonwealth of Pennsylvania v. Copenhefer,* 587 Atl. 2d 1353 (Pa. 1991), upheld the recovery by police of files which the defendant had erased from his hard disk (see Chapter 6 for a discussion of erased files). The court held that the defendant did not have a heightened expectation of privacy based on his attempt to erase the evidence. If attempting to erase files stored within a computer does not create an additional expectation of privacy, then neither does storing those files on the computer in the first place.

Other cases lead to the same conclusion. *See State v. Petrone,* 468 N.W. 2d 676 (Wis. 1991) (police may develop film seized pursuant to a search warrant without obtaining a second warrant; development of the film is simply a form of examination of evidence already seized); *United States v. Gomez-Soto,* 723 F.2d 649 (9th Cir. 1984) (any container found on the premises may be searched pursuant to a warrant allowing a search of those premises).

7.22 If you have a warrant to search the premises where a computer is located, you may also search the computer

If you have permission from a magistrate to search the premises, you are free to search computers without any special permission in

---

12. There are exceptions to this observation. In computer intrusion cases, for example, the computer hardware itself may be the target of the seizure because the hardware (e.g., computers, modems) may be evidence that the intruder was capable of dialing into the victim's computer. Other cases may involve the use of a search warrant to recover stolen components.

your search warrant, just as you would search file cabinets located at a business. (Seizing computers is a very different issue and is discussed in detail later in this chapter.)

Note that the rule just stated begins with the words, "if you have permission from a magistrate to search the premises." The owner of any container, including a file cabinet, a wall safe, or a computer, enjoys an expectation of privacy in that container and its contents.

The only reason you are allowed to search that container is that you have a search warrant authorizing you to search it, or a warrant authorizing you to search an entire location or premises (e.g., an automobile or house) for responsive evidence. Permission to search given by someone who is not an owner of the computer does not allow you to search that computer without a warrant.

For example, assume that you are investigating John Doe, an employee of Xcorp, for passing trade secrets to a competitor. If John Doe has his own personal computer (not owned by Xcorp) at his Xcorp office, you may not search that computer without a warrant even if Xcorp invites you to do so. John Doe retains his expectation of privacy in his computer (and its contents—i.e., the data), and you will need to obtain a search warrant.[13]

Finally, as discussed in Chapter 8, in cases involving communications (e.g., E-mail) or electronic publishers, federal laws may limit your search even where you have permission to search the premises.

7.23 Computers and probable cause

As discussed above, your affidavit must demonstrate probable cause to believe that the property to be seized is likely to:

- be found at the premises to be searched; and

- constitute evidence of a crime.

The next sections discuss these requirements.

---

13. It is unclear whether employees who are given their own "space" for personal files on a company computer enjoy an expectation of privacy in that space and its contents. To be safe, you should obtain a search warrant before examining the data in that space, especially if the company has not announced a policy designed to eliminate any expectation of privacy.

Jurisdiction in cyberspace

What should you do when you discover that the computer you have found is part of a wide area network (WAN), and the server is located in another state? Can you use the workstation at the scene to download data from the server, even though that server is located outside the jurisdiction of the magistrate who issued your warrant? After all, the operators of the workstation can certainly access, and perhaps critically, download, the data by their actions wholly within your jurisdiction.

Courts have yet to provide a solution to this problem. If you are unable to obtain a warrant in the other jurisdiction (e.g., you did not know that the WAN existed), an interesting case can be made for excusing a warrant on the grounds of exigency. Furthermore, there is a persuasive argument that the only parties having standing to object to the search are the owners of the computer in the other state.

Finally, you might argue that the expectation of privacy of the owner of the data is limited by the ability to access the data from another state. The owner's expectation of privacy does not include freedom from having someone access the data from the computer at the other end of the telephone line. The search warrant authorizes law enforcement to use that computer at the other end of the line, and the owner is left with no Fourth Amendment right.

Note that each of these arguments is extremely risky, and you would risk suppression of the evidence, and perhaps even civil liability, if a court were to reject them.

7.23–a   *Showing probable cause that the property is likely to be found at the premises to be searched*

In most cases, you are searching for property (e.g., records) which may be found in documentary form or on magnetic media. The issue is whether you would expect that information, in whatever form, to be located where you are searching. It is usually easy to satisfy this requirement.

For example, if you are searching for business records, the issue is whether someone is likely to keep business records in their residence or office, not whether those records are likely to be found on a computer. That a suspect's records may be computerized does not affect the likelihood that you will find them at his or her home.

Out of an abundance of caution, however, you should note in your affidavit that you are aware that the evidence which you seek is capable of being stored on a computer. This will eliminate any claims that you should not have expected to find any evidence on a computer.[14]

As discussed in Chapter 9, the affiant usually has sufficient training and experience to state that computer users often make backups of their computer files and store them away from their computer for safekeeping. The affiant may also note that automobiles are often used to transport software (particularly backups) to and from computers. Investigators new to this field may wish to seek out, and quote, expert opinion on these points to allow them to search residences and automobiles.

7.23–b   Showing probable cause to believe that particular property is likely to be evidence of a crime

In addition to explaining why you believe that evidence will be found on the premises, you must show probable cause that the property to be seized is, or contains, evidence of the crimes described within the affidavit. If you have shown probable cause that business records will contain evidence of a crime, then you have shown probable cause for seizing such business records stored within a computer.

---

14. *Compare Stanley v. Georgia*, 394 U.S. 557, 569–72 (1969) (Stewart, J., concurring) (Justice Stewart would have suppressed evidence obtained by viewing films found at the scene on a projector because there was no showing suggesting that films might contain evidence of a crime); *United States v. Giannetta*, 909 F.2d 571 (1st Cir. 1990) (police may look wherever evidence of a crime can be expected to be found); *United States v. Guy*, 903 F.2d 1240 (9th Cir. 1990) (police may seize safe at the premises because the evidence justifying the issuance of the warrant suggested that the safe was being used for criminal activity); *United States v. Wright*, 667 F.2d 793 (9th Cir. 1982).

However, establishing probable cause to seize *non-documentary* evidence may require special care.

For example, seizing a modem may prove that a cracker had the ability to dial into the victim's computer. But without such an explanation in the affidavit, you must rely on the court to find that it was obvious from the facts of your case that the modem was relevant evidence. You should explain in your affidavit the connection between seemingly irrelevant property and the facts of your case.

7.24 Computers and particularity

The particularity requirement is a dangerous obstacle to writing valid search warrants to obtain computer evidence. The authors of a legal treatise provide the following advice to criminal defense attorneys seeking to challenge the admission of evidence seized pursuant to a search warrant:

> In computer crime cases, the government may have difficulty in specifically describing the items sought, since a computer operation can be too complicated and technical for the average lay person to grasp, particularly in complex financial frauds.... Although federal authorities can often call on their own computer experts for assistance when drafting a search warrant in a computer crime case, their local counterparts often cannot. Local authorities usually have no such experts on their staffs and often lack the resources to retain outside consultants. Thus, counsel should scrutinize carefully the manner in which the warrant describes the material sought.[15]

As discussed in the previous section, a search warrant is overbroad unless the description of the property is:

- sufficiently clear and detailed to allow any police officer to identify the property to be searched for and seized; and

- includes only that property which could be searched based upon the probable cause shown by the affidavit.

---

15. S. Arkin et al., *Prevention and Prosecution of High Technology Crime* (New York: Matthew Bender, 1992), at 8–18.

In most cases, the fact that the evidence is stored on a computer does not make it more difficult to describe that property. If you are searching for spreadsheets and databases describing money laundering and cocaine sales, your description of those items will be similar to the descriptions you use for ledgers and business records. You should have no problem if you describe the evidence as it would appear in documentary form.

However, many high-technology crime investigations involve unusual evidence, such as software. You must be very careful to describe such evidence in terms sufficient to allow a police officer to find and seize that evidence.

Chapter 9 discusses several techniques for describing such property and recommends obtaining a court order allowing an expert to identify that property for police. When using such an expert, the description in the search warrant must be sufficiently specific to allow an expert to identify that property.

7.25 Removing computers and media for examination off-site

Investigators with experience in this area may be puzzled by the emphasis placed in this chapter on the importance of carefully describing the property likely to be found on magnetic media. After all, many law enforcement agencies active in this field routinely seize all computers, magnetic media, and peripherals on the premises after including a blanket authorization to do so in their search warrants. They examine that equipment only after they have brought it back to the police station.

If it is legal to seize all computer equipment and software found on the premises, why worry about describing a particular piece of software contained within a computer?

The problem is that there is a critical difference between seizing a computer after you have searched it on-site and found property listed in the search warrant (e.g., a narcotics ledger) and seizing that computer without searching it because you *expect* it to contain such property. As discussed in the next few sections, special rules apply when you seize computers without searching them first.

7.25–a   Seizing a computer after a search reveals property listed in the warrant

If you have searched a computer on-site and found evidence listed in the warrant on the hard drive (such as stolen software listed in the property description), you may seize the computer because it contains that evidence and keep the computer pending trial.

7.25–a(1)   Responding to claims that seizing a computer is illegal because that seizure inevitably includes additional property not encompassed by the warrant

Some lawyers argue that allowing police to seize a computer after finding even a tiny amount of property described in the warrant allows abuses. They fear that police may seize a mainframe computer containing thousands of unrelated files in order to seize one cracker's data. They argue that investigators should be required to download the relevant information and leave the hard drive behind.

Case law refutes their position. Courts have consistently held that investigators may seize evidence unrelated to the warrant where that evidence is part of a "single unit"—a single physical object, such as a book or ledger. These cases note that a contrary rule would greatly increase the intrusiveness of the search by requiring officers to search all of the records within that object and painstakingly remove only those items which were demonstrably covered by the warrant.[16] These cases are particularly appropriate here, where investigators could easily spend weeks searching a server for relevant files.

Furthermore, the entire computer in such cases is evidence. The way in which certain data was stored on the hard drive relative to other information, even if that information is less relevant, is itself evidence.

Moreover, the computer is the "best evidence." A copy of the hard drive is just that—a copy. Even assuming that the copy is made properly, such copies are open to legal challenges because they are not the

---

16. *See United States v. Schandl,* 947 F.2d 462 (11th Cir. 1991); *Crooker v. Mulligan,* 788 F.2d 809 (1st Cir. 1986); *United States v. Slocum,* 708 F.2d 587 (11th Cir. 1983); *United States v. Wuagneux,* 683 F.2d 1343 (11th Cir. 1982); *United States v. Beusch,* 596 F.2d 871 (9th Cir. 1979).

"best evidence." That those challenges must fail for various reasons does not mean that law enforcement must take the risk of an exceptional case where the challenge succeeds.[17] At this date, there are no cases suggesting that officers have a duty to leave the computer behind in favor of attempting to copy the evidence.

However, there are probably some limits to seizing computers containing evidence. Courts retain the power to suppress evidence on the grounds that police acted outrageously in serving the warrant. For example, jackhammering through floors to find narcotics without reason to believe that narcotics might be found underneath the floor might be considered outrageous. A court might conceivably suppress a search for computer evidence on such "due process" grounds in the most extreme case, such as where investigators seize a mainframe computer to obtain a few marginally relevant files. Of course, as explained in Chapter 6, you have little incentive to seize mainframe computers anyway.

7.25–b   Seizing a computer before any search reveals property listed in the warrant

What if you seize the computer without searching it first? What happens if, following the advice of many experts, you immediately pull the plug and take the system away for analysis in a properly equipped computer lab? (Chapter 6 also recommends this approach in many situations.)

The defense will claim that you seized the computer without probable cause, and file a motion to suppress any evidence found within that computer. Their claim is that since you had no idea whether the computer contained evidence, you could not seize it, anymore than you could seize every desk and file drawer in an office and cart them away to look for business records.

You cannot solve this problem by including in your warrant a blanket authorization to seize computers. If you had no probable cause to seize the computer, having the magistrate sign a warrant allowing seizure of all computers does not cure that defect.

---

17. See Chapter 6, § 6.43–c(2)(i), beginning on page 290.

There are four answers to the defense challenge. First, you can argue that the facts related in your affidavit strongly suggest that the computer was *itself* evidence. For example, in a cracker case, you might argue that it was obvious that any computer found on the premises would itself be evidence of the cracker's ability to access the victim's computer.

However, this argument will be available only in a minority of cases. Most cases will involve evidence which just happens to be stored on a computer (e.g., narcotics ledgers, correspondence); the computer itself will not have been used to commit a crime.

Second, you can argue that the facts of your case strongly suggested that the evidence you sought (e.g., business records) would be found on the computer. But that argument could also justify seizing 100 file cabinets from a warehouse without opening a single file drawer, based on evidence that the warehouse was used to store the suspect's business records. A search warrant based on that theory would be overbroad.[18]

Third, you will prevail in the unusual case where the criminal activity was so widespread that it justified a search warrant allowing seizure of all of the records at the premises. If the affidavit provides probable cause that the entire records of the business will present evidence of criminal activity, then courts will allow police to seize the computer along with the rest of the business.[19]

Finally, as discussed in the next section, the argument that wins the day is that officers are not really seizing the computer in the traditional sense—they are *removing* it from the premises to another location in order to perform the search authorized by the warrant. The

---

18. In many cases, the mere existence of a computer at the premises does not suggest that the computer is being used to store or create evidence of a crime. *But see United States v. Guy*, 903 F.2d 1240 (9th Cir. 1990) (allowing police to seize a safe because the evidence justifying the issuance of the warrant suggested that the safe was being used for criminal activity). Furthermore, while seizing a small item like a ledger book may not rise to the level of a "general search," seizing a computer system containing the equivalent of 100,000 pages certainly might.

19. *See United States v. Henson*, 848 F.2d 1374 (6th Cir. 1988) (agents not required to segregate the few computer files which were not inculpatory); *United States Postal Service v. C.E.C. Services*, 869 F.2d 184, 187 (2d Cir. 1989); *United States v. Wuagneux*, 683 F.2d 1343 (11th Cir. 1982).

police are not "seizing" the computer as evidence, but moving the location of the ongoing "search" to the police station.

> *7.25–b(1)   The law allows police to remove property for further examination off-site when it would be impractical to search that property at the scene*

Although there is very little case law relating to this issue, several courts have decided that the Fourth Amendment allows officers to remove property to another site for further examination when it would be impractical to search that property at the scene to determine whether it is, or contains, evidence.[20]

For example, in *United States v. Santarelli*,[21] officers chose to remove thousands of documents to the police station for further examination. The court denied a motion to suppress evidence found in the documents.

The court observed that police could have examined those documents at the scene. The court reasoned that removing documents for examination was less intrusive than the alternative, which was for the agents to occupy the premises for several days. Other courts have accepted this reasoning.[22]

The same rationale applies to cases involving computers because a thorough search of a single computer capable of holding hundreds of thousands of pages can take weeks, or even months.

Another line of cases allows officers to remove property when they discover items described in the warrant, only to find that those items are thoroughly intermingled with unexamined items. Courts

---

20. *See United States v. Santarelli*, 778 F.2d 609, 615, 616 (11th Cir. 1985); *United States v. Hughes*, 823 F.Supp. 593, 604 (N.D. Ind. 1993); *United States v. Searle*, 804 F.Supp. 1437 (D. Utah 1992); *Naugle v. Whitney*, 755 F.Supp. 1504 (D. Utah 1990), *rev'd on other grounds*, 997 F.2d 819; *State v. Petrone*, 468 N.W. 2d 676 (Wis. 1991) (police may remove undeveloped film to a laboratory for development).

21. 778 F.2d 609, 615, 616 (11th Cir. 1985).

22. *See United States v. Hughes*, 823 F.Supp. 593, 604 (N.D. Ind. 1993) ("[t]he underlying supposition is that a wholesale seizure of all property of a certain ilk for subsequent filtering and classification elsewhere is less intrusive and more feasible than an extended police presence for a substantial period of time upon the premises searched").

have reasoned that officers in such cases have already seen incriminating evidence in "plain view" and are merely taking other evidence which is probably incriminating.[23] In theory, this line of cases should not apply where officers seek to seize a computer without first discovering *any* material described by the warrant on the hard drive. However, prosecutors may still cite those cases for the principle that police may remove unexamined material to another location.

> *7.25–b(2)   The law may require investigators to obtain authorization in the warrant to remove computer evidence*

The Ninth Circuit Court of Appeals has suggested that removal of records off-site for further examination without specific authorization in the warrant to do so constitutes a "general search." In *United States v. Tamura,*[24] decided *before* the cases discussed in the previous section, federal agents executed a warrant calling for seizure of certain accounting records. After the suspects refused to assist agents in separating those records from their thousands of other accounting records, agents seized all of the records.

Apparently offended by the agents' conduct, the court stated that the removal was an improper general search. The court's language is especially forbidding:

> [T]he wholesale seizure for later detailed examination of records not described in a warrant is significantly more intrusive [than mere inspection at the scene], and has been characterized as "the kind of investigatory dragnet that the Fourth Amendment was designed to prevent [citation omitted]." We cannot sanction the procedure followed by the Government in this case.[25]

---

23. *See United States v. Blakeney,* 942 F.2d 1001 (6th Cir. 1991); *United States v. Fawole,* 785 F.2d 1141, 1144 (4th Cir. 1986) (agent who found a briefcase containing 150 different items was allowed to remove that briefcase from the premises to perform a more thorough examination).

24. 694 F.2d 591 (9th Cir. 1982).

25. *United States v. Tamura,* 694 F.2d 591, 595 (9th Cir. 1982).

This decision appears to conflict with the other decisions cited previously, and should not be followed.

However, even the *Tamura* decision appears to allow removal if the magistrate issuing the warrant authorizes removal when signing the warrant. The court stated that such authorization "should be granted by the magistrate issuing the warrant only where on-site sorting is infeasible and no other practical alternative exists."[26]

This approach is consistent with *Santarelli*, which authorized removal on the theory that the alternative, an on-site search requiring agents to remain on the premises for hours or days, represented a greater intrusion into the suspect's privacy rights. As discussed later in this chapter and in Chapter 9, this restriction should not prevent removal. You can easily demonstrate that "on-site sorting" of a possibly rigged computer with a 500 MB hard drive is "infeasible, and [that] no other practical alternative exists."

The next sections discuss the steps you should take to comply with the Fourth Amendment when removing computers and media for later examination.

7.25–c   How to comply with the rules governing removal of computer evidence

You may remove computer evidence to an off-site location without reviewing it first if you:

- demonstrate that the removal was reasonable;

- search the computer evidence promptly after removing it; and

- return any computer evidence that is not encompassed by your search warrant promptly.

7.25–c(1)   The removal must be reasonable

You can easily show that "removal" is necessary to conduct a competent search of the computer. As discussed in Chapter 6, there are many reasons why searching a computer on-site is fraught with

---

26. *Tamura*, at 596.

peril. Moreover, courts allow removal because it is preferable to having police remain at the premises for hours or days. A competent search of a computer system can take anywhere from a week to several months.

Unfortunately, courts have yet to address this issue. There is no guarantee that your judge will understand computer technology, or accept that it is often foolhardy to search a computer on-site. The problem is particularly acute where computer bulletin boards are involved because civil libertarians argue that seizing such a board is akin to shutting down a printing press, and is automatically unreasonable.

You can avoid this problem by addressing it in your affidavit. By justifying in your affidavit your removal of computers found at the premises, and asking the magistrate to approve that removal, you put the defense attorney in a difficult position. Any attack on the warrant may be perceived as an attack on the magistrate's judgment in issuing the warrant approving that removal.[27] Chapter 9 includes sample language addressing this issue.

7.25–c(2)   *The removal must be temporary, and irrelevant items must be returned promptly*

Although you are allowed to remove a computer, you must search it promptly. The reason for this rule is that you do not know whether the computer contains evidence until you search it. Your search must be "ongoing"—until you find evidence on that computer, you have no basis for keeping it. Moreover, once you have determined that certain computer evidence is not encompassed by the search warrant, you must return it promptly.

Experience has shown that it is very tempting to delay searching seized equipment in favor of completing other parts of an investigation, or even working on other cases. You must resist that temptation because delaying your search creates two unacceptable risks.

First, the owner of the computer may go to court and demand that you return the computer immediately. The standard reply that you are

---

27. *See United States v. Tamura*, 694 F.2d 591 (9th Cir. 1982). You will also demonstrate good faith, which may reduce the risk that you will be found liable for any disruption caused by your removal.

retaining the computer as evidence until the end of the case is unavailable because you have yet to find any evidence. The court will order you to complete your search of the "removed" computer immediately. Such an order entered at an inconvenient time may prevent you from completing more urgent parts of your investigation. In extreme cases, you may not have time to search the computer.

Second, a canny defense lawyer may simply do nothing, and wait for a few months while you work on other cases. At some point, the defense will move to suppress the results of any subsequent search of the computer on the grounds that the delay in returning the "removed" computer transformed a removal into a seizure unsupported by probable cause.

Your "removal" was supposed to be a continuation of the search. If you failed to make that search, then your retention of the computer may be deemed to have been a seizure without probable cause. Although you can make a persuasive argument that the defense waived any objection by failing to demand the return of the computer, you may lose.

The clock starts ticking when you seize a computer without searching it first. It does not stop ticking unless and until you find evidence allowing you to hold the computer until trial. Thus, you must examine "removed" computer evidence promptly. If the computer contains evidence listed in the warrant, then the computer becomes "evidence" in the case, and you do not have to return it pending trial.

In addition to removing computers, you should also remove associated equipment necessary to complete your search off-site. You should take documentation explaining how to operate the computer and software necessary to complete your search.

Various peripherals, such as printers, may be necessary to your search. Although this may sound extreme to someone not versed in searching and seizing computers, many experts recommend taking everything connected to a computer, including the printer, because it is quite possible a computer will not operate properly unless it is set up in the same "configuration" that it was in when it was seized.

However, taking such materials poses another problem. The Fourth Amendment allows you to remove property which you have probable cause to believe contains evidence listed in the warrant.

Does it also allow you to seize objects which probably do not contain evidence, but are useful, or even necessary, to allow you to complete your search? For example, can you seize printers to help you print evidence, or documentation to help you operate the computer?[28]

Although there are no cases directly addressing this question, it seems reasonable to allow police to seize items necessary to conduct the search. For example, if a safe were removed from the premises for further examination, it would appear reasonable for officers to seize any keys to that safe.

However, a court may interpret a seizure of documentation or printers as evidence that officers were engaged in a "general search," and were using the warrant as a "pretext," or excuse, to search and seize everything located at the premises.

You should address this problem in your affidavit. If you need those items to complete your search, say so. By justifying the seizure, you reduce any suspicion that you seized items simply because they were present at the scene.

You should use the standard language included in Chapter 9 (i.e., stating that the documentation will assist you in operating the computer), and mention any facts particular to your case which support the seizure (e.g., the computer owner uses an off-brand printer; police would not be able to obtain a similar printer and would have difficulty printing documents).[29]

You may also characterize certain components as a part of the physical object (the computer) which you are seizing. Monitors, mice and trackballs, removable media drives, and external tape drives would normally be considered part of the computer—modems, printers, fax machines, and telephones would probably not be included. In addition, documentation would be considered to be part of the computer, just as instructions are part of a kitchen appliance.

---

28. Although it is theoretically possible to store data in a printer's memory, the odds of a suspect's doing so are remote.

29. You can also justify seizing documentation on the grounds that such materials may demonstrate that the suspect owns the computer (e.g., a manual with the owner's name or handwritten notes in it).

What components are part of the computer?

There is no satisfactory test for determining which items should be considered part of the computer. Some state laws define "computer" broadly, so as to include peripherals. One test would be whether those items are usually needed to perform the normal functions of a computer or merely add optional features. While a monitor may be disconnected from a computer, the monitor is used every time the computer is booted up. Extra storage devices (and, stretching a little, devices such as tape backup units used to effectuate that storage) are also needed. However, a user can operate a computer without printing output and without communicating with other computers.

A defense argument that a computer consists of only those components necessarily included within a computer as purchased from a store is defeated by the observation that computers are frequently sold as components alone (e.g., motherboards, disk drives, memory chips). A car can also be purchased piecemeal, yet police are still allowed to seize the car without removing the radio.

However, another test might be to allow seizure of the computer case and its contents only. Under this test, the monitor, mouse, and printer could not be seized because they are easily left behind.

In appropriate cases, you may argue that the other items are evidence of how the suspect used the computer. A printer used to forge checks is an instrumentality. In cracker cases, the modem is an instrumentality. A modem is evidence that the cracker was able to dial the victim's computer; it may also be evidence of a conspiracy (i.e., communication with other suspects).

Finally, seemingly innocuous items can be characterized as potential sources of evidence. For example, as discussed in Chapters 6 and 9, you should always obtain permission to seize *all* loose media, including disks labeled as original software disks (e.g., the suspect's copies of DOS, WordPerfect, etc.), because those disks can be used to store other data.

7.25–c(3)   *Accounting for removed items in the return to the search warrant*

When "removing" computers and peripherals, file a return with the court which, in addition to accurately describing all items seized pursuant to the search warrant, includes the removed items. As you complete your examination, you should also file a separate return for any computers and peripherals which you are formally "seizing" as instrumentalities of the crime or repositories of evidence.

8

Federal Privacy Laws

8.00 Introduction

8.01 It is usually easy to comply with federal privacy laws

Do not get overwhelmed by the length of this chapter or the complexity of the federal laws involved. Most investigations will not involve federal privacy laws at all.

In the few cases where those laws are important, law enforcement investigators will usually be able to obtain the evidence they seek by using a carefully drafted search warrant. Corporate investigators will be able to comply with these laws by using caution and common sense.

The main point of this chapter is to ensure that you recognize when those laws may apply.

8.02 This chapter is organized differently—you may only need to read a few pages to find what you need

This is the only chapter in the book which is not written to be read from start to finish.

Although every reader should read the introductory sections (§§ 8.03, 8.04, 8.05, and 8.06), most law enforcement and corporate investigators will need only to consult a few sections to understand how federal privacy laws affect their particular investigations. Prosecutors and investigators responsible for their agencies' compliance with those laws should read the entire chapter.

The next section is intended to help you find the information you need for your investigation.

8.03 This chapter at a glance

Tables 8–1 and 8–2 summarize the types of law enforcement investigative activities which may require compliance with federal privacy laws. Corporate investigators (and investigators employed by universities) should use Table 8–3 as a guide to the portions of this chapter discussing the impact of federal privacy laws on private parties.

Table 8–1: Law enforcement investigators and the Omnibus Act

Title III of the Omnibus Crime Control and Safe Streets Act applies where a law enforcement investigator:	You should read the following sections of this chapter before proceeding with your investigation:
Intercepts a communication while it is actually taking place (e.g., recording commands sent by intruders, intercepting cordless and cellular telephones, tapping data lines).	§§ 8.10, 8.20, 8.31, 8.33
Searches, seizes, or requests disclosure of a communication stored by an electronic communication service or remote computing service (including companies such as CompuServe and MCI Mail, *and any computer used as a BBS or used to provide E-mail services*), or requests information about such a communication. This *may* include attempts to obtain E-mail stored by a business or university.	§§ 8.10, 8.40
Searches or seizes a computer bulletin board (a BBS).	§§ 8.10, 8.20, 8.31, 8.33, 8.40
Requests installation of a trap and trace or a pen register.	§ 8.50
Requests telephone subscriber records.	§ 8.60

Table 8–2: Law enforcement investigators and the Privacy Protection Act

The Privacy Protection Act applies where a law enforcement investigator:	You should read the following section of this chapter before proceeding:
Searches a BBS or any person or entity able to claim an intent to publish information to the public in paper or electronic form. (The law does not apply to private parties.)	§ 8.70

Table 8–3: Corporate investigators and the Omnibus Act

Title III of the Omnibus Crime Control and Safe Streets Act applies where a private party:	You should read the following sections of this chapter before proceeding:
Intercepts a communication while it is actually taking place (e.g., recording commands sent by intruders, wiretapping, tapping cordless or cellular telephone conversations, tapping data lines).	§ 8.32
Monitors or discloses communications being sent from, received by, or stored in its computer, or discloses information about the sender or recipient of such a communication. This material is aimed at businesses intending to read employee E-mail, universities intending to monitor activities of their computer users, and companies (e.g., MCI Mail) providing communication services.	§§ 8.32, 8.40. Businesses and universities should pay particular attention to § 8.47–a.

8.04 Updating the Fourth Amendment—why we have federal privacy laws protecting computer technology

Law reacts to changes in technology in a slow and unpredictable way. For example, although eavesdropping has always been considered an invasion of privacy, for centuries evidence obtained by eavesdropping was admissible in court. This began to change with the introduction of long-distance communication technology, as concerns arose that eavesdropping was becoming harder to detect and prevent.

The introduction of more sophisticated electronic surveillance devices in the early 20th century, such as phone taps and bugs, enabled individuals to eavesdrop on spoken conversations unobtrusively and from a distance. This new capability raised questions about the boundaries of the Fourth Amendment. The Fourth Amendment generally prohibits police from entering a house to observe a conversation conducted inside. Is the use of surveillance devices to eavesdrop on communications within a house, or a telephone booth, a "search"?

The United States Supreme Court decided in 1928 that the Fourth Amendment did not apply to wiretapping because the mere act of listening to a conversation did not involve a physical trespass or a seizure of anything tangible.[1] Forty years later, the Court reversed itself.

In *Katz v. United States*,[2] the Court ruled that the Fourth Amendment applies to wiretapping because persons talking on the telephone enjoy an "expectation of privacy" in their conversation. Any attempt to capture that conversation was deemed to be a "search."[3] This is the rule today, and it means that whenever a new type of communication is introduced, the courts must determine whether persons using that new technology enjoy an expectation of privacy.

Unfortunately, this interpretation of the Fourth Amendment raises new issues. When *Katz* was decided, long-distance voice communication was generally limited to speech transmitted on a

---

1. *See Olmstead v. United States*, 277 U.S. 438 (1928).

2. 389 U.S. 347 (1967).

3. The Court also ruled that the Fourth Amendment applies to electronic eavesdropping on oral conversations (e.g., "bugging" a room). *See Bergen v. New York*, 388 U.S. 41 (1967).

telephone connected to a wire. Today, in addition to traditional telephones, we use pagers, cordless telephones, and cellular telephones to communicate via radio waves.

While intercepting a wire communication requires sophistication and special equipment, intercepting a conversation held on a cordless telephone requires only a cheap scanner and patience. Does the Fourth Amendment apply to both communications? If so, how do we define a reasonable expectation of privacy for a cordless telephone communication which is so easy to intercept?

Not only the means of communication has changed—so too has the form of the information communicated. In addition to voice, we now send data over telephone lines, by satellite, and between computers located within the same room or building. That data may be indistinguishable from traditional forms of communication.

For example, computer users now send "electronic mail," or E-mail, from one computer to another. Fax machines are also used to send messages. Are these new forms of communication protected by the Fourth Amendment?

Another problem is that some new forms of communication retain a physical presence after the communication has ended. A telephone conversation, unless taped, ceases to exist after the last words are spoken. But electronic mail, like regular mail, remains on some medium (usually a hard disk) after the communication is completed; and it can be located, examined, and seized after the message has been received.

Indeed, many companies (such as MCI and CompuServe) offer to serve as waystations for electronic mail by storing messages in "electronic mailboxes" for customers. This means that it may be possible for persons with access to such mailboxes to obtain a communication before the intended recipient receives it.

In addition to the messages in the mailboxes, those companies may also create and maintain backup copies of those messages long after they have been sent, received, and deleted by the recipient. Are such "stored communications" protected by the Fourth Amendment?

Finally, just what does it mean to "intercept" a communication? Is it a violation of the Fourth Amendment to read messages stored on a pager found at a crack house? May private parties or law enforcement investigators trap commands sent to a computer by an intruder? May the owner of a university computer system monitor account activity of users accessing the Internet? May a business or police search the company's computer system for E-mail messages transmitted by employees to each other, or to other companies?

Congress has responded to these issues by enacting new laws designed to protect certain newer forms of communication from interception. This chapter explores those laws and discusses how investigators and communication service providers (defined later in this chapter) can comply with them during a criminal investigation.

8.05 This chapter discusses two statutes: Title III of the Omnibus Crime Control and Safe Streets Act and the Privacy Protection Act.

8.05–a   Description of Title III of the Omnibus Crime Control and Safe Streets Act

Congress passed Title III of the Omnibus Crime Control and Safe Streets Act of 1968 in response to the *Katz* decision. Although Title III originally regulated interception of oral and wire communications, Congress eventually decided to provide rules governing interception of newer forms of communication, particularly electronic communications.

In 1986, Congress amended Title III by enacting the Electronic Communications Privacy Act (ECPA). This chapter refers to the resulting collection of statutes as "the Act."[4] The Act is huge, consisting of over thirty statutes grouped within Title 18 of the United States Code.[5]

---

4. Many high technology crime investigators and prosecutors use ECPA, or Title III to refer to these statutes, and for that reason the index to this book collects references to it under the heading "ECPA." However, a few important statutes were never amended by the ECPA, and Title III is more closely associated with restrictions on wiretapping.

5. *See* 18 U.S.C. 2510–2521, 2701–2711, 3121–3127. Sections 2510–2521 regulate interception of electronic communications. Sections 2701–2711 regulate governmental access to stored electronic communications (e.g., E-mail). Sections 3121–3127 regulate use of trap and trace devices and pen registers.

Congress periodically amends portions of the Act to keep pace with new technology and to repair drafting errors.

The Act applies to all law enforcement personnel, *and to private parties*, and a violation can be costly. Unauthorized interception of protected communications is punishable by fine and/or imprisonment. The Act also allows "aggrieved persons" to obtain civil damages. In addition to the actual loss suffered by the victim, the statute provides for an award of damages of as much as $10,000 regardless of actual loss, *plus* attorneys fees and costs of litigation.[6]

As discussed later in this chapter, certain evidence gathered in violation of the Act may be inadmissible in court.

8.05–b   Description of the Privacy Protection Act

The Privacy Protection Act[7] is a different type of statute. (To avoid confusion with the Omnibus Act, this chapter refers to the Privacy Protection Act by its full name or as the PPA.)

While the Act seeks to protect communications based on their form (e.g., electronic communications receive protection different from wire communications), the PPA was enacted to protect a group of communicators: the media.

The PPA restricts the government's ability to use a search warrant to seize materials belonging to persons who intend to disseminate information to the public. (The law does not apply to private parties.) The PPA is relevant to high-technology crime investigation because, in addition to traditional newspapers, many people sending and receiving electronic communications (including bulletin board sysops) may also be treated as publishers under the PPA.

The PPA is not to be taken lightly. In a recent case that shook the law enforcement community, the Secret Service was ordered to pay a Texas game company $50,000 in damages, $195,000 in attorney's fees, and $57,000 in costs for violating the law. The Secret Service had seized the company's computers while investigating a suspected

---

6. *See* 18 U.S.C. 2520.

7. 42 U.S.C. 2000aa *et seq.*

computer intrusion involving an employee. The agent who violated the PPA testified that he was not aware of the law.[8]

8.06 Warnings

These federal statutes do not replace the Fourth Amendment, but supplement it. Congress may not limit the protections provided by the Fourth Amendment, and there is no guarantee that a search permitted by a federal statute will not violate the Fourth Amendment. However, if you comply with federal law (along with applicable state constitutional and statutory law) governing an *existing* type of communication, the courts will most likely find that you have also satisfied the requirements of the Fourth Amendment.[9]

In addition, states are free to add protections beyond those provided by federal law, and some have done so. This book cannot cover the law in every state. You should therefore examine applicable state law whenever your investigation may result in the interception or seizure of communications.

Finally, bear in mind that these laws are not only complex, but are also unclear in several vital areas. Courts have yet to resolve many questions, and this book can only give you guidance—not ironclad answers. *Investigators should consult a lawyer (preferably a prosecutor) in cases where it appears that one of these statutes may apply.*

8.10 A summary of the Act

Here is the Omnibus Act in a nutshell:[10]

---

8. *See Steve Jackson Games v. United States Secret Service*, 816 F.Supp. 432 (W.D. Tex. 1993), *affirmed* 36 F.3d 457 (5th Cir. 1994). The company was not suspected of any wrongdoing.

9. *See, e.g., United States v. Bailey*, 607 F.2d 237 (9th Cir. 1979). However, if you intend to intercept a new form of communication not covered by the Act, you must determine whether the parties to that communication enjoy an expectation of privacy guaranteed by the Fourth Amendment.

10. Federal investigators should also obtain a copy of the guidelines recently issued by the Department of Justice. *See* United States Department of Justice, *Federal Guidelines for Searching and Seizing Computers* (Department of Justice, 1994).

- Law enforcement investigators must obtain a special court order before intercepting any electronic communication, including E-mail, when that communication is actually taking place (i.e., when it is "in transmission"). An application for such an order must meet a standard higher than that required for an ordinary search warrant. Private parties may not intercept certain electronic communications in transmission.

- The Act protects *only* those communications which are in transmission (i.e., it does not protect E-mail after it has been "delivered" to the suspect's hard drive), with one large exception.

  The Act protects any electronic communication "stored" by an "electronic communication service" for eventual transmission to the intended recipient. For example, law enforcement investigators must obtain a warrant, court order, or subpoena to obtain E-mail held for a customer by a company such as MCI Mail. Investigators must obtain similar legal process in order to compel a "remote computing service" (a "data bank") to disclose data stored for a customer.

- Investigators must obtain a court order before installing pen registers and traps and traces on telephone lines. Although the Act allows investigators to obtain those orders by stating under oath that the results will be relevant to an ongoing investigation, certain states, such as California, require investigators to obtain a search warrant.

- The Act prevents telephone companies from disclosing toll records without a search warrant, subpoena, or court order. Again, certain states require a search warrant.

8.20 The Act protects wire, oral, and electronic communications—most investigations involve electronic communications

The Act covers three types of communication: wire, oral, and electronic. A wire communication is any transfer of the human voice made in whole or part through the use of facilities designed to transmit communications by wire or cable.[11] A wire communication includes telephone conversations transmitted to or from a telephone company (e.g., on a telephone), *including cellular and cordless telephone conversations.*[12] It does not include communications transmitted on systems which are not connected with the outside world.[13]

Congress defined an oral communication as "any oral communication uttered by a person exhibiting an expectation that such communication is not subject to interception under circumstances justifying such expectation."[14] Think of an oral communication as including any speech uttered in apparent secrecy. Congress appears to have been concerned about the use of surveillance techniques such as bugs and parabolic microphones which can intercept speech even where the speaker assumes that the communication is private.

The ECPA added "electronic communications" as a separate category of communications protected by the Act, and it is this type of communication which creates the most problems during high-technology crime investigations. An electronic communication is "any transfer of signs, signals, writing, images, sounds, data, or intelligence of any nature transmitted in whole or in part by a wire, radio, electromagnetic, photoelectronic, or photooptical system."[15]

---

11. 18 U.S.C. 2510(1).

12. *See* 18 U.S.C. 2510(1) (specifically including communications transferred through switching stations). Congress recently changed the Act to prohibit interception of the radio transmission between a cordless handset and its base unit. *Investigators seeking to "listen in" to those conversations must obtain a court order. See § 8.33.*

13. *See* 18 U.S.C. 2510(1) ("wire communication" includes only communications through facilities operated or provided for the transmission of communications which affect interstate or foreign commerce).

14. 18 U.S.C. 2510(2). Leave it to Congress to define a term by using that term in the definition!

15. 18 U.S.C. 2510(12). Congress excluded three types of communication from this category. First, a wire communication cannot also be an electronic communication; if a human voice is being transmitted, then the communication is either a wire or an oral communication. Second, radio transmissions readily accessible to the general public, such as AM-FM broadcasts and other unscrambled, unencrypted broadcasts (such as police communications), are not electronic communications. Third, messages to tone-only paging devices (now obsolete) are not electronic communications.

This definition is broad, and includes fax transmissions, E-mail, data transferred between computers, and most communications between pagers and pager companies.

8.30 Requirements for intercepting communications in transmission

8.31 The communication must be in transmission

The Act protects a communication from interception while it is in transmission. A communication is "in transmission" when the speech, electrical impulses, radio waves, etc., making up that communication are moving from one party to the communication to another party.

A communication stops being "in transmission" when: (1) the communication is received by the other party to the communication; or (2) the communication is "stored" by an electronic communication service provider as an interim step in providing the message to the intended recipient. (The definition of such service providers is broad. For now, think of a provider as MCI Mail, CompuServe, or another company which allows customers to send or receive E-mail.)

Examples of communications in transmission include communications to a digital pager, fax transmissions in progress, and most important, any data (including commands) traveling from one computer to another. If you intercept packets on the Internet, you are intercepting a communication in transmission.

Investigators rarely need to intercept communications in transmission. Some interceptions, while useful, are not feasible. For example, while tapping a fax line might prove useful, most investigations will not justify the time and expense of doing so.

Furthermore, investigators are usually able to delay obtaining the contents of a communication until after that communication is no longer in transmission. For example, you usually do not need to intercept a phone number on its way to a pager; you need only read the display on that pager after the message has been received. Although the communication from the paging company to the pager is an electronic communication in transmission, the readout on the pager displaying the stored message is not. And while searching the pager for that information is a search and seizure under the Fourth Amendment, the search is not an interception of an electronic communication as defined by the Act.[16]

The same principle applies to electronic communications between computers. In most cases, you will be searching computer records of a communication which has already been transmitted.

For example, it is possible to intercept E-mail sent between computers by tapping a data line, and such an interception would be covered by the Act. However, you are more likely to encounter E-mail after it has been received and stored on a suspect's personal computer; as discussed later, such a search of the suspect's hard drive would not be covered by the Act.

The prohibition in the Act against intercepting electronic communications *does not apply* to searches of communications not in transmission, although, as discussed later, the Act does regulate searches of communications stored by individuals or institutions providing communication services to the public (e.g., CompuServe, MCI Mail). *A typical search of a computer in a residence or a business does not involve the Act.*[17]

8.32 Interception by private parties

Notwithstanding the fact that many investigations can be completed without intercepting electronic communications in transmission, there are several situations in which private parties may want to intercept such communications:

- A computer owner seeks to *keystroke monitor* the activities of an intruder who is breaking into the owner's computer. *Keystroke monitoring* refers to monitoring (and recording) the typewritten

---

16. *See People v. Bullock*, 226 Cal. App. 3d 380 (Cal. Ct. App. 1990) (the contents of a pager are protected by the Fourth Amendment); *United States v. Meriwether*, 917 F.2d 955 (6th Cir. 1990) (the Act does not prohibit police from reading messages stored within a digital pager).

17. As discussed later in this chapter, an exception is where that computer is being used as a bulletin board and/or electronic communication service.

commands (the keystrokes) sent by an intruder to another computer system.

- A computer owner seeks to monitor a user who is using the owner's computer to break into other computers. For example, a cracker has an account with America Online which provides Internet access. He is using that account to break into a University of Washington computer system. System administrators at America Online wish to use their computers to keystroke monitor the cracker's commands sent to the University of Washington computer system.

- A business seeks to intercept E-mail sent between employees, and between employees and persons outside the company. The employer may be concerned about employees' sending unauthorized personal messages, using the company's computer system to break into other computers, or sending proprietary information outside the company. For example, a recent criminal case in California involved an executive who allegedly used his company's E-mail to transfer proprietary information to a competitor.

The Act does not address any of these scenarios directly. Rather, it sets forth a general rule prohibiting all interceptions, along with a series of exceptions to that rule.

The next section summarizes the rights of computer owners to intercept electronic communications, and then examines each of those exceptions individually.

8.32–a *Summary of rights of private parties to intercept electronic communications*

The Act appears to allow computer owners to perform the following interceptions.

- A computer owner may intercept communications between an intruder and that owner's computer system.

- A computer owner providing others with the ability to use that computer to communicate with other computer systems may:

- •• Make routine backups and perform other routine monitoring (terminating classes of communications which are not allowed, such as background processes running after the user has logged off) necessary to provide computing services.

- •• Intercept those communications with the prior consent of the user.

- •• Intercept those portions of communications necessary to determine their origin and destination on the Internet.

- •• Intercept communications where necessary to protect the owner's rights or property (e.g., against intrusion, fraud, or civil liability arising from someone using the owner's system to break into other computers).

- •• Disclose to law enforcement any communications inadvertently discovered which reveal criminal activity.

- • A business may monitor employee communications using its computer system where:

  - •• Employees have no right to use the computer for any reason.

  - •• The employer's policy unambiguously states that the employer will monitor all employee communications. If the employer's policy states that only certain communications will be monitored, then the employer may perform any monitoring authorized by that policy.

  - •• The employer monitors communications as part of a legitimate investigation of criminal misconduct by an employee and performs that monitoring for a limited period of time using equipment provided by the telephone company (i.e., the PBX).

  - •• As discussed in § 8.47–a, employers and universities may have additional rights to monitor communications, depending upon whether they are deemed to be electronic communication providers.

You should be cautious in relying upon this list to justify an interception. As noted in the next few sections, the rules in this area are ambiguous, and there is little or no case law to guide you. If in doubt, ask a law enforcement agency to obtain a court order authorizing an interception.

The next section explores the exceptions to the Act.

8.32–b   Exceptions to the rules protecting communications in transmission

8.32–b(1)   A party to a communication may intercept that communication

Section 2511(2)(d) allows any party to a communication to intercept that communication.[18] Does this exception allow a private party to monitor and record commands sent by an intruder to the party's computer? Although the United States Department of Justice has declined to take a position on this issue, there is a compelling argument that computer owners may capture intruders' commands.[19]

If the intruder is communicating with the owner's equipment, then the owner is a party to the communication and may intercept it. You do not communicate with a telephone—you communicate with the person holding the telephone. Therefore, a computer owner should be considered a party to any communication between an intruder and the owner's computer, and thus entitled to intercept those communications.

The history of the Act supports keystroke monitoring. The sponsor of § 2511(2)(d) stated that it allowed interceptions when "the

---

18. The Fourth Amendment does not prohibit such interceptions—a party to a communication assumes the risk that another party will report that communication to police. *See United States v. White*, 401 U.S. 745 (1971). Note that private parties not acting "under color of law" (i.e., under police direction) may not intercept a communication for the purpose of committing a crime or a civil wrong. *See* 18 U.S.C. 2511(2)(d).

19. In CERT Advisory CA-92:19, December 7, 1992, the Department stated that although it believed that keystroke monitoring was defensible under the Act, the Act did not expressly authorize such monitoring. As discussed in the next section, the Department suggests that owners post "banners" advising all users that the owner reserves the right to monitor communications.

party records information of criminal activity by the other party with the purpose of taking such information to the police as evidence."[20]

Two cases support keystroke monitoring. The most important case is *United States v. Seidlitz*,[21] in which the court allowed a computer owner to perform keystroke monitoring on the grounds that the owner was a party to the communication per § 2511(2)(d). Although *Seidlitz* was decided before Congress amended the Act to protect electronic communications, those amendments do not affect the court's interpretation of § 2511(2)(d).

In *United States v. Meriwether*,[22] the defendant sought to suppress the contents of a digital pager discovered by an agent during the execution of a search warrant. The court first denied the request because the communication was no longer in transmission when displayed by the agent. The court also held that *the agent became a party to the communication* by possessing the pager.[23] *Meriwether* suggests that the owner of a device, be it a pager or a computer, is a party to any communication with that device.

However, computer owners should not be able to use this exception to justify monitoring communications sent by employees to other computer systems. An employee does not communicate with the owner's computer, but merely uses it as a medium to communicate with another party. The owner is therefore not a party to the communication.

> *8.32–b(2)   A communication may be intercepted where any of the parties to that communication has given prior consent*

Section 2511(2)(d) allows interception of a communication when any party to that communication has consented to that interception.

---

20. 114 Congressional Record 14694 (May 23, 1968), *see* Fishman, Clifford S., *Wiretapping and Eavesdropping* (New York: Clark Boardman Callaghan, 1994) (Supplement), § 25.4, at 252.

21. 589 F.2d 152, 158 (4th Cir. 1978).

22. 917 F.2d 955 (6th Cir. 1990).

23. *Id.*, at 960. *See also United States v. Diaz-Lizaraza*, 981 F.2d 1216 (11th Cir. 1993).

If the owner has posted a notice indicating that all communications are monitored, then any intruder communicating with the computer has given prior consent to interception. Of course, this argument is useful only when the owner had the foresight to post notices before the intrusion. (Posting such a notice in the middle of an incident will warn off the intruder.)[24]

Even without such notices, computer owners *may* be able to justify interception based upon on a theory of implied consent. You can argue that an intruder can expect larger computers to have a monitoring system which, at a minimum, tracks commands sent to the computer. Such knowledge *may* be equivalent to consent.[25]

This consent exception may also allow providers of computing services to monitor communications by permissive users to other computer systems. However, courts will probably require evidence that the user gave prior written consent to such interceptions.

Finally, this exception may allow businesses to monitor employees' communications. However, businesses should proceed extremely cautiously in claiming consent.

That employees are, or should be, aware that employers are capable of monitoring communications probably does not equal consent.[26] Consent is difficult to prove in the absence of a widely circulated and carefully drafted policy governing employees' use of the computer.

---

24. In the CERT advisory cited in footnote 19, the Department of Justice suggests that computer owners post such banners. Unfortunately, depending upon the computer system, it can be impossible to "post" such notices on every "route" an intruder can use to access that computer.

25. *See United States v. Seidlitz*, 589 F.2d 152, n. 20 (4th Cir. 1978) (expressing "serious reservations" that an intruder enjoys a Fourth Amendment expectation of privacy). The argument is that if an intruder has no expectation of privacy, then that lack of privacy interest is equivalent to consent.

26. *See, e.g., Watkins v. L.M. Berry & Co.*, 704 F.2d 577 (11th Cir. 1983) (allowing employer monitoring to guard against unauthorized use of company telephones, but prohibiting interception of personal calls to determine the contents of those calls). The court found that employees had consented only to monitoring of business calls; their knowledge that the employer was capable of monitoring all communications did not imply consent. The result in *Watkins* is ironic, in that the employees maintained a privacy interest when exceeding the employer's consent to use its equipment, but lost that privacy interest via "consent" when making a business call.

Determine whether: (1) the employee consented to any monitoring; and (2) any consent was limited to allowing management to "peek" at messages to determine whether communications were company business, or permitted full-fledged monitoring of all communications, business or personal.

Moreover, businesses have more than the Act to worry about. Congress is considering legislation to strengthen privacy protections, and several lawsuits pending at the time of this writing raise objections to such monitoring based on federal and state constitutional and common law arguments.[27]

> *8.32–b(3)*   *Equipment furnished by the telephone company to any subscriber or user of such service may be used in the ordinary course of business to intercept communications*

Although the Act prohibits interception of communications, the definition of "interception" creates an interesting exception to that general rule. Section 2510(4) defines an interception as the "acquisition of the contents of any wire, electronic, or oral communication through the use of any electronic, mechanical, or other device." Section 2510(5) defines an "electronic, mechanical, or other device" as any device *except*:

> [A]ny telephone or telegraph instrument, equipment, or facility, or any component thereof furnished to the subscriber or user by a provider of wire or electronic communication service in the ordinary course of its business and being used by the subscriber or user in the ordinary course of its business or furnished by such subscriber or user for connection to the facilities of such service and used in the ordinary course of its business.

This exception, known as the *business-extension exception*, allows the use of equipment provided by the telephone company to its customers to intercept communications, so long as that equipment is

---

27. *See* Traynor, "Computer E-Mail Privacy Issues Unresolved," *National Law Journal*, January 31, 1994.

being used "in the ordinary course of business." This exception has been interpreted as allowing businesses to use their telephone equipment to monitor employee telephone calls without consent.

However, courts have ruled that this exception allows monitoring only for a legitimate business purpose and for a limited period of time. Courts have disallowed wholesale monitoring of all phone calls, but have approved limited monitoring designed to ensure that employees are using the phone for business, or as part of an investigation of suspected misconduct.[28]

Can businesses use this exception to intercept outgoing E-mail? If the statute is interpreted literally, any interception would have to be accomplished by using equipment supplied by the telecommunications company, as opposed to an interception accomplished solely "within" the employer's computer. The business would have to perform the interception using the PBX.

Furthermore, any such interception would face the same scrutiny as monitoring of telephone conversations. *Remember that the Act is only one obstacle to monitoring—your state law or constitution may prohibit it outright.*[29] You should determine both the technical details of the interception and the company's E-mail policy (generally, and in your specific case) before relying on this exception. You should try to use the "consent" exception instead where applicable.

> *8.32–b(4)*   *A provider of wire or electronic communication services may intercept an electronic communication where necessary to provide communication services or to protect the provider's rights or property*

---

28. *Compare Deal v. Spears*, 980 F.2d 1153 (8th Cir. 1992); *Epps v. St. Mary's Hospital, Inc.*, 802 F.2d 412 (11th Cir. 1986); *Watkins v. L.M. Berry & Co.*, 704 F.2d 577 (11th Cir. 1983); *Briggs v. American Air Filter*, 630 F.2d 414 (5th Cir. 1980) (employee suspected of leaking confidential bidding information); *Burnett v. State*, 789 S.W. 2d 376 (Tex. Ct. App. 1990).

29. For example, California prohibits wiretapping unless both parties consent to the interception. *See* California Penal Code Sections 632, 633.5; *People v. Otto*, 2 Cal. 4th 1008 (Cal. 1992). Although those laws apply to wire communications only, defendants will seek to extend those protections to electronic communications.

Section 2511(2)(a)(i) allows telecommunications companies and providers of electronic communication services to intercept electronic communications[30] where necessary to provide communication services or to protect "the rights or property of the carrier."[31] This type of exception is crucial for electronic communication service providers because they regularly monitor account activity and make backup tapes (making such tapes may intercept communications).[32]

The exception is also very important because it allows providers to intercept outgoing communications (including commands or viruses sent by crackers) on the grounds that the victim could sue the provider for providing the cracker with the means to access the victim's computer. The interception is thus justified by the provider's need to prevent its computer system from being used to commit crimes or civil wrongs. Similarly, the provider can intercept incoming communications as necessary to protect its rights or property.

The definition of electronic communication service provider becomes critical at this point because only such providers may use this exception. It is clear that companies which charge customers for the ability to send E-mail, such as America Online, MCI Mail, and Internet service providers generally, qualify under this exception.

However, as discussed later in this chapter (at § 8.47–a, beginning on page 381), some commentators believe that businesses providing communication services (e.g., E-mail) to employees, or universities providing such services to students, also qualify as electronic communication service providers.

---

30. Until recently, § 2511(a)(2) stated that only providers of wire communications could examine electronic communications. Congress recently made a "technical correction" to clarify that electronic communication service providers may also examine those communications. *See* P.L. 103-414, 108 Stat. 4279, 4291 (1994).

31. *See United States v. Goldstein*, 532 F.2d 1305 (9th Cir. 1976); *United States v. Clegg*, 509 F.2d 605, 612 (5th Cir. 1975); *United States v. Freeman*, 524 F.2d 337 (7th Cir. 1975).

32. "The provider of electronic communications services may have to monitor a stream of transmissions in order to properly route, terminate, and otherwise manage the individual messages they contain. These monitoring functions, which may be necessary to the provision of an electronic communication service, do not involve humans listening in on voice conversations. Accordingly, they are not prohibited." Sen. Rpt. 99-541, at 20, 1986 U.S.C.C.A.N. 3574.

This issue is complex and unsettled, and businesses and universities should proceed with great caution. Private parties contemplating monitoring communications of permissive users or employees should prepare and circulate a carefully drafted policy which obtains the consent of their users to monitoring.

> *8.32–b(5)*   *A provider of electronic communication services may provide to law enforcement any communication inadvertently obtained by that provider which appears to pertain to criminal activity*

Section 2511(3)(b)(iv) applies only to electronic communication service providers and is helpful where the provider has stumbled across illegal activity during routine system administration. Such activity may include war dialer or password acquisition programs left active after the user has logged off the system. The provider must truly stumble across the activity—a provider who monitors communications to determine whether criminal activity is occurring does not qualify for the exception.[33]

> *8.32–b(6)*   *It is not an interception to examine only that part of an electronic communication which reveals its source or destination, as opposed to its contents*

System administrators dealing with an intruder using the Internet need to examine the intruder's communications to determine the origin or destination of those communications. In addition, system administrators often employ source logging devices, which monitor the source and destination of traffic on their networks.

Section 2510(4) defines interception as the acquisition of the "contents" of the communication. Other portions of an electronic communication, such as information concerning the destination or

---

33. *See* Sen. Rpt. 99-541, *supra*, at 26, 1986 U.S.C.C.A.N. 3580. Again, state law may nullify such exceptions. *See, e.g., Tavernetti v. Superior Court*, 22 Cal. 3d 187 (Cal. 1978). Note that several cases hold that this exception allows a telephone operator who inadvertently overhears an incriminating conversation to stay on the line to determine the nature of that conversation. *See Adams v. Sumner*, 39 F.3d 933 (9th Cir. 1994); *United States v. Savage*, 564 F.2d 728 (5th Cir. 1977).

source of the communication, are not part of the "contents" of the communication. Thus, § 2510(4) appears to allow the examination of portions of the communication which do not reveal the contents of that communication.

Does such examination constitute an illegal trap or trace under the Act? As discussed below, the use of a device to acquire analogous information (i.e., pen registers and traps and traces) is covered by other portions of the Act. However, those provisions appear to apply only to devices which record telephone numbers, and therefore do not prohibit source/destination monitoring of electronic communications.[34]

Finally, do state privacy laws prohibit the gathering of source/destination information? Such privacy laws probably do not apply. First, like the Act, many such laws (i.e., wiretapping laws) do not specifically protect information which is unrelated to a traditional telephone conversation.

Second, those laws which simply protect "privacy" apply only where the user has a strong expectation of privacy in that activity. It is unlikely that courts will find that persons who communicate electronically have a sufficiently strong privacy interest in masking the source or destination of their communications. However, it is always possible that the debate over CallerID may prompt a court to find such a privacy interest in an unusual case.

---

34. Section 3127(3) defines a "pen register" as a separate device which identifies the "*numbers* dialed or otherwise transmitted on the telephone line to which such device is attached." Section 3121(c), added in 1994, requires a government agency to ensure that any pen register it uses "restricts the recording or decoding of electronic or other impulses *to the dialing and signaling information utilized in call processing*." These phrases appear to refer to traditional telephone calls only. Similarly, the definition of a trap and trace refers to capturing the impulses which identify the originating *number* or device from which a communication was transmitted.

Although these definitions are ambiguous (particularly since Internet addresses *are* numbers), the glossary to the Senate Judiciary Report discussing the ECPA confirms the limited nature of pen registers and traps and traces. "Pen registers are devices that record *the telephone numbers* to which calls have been placed *from a particular telephone*. These capture no part of an actual *telephone conversation*, but merely *the electronic switching signals that connect two telephones*. The same holds true for trap and trace devices, which record the numbers of telephones from which calls have been placed to a particular telephone." Sen. Report 99-541, at 10, 1986 U.S.C.C.A.N. 3564 (emphasis added).

8.32–c   Disclosure of lawfully intercepted communications by private parties

A private party who lawfully intercepts an electronic communication may disclose that communication, with two exceptions.

First, an electronic communication service provider that intercepts a communication may disclose it only where necessary to protect its rights and property or to render normal service. Second, a service provider that inadvertently intercepts a communication revealing criminal activity may disclose that communication to law enforcement personnel only.[35]

8.33   Interception of communications in transmission by law enforcement

Law enforcement investigators may intercept communications in transmission only after obtaining a court order. The Act distinguishes between intercept orders issued by federal courts and state courts.

Warning: the details of how to obtain an intercept order are complex and mind-numbing. Readers who do not need to intercept communications in transmission are advised to skip ahead to § 8.34, beginning on page 361.

8.33–a   Federal court orders

The United States Attorney General and certain of his or her deputies may apply to a federal judge for an order allowing interception of wire or oral communications where those communications may reveal evidence of one or more enumerated federal crimes.[36]

The rule is more lenient for electronic communications—any United States Attorney may apply to a federal judge for an intercept

---

35. *See* Fishman, *Wiretapping and Eavesdropping* (New York: Clark Boardman Callaghan, 1994) (Supplement), § 25.7 (collected authority). Note that the rules are different for "stored communications"; those rules are discussed later in this chapter.

36. *See* 18 U.S.C. 2516(1) (the list of crimes is extensive). Congress recently amended the Act to allow an "acting" deputy to make the application.

Call an experienced prosecutor for help

Orders authorizing interception of electronic communications are very similar to standard federal wiretap orders; most of the provisions of the Act apply to interceptions of both wire and electronic communications. Large treatises have been written on the legal issues in this area, and novices may soon find themselves overwhelmed.

If you need an order to intercept electronic communications, contact a prosecutor with experience in this area, preferably a United States Attorney with experience in drafting wiretap applications under the Act.

---

order where electronic communications may reveal evidence of a federal felony offense.[37]

8.33–b   State court orders

As discussed in this section, the Act places state law enforcement officials at a disadvantage. Those officials should consider seeking assistance from federal agencies when seeking to intercept communications covered by the Act.

State and local law enforcement officials may apply only to state courts of "general jurisdiction" for interception orders (i.e., generally not justice or municipal courts).[38]

Those officials must meet three conditions to obtain an order. First, the applicant must be "authorized by a statute of that State to

---

37. *See* 18 U.S.C. 2516(3). Magistrates may not be able to authorize such orders. *See In re United States*, 10 F.3d 391 (2d Cir. 1993). Magistrates may issue orders authorizing pen registers and trap and traces. *See* 18 U.S.C. 3127(2)(A).

38. 18 U.S.C. 2516(2) allows state officials to petition a state court of "competent jurisdiction." That phrase is used throughout the Act (*see, e.g.,* §§ 2703(d), 3122(a)), and is defined as a court of "general criminal jurisdiction." *See* 18 U.S.C. 2510(9), 2703(d), 3126(2)(a), and 3127(2). That definition probably excludes municipal and justice courts.

make application to a State court judge of competent jurisdiction for an order authorizing or approving the interception of a wire, oral, or electronic communication."[39]

Congress appears to have intended this provision to encourage states to enact even tougher restrictions on interceptions of communications. However, the result may not be what Congress intended.

Some states, such as California, have enacted statutes which refer to interceptions of wire communications only. Those laws do not mention electronic communications. Thus, if the Act requires a special court order to intercept an electronic communication in transmission, law enforcement agencies in those states may not obtain such an order from a state court judge.[40] They must ask federal authorities to obtain that order from a federal court.

Second, in addition to meeting the requirements set forth by the Act, the application must meet the standards required by the state law authorizing interception of communications.[41]

This means that restrictive state laws may prevent local police officers from obtaining court orders from state judges, but allow those officers to use federal attorneys and federal law enforcement officials to obtain orders from federal judges where federal crimes are involved.

The Act on its face does not appear to allow state law enforcement officials to apply to federal courts for intercept orders. Moreover, the Act does not allow state law enforcement officials to

---

39. *See* 18 U.S.C. 2516(2).

40. The structure of 18 U.S.C. 2516 appears to contemplate that a state must authorize the precise type of interception requested. A state agent seeking to intercept an electronic communication must have the authority under state law to intercept an electronic communication, as opposed to a wire or oral communication.

Moreover, even if the authority to intercept any communication were sufficient to intercept an electronic communication, California law enforcement agencies would still be out of luck in most cases because California prohibits wiretapping unless authorities have probable cause to suspect drug trafficking. *See* California Penal Code Section 629.02(1); *see also Vance*, "Almost Everything You Wanted to Know About Cellular and Cordless Telephones, Tone, Voice and Digital Pagers and Pen Registers," Prosecutor's Brief (published by the California District Attorneys' Association) (November, 1992).

41. *See* 18 U.S.C. 2516(2).

intercept communications based on a federal court order unless those state officials are working under the supervision of federal agents.[42]

Third, the application must demonstrate that the communications may reveal evidence of one or more enumerated crimes under state law. This list of enumerated crimes differs from the list of federal crimes which governs applications by federal attorneys to federal courts. The list of state crimes includes a catch-all provision allowing interceptions in cases involving crimes "dangerous to life, limb, *or property*," so long as those crimes are "punishable by imprisonment for *more* than one year."[43]

8.33–c   Exception for exigent circumstances

There is an "emergency" exception to the requirement that law enforcement officers obtain a court order before intercepting communications, but law enforcement investigators must use it with extreme caution. The exception applies where there is immediate danger of death or serious physical injury, or evidence of "conspiratorial activities" which threaten national security or are characteristic of organized crime.

Investigators must have grounds for a normal interception order before intercepting any communication and must file an application for such an order within 48 hours after the interception. If the application is denied, the interception must cease, and investigators are considered to have violated the Act.[44]

8.33–d   Applications for court orders

If you thought that search warrants were burdensome, consider the Act. The Act requires that an application for a court order allowing

---

42. *See, e.g., United States v. Bynum*, 763 F.2d 474 (1st. Cir. 1985); *United States v. Barker*, 623 F.Supp. 823 (D.C. Col. 1985).

43. 18 U.S.C. 2516(2). This provision appears to encompass common property crimes, such as larceny, and invasions of computer systems which could damage property.

44. *See* 18 U.S.C. 2518(7).

interception of communications in transmission contain the following information:

- a showing of probable cause that a particular offense will be committed;

- the identity of the suspect, if known;

- the identity of the person whose communications will be intercepted;

- a particular description of the location of the point of interception (which telephone, computer, or room will be the subject of surveillance), or the facilities to be used in making that interception (e.g., the telephone company);

- the period of time for which the interception is to be maintained;

- the existence of earlier applications for such orders made during the course of the investigation; and

- a showing of good cause as to why other less intrusive investigative techniques (e.g., informants) are either unlikely to succeed or are too dangerous.[45]

An application for an order allowing interception of communications in transmission must meet a standard higher than that required for an ordinary search warrant. In addition to showing probable cause that the suspect is involved in criminal activity, the application must demonstrate that investigators pursued all other avenues which could have reasonably avoided the need for an interception. Remember, too, that relevant state laws may impose additional requirements governing applications to state courts for intercept orders.

A court may issue an order per the Act after finding the following:

- that there is probable cause to believe that one of the crimes enumerated within the applicable part of the Act has been, is, or is about to be, committed;

---

45. *See* 18 U.S.C. 2518(1). Great care should be taken when drafting the application to provide good reasons why the same results cannot be obtained without the interception.

- that there is probable cause that particular communications relating to that crime will be obtained through the requested intercept;

- that the facilities at which the interception is authorized by the order are the facilities being used for the communication; and

- that normal investigative procedures either were tried and failed, or appear to be unlikely to succeed or unacceptably dangerous.[46]

The order must include the following:

- the identity of the person whose communication is to be intercepted;

- the nature and location of the communication facilities where the interception will take place;

- a description of the type of communication to be intercepted;

- a description of the offense to which the communication relates;

- the identity of the applicant, and of the agency authorized to intercept the communication;

- an order that the interception shall be conducted in such a way as to minimize interception of irrelevant communications, and shall terminate as soon as the objective of that interception has been achieved. *The Act may require that law enforcement officers conducting the interception sanitize any communications obtained to eliminate irrelevant matter before showing those communications to other officers (see box on next page);*

- the period of time for which interception is authorized, and whether that authorization terminates immediately after a specific communication has been obtained;[47]

---

46. *See* 18 U.S.C. 2518(4). Those findings should be recited in any proposed order presented to a judge for signature.

47. *See* 18 U.S.C. 2518(5). No order may authorize an interception during a period longer than 30 days after issuance, counting the first day as ten days after the order was signed, or on the first day an interception is commenced; the Act authorizes a one-time extension of 30 days for good cause.

- an order that the interception shall begin as soon as possible; and

- if requested by the applicant, an order requiring communications providers to assist in the interception; the applicant must pay reasonable costs.

Applying the minimization requirement to electronic communications

Congress has required investigators to take precautions to make sure that they only intercept communications which are relevant to their investigation. Thus, investigators tapping telephones are required to stop monitoring conversations which, after initial monitoring, appear to be "innocent."

This concept is difficult to apply to monitoring of electronic communications because the interception of an electronic communication occurs all at once; investigators only discover the content of the communication after they have intercepted all of it. The Senate Judiciary Committee has offered a "suggestion" on this issue.

The Committee suggests that "minimization for computer transmissions would require a somewhat different procedure from that used to minimize a telephone call. Common sense would dictate, and it is the Committee's intention, that the minimization should be conducted by the initial law enforcement officials who review the transcript (*sic.*: of course, there is usually no transcript of an electronic communication). Those officials would delete all non-relevant materials and disseminate to other officials only that information which is relevant to the investigation." Sen. Rpt. No. 99-541, at 31, 1986 U.S.C.C.A.N. 3585.

It would be prudent to follow the Committee's suggestion—courts may decide that Congress incorporated that suggestion into the Act as a requirement.

8.33–e   After the order is issued

The Act contains three important provisions which may surprise the unwary investigator. First, anyone conducting an authorized interception must, if possible, record the intercepted communication on appropriate media.[48] Such recordings must be provided to the judge *immediately upon expiration of the period of time for which the interception is authorized,* and retained by the court under seal for ten years. The investigator may make duplicate copies of that information, but must guard that information from disclosure as described below.

The idea behind this requirement is to ensure that there is never a basis for a claim that investigators tampered with the evidence after the interception. (To be blunt, the fear is that law enforcement investigators will tamper with intercepted evidence before seeking to admit it in court.)

Courts construe these provisions very strictly.[49] As discussed in the next section, failure to provide the court with the intercepted evidence promptly may result in suppression of that evidence.

Second, there are restrictions on dissemination of information intercepted pursuant to the Act. Law enforcement investigators may disclose such information only to other law enforcement investigators (not to the victim) and may use such information only as appropriate to the performance of their official duties.[50]

Third, within 90 days after an application has been denied or an order authorizing interception has terminated, the court must inform the suspect of the interception of the application for an order and of all attempted and actual interceptions. An applicant may seek to postpone disclosure by seeking an order from the court *ex parte* (i.e., without telling the suspect).[51]

---

48. *See* 18 U.S.C. 2518(8)(a).

49. *See, e.g., United States v. Ojeda Rios,* 495 U.S. 257 (1990); Fishman, *Wiretapping and Eavesdropping* (New York: Clark Boardman Callaghan, 1994) (Supplement), at §§ 191–94.

50. *See* 18 U.S.C. 2517(1) and (2).

51. *See* 18 U.S.C. 2518(8)(b).

8.34 Suppression of an unauthorized interception of an electronic communication in transmission by law enforcement or private parties

Intercepting an electronic communication in transmission in violation of the Act can result in costly civil penalties and possible criminal sanctions. But does the Act prevent the prosecution from using the communication as evidence in a criminal prosecution?

For those who would prefer to skip the legal analysis and proceed to the next section (beginning on page 363), the answer is no, although state law may still require suppression of those communications.

Section 2515 sets forth the suppression remedy:

> Whenever any *wire or oral communication* has been intercepted [in violation of the Act], no part of the contents of such communication and no evidence derived therefrom may be received in evidence in any trial, hearing, or other proceeding in or before any court, grand jury, department, officer, agency, regulatory body, legislative committee, or other authority of the United States, a State, or a political subdivision thereof.[52]

Notice that the words "electronic communication" do not appear in that clause. Nor do they appear in § 2518(10)(a), which allows suppression motions where errors were made in following the procedures mandated by the Act for intercepting communications.

Equally important is the unequivocal language of § 2518(10)(c), which states that the remedies and sanctions described in the Act with respect to *electronic communications* are "the only judicial remedies and sanctions for nonconstitutional violations of this chapter involving such communications."[53]

The addition by Congress of § 2518(10)(c) in 1986 as part of the Electronic Communications Privacy Act indicates that Congress intended to exempt electronic communications from the suppression

---

52. Section 2515 (emphasis added).

53. The phrase "nonconstitutional violations" appears to include only violations of the Act—Congress did not intend to foreclose Fourth Amendment and state constitutional challenges based on conduct which also violates the Act.

provisions of the Act. Furthermore, the Senate Judiciary Committee Report on the ECPA says as much:

> Subsection 101(e) of the Electronic Communications Privacy Act amends subsection 2518(10) of title 18 to add a paragraph (c) which provides that with respect to the interception of electronic communications, the remedies and sanctions described in this chapter are the only judicial remedies and sanctions available for nonconstitutional violations of this chapter involving such communications. In the event that there is a violation of law of a constitutional magnitude, the court involved in a subsequent trial will apply the existing Constitutional law with respect to the exclusionary rule. *The purpose of this provision is to underscore that, as a result of discussions with the Justice Department, the Electronic Communications Privacy Act does not apply the statutory exclusionary rule contained in the Act of the Omnibus Crime Control and Safe Streets Act of 1968 to the interception of electronic communications.*[54]

The Sixth Circuit Court of Appeal understood the intent of Congress when it held in 1990 that "the ECPA does not provide an independent statutory remedy of suppression for interceptions of electronic communications."[55]

However, the United States Supreme Court stated in the same year that Congress intended to suppress illegally intercepted electronic communications.[56] The Court made its pronouncement in a footnote in the course of considering other issues relating to the sealing of lawfully intercepted communications:

> [The Act] also contains a general suppression remedy, not applicable in this case, that provides for suppression when electronic communications have been unlawfully intercepted, were intercepted pursuant to a court order that is facially invalid, or were not

---

54. Sen. Rpt. 99-541, *supra*, at 23, 1986 U.S.C.C.A.N. 3577 (emphasis added).

55. *United States v. Meriwether*, 917 F.2d 955, 960 (6th Cir. 1990) (citing the same legislative history discussed above); *see* Fishman, *Wiretapping and Eavesdropping* (New York: Clark Boardman Callaghan, 1994) (Supplement), at § 252.1.

56. *See United States v. Ojeda Rios*, 495 U.S. 257, 259, n.1 (1990).

intercepted in conformity with the order of authorization. *See* 18 U.S.C. 2518(10).[57]

But the Court did not discuss § 2518(10)(c) or the legislative history plainly stating that no such suppression remedy exists. Indeed, it is puzzling why the court made the comment at all, since the case before it only involved interception of wire communications. Because the Supreme Court made this comment only in *dicta* (in passing), it is not clear whether other courts will consider the Supreme Court's view to be binding precedent.

The latest court to address the issue noted, again in *dicta*, that there is no suppression remedy available for unlawful seizures of electronic communications.[58] Although certainty is impossible in this area, it appears that there is no suppression remedy under the Act for an illegal interception.[59] Nonetheless, it bears repeating that *state law* may prohibit certain interceptions, and require suppression of evidence obtained from such interceptions.[60]

8.34–a *Failure to comply with "after-interception" requirements of the Act may result in suppression*

What happens if investigators obtain a valid order to intercept an electronic communication but fail to comply with the "after-interception" requirements (e.g., they do not deliver the evidence to the court)?

Notwithstanding the legislative history stating that Congress agreed not to "apply the statutory exclusionary rule contained in the Act of the Omnibus Crime Control and Safe Streets Act of 1968 to the interception of electronic communications,"[61] the Fourth Circuit

---

57. *United States v. Ojeda Rios, supra*, 495 U.S. 257, at 259 n.1.

58. *Steve Jackson Games, Inc. v. United States Secret Service*, 36 F.3d 457, n.6 (5th Cir. 1994).

59. *See also* Fishman, *Wiretapping and Eavesdropping* (New York: Clark Boardman Callaghan, 1994) (Supplement), at § 252.1.

60. *Compare Tavernetti v. Superior Court*, 22 Cal. 3d 187 (Cal. 1978), with 18 U.S.C. 2511(3)(b)(iv).

61. Sen. Rpt. 99-541, *supra*, at 23.

Court of Appeal in *United States v. Suarez,*[62] suggested that suppression would be required.

Although § 2518(8)(a) explicitly mentions electronic communications as well as wire communications, the court's interpretation should be rejected because it creates an absurd result. Section 2518(8)(a) requires only that investigators bring evidence to the court which has been intercepted in accordance with the Act. Therefore, the court's interpretation would mean that evidence seized illegally (and not delivered to the court) would be admissible, but evidence seized legally, but not delivered to the court, would be inadmissible.

8.40   Obtaining stored communications

8.41   Stored communications explained

The provisions of the Act governing stored communications were added by Congress in response to changes in technology.[63] Instead of using the postal service or the telephone, computer users began sending each other messages. Large companies, such as MCI and CompuServe, now serve as waystations for messages by acting as electronic "mailboxes." These companies are referred to as electronic communication service providers.

Messages are transmitted in two phases. First, the sender transmits a message to the service provider, and the provider stores the message in a "mailbox." That message is now a *stored communication.* The second phase occurs when the intended recipient contacts the provider and obtains the message. That intended recipient is usually a "customer" of the service (i.e., the recipient pays to maintain a mailbox on the provider's computer).

Note that the communication is not "stored" until it arrives at the service provider. If Mr. A sends a message to Mr. B, and Mr. Crook taps the data line leading to the service provider, Mr. Crook has not obtained a stored communication. Rather, he has intercepted a communication in transmission, as discussed above.

---

62. 906 F.2d 977, n.11 (4th Cir. 1990).

63. *See* 18 U.S.C. 2701–2709.

As part of the first phase, the service provider will make a backup copy of the stored communication to guard against a system failure. Thus, there will be at least two copies of the stored communication held by the provider: (1) the message stored awaiting review by the recipient in an electronic "mailbox" residing on the provider's computer; and (2) backup copies of the message maintained by the provider.

Figure 8-1: Typical E-mail

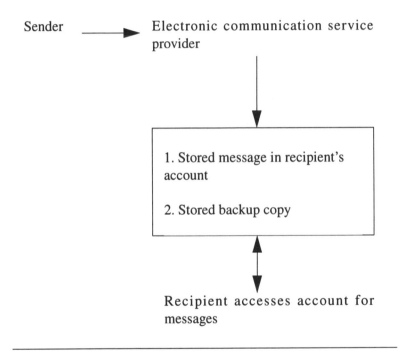

Sender ⟶ Electronic communication service provider

1. Stored message in recipient's account

2. Stored backup copy

Recipient accesses account for messages

The Act protects those communications when they are in "electronic storage." Section 2510(17) defines storage as "any temporary, intermediate storage of a wire or electronic communication incidental to the electronic transmission thereof" and any backup copy of such a communication made by the provider.

The Act protects only communications in the possession of the provider. The Act does not protect communications which have been downloaded by the addressee to another computer not maintained by the provider.

For example, if Mr. A sends Mr. B a message to Mr. B's MCI Mail account, that message is protected when it is stored in Mr. B's account. The copy of the message residing in Mr. B's MCI Mail account, and any backup copies retained by MCI, are protected under the Act, even after Mr. B contacts the provider and reads the message.

However, if Mr. B downloads a copy of that message to his home computer, the message residing on that home computer is *not* protected by the Act. Thus, the same message may be protected in one place and not in another.

As depicted in Figure 8–2:

- A message on its way to a service provider is protected from interception, as discussed in the first part of this chapter.

- A message which has arrived at the service provider, and is "stored" by that provider, is protected as a "stored communication," as described in this section. Backup copies held by the provider are also protected.

- A message which is stored on the recipient's own computer is not protected by the Act, even though it was once a communication (e.g., E-mail). Of course, law enforcement investigators must still comply with the Fourth Amendment when obtaining that message.[64]

8.42 An overview of the Act's protection of stored communications

The Act protects electronic communications maintained by two types of providers: (1) electronic communication services; and (2) remote computing services. An electronic communication service provides users with the capability of sending and receiving electronic communications (e.g., E-mail services).

---

64. *See United States v. Meriwether*, 917 F.2d 955 (6th Cir. 1990); *Steve Jackson Games, Inc. v. United States Secret Service*, 36 F.3d 457 (5th Cir. 1994) (reviewing stored communications does not constitute an interception of the message).

Figure 8–2: Stored communications protected by the Act

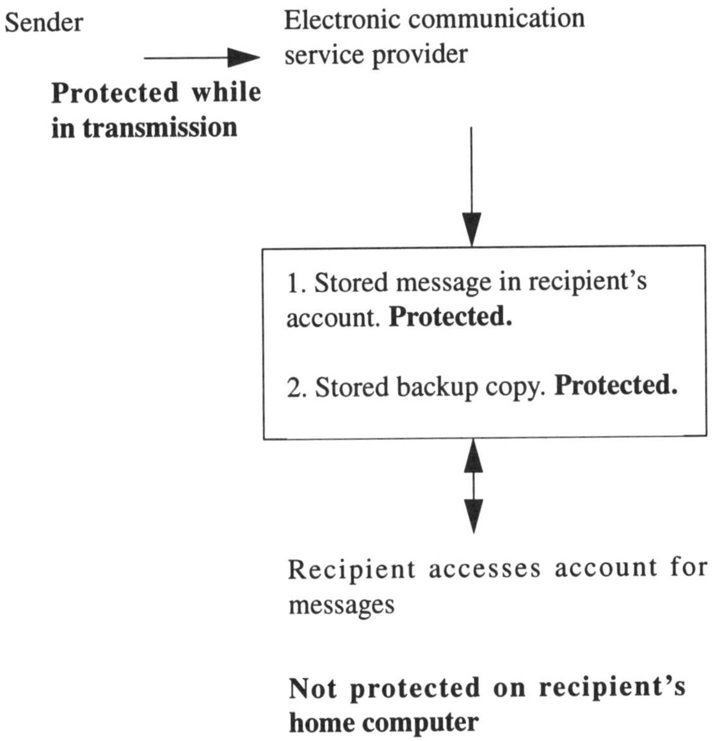

Sender   Electronic communication
         ⟶   service provider

**Protected while
in transmission**

> 1. Stored message in recipient's account. **Protected.**
>
> 2. Stored backup copy. **Protected.**

Recipient accesses account for
messages

**Not protected on recipient's
home computer**

Although we have talked about stored communications as if they were all E-mail messages, the Act also protects data stored for safe-keeping in a "remote computing service."

A remote computing service is a "data bank." Customers pay to store data off-site and access that data from their own computers. As discussed later in this chapter, these accounts are basically Swiss bank accounts for data. The Act protects data placed in such an account and the identity of the holder of that account.[65]

---

65. *See* 18 U.S.C. 2510(12), 2702(a)(2), and 2703(b).

The Act prohibits both types of service providers from disclosing the contents of an electronic communication to anyone, with several exceptions. The major exception is that law enforcement can compel that information from both electronic communication services and remote computing services by using legal process, such as a search warrant or subpoena. The type of legal process required by the Act depends upon the age of the communication and the willingness of the government to inform the customer of the service of the request.

The Act also prohibits service providers from disclosing information about their customers to a governmental entity without legal process.[66] Such information would include the identity of the sender of an electronic communication, the place from which the communication originated, and the identity of the recipient.

As discussed later in this chapter, the language of the Act indicates that a communication obtained in violation of its provisions will *not* be suppressed. However, aggrieved parties may still sue violators civilly and obtain large damage awards.

This is a very complex area, and it is easy to get lost in the detail. The following summary provides the "big picture," which you should keep in mind when attempting to seize stored communications and related information.

8.43 Summary: seven important points concerning stored communications

- The provisions of the Act protecting "stored communications" protect only communications stored on the service provider's computer or communications maintained on backup media created by that provider. They do not protect communications residing on a suspect's computer (i.e., after the suspect has downloaded those communications from the provider). *See* §§ 8.41, 8.42, 8.44.

- The Act also protects "transactional information" relating to stored communications (i.e., information about who sent or received a stored communication). *See* page 375.

---

66. *See* 18 U.S.C. 2703(c)(1)(A). Apparently Congress only wanted to protect customers from the government, and not from telemarketers.

- Law enforcement investigators should use search warrants (instead of subpoenas) to obtain stored communications. *See* § 8.46–a (at page 376).

- Law enforcement investigators must not rely on standard warrants alone to obtain stored communications. The appropriate search warrant includes: (1) a request to seize communications; and (2) evidence demonstrating probable cause to obtain the communications (i.e., evidence suggesting that those communications may include evidence of a crime). *See* § 8.46–b (at page 378).

- Law enforcement investigators should use search warrants even when businesses or universities offer to disclose stored communications voluntarily. *See* § 8.47–a (at page 381). Businesses and universities should consider demanding a search warrant, subpoena, or court order before disclosing such communications or transactional information.

- Law enforcement investigators who do not seize magnetic media containing communications should require providers to create backup copies of those communications. *See* § 8.46–d (at page 379).

- Law enforcement investigators should consider delaying examination of any stored communications seized pursuant to a warrant to allow aggrieved parties time to object, particularly when searching a bulletin board. *See* § 8.47–b (at page 387).

8.44   The Act defines an "electronic communication service" broadly

The typical scenario involves law enforcement investigators seeking to obtain electronic communications from an E-mail service, such as MCI Mail or CompuServe. However, the Act defines an electronic communication service broadly, as "any service which provides to users thereof the ability to send or receive wire or electronic communications."[67]

---

67. 18 U.S.C. 2510(15).

This means that the Act can apply to bulletin board systems which offer E-mail services. As discussed later in this chapter, the Act may also apply to universities and to businesses which allow employees to use the company computer system to exchange E-mail.

8.45 The Act defines a "remote computing service" broadly

A remote computing service provider includes anyone who provides "to the public ... computer storage or processing services by means of an electronic communication system."[68] *This also means that a bulletin board may serve as a remote computing service covered by the Act.*[69]

8.46 Protections for stored communications

This section discusses how law enforcement investigators can obtain information from electronic communication services and remote computing services.[70] It also summarizes the Act's restrictions on the ability of those services to disclose stored communications generally. Unless otherwise stated, the term "provider" refers to both electronic communication services and remote computing services.

---

68. 18 U.S.C. 2711(2).

69. *See Steve Jackson Games v. United States Secret Service,* 816 F.Supp. 432 (W.D. Tex. 1993), *affirmed* 36 F.3d 457 (5th Cir. 1994) (bulletin board offering information about computer game company's products and activities, which also offered E-mail services, was a remote computing service within the definition of 18 U.S.C. 2711). Indeed, many bulletin boards will qualify as both electronic communication service providers and remote computing services

70. Note that § 2701(a) punishes persons who break into an electronic communication service provider's computer system, even if they do not obtain stored communications. Section 2701(a)(2) punishes persons who exceed their authorization to access such a facility *and* obtain, alter, or prevent authorized access to stored communications.

However, § 2701 does not prohibit police from using an informant to access a publicly available BBS which offers E-mail services. *See Sega Enterprises Ltd., et al. v. MAPHIA BBS, et al.,* 30 U.S.P.Q. 2d 1921 (N.D. Cal. 1994) (§ 2701 did not apply where Sega used an informant to collect evidence of software piracy from a pirate BBS, because the BBS was available to the public). Again, state laws may impose additional restrictions.

Section 2702 of the Act prohibits providers from disclosing stored communications to *anyone* other than the intended recipient, including but not limited to law enforcement investigators, unless:

- either the sender or recipient of the communication consents to disclosure (meaning that investigators can read messages posted on public bulletin boards, such as CompuServe or Usenet);

- disclosure is necessary to process the communication, or, more significantly, to protect the rights or property of the provider;

- the provider *inadvertently* obtains a communication which pertains to the commission of a crime, in which case it may disclose the communication to law enforcement; or

- the provider is required to do so by the government, as provided for in Section 2703.

The last exception is the most common means by which law enforcement investigators obtain stored communications.

Section 2703 is an interesting piece of legislation, in that the degree of privacy afforded the electronic communication depends upon the age of the communication, what measures the government is willing to use to obtain it, and whether the government wants the affected parties to know that it has obtained it.

Table 8-4 summarizes the rules governing the authority of law enforcement investigators to obtain the contents of stored communications from providers. The table also notes the requirements for obtaining customer records.

The government may obtain any stored communication, no matter how recent, by serving the provider with a search warrant for that communication.[71] *This means that law enforcement investigators can always comply with the Act by including language in a search warrant affidavit stating that they intend to seize certain stored communications, accompanied by facts demonstrating probable cause that those communications may be evidence of a crime.* (Using a warrant to obtain stored communications is discussed later in this chapter.)

---

71. 18 U.S.C. 2703(a) and (b).

Table 8–4: Requirements to obtain stored communications

Law enforcement may obtain the following material:	With the appropriate authorization:	And with the following notice to the customer:
1. Communications held by an electronic communication service provider for less than 180 days.	A search warrant expressly granting permission to obtain those communications. §§ 2703(b) and (c).	The government is not required to give notice to the customer, and it can prevent the provider from doing so upon showing that notification would cause an "adverse result." § 2703(c)(2), § 2705(b).
2. Any communication held by a remote computing service, regardless of age, and any communication held by an electronic communication service provider for more than 180 days.	A search warrant, grand jury subpoena, administrative subpoena, or trial subpoena. Can also obtain communications via a court order by presenting specific and articulable facts showing that there are reasonable grounds to believe that the contents of the communication are relevant and material to an ongoing criminal investigation. §§ 2703(b) and (d).	If it does not use a search warrant, the government must give notice to the customer unless the requesting agency certifies (or, to obtain a court order, demonstrates) that notification would cause an "adverse result," in which case notification is delayed for 90 days, with additional 90-day extensions available upon court approval. The government may obtain a court order preventing the provider from informing the customer of the request for records. § 2705.

Law enforcement may obtain the following material (cont.):	With the appropriate authorization (cont.):	And with the following notice to the customer (cont.):
3. Subscriber's name, address, and "telephone number *or other subscriber number of identity*" (presumably Internet address), as well as *telephone* billing records and a description of the type of services used by that subscriber.	A search warrant, grand jury subpoena, administrative subpoena, or trial subpoena. Can also use the same court order that is required to obtain more specific information about the communication (see row 4 below). § 2703(c)(1)(C).	The government is not required to give notice to the customer, and it can prevent the provider from doing so upon showing that notification would cause an "adverse result." § 2703(c)(2), § 2705(b).
4. Record of the destination and recipient of a particular electronic communication.	A search warrant, or a court order obtained by presenting specific and articulable facts showing that there are reasonable grounds to believe that the records are relevant and material to an ongoing criminal investigation. § 2703(c)(1)(B).	The government is not required to give notice to the customer, and it can prevent the provider from doing so upon showing that notification would cause an "adverse result." § 2703(c)(2), § 2705(b).

By using a search warrant, the government avoids the difficult task of notifying the provider's customer (see box on next page).

The warrant can also prohibit the provider from notifying the customer if the government can demonstrate in the affidavit that notice may produce an "adverse result."[72] The government must show that there is reason to believe that such notice may endanger lives, cause flight from prosecution, cause destruction of, or tampering with, evidence, allow intimidation of witnesses, or seriously jeopardize an investigation or unduly delay a trial.[73]

If you are required to notify the customer,
how do you comply?

The Act is unclear on how the government is to provide notice to any "customer or subscriber" of an electronic communication service. The terms "customer" and "subscriber" are not defined within the Act, and could be construed to refer to every party to an electronic communication, rather than to the person who pays for the electronic communication service. For example, 18 U.S.C. 2510(13) defines a "user" as anyone authorized by the provider to "use" the service. This could refer to the customer who has a formal agreement with the service, or less persuasively, to anyone allowed to send a message to the provider for forwarding to such a customer.

Many times the government will not know the identity of all of the parties to a particular communication. Indeed, the government may not know the true identity of the customer (usually the recipient) of that service. Using a search warrant avoids this headache.

If the communication is more than 180 days old, *or* if the communication is held by a remote computer service (in which case Congress has deemed the age of the data to be irrelevant), the government may forgo using a search warrant in favor of a grand jury subpoena, administrative subpoena, or trial subpoena (i.e., a subpoena *duces tecum*).[74]

---

72. 18 U.S.C. 2703(b)(1)(B)(ii), 2705.

73. 18 U.S.C. 2705.

74. 18 U.S.C. 2703 (a) and (b).

The government may also obtain a court order requiring disclosure by presenting specific and articulable facts showing that there are reasonable grounds to believe that the contents of the communication are relevant and material to an ongoing criminal investigation.

Why did Congress afford certain communications more protection than others?

Congress appears to have drafted the provisions on stored communications based on an analogy between E-mail and regular mail. A communication which is stored for a short period of time is similar to a letter in the U.S. mail system—the government must obtain a warrant for such "mail." A letter which has been "sitting" for over 180 days is less like mail in transit and more like property in a storage locker, or mail held by a third party for storage purposes.

In more traditional contexts, such as tax records held by an accountant, the government has been able to use a subpoena to obtain such "stored" information. Congress also used this analogy in drafting the rules for obtaining information stored in a remote computing service. *See* Fishman, *Wiretapping and Eavesdropping* (New York: Clark Boardman Callaghan, 1994) (Supplement), at § 449.

Although these procedures are less burdensome, there is a trade-off—the government must notify the subscriber or customer of the request before demanding the communication unless the government can convince the court that such notice will produce an "adverse result."[75]

Finally, the Act protects "a record or other information pertaining to a customer [or subscriber]" from unauthorized disclosure.[76] The Act distinguishes between two types of "transactional information."

---

75. 18 U.S.C. 2703. Per § 2705, the provider may object to producing the records on hardship grounds.

76. 18 U.S.C. 2703(c).

The government may use a search warrant, grand jury subpoena, administrative subpoena, or trial subpoena to obtain the subscriber's name, address, and "telephone number or other subscriber number of identity" (presumably the subscriber's Internet address), plus the *telephone* billing records and a description of the type of services used by that subscriber.[77] In other words, the government can discover the name, address, and telephone number of the customer, and a general description of the types of services (e.g., Internet access) used by that customer.

However, in order to obtain a record of the destination and recipient of a particular electronic communication, the government has only two options. First, the government may obtain a search warrant. Second, the government may obtain a court order by presenting specific and articulable facts showing that there are reasonable grounds to believe that the records are relevant and material to an ongoing criminal investigation.[78]

A provider who discloses communications or information in compliance with legal process is immune from liability to the customer.[79]

8.46–a   Use a warrant instead of a subpoena to obtain stored communications

Although the government can obtain stored communications by using a subpoena, law enforcement investigators should always use a search warrant to obtain those communications.

The reason for this advice is that in most cases you will not know whether there are messages held by the electronic communication service provider which are less than 180 days old. Therefore, you should always use a warrant unless you are targeting specific communications over 180 days old and are able to subpoena only those communications, or you are targeting a remote computing service.

As noted above, another advantage to using a warrant instead of a subpoena is that you can avoid giving notice to the provider's customer.

---

77. 18 U.S.C. 2703(c)(1)(C).

78. 18 U.S.C. 2703(c)(1)(B).

79. 18 U.S.C. 2703(e).

Law enforcement investigators concerned about suspects erasing communications should ask the provider to make a backup copy while investigators obtain a search warrant.

The Act prohibits providers from disclosing communications. However, it does not specifically prohibit them from *copying* communications, although it protects any such copies as if they were the original communication. Therefore, law enforcement investigators concerned that a suspect may access a service provider and erase communications or data before investigators can prepare and serve a search warrant should ask that provider to make a backup copy and hold it while investigators obtain a warrant.

Note that the Act does not require providers to comply with that request, so you must rely on their good will. Furthermore, providers receiving such a request must be careful.

Because there is no legal authority requiring providers to make such copies unless and until they have been served with appropriate legal process under § 2704 (i.e., an order accompanying the service of a search warrant), providers must make sure they have not made any representations to customers which might make them liable for making backup copies. This is of particular concern to remote computing services, which may promise to hold customers' data inviolate.

The warrant can also include an order prohibiting the provider from notifying the customer of the interception.

Using a warrant instead of a subpoena may also avert disaster if you unwittingly search a computer used to store communications. A criminal using a computer to transmit child pornography may also be using that computer to provide a cut-rate, and legitimate, electronic communication service.

Although the Act only penalizes intentional access of a communication service, it is unclear whether intentional access of a computer which turns out to be part of a communication service constitutes a violation.[80]

Finally, using a warrant precludes any argument that the search violated the Fourth Amendment prohibition against warrantless searches. A subpoena may not be sufficient to allow a search which, per the Fourth Amendment, requires a search warrant.[81]

8.46–b   Your warrant must justify seizure of stored communications

Do not rely on your standard warrant alone to obtain stored communications. You must include in your warrant: (1) a request to seize communications; and (2) evidence demonstrating probable cause to obtain the communications (i.e., evidence suggesting that those communications may include evidence of a crime). Failure to do so may violate the Act.[82] Chapter 9 includes language designed to allow you to obtain stored communications.

---

80. *See* 18 U.S.C. 2701(a). The district court's decision in *Steve Jackson Games v. United States Secret Service*, 816 F.Supp. 432 (W.D. Tex. 1993), *affirmed* 36 F.3d 457 (5th Cir. 1994), suggests that the Act does not apply where officers do not know that the computer contains stored communications.

81. This is particularly the case with rights guaranteed by state constitutions. The Senate Judiciary Report states that the Act "provides no authority for the issuance of a state subpoena that is prohibited under the law of such state." Sen. Rpt. 99-541, *supra*, at 39, 1986 U.S.C.C.A.N. 3593. Thus, state constitutional guarantees of privacy and state statutes may present additional barriers. *See, e.g.,* 18 U.S.C. 2703(d) (court order shall not issue where applicant is a state official who could not obtain such an order under more restrictive state law). While such barriers may apply to subpoenas, they generally permit the same search if accomplished via a search warrant. *See, e.g., People v. Larkin*, 194 Cal. App. 3d 650 (Cal. Ct. App. 1987) (prohibiting use of a court order to obtain a trap and trace, but allowing installation of same pursuant to a search warrant).

82. *See* 18 U.S.C. 2703; *Steve Jackson Games v. United States Secret Service*, 816 F.Supp. 432 (W.D. Tex. 1993), *affirmed* 36 F.3d 457 (5th Cir. 1994). Note that the court was unsympathetic to the claim that the officers relied in "good faith" on the warrant that allowed seizure of the magnetic media containing the communications. The court stated that "the Court declines to find this defense by a preponderance of the evidence in this case." This language suggests that while such a defense might be available in the appropriate case, it is not available where officers knew or should have known that the Act applied.

*8.46–c   The Act does not require suppression of stored com-
munications obtained in violation of its provisions*

The language of the Act indicates that a communication obtained in violation of its provisions will *not* be suppressed.[83] However, aggrieved parties may still sue violators civilly, and obtain damages.

*8.46–d   If you are seeking communications from a remote
computing service provider via a subpoena or court
order, require that provider to create a backup copy*

In some cases it will be impractical to seize magnetic media held by a remote computing service (e.g., where the media is contained within a mainframe). If you must use a subpoena or court order, in addition to prohibiting the provider from notifying the customer, you should require that provider to create a backup copy of the stored communication.

Unlike the backup discussed above, which you ask a friendly service provider to make while you obtain a warrant, this backup is performed at the time the communication is produced pursuant to legal process.

Section 2704 allows the government to include in a court order or subpoena an order requiring a remote computing service to make a backup copy of any communication encompassed by that legal process. The only requirement for such an order is that the government, *in its sole discretion*, believes that its subpoena or court order may prompt someone to destroy or tamper with the communication.[84] You should always include such an order in any subpoena or court order directed toward a remote computing service.

The provider must make that copy, without notifying the customer, "as soon as practicable consistent with its regular business practices," and in no event later than two business days after service of the order.[85] Unless the government obtains delayed notification

---

83. *See* 18 U.S.C. 2708; Fishman, *Wiretapping and Eavesdropping* (New York: Clark Boardman Callaghan, 1994) (Supplement), at § 456.

84. 18 U.S.C. 2704(a)(1), (5).

85. 18 U.S.C. 2704(a)(1).

pursuant to § 2705 (as discussed earlier), it must notify the customer of the backup preservation order three days later. The service provider must release that backup copy to the government no later than 14 days after receiving the order, unless the provider or the customer challenges that order in court.[86]

8.47 Special problems relating to stored communications

Many parts of the Act are new, and we are just starting to see problems emerge. This section discusses two areas which may trouble investigators and lawyers in the near future.

First, it is unclear whether businesses and universities which provide communication services (e.g., E-mail) to their employees or students are electronic communication service providers. If they are classified as providers, they may not disclose communications to law enforcement investigators without legal process. However, as noted later in this chapter, they may gain the right to monitor communications sent or received by employees and students as necessary to provide the communication service and to protect their rights or property.

Section 8.47–a suggests that law enforcement investigators should use a search warrant even when a business or university offers to disclose stored communications voluntarily. Private parties unable to defend an interception of electronic communications based on consent or another exception to the Act may wish to consider whether a court will "rescue" them by deeming them to be a service provider under the Act.

Second, a recent court decision, combined with some ambiguous language in the Act, may encourage lawsuits against investigators who seize computers being used to provide electronic communications or remote computing services (e.g., bulletin boards). Section 8.47–b analyzes the theory behind such potential lawsuits (none has been filed as yet) and suggests that law enforcement investigators consider delaying examination of any evidence seized pursuant to a warrant to allow aggrieved parties to object, particularly when searching a bulletin board.

---

86. 18 U.S.C. 2704(4).

*8.47–a   A business or university offering E-mail may be an
electronic communication service provider*

It is unclear whether businesses and universities which provide E-mail or other communication services for use by employees and students are communication service providers under the Act.

If they are service providers, the same rule applies to them as to all other service providers: they may not disclose stored communications to law enforcement investigators without legal process. This means that all of the information in the previous sections about investigators obtaining legal process would apply, not just to a request for communications held by MCI Mail, but also to attempts to obtain an employee's E-mail residing on a company's computer, or E-mail residing in a student's account at a university computer center.

There is another consequence to the argument over whether businesses and universities are communication service providers. If they are communication service providers, they are allowed to read all E-mail they transmit or receive as necessary to protect their rights or property.

The safest course through this minefield is to assume the worst. If you are a business or university, act as if you: (1) may not disclose any communications without legal process (i.e., as if you are a provider); and (2) may not monitor communications simply because you own the computer system transmitting the message (i.e., as if you are *not* a provider).

If you are a law enforcement investigator, act as if the business or university may not disclose any communications without legal process. The next few pages explain the issue in greater detail, *and may be of interest primarily to lawyers.*

*8.47–a(1)   The Act does not clearly define what constitutes
an electronic communication service*

The Act broadly defines an electronic communication service as "any service which provides to users thereof the ability to send or receive wire or electronic communications."[87] Is an organization which

---

87. 18 U.S.C. 2510(15).

provides communication services to its own employees an "electronic communication service provider" subject to the Act? What about a university which provides its students with mailboxes for receiving E-mail?

The language of the Act is ambiguous. For example, § 2510(15), defining "electronic communication service," does not confine the term to commercial services. Furthermore, several sections of the Act appear to distinguish between "public" and "private" providers.

For example, § 2511(2)(a)(1) includes private switchboard operators as one of the groups of providers allowed to monitor certain communications in transmission. Section 2711(2) restricts the definition of a remote computing service to providers of computer storage or processing services to the public. These two sections suggest that Congress intended to include private providers within the Act, but treat them differently.[88]

However, the language of the Act also suggests that Congress intended only commercial services to fall within the Act. For example, the word "service," in conjunction with "subscriber" and "customer," appears to suggest a fee-based operation. This reading would exclude any business which maintains an E-mail capability as part of its computer operations for employees' use. (However, it might not exclude a university that provides its tuition-paying students with E-mail services for no additional charge.) Similarly, the Act also refers frequently to the "subscriber" and "customer" of such a service[89]—

---

88. Similarly, as discussed in more detail below, both § 2511(3) (disclosure of communications transmitted by service provider) and § 2702 (disclosure of stored communications by service provider) distinguish between "private" and "public" providers. However, note that the phrase "to the public" is included not only within § 2702(a)(1) (restricting communication services), but also within subdivision (a)(2) (restricting remote computing services). Given that Congress used the same phrase for remote computing services, which by definition (*see* § 2711(2)) must provide services to the public, it is also possible that Congress simply forgot to draft the definition of electronic communication service so as to exclude such private providers from coverage.

89. *See, e.g.,* 18 U.S.C. 2703(b)(1)(A), 2703(c), 2704(5); *see also* Senate Report, 99-541, at 20, 1986 U.S.C.C.A.N. 3574 (stating that Congress intended to allow service providers to intercept communications to protect themselves and their customers).

commercial terms which would appear to exclude businesses, and perhaps universities.

Unfortunately, just as various sections of the Act appear in conflict, the legislative history (which courts examine to understand the intent of Congress) is also ambiguous.[90] Courts have yet to rule on this issue, and commentators are divided.[91]

There is one persuasive argument against including private providers under the Act—such an interpretation would allow businesses to monitor employees' E-mail. (Indeed some of the commentators cited in note 91 above, apparently eager to avoid this result, argue that

---

90. Consider two passages from the Senate Judiciary Report on the ECPA:

"Electronic mail is a form of communication by which private correspondence is transmitted over public and private telephone lines. In its most common form, messages are typed into a computer terminal, and then transmitted over telephone lines to a recipient computer operated by an electronic mail company. If the intended addressee subscribes to the service, the message is stored by the company's computer 'mail box' until the subscriber calls the company to retrieve its mail, which is then routed over the telephone system to the recipient's computer. If the addressee is not a subscriber to the service, the electronic mail company can put the message onto paper and then deposit it in the normal postal system. Electronic mail systems may be available for public use *or may be proprietary, such as systems operated by private companies for internal correspondence.*" Senate Judiciary Report 99-541, at 8, 1986 U.S.C.C.A.N. 3562 (Glossary) (emphasis added).

However, consider another portion of that same report: "[a]n 'electronic communication service' is defined in proposed subsection 2510(15) of title 18 as a service which provides its users the ability to send or to receive wire or electronic communications. Such services can be provided through the same facilities. Existing telephone companies and electronic mail companies are providers of electronic communication services." *Id.*, at 14, 1986 U.S.C.C.A.N. 3568.

This second passage suggests a more commonplace definition of "service." The two passages can be reconciled by suggesting that the Glossary merely describes how electronic mail can be used, while the second passage defining electronic communication service specifies that such services only include commercial services designed to transfer such mail for a fee.

91. *Compare* Morris, "Privacy and Defamation in Employment," American Law Institute (1994); Kane, "Electronic Mail and Privacy," Practicing Law Institute, 15th Annual Computer Law Institute (1993); Note, "Privacy Issues in the Private Sector Workplace: Protection from Electronic Surveillance and the Emerging Privacy Gap," 67 S. Cal. L. Rev. 451–56, 469 (1994); Comment, "Terminally Nosy: Are Employers Free to Access Our Electronic Mail?", 96 Dick. L. Rev. 545 (1992).

businesses which provide E-mail for use by employees are *not* service providers under the Act.)

The first part of this chapter discussed a company's right to intercept employees' communications in transmission (i.e., monitoring E-mail sent by employees) and concluded that the Act allowed such monitoring only under limited circumstances.

However, that conclusion must be discarded if businesses are communication service providers under the Act. If an organization is to be considered a provider for purposes of being required to guard stored communications from disclosure, it must also be allowed to examine communications transmitted by its computers on the same terms and conditions afforded any other provider.

Thus, the Act would not prohibit a business that is deemed a provider from monitoring its employees' outgoing E-mail as necessary to protect the business's rights and property, per § 2511(2)(a)(1).[92] It would also allow businesses to read internal and incoming E-mail in all cases, per § 2701(c)(1).[93] Of course, as discussed above, state privacy laws might prevent such monitoring.

Courts tempted to classify businesses and other private organizations as electronic communication services covered by the Act may hesitate in light of the consequences of such a ruling.

8.47–a(2) If an organization is deemed a provider under the Act

Even if a business is included under the Act as a provider, § 2702 states that only those providers which offer services "to the public" are limited in their ability to disclose electronic communications. This means that a private provider, unlike a provider that offers services to

---

92. Indeed, § 2511(2)(a)(1) prohibits only providers of *wire* communication services from monitoring randomly.

93. The employer's right to read incoming E-mail may not depend upon whether the employer is a provider. If the employer is a provider, then § 2701(c)(1) authorizes the employer to read that communication. If the employer is not a provider, then the employer, as the owner of the computer, is the recipient of that communication per § 2511(2)(c) and should be allowed to intercept it. However, this last conclusion is uncertain at best.

Does the Act allow a business to monitor all internal and incoming E-mail?

There is an apparent loophole in the Act which bears mentioning, although relying upon it to justify businesses' reading employees' E-mail seems risky. When one employee sends another employee a message, that message is held at the server for the recipient to read. Thus, that message appears to fit within the definition of a communication in electronic storage. However, the Act does not appear to protect that communication at all.

If the employer is a service provider, § 2701(c)(1) allows the employer to look at the message. If the employer is not a provider, does the employer violate § 2511 by "intercepting" the communication? The answer is apparently not; an appellate court recently ruled that reading a stored communication is not an "interception" under the Act. *See Steve Jackson Games, Inc. v. United States Secret Service*, 36 F.3d 457, 461-62 (5th Cir. 1994). Thus, it appears possible for a communication to be held in storage by a non-provider, which that non-provider may read with impunity.

This same reasoning would apply to E-mail sent from outside the owner's computer to that system. That message would come to rest in electronic storage, where it would be unprotected.

Of course, courts might decide that Congress intended to allow only service providers to access communications in electronic storage, and to prevent anyone else, including the owner of the computer storing the message, from reading that message. Another risk is that state privacy laws might prevent such monitoring.

the public, would not violate the Act by voluntarily disclosing stored communications to law enforcement without first receiving any legal process.

The Act does not clearly define the phrase "to the public." Does connecting to the Internet, and allowing outsiders to communicate with employees or students, constitute providing a service to the public?[94] If so, do the restrictions of § 2702 apply to *all* communications, even those solely between those persons who are not "the public" (e.g., employees)?[95]

What about a university with a network connecting all its students? Does it matter whether the university is funded by the state? What about student bulletin boards on campus?

The most recent guidelines promulgated by the United States Department of Justice suggest that organizations connecting to the Internet should not be considered "public" providers.

> It is probably safe to assume that any service permitting "guest" or "visitor" access is "public." On the other hand, the term should not be read to cover business networks open only to employees for company business. If that business network is connected to the Internet ... it may be part of a "public" system, but this does not necessarily mean that the corporate LAN ... becomes a "public" service.[96]

Common sense suggests that merely allowing the public to communicate with employees does not create an electronic communication service providing services to the public, any more than plugging in a telephone at your business would make your business a telephone company.

---

94. *See* Kane, "Electronic Mail and Privacy," Practicing Law Institute, 15th Annual Computer Law Institute (1993) (suggesting that businesses which allow communications with non-employees may lose their "private" status).

95. The court in *Bunnell v. Superior Court*, 21 Cal. App. 4th 1811 (Cal. Ct. App. 1994), suppressed wiretaps of a prison telephone because the phone could be used to place and receive outside calls if the switchboard operator at the prison "could be persuaded to do so." (Some of the intercepted calls were in fact outside calls.) That case is not quite apposite here, since the issue in *Bunnell* was whether the line qualified as an instrument capable of placing interstate calls. *See* 18 U.S.C. 2510(1). In an employment context, the issue might be somewhat different: even if an employer is a provider, and the employer's computer is capable of accessing outsiders, is it reasonable to treat the employees as using a "public" service even when communicating among themselves? The answer should be no.

96. United States Department of Justice, *Federal Guidelines for Searching and Seizing Computers* (Washington, D.C., 1994), at 82.

However, there are no cases on the subject. Furthermore, the Department of Justice guidelines are not "the law"—they are just another, albeit respected, opinion.

Moreover, some organizations may appear to serve the public. For example, courts may view any large university computing center (even with a network limited to students sending mail to other universities) as providing communication services to the public. Thus, relying on an organization's "private provider" status may not be prudent if that organization allows outside access.

Finally, employees (and to a lesser extent, students) *may* have a right of privacy under your state's law which, in some circumstances, would protect both their outgoing E-mail from interception and their internal E-mail from disclosure. A business or university might be sued by an aggrieved party whose "mail" was delivered to police.

In light of this uncertainty, organizations such as businesses and universities should consider requiring law enforcement to obtain legal process before disclosing E-mail, particularly if that E-mail involves communications with non-employees (or non-students). This decision should take into account the organization's E-mail policy, and, for communications to or from non-employees or unauthorized users, the extent to which such persons are informed of that policy.

Law enforcement investigators should also be cautious. The safest course is to apply for a search warrant to obtain communications stored by any organization or individual which could be characterized as providing an electronic communication service to the public.[97]

> *8.47–b* *When seizing computers used to provide electronic communication services, such as bulletin boards, consider delaying examination of the seized communications to allow aggrieved parties to object*

This section is written for law enforcement investigators and lawyers, and applies where investigators intend to seize computers being

---

97. Although the language of § 2703 only restricts the government from *requiring* the service provider to disclose communications, a provider voluntarily disclosing a communication in violation of § 2702 might prompt a lawsuit against both the provider and the agency which accepted that communication.

used to provide electronic communication or remote computing services (e.g., bulletin boards).

For the reasons stated below, if you intend to seize such computers, you should consider including in your warrant a request for permission to delay your examination of the communications until the computer owner or any interested third party (i.e., a party to a stored communication) has an opportunity to object to the seizure.

> *8.47–b(1)* *The Act may encourage lawsuits against investigators who seize a computer being used to provide communication or remote computing services*

This issue does not arise when law enforcement investigators seek to obtain a stored communication from a large provider, such as MCI Mail, because investigators have little interest in seizing the mainframe computer containing the stored communication. However, in many cases, law enforcement investigators intend to seize the magnetic media as part of a broader search for incriminating evidence (e.g., pirated software or stolen access codes).

Those searches are often covered by the Act because the definitions of "electronic communication service provider," "remote computing service," and "stored communication" are broad and include system operators ("sysops") running bulletin boards that are configured to allow subscribers to exchange E-mail.

There is a risk that a court might misinterpret the Act as prohibiting investigators from seizing a computer containing stored communications, *even with a warrant.* Although there is no suppression remedy for illegally seized stored communications,[98] the owner of the computer *and* parties to any seized communications not specifically identified in the warrant might sue the investigators and their agencies for damages.

A recent court decision so muddies the waters in this area that you should consider delaying your review of seized media containing

---

98. *See* § 8.46–c (at page 379).

stored communications until the suspect and other aggrieved parties have a chance to object to that review.

> *8.47–b(2)   The problem is caused by the language of the Act and a recent court decision*

This section may be of interest only to lawyers. Other readers may wish to skip to the next section.

There is an argument that under the Act a search warrant does not allow seizure of media containing communications, but is merely another form of court order compelling the provider to *disclose* the content of those communications.

Section 2703 does not mention the word "seize"—rather, it provides for "disclosure" of the contents of the communication. Thus, the government may "require *the disclosure* by a provider of ... the contents of an electronic communication [in storage fewer than 180 days] ... only pursuant to a [search] warrant."[99] This exclusive use of the term "disclosure" leaves room for lawyers to argue that Congress intended to limit the government to obtaining the content of communications, not the media on which those communications reside.

Courts should reject this argument. It would be odd for Congress to prohibit the government from obtaining a stored communication after the government has satisfied the Fourth Amendment by establishing probable cause to seize it. It would be particularly unusual for Congress to do so without explicit language to that effect. Furthermore, had Congress intended to limit the use of a search warrant in this fashion, it would have included warrants within the ambit of those court orders which could be challenged by the provider in court before those orders took effect.[100]

Moreover, § 2704 by its terms applies only to subpoenas and court orders, suggesting that Congress recognized that the government would not need a backup copy when it chose to seize the original media with a search warrant. Finally, note that an adverse interpretation should not prevent law enforcement from obtaining

---

99. 18 U.S.C. 2703(a) (emphasis added).

100. *See* 18 U.S.C. 2703(d).

media via a search warrant on other grounds (i.e., that files other than those containing electronic communications contain evidence of a crime). In such cases, the communications would simply "come along for the ride."

Unfortunately, a recent court decision creates additional risk for investigators. In *Steve Jackson Games, Inc. v. United States Secret Service*,[101] the Secret Service seized a bulletin board operated by a game company. The board offered E-mail services to subscribers. Agents believed that an employee of the company had downloaded confidential telephone company documents onto the board. The Secret Service was searching for stolen trade secrets and evidence of a conspiracy to disseminate that information.

Although the Secret Service's warrant authorized the seizure of the computer containing that E-mail, the court found that the affidavit did not indicate that there were stored communications within that computer or request permission to seize those communications. Thus, the warrant was not sufficient under the Act to obtain the stored communications.[102]

The language of the opinion is interesting because it appears to distinguish between compelling disclosure of communications and seizing the media containing those communications.

> Steve Jackson Games, Inc., through its Illuminati bulletin board services, was a "remote computing service" within the definition of Section 2711, and, therefore, the only procedure available to the Secret Service to obtain "disclosure" of the contents of electronic communications was to comply with this statute. See, 18 U.S.C. 2703. *Agent Foley and the Secret Service, however, wanted more than "disclosure" of the contents of the communication.* As the search warrant application evidences, the Secret Service wanted *seizure* of all information and the authority to review and read all electronic communications, both public and private. A court order *for such disclosure* is only to issue if "there is a reason to believe

---

101. 816 F.Supp. 432 (W.D. Tex. 1993), *affirmed* 36 F.3d 457 (5th Cir. 1994).

102. *Steve Jackson Games, supra,* at 442–443, *affirmed* 36 F.3d 457 (5th Cir. 1994). The court also held that the Secret Service failed to comply with the Privacy Protection Act. That law is discussed later in this chapter.

the contents of a[n] . . . electronic communication . . . are relevant to a legitimate law enforcement inquiry." See, 18 U.S.C. § 2703(d).

. . .

The procedures followed by the Secret Service in this case virtually eliminated the safeguards contained in the statute. For example, no Plaintiff was on notice that the search or seizure order was made pursuant to this statute and that Steve Jackson Games, Incorporated could move to quash or modify the order or eliminate or reduce any undue burden on it by reason of the order. See, 18 U.S.C. s 2703(d). The provisions of the statute regarding the preparation of backup copies of the documents or information seized were never utilized or available. See, 18 U.S.C. s 2704. Agent Foley stated his concern was to prevent the destruction of the documents' content and for the Secret Service to take the time necessary to carefully review all of the information seized. He feared Blankenship could possibly delete the incriminating documents or could have programmed destruction in some manner. Notwithstanding that any alteration or destruction by Blankenship, Steve Jackson, or anyone else would constitute a criminal offense under this statute, Foley and the Secret Service *seized—not just obtained disclosure of the content*—all of the electronic communications stored in the Illuminati bulletin board involving the Plaintiffs in this case. This conduct exceeded the Government's authority under the statute.[103]

The first excerpt could be read as indicating that once the government has obtained a search warrant to obtain disclosure of stored communications, it may use that warrant to obtain disclosure by seizing the magnetic media containing those communications. Or, to put it another way, that the Act does not prevent the use of a search warrant to seize media containing stored communications if the warrant provides probable cause for seizing those communications. This interpretation is a logical and persuasive reading of the Act.

Unfortunately, the second excerpt appears to contradict the first. The court seems to be suggesting that the search warrant, even if

---

103. *Steve Jackson Games, supra*, at 443 (emphasis added).

valid, could only have served the same function as a subpoena. The communication service provider would have been able to contest the warrant in court, and then, only if the Service prevailed, turn over the communications. It is this excerpt which would fuel any lawsuit against an investigator who seizes a computer used to operate a communication service.

There are several problems with the court's opinion. The first problem is glaring—the court referred to the wrong part of the Act. Although the court chastised the Service for not obtaining a proper court order under § 2703(d), the Service was purporting to act pursuant to § 2703(a), which allows "disclosure" of communications via a search warrant. The court was correct that under § 2703(d), the provider has an opportunity to move to set aside, or "quash," an order if compliance would be burdensome. But § 2703(a), unlike § 2703(d), does not appear to provide such a right.

Second, the backup procedures set forth in § 2704, which also contemplate the provider's turning over copies of communications, are available only when the government uses a "subpoena or court order," not a warrant.[104] This omission can only be explained by the fact that there is no need (or ability) to make a backup copy if the government has seized the original. Thus, § 2704(a)(1) appears to suggest that a warrant may be used to seize materials, and not just as a glorified subpoena.

Third, there is no language in the Act limiting "disclosure" to the provision of copies of the communication. It is equally plausible that "disclosure" includes the seizing of the communications themselves.

Finally, the first excerpt quoted above appears to suggest that the court believed that the Service *could* have seized the materials under § 2703(d) had it complied with that statute. However, a court order pursuant to § 2703(d) (before it was amended in 1994) was actually *easier* to obtain than a search warrant. A properly drafted warrant requires more than a reasonable belief that the communications were relevant—the affiant must demonstrate probable cause to believe that the communications are evidence of a crime. Thus, the first excerpt

---

104. *See* § 2704(a)(1).

suggests that a properly drafted warrant allows investigators to seize computers containing stored communications.

8.47–b(3)   Play it safe—seize and don't look

The Act appears to allow seizure of magnetic media containing stored communications upon a showing that there is probable cause that those communications may contain evidence of a crime. However, there is always the risk of a lawsuit.

A more cautious approach is to insert language in the warrant which allows you to seize the media containing the communications and hold it for a short period of time (say two days) without examining those communications. Chapter 9 includes language designed for this purpose.

This approach demonstrates your concern for the rights of persons not involved in your investigation whose privacy otherwise would be jeopardized, and provides a convincing showing of good faith should you be sued. Although you will have seized those communications, you will have maintained the status quo by not examining them. Any violation of the Act is hypertechnical at best because aggrieved parties still have whatever rights they otherwise have under 18 U.S.C. 2703(d) to ask a court to order the communications returned unread.

You are justified in seizing those communications in order to prevent the sysop from tampering with, or destroying, those messages. You must specify a short period of time because those communications are not evidence; you have "removed" the communications without formally seizing them, and you have no other basis for delaying the ongoing search.[105] Allowing aggrieved parties only two days to object is in keeping with § 2703(d), which requires that objections to court orders mandating disclosure be filed "promptly."[106]

---

105. This problem is discussed in Chapter 7.

106. You might consider including an order in the warrant requiring the suspect (or owner of the computer) to personally notify all parties to communications contained within the seized media of the seizure. You can justify this request by suggesting that the service provider should know who has been communicating via his computer.

Where you anticipate seizing both communications and other evidence (e.g., access codes or pirate software), your warrant should give you permission to examine the media, conditioned on your exercise of best efforts to avoid reading any communications pending an objection by any aggrieved party.

8.50   Pen registers and traps and traces

The next two sections on identifying the source or destination of telephone calls are (mercifully) straightforward. The Act allows law enforcement investigators to obtain such records by using legal process. Some states, like California, require investigators to use a search warrant.

A *trap and trace* is a procedure whereby a telephone company uses its switching equipment to "trace" a call to the location of the party placing the call. As discussed in Chapter 4, the most common use of a trap and trace in high-technology crime investigations is to determine the location of an intruder illegally accessing a computer.

A *pen register* is a device which, when connected to a phone line, records phone numbers dialed by a phone connected to that line. Telephone companies can use their switching equipment to initiate a pen register. In addition to using pen registers in computer intrusion cases, law enforcement investigators use them to determine a drug dealer's confederates, suppliers, and customers.

8.51   The Fourth Amendment does not apply to traps and traces or pen registers

The United States Supreme Court has held that the Fourth Amendment does not prohibit warrantless traps and traces because the customer is deemed to have provided the phone company with the information pinpointing the phone the customer is using to place the call.[107] Similarly, the Fourth Amendment does not apply to warrantless pen registers because the customer voluntarily transmitted the

---

107. *See United States v. Miller*, 425 U.S. 435 (1976); *United States v. White*, 401 U.S. 745 (1971).

phone numbers intercepted by the register for the purpose of making the telephone call.[108]

8.52 The Act expands upon the Fourth Amendment by requiring court orders

As discussed at the beginning of this chapter, the Act expands upon the Fourth Amendment in certain areas. This is one of those areas—the Act requires a court order in order to perform either procedure, with certain limited exceptions.[109]

Taking the exceptions first, there are three cases where no order is required by the Act. First, no order is required where the party seeking to install the trap and trace or pen register is a communications carrier performing routine maintenance, protecting its rights or property, or protecting its users against fraud and abuse.[110]

Second, no order is required where the subscriber consents to the installation.[111] Thus, a computer owner could consent to a trap and trace to determine the location of an intruder; no order would be required under the Act.

Finally, § 3125 authorizes a temporary installation without an order where there is an immediate danger of death or injury, or where there are conspiratorial activities characteristic of organized crime.

Where no exceptions apply, a federal or state (including local) law enforcement official must apply in writing, under oath, to a court of competent jurisdiction for a court order allowing installation of a trap and trace or pen register. Federal magistrates can issue such orders.[112] The official need only certify that "the information likely to be obtained by such installation and use is relevant to an ongoing criminal investigation."[113]

---

108. *See Smith v. Maryland*, 442 U.S. 735 (1979).

109. *See* 18 U.S.C. 3121–3126.

110. *See* 18 U.S.C. 3121(b)(1).

111. *See* 18 U.S.C. 3121(b)(3).

112. *See* 18 U.S.C. 3127(2)(A).

113. *See* 18 U.S.C. 3123(a).

The order must include the identity of the person leasing or associated with the telephone line to be monitored, the identity, if different, of the suspect, the number and the physical location of the telephone line, and a statement of the offense under investigation. (The application should also include this information.)

The order may allow installation for a maximum of 60 days; law enforcement may seek additional extensions.

The order should direct the telephone company to install the pen register and/or trap and trace, and not to disclose the installation to anyone. The order should be filed under seal. The law enforcement official seeking the installation must reimburse the telephone company for the reasonable cost of the installation.[114]

8.53 Some states require search warrants to perform pen registers and traps and traces

The Act does not require investigators to use a search warrant to install a pen register or trap and trace. However, just as Congress giveth, the state taketh away.

Many states, most notably California, interpret their state constitutions as requiring a search warrant in order to install either a pen register or trap and trace.[115]

---

114. Congress recently changed the Act to explicitly require any government agency installing a pen register to use "technology reasonably available to it that restricts the recording or decoding or electronic or other impulses to the dialing and signaling information utilized in call processing." 18 U.S.C. 3121(c).

115. *See, e.g., People v. DeLaire*, 610 N.E.2d 1277 (Ill. Ct. App. 1993) (dicta); *Richardson v. State*, 865 S.W. 2d 944 (Tex. Ct. App. 1993) (suggesting that a warrant *may* be required); *State v. Thompson*, 760 P.2d 1162, 1165 (Idaho 1988); *People v. Larkin*, 194 Cal. App. 3d 650 (Cal. Ct. App. 1987) (relying upon *People v. Blair*, 25 Cal. 3d 640 (Cal. 1975); *Commonwealth v. Melilli*, 555 A.2d 1254 (Pa. 1989); *Commonwealth v. Beuford*, 475 A.2d 783 (Pa. 1984); *People v. Sporieder*, 666 P.2d 135 (Col. 1983); *see* Fishman, *Wiretapping and Eavesdropping* (New York: Clark Boardman Callaghan, 1994) (Supplement), at § 28.9. A persuasive argument can be made that these decisions should not apply in cases of computer intrusion—unauthorized callers to a computer system protected by a password or other indication that access is prohibited should not enjoy the same level of privacy as other users of telephone services. *See United States v. Seidlitz*, 589 F.2d 152, 158 (4th Cir. 1978).

The Act does not exempt law enforcement officials from obtaining search warrants in those states.[116]

8.60 Obtaining toll records from a telephone company or other electronic communication service

As discussed earlier in this chapter, § 2703 of the Act prevents a provider of electronic communication services from disclosing records concerning subscribers without a search warrant, subpoena, or court order. While § 2703 was discussed with respect to records relating to stored communications, it also applies to ordinary telephone billing information.

Congress defined electronic communication service providers as including any provider which "provides to users [of the service] the ability to send or receive *wire* or electronic communications."[117] Thus, § 2703(c) of the Act prohibits telephone companies from divulging toll records without legal process.

As discussed above, the government may forgo using a search warrant to obtain such records in favor of using a grand jury subpoena, administrative subpoena, or trial subpoena.[118] The government may also obtain a court order requiring disclosure by presenting specific and articulable facts showing that there are reasonable grounds to believe that the contents of the communication are relevant and material to an ongoing criminal investigation.

The same reasons for using a search warrant instead of a subpoena apply to a request for toll records. In most cases, it is better for investigators to use a search warrant, and to include in that warrant an order prohibiting the telephone company from disclosing the existence of the warrant.

---

116. "To the extent that state law currently provides that a pen register or trap and trace device may only be installed or used by a state official based on some other, higher standard of proof, that law will continue in effect with respect to such officials." Sen. Rpt. 99-541, *supra*, at 46, 1986 U.S.C.C.A.N. 3600.

117. 18 U.S.C. 2510(15) (emphasis added).

118. 18 U.S.C. 2703(a) and (b).

Again, the Act does not "preempt," or eliminate, any state law requiring a search warrant to obtain such records.

8.70   The Privacy Protection Act

8.71   Introduction to the PPA

The Privacy Protection Act (PPA) seeks to protect activities relating to publishing. You must be aware of the PPA because its provisions apply not only to searches of traditional newspapers, but also to searches of anyone who can reasonably claim to be a publisher. This includes purveyors of obscene publications and anyone clever enough to provide information to the public as part of operating a criminal enterprise.

You must be extremely careful before using a search warrant to obtain evidence from persons who are able to claim that they publish information to the public (e.g., bulletin board sysops).

Congress passed the Privacy Protection Act[119] in response to the United States Supreme Court 1978 decision in *Zurcher v. Stanford Daily.*[120] Police in *Zurcher* served a search warrant on a campus newspaper to obtain photographs of participants in a demonstration. The newspaper challenged the seizure of the photographs on the grounds that the police gave no notice before serving the warrant.

Plaintiffs argued that the search of a newspaper posed such a threat to First Amendment freedoms that the newspaper should be provided an opportunity *before the search* to ask a court to prevent that search. Plaintiff suggested that police should be forced to use a subpoena, which provides that opportunity, instead of a search warrant.

The lower courts agreed and suppressed the search. The United States Supreme Court reversed, on the sensible ground that giving notice would defeat the whole purpose of a search warrant, which is to obtain evidence before it can be destroyed.

Congress reacted to the decision by passing the Privacy Protection Act, which seeks to strike a middle ground between the First

---

119. 42 U.S.C. 2000aa.
120. 436 U.S. 547 (1978).

Amendment concerns of newspapers and the concern that suspects will destroy incriminating evidence. As you will see, while the *Zurcher* decision involved a traditional newsroom, Congress went much further by enacting a law which applies to almost anyone claiming an intent to distribute information to the public.

8.71–a   The PPA applies only to law enforcement

Congress was concerned about governmental searches of institutions protected by the First Amendment; the PPA therefore applies only to searches by law enforcement.

8.71–b   The PPA provides for damages even where officers acted in good faith

Violating the Privacy Protection Act can be expensive. A "person aggrieved by a search for or seizure of materials" in violation of the PPA may sue the officer individually, along with the officer's governmental employer. The "aggrieved party" may collect actual damages (in an amount no *less* than $1,000) and attorneys fees. For example, the United States Secret Service was recently ordered to pay $50,000 in damages, $195,000 in attorney's fees, and $57,000 in costs for violating the PPA.[121]

The officer is immune if he or she had "a reasonable good faith belief in the lawfulness of his [or her] conduct." However, that defense excuses only the officer; the government is liable regardless of the intent of its employee. In other words, you get to keep your house, but your agency pays for your conduct. And it does not stop there for federal officials. The Privacy Protection Act also requires the Attorney General to convene an administrative inquiry whenever a federal official violates the PPA, and to impose sanctions in appropriate cases.[122]

In addition, Congress required the Attorney General to set forth separate guidelines regulating the activities of federal officials in relation to searches involving the media. These official guidelines are

---

121. *See Steve Jackson Games v. United States Secret Service*, 816 F.Supp. 432 (W.D. Tex. 1993), *affirmed* 36 F.3d 457 (5th Cir. 1994).

122. *See* 42 U.S.C. 2000aa-6(b), (c), and (g).

contained within the Code of Federal Regulations.[123] Although this chapter does not discuss those guidelines, federal prosecutors and investigators should review them, along with any internal regulations and policies promulgated by their separate agencies.[124]

The official guidelines are not binding on state and local investigators, and should not be given any effect in cases not involving federal agents.

8.72 Overview of the PPA

The following section is a brief overview of the PPA.

- The Privacy Protection Act regulates searches or seizures of "work product materials" or "documentary materials."[125] "Work product materials" include any mental impressions, theories, or conclusions which a person created with the intent to communicate those matters to the public (e.g., reporters' notes for a story). Documentary materials include any recorded information (e.g., videotapes of the Rodney King beating). However, as discussed below, the language of the PPA is so broad that you should assume that the law covers virtually any evidence.

- Law enforcement officials may not search or seize work product or documentary materials (i.e., just about anything) from any person who intends to publish information to the public. As discussed below, the PPA may allow virtually anyone to claim that he or she is a publisher.

- Officers seeking to search or seize certain material protected by the PPA must serve the target with a subpoena, which the publisher may seek to have quashed (struck down) by a court. The effect of the PPA may be to prohibit you from using a search warrant to obtain records from anyone who can plausibly claim that he or

---

123. *See* 29 CFR 58.

124. Unfortunately, the rules are so general as to be useless. Federal employees should review them so that they can report, if asked, that they reviewed them.

125. *See* 42 U.S.C. 2000aa(a) (work product materials) and (b) (documentary materials).

she publishes information to the public (e.g., a bulletin board sysop).

- Congress included some common-sense exceptions within the PPA. *Your job is to draft your affidavit to fit within one of those exceptions.* Chapter 9 includes language designed for this purpose.

  - •• Congress excluded from the definition of work product materials or documentary materials any "contraband or the fruits of a crime or things otherwise criminally possessed, or property designed or intended for use, or which is or has been used, as the means of committing a criminal offense."[126]

  - •• The PPA also allows officers to use a search warrant where:

    - ••• the materials relate to a criminal offense (other than possession of the materials themselves);

    - ••• immediate seizure of the materials is necessary to save lives;

    - ••• *in the case of documentary materials only,* service of the subpoena would result in destruction, alteration, or concealment of evidence; or

    - ••• *in the case of documentary materials only,* a court order requiring production of the documents pursuant to a subpoena was not complied with, and either appellate remedies are exhausted or further delay would threaten the interests of justice.

The next section takes you through the PPA a step at a time and emphasizes the exceptions which allow you to search and seize bulletin boards in certain cases. First, however, you may find the following chart helpful in complying with the PPA.

---

126. 42 U.S.C. 2000aa-7.

Figure 8–3: Complying with the PPA

- Is it reasonable to believe that the target intends to publish information to the public?

  •• If no, then the PPA does not apply to your case. However, be absolutely certain that you can defend your position. If you discover after the seizure that the target intended to publish materials to the public, return copies of that material upon request, and stop reading any materials you seized until after the target has had the opportunity to contest the seizure in court.

  •• If yes, even if some of the materials you want to seize are not protected under the PPA, consider seizing the target's computer but not examining it until after the owner has been given an opportunity to contest the seizure in court.

    The answer is almost always yes when the target runs a bulletin board.

- Are the materials you want to seize either work product or documentary materials?

  •• *The answer is always yes when you have reason to believe that the suspect may be storing materials relating to his or her publishing activities on the computer you intend to search or seize.*

- *Exemptions.* If the materials you expect to seize fall within the categories listed below, you may use a search warrant to seize those materials:

  •• The materials are contraband, stolen property, or property used to commit a crime.

  •• There is probable cause to believe that the target has committed, or is committing, a criminal offense to which the

Figure 8–3, cont.

> materials relate, *other than* a criminal offense based on the mere possession of the materials themselves.

> •• It reasonably appears that immediate seizure of the materials is necessary to prevent death or serious bodily injury.

- If you are seizing documentary materials which do not fall within the exemptions listed above, you may still use a search warrant to seize them (*and only documentary materials*), if your affidavit establishes that there is reason to believe that serving a subpoena would result in the destruction, alteration, or concealment of those documentary materials.

8.73   Exploring the PPA

8.73–a   The PPA protects work product and documentary materials

The PPA prohibits a government official from searching or seizing work product materials. Work product materials are materials which:

- are prepared, produced, authored, or created in anticipation of communicating such materials to the public;

- are possessed for the purpose of communicating those materials to the public; and

- include mental impressions, conclusions, opinions, or theories of the person who prepared, produced, authored, or created such material.[127]

8.73–b   Work product materials can include almost anything

It appears that Congress intended work product materials to include reporters' interview notes, draft stories, research, and the

---

127. *See* 42 U.S.C. 2000aa-7(b).

like.[128] However, anybody running a bulletin board can easily claim that he or she intended to communicate material found on the board's hard disk (or server) to the public.

8.73–c Documentary materials can mean almost anything, too

Documentary materials include "materials upon which information is recorded, and includes, but is not limited to, written or printed materials, photographs, motion picture films, negatives, video tapes, audio tapes, and other mechanically, magnetically, or electronically recorded cards, tapes, or discs."[129]

Any piece of paper, floppy disk, or hard drive may be "documentary material" because it is material "upon which information is recorded." However, the word "recorded" may narrow the meaning of "documentary material." The legislative history suggests that Congress intended to include only those materials which record information forming the basis for news stories, such as photographs or videotapes of events.[130] Nonetheless, this language is ambiguous, and you must assume that a court may find that virtually any computer evidence you seize is "documentary material."

8.73–d The PPA does not protect contraband, stolen property, or property used to commit a crime

The PPA excludes any information which is "contraband or the fruits of a crime or things otherwise criminally possessed, or property designed or intended for use, or which is or has been used, as the means of committing a criminal offense."[131]

This exclusion allows you to use a warrant to obtain stolen data (e.g., telephone access codes or trade secrets). However, you must

---

128. *See* Sen.Rep. No. 874, 96th Cong., 2nd Sess., 10 (1980), reprinted in 1980 U.S.C.C.A.N. 3950 (Sen. Rpt. 96-874).

129. 42 U.S.C. 2000aa-7(a).

130. *See* Sen. Rpt. 96-874, relating to comments about Section 107(a).

131. 42 U.S.C. 2000aa-7.

explain in your affidavit why the materials you seek fit within this exclusion.

For example, if you are seeking obscene materials, your affidavit should include evidence that those materials are contraband and/or fruits of child molestation, pimping, or pandering. If you are seeking stolen data or pirated software, the affidavit should include evidence indicating that those materials may be found on a computer belonging to the suspect "publisher."

Furthermore, the exclusion applies only to the actual contraband or stolen property, and not to related materials. An obscene picture may be contraband; a letter talking about purchasing such pictures is "related material." Such material is covered by another section of the PPA, discussed below at footnote 141 on page 408.

8.73–e   The PPA protects materials possessed by persons who intend to publish information to the public

8.73–e(1)   Anyone with a computer may be a publisher

Assuming that certain material is work product or documentary, the next issue is whether the person possessing that information is a publisher. The PPA defines such a person as one who has a purpose "to disseminate to the public a newspaper, book, broadcast, *or other similar form of public communication*, in or affecting interstate or foreign commerce."[132]

The words "other similar form" appear to include electronic communications, and the words "public communication" appear to include communications by bulletin board sysops to persons accessing their boards.[133]

---

132. 42 U.S.C. 2000aa(a) (emphasis added). This language also appears in § 2000aa(b).

133. *Cf. Steve Jackson Games v. United States Secret Service,* 816 F.Supp. 432, at 439-40, n.7 (W.D. Tex. 1993), *affirmed* 36 F.3d 457 (5th Cir. 1994) (decision can be read as suggesting that announcements and newsletters posted on a bulletin board are protected by the PPA). Although the PPA also requires that the intended publishing activities affect interstate or foreign commerce, bulletin boards can be accessed from anywhere in the country.

8.73–e(2)   The materials must be intended for publication

Section 2000aa-7(b)(2), defining work product materials, includes only those materials "possessed for the purposes of communicating such materials to the public." Section 2000aa(b) only prohibits law enforcement officials from seizing documentary materials "possessed by a person *in connection with* a purpose [to publish material to the public]."[134]

8.73–e(3)   The government may seize materials where investigators "reasonably believe" that the holder of those materials is not a publisher who intends to publish those materials

Section 2000aa(a) states that law enforcement investigators may not search or seize any work product materials possessed by a person "reasonably believed" to be a publisher. Congress appears to have provided a defense of lack of knowledge where the investigator reasonably believes that he or she is not seizing work product or documentary materials intended for publication.

> The Committee recognized a problem for the law enforcement officer, who seeking to comply with the statute, might be uncertain whether the materials he sought were work product or non-work product *and* that they were intended for publication. Therefore, in the interests of allowing for some objective measure for judgment by the officer, the Committee has provided that the work product must be possessed by someone "reasonably believed" to have a purpose to communicate to the public.[135]

In *Steve Jackson Games v. United States Secret Service*,[136] the only case discussing the Privacy Protection Act in the context of searches of computer evidence, the court applied an "objective"

---

134. Section 2000aa(b) (emphasis added).

135. Sen. Rep. 96-874., 1980 U.S.C.C.A.N. 3950, 3957 (emphasis added). The word "and" suggests that investigators may rely on their reasonable belief that the work product materials were not intended to be disseminated to the public.

136. 816 F.Supp. 432 (W.D. Tex. 1993), *affirmed* 36 F.3d 457 (5th Cir. 1994).

standard based on what the officer knew, or should have known, about the activities of the owner of the computer.[137]

Most important, the court found that while the Secret Service did not know in advance that Steve Jackson Games was a publisher, the company's documented claim it was a publisher put the Service on notice. The court held that the PPA operated at that point and that the law required the agents to return copies of the seized work product materials immediately upon request.[138]

Finally, note that § 2000aa(b), governing seizure of documentary materials, does not include the phrase "reasonably believed." Moreover, the legislative history quoted above refers only to work product materials.

However, there is no reason to distinguish between work product and documentary materials in terms of whether the investigator knew that the holder of those materials was a publisher. Investigators cannot avoid seizing protected materials unless they are aware that those materials are protected. Therefore, courts will likely allow investigators to raise the defense of a lack of knowledge in cases involving both work product and documentary materials.

8.73–f   The PPA prohibits search and seizure of protected materials; law enforcement must serve a subpoena for those materials instead

Law enforcement officials may not search for, or seize, materials protected by the PPA. *This means that officers may not use a search warrant to obtain those materials.* Instead, officers must serve the person possessing those materials with a subpoena, which allows that person to challenge the request in court.[139]

8.73–g   Exceptions to the subpoena requirement for work product materials

---

137. *Id.*, at n.8.

138. *Id.*, at 441.

139. Note, however, that a violation of the PPA does not make evidence obtained in violation of that law inadmissible. *See* 42 U.S.C. 2000aa-6(e). Please do not take this as a license to violate the PPA—you may lose your job and all your assets.

Congress provided certain exceptions to the PPA for work product materials (e.g., reporters' notes) and others for documentary materials (e.g., videotapes).

Officers may seize work product materials where:

- there is reason to believe that immediate seizure of the materials is necessary to prevent death or serious bodily injury;[140] or

- there is probable cause to believe that the person possessing the materials has committed, or is committing, a criminal offense to which the materials relate, other than a criminal offense based on the mere possession of the materials themselves.

The first exception will not apply in most cases. The second exception is more useful. As discussed above, the PPA already excludes from protection contraband, stolen property, and property which is an instrumentality, or result, of an offense. The second exception is relevant when the materials sought provide evidence relating to a criminal offense. For example, E-mail between a sysop and a subscriber in which the sysop admits stealing access codes is related to the crime of theft of access codes, but it is not contraband, stolen property, or an instrumentality of a crime.[141]

Particularity is critical when drafting your affidavit. Any description of property to be seized must be so narrow that each and every item encompassed by that description can be shown to relate to the crime(s) discussed in the affidavit. Otherwise, a court may find

---

140. *See* 42 U.S.C. 2000aa(a)(1) and (2).

141. This exception does not allow searches or seizures of work product materials where the only criminal offense to which the materials relate "consists of the receipt, possession, communication, or withholding of such materials or the information contained therein." 42 U.S.C. 2000aa(a)(1). (The same section provides an exception to this exclusion in cases where the materials relate to the national defense or other sensitive areas relating to national security.)

There are probably few, if any, cases in which possession of property is a crime where the property does not qualify as contraband, stolen property, an instrumentality of a crime, or the fruits of a crime. Should you encounter one of those cases, remember that if possession of the item is a crime, then that item is probably also related to other crimes. For example, possession of child pornography may also be evidence of child abuse, pimping, and pandering.

a violation of the PPA because the warrant authorized a search for work product material not falling within the exception.

For example, a request in a warrant for "all E-mail addressed to John Doe" may violate the PPA even where John Doe is suspected of using the board to post stolen access codes delivered by E-mail, because some E-mail might have nothing to do with access codes. The request could be drafted to avoid the problem—the request could call for "all E-mail to John Doe relating to unauthorized use of AT&T access codes." An investigator executing the warrant would still be justified in looking through all E-mail addressed to John Doe in order to determine whether that E-mail related to the use of AT&T access codes.

8.73–h   Exceptions to the subpoena requirement for documentary materials

The same two exceptions relating to work product materials apply to documentary materials.[142] In addition, Congress provided two more exceptions for documentary materials; those exceptions allow search warrants where:

- there is reason to believe that serving a subpoena would result in the destruction, alteration, or concealment of documentary materials; or

- a court order requiring production of the documents pursuant to a subpoena has not been complied with, and either:

  - •• all appellate remedies are exhausted; or

  - •• further delay required to litigate the subpoena would threaten the interests of justice.

Taking these in reverse order, the second exception is really not an exception at all; it applies where investigators have already served a subpoena without success. However, the exception relating to destruction of evidence is very useful. Obviously, the main advantage of a search warrant is surprise. If you can show that your "publisher"

---

142. *See* 42 U.S.C. 2000aa(b)(1) and (2).

is a crook, you will fall into this exception easily. You may also be able to take advantage of this exception where the publisher is a third party tied to the suspect. In either case, you must include evidence supporting this exception in your affidavit.

Remember: the "destruction of evidence" exception applies only to documentary materials. This exception is not available for searches and seizures of work product materials.

8.74 Special problems created by the Privacy Protection Act

8.74–a Commingled materials

Sloppy language in the PPA creates problems which have not been resolved. The first problem is that magnetic media may contain evidence of a crime "commingled" with work product or documentary materials. The Privacy Protection Act states that it is unlawful for law enforcement investigators to "search for *or* seize" protected materials. It is the prohibition against seizure which causes problems.

Law enforcement agencies routinely seize hard drives because a small portion of the drive contains relevant evidence. Indeed, as noted in Chapter 6, many law enforcement agencies remove computers without examining them first. What happens if that hard drive also contains protected materials?

Assume that investigators serve a search warrant at a house occupied by a sysop suspected of paying for, and posting, pirated software on a pirate bulletin board. Mindful of the prohibition against searching for work product materials, investigators do not search for anything other than pirated software.

To make the example even better, assume that the investigators use software (such as Magellan or ZyIndex) to search for key words connected with the software (e.g., the title, file names, etc.); they examine only files in which those words appear. They find several files containing access codes, and seize the entire computer as evidence.

Have investigators violated the PPA if another portion of that drive contains an article discussing programming techniques which the sysop planned to publish on the bulletin board? What if investigators had no reason to believe that the drive contained such materials? Do investigators have a duty to examine each and every file contained on a computer before removing that computer from the premises? Are investigators prohibited from seizing the entire computer because by doing so they also seize protected materials?

There are no easy answers to these questions. The court in *Steve Jackson Games*[143] appeared to suggest that officers do not violate the PPA by seizing work product materials unless they are aware that they are doing so.

But even if other courts follow this reasoning, what about cases where officers are aware that the computer owner is operating a bulletin board? Common sense suggests that investigators are entitled to seize evidence of a crime even if the object containing that evidence also contains material arguably protected by the First Amendment. The alternative is to allow criminals to conceal their activities by inserting a "letter to the editor" within an obscure file in each computer they own.

Unfortunately, the counterargument may be appealing to those who support the PPA. Without a strict interpretation of the law, police may seize computers used to publish information on the grounds that there is evidence of a crime on a small portion of the disk. The publication would be shut down when police could have merely copied the relevant information onto a floppy disk.[144]

Thus, investigators should hesitate before seizing a computer in cases where they are aware of facts suggesting that the owner could claim to be a publisher. If investigators must seize the computer to

---

143. *Steve Jackson Games v. United States Secret Service* 816 F.Supp. 432 (W.D. Tex. 1993), *affirmed* 36 F.3d 457 (5th Cir. 1994).

144. This argument ignores the fact that investigators are not able to identify all relevant material on the hard drive while at the scene executing a search warrant; a thorough examination of a personal computer can take days or weeks. This fact alone mandates against prohibiting seizure of commingled evidence.

The argument also ignores the risk that mere copying may raise evidentiary problems (i.e., how do we know that the copy faithfully reflects the original) and claims that police overlooked exculpatory evidence in the form of information on the "unseized" disk which would place the seized evidence in an "exculpatory" context. Although the evidentiary problems are usually manageable, it is always safer to have original evidence than a copy. More to the point, law enforcement should not bear the risk of loss of evidence in such cases.

preserve the integrity of the evidence, they should consider not examining it until the computer owner has had an opportunity to contest the seizure in court. That opportunity should be arranged within days, if not hours, of the seizure.

This approach is consistent with the aims of the PPA because it allows the aggrieved publisher an opportunity to prevent inspection of materials by seeking judicial relief. Chapter 9 includes language intended for this purpose.

8.74–b   The PPA conflicts with the Omnibus Act

The Omnibus Act requires a search warrant before officers may intercept "stored communications" where those communications are less than 180 days old. Yet those very same providers of electronic communication service or remote computing service may be publishers entitled to protection under the PPA. And the PPA prohibits the use of a search warrant to obtain "documentary materials."

What happens when police want to search a bulletin board suspected of disseminating child pornography when the sysop is using the board to publish articles advocating lowering the age of consent to eight? The sysop will claim he is a publisher under the PPA. The sysop will also claim that he provides a communication service allowing "subscribers" (i.e., pedophiles) to send messages to each other (including .GIF files depicting naked children).[145]

Police seeking to search the bulletin board for evidence, including the messages, are stuck between two contradictory laws. The Omnibus Act demands that they use a warrant. The PPA prohibits use of a warrant, requiring a subpoena instead.

There are no easy answers to this dilemma. In this case, you could probably draft your affidavit to fit within the exceptions for: (1) work product materials related to an offense (possession of child pornography); and (2) documentary materials in the hands of someone who is

---

145. GIF (graphic interchange file) is the three-letter extension denoting a particular graphics file format. Just as .exe denotes a file which can be executed by a computer (usually the main file in a program), a .gif file indicates a type of graphics file which may be viewed with the appropriate software.

prepared to destroy them (the sysop). But you may not be able to find an exception in other cases.[146]

The safest answer is to use a subpoena whenever possible. The subpoena should be supported by an affidavit showing probable cause for the seizure. You should obtain court approval before accepting records pursuant to that subpoena. A court order enforcing a subpoena supported by probable cause should be equivalent to a warrant under the Omnibus Act, but there are no guarantees.

However, "safe" does not always mean "best." If you believe that the risk of the "publisher" destroying the evidence is high, consider using a search warrant. Note in your affidavit any exceptions which may allow you to use a warrant under the Privacy Protection Act, and in any event, include an order prohibiting you from examining the materials for at least two days to allow aggrieved parties to object.

---

146. Cases involving pirate bulletin boards may pose problems. Assume you want to seize a bulletin board to track down persons who are sending pirate software. If the sysop provides communication services to subscribers, and also publishes a newsletter, how do you obtain stored communications that are less than 180 days old? Although the software is pirated, the stored communications identifying participants are not contraband, and are thus protected by both the ECPA and the PPA. The ECPA prohibits you from obtaining those communications without a warrant, and the PPA prohibits you from using a warrant.

9

Drafting Search Warrants in Cases Involving Computers

9.00 Introduction

You should begin writing your affidavit as early in your investigation as possible.[1] In complex cases, you will need several days, or even weeks, to complete your affidavit—you need as long a head start as possible.

Before visiting the courthouse to obtain a search warrant, recruit other officers to proofread your affidavit and warrant. Search warrants in cases involving computers are typically lengthy and complex. In addition to saving you from embarrassing and potentially devastating errors, such peer review may provide evidence of your good faith sufficient to save your warrant and avoid liability under federal civil rights laws.[2]

9.01 The language suggested in this chapter also appears in Appendix B

Both this chapter and Chapters 4 and 5 suggest language you may use to draft search warrants for computer evidence. That language is also included in Appendix B.

---

1. As with Chapter 7, this chapter is aimed at law enforcement investigators and prosecutors who are charged with writing search warrants. However, corporate investigators and counsel may find this information helpful in assisting police departments which are not experienced in this area.

2. *See, e.g., United States v. Leon*, 468 U.S. 897 (1984); *Malley v. Briggs*, 475 U.S. 335 (1986).

9.02   The affidavit contains several elements

An affidavit can be divided into four sections:

- preliminary matters;

- property description;

- probable cause to search and/or seize each item of property described in the property description; and

- requests for orders dictating how the warrant will be executed, also referred to as "protocols."

9.10   Preliminary matters

The term "preliminary matters" refers to information, apart from a showing of probable cause, which must be included in order to comply with the Fourth Amendment. For example, every warrant must include a statement indicating the basis for searching and/or seizing property (e.g., the property is stolen or constitutes evidence of a crime) and a description of the premises to be searched (e.g., "a single-story residence, brown in color; a 1982 Toyota pickup, license plate #XYZ").

The language you use in your typical search warrant will suffice for high-technology cases. In complex cases, however, you might consider adding a separate section defining technical terms for the magistrate. (An acceptable alternative is to define each term as it appears in the warrant. If you are short on time, defining each term as it appears is usually faster.)

You should assume that the magistrate is aware of, but not familiar with, computers. For example, while you do not have to define "computer," you should consider defining "modem" (e.g., "a device used to allow one computer to communicate with another").

9.20   Property description

Your property description must achieve two goals:

- it must be broad enough to justify searching and seizing all computer evidence relevant to your investigation; and

- it must be narrow enough to prevent officers from searching and seizing material irrelevant to your investigation.

9.21 Drafting the warrant to include all computer evidence

You can meet your first objective by stating that your warrant encompasses all media. Consider relying upon your state's Evidence Code definition of what constitutes a "writing." You might insert the following language at the beginning of your property description:[3]

> The following personal property has been grouped into categories for clarity. Each category contains a group of personal property, information, and other items to be searched/seized, regardless of the media which they appear in or on.
>
> The term "media" encompasses all "writings," as that term is defined by section _____ of the _____ Evidence Code [*the statute in your state which defines "writing"; that statute will usually cover every conceivable medium*], and [*just to cover any media not defined as a "writing"*] documents and records, magnetic media (e.g., floppy disks, hard disks, cassette tapes, magnetic tapes, removable media, tape and/or data cartridges), photographic media (e.g., film, microfilm, photocopies, faxes), optical media (e.g., CD-ROMs), and all information stored within a computer or computer peripheral in any form.

You should also include computers and associated peripherals as property you intend to seize:

> Computer systems, computer hardware (including peripherals), software, and data, including, but not limited to, central

---

3. Text in italics in this chapter is either commentary relating to suggested language or a description of the type of information you should insert at that point.

processing units (CPUs), hard disk drives, floppy disk drives, tape drives, removable media drives, optical/CD-ROM drives, servers, workstations, display screens, input devices (including but not limited to keyboards, mice, and track-balls), printers, modems, peripherals, floppy disks, magnetic tapes, cassette tapes, removable storage media, and/or optical/CD-ROM disks or cartridges, found together or separately from one another.[4]

Remember that computers can be found in unusual places. As discussed in Chapter 6, in addition to personal computers, you may need to search or seize memory telephones, fax machines, copiers, and wristwatches. If you want to seize such property, do not forget to list it in your property description. For example:

Any and all records of telephone numbers stored within telephones, fax machines, and timepieces [*choose one or all of these depending upon the facts of your case*] capable of storing and/or automatically dialing pre-programmed phone numbers, including numbers stored as part of an "automatic dialing feature." [*If you can make the case elsewhere in your affidavit for taking the equipment and searching it off-site, ask for the equipment itself: "telephones, fax machines, and timepieces capable of storing and/or automatically dialing pre-programmed phone numbers, including numbers stored as part of an automatic dialing feature." Of course, if you find evidence within equipment, you can seize that equipment.*]

Finally, you need to include language authorizing seizure of peripherals and documentation needed to aid in your examination of the seized computer:

---

4. Bear in mind that magistrates may be concerned that you are taking computer equipment which you do not need. Consider narrowing this list when you request the warrant.

Documentation or other material describing the operation of any computer systems, computer hardware, software, and/or computer peripherals found at the premises, including instructions on how to access disks, files, or other material stored within same, including but not limited to computer manuals, printouts, passwords, file name lists, "readme" and/ or "help files."

Remember that the property description lists only the property you wish to take; you still need to provide justification for taking it. That justification is discussed later in this chapter.

9.22 Drafting the warrant to be sufficiently "particular" as required by the Fourth Amendment

Listing "all computers" as property to be searched and/or seized is, by itself, meaningless. You are generally not looking for containers—you are looking for information. If your warrant lists computers as the only property to be searched and/or seized, your evidence may be suppressed, just as if your property description listed only "all desks and file cabinets."

The risk is that your warrant may be classified as a "general search." As discussed in Chapter 7, the concept of the general search arose out of the writs of assistance denounced by the Framers of the Fourth Amendment. Such writs allowed a general search of a residence without listing any particular property to be searched for and seized. Warrants authorizing a general search are invalid.

Defense lawyers will argue that your property description was so broad as to give you a "fishing license" to examine all computers and floppy disks for anything which might prove incriminating. They will contend that your warrant was nothing more than a writ of assistance allowing a general search of all magnetic media.

Of course, you want to be able to search all magnetic media and seize any information which may be relevant to your case. Fortunately, the nature of computer evidence provides you with an overwhelming advantage.

Computers contain an enormous amount of information within one physical object. Under current search and seizure law, if you have permission to search any part of an object (e.g., a book) for evidence, you may search all parts of that object (e.g., every page) until you find it. Therefore, if you are searching a computer, and your property description is not overbroad, you may search the entire hard drive to find property encompassed by that request.

If you find any such property, you may seize the entire hard drive as evidence. Once you have seized the hard drive pursuant to a valid search warrant, you may examine all of it. You may use any evidence you find, even if that evidence was not encompassed by your property description.[5]

At the same time, however, if many of your requests are overbroad, a court may decide that your warrant was nothing more than an excuse to rummage through the subject's computers. Your entire warrant, including the properly drafted requests, could be struck as overbroad, and your evidence suppressed.

Thus, the rule is simple: play it safe. If you draft your requests very narrowly, you usually will be able to search the whole hard drive to your heart's content.[6]

How do you ensure that your property description is sufficiently narrow? Courts require a warrant to provide a police officer with very little discretion as to what should be taken and what should be left behind. Think of the police officer as a robot, mechanically carrying out your orders to seize *everything* covered by your property description.

---

5. As discussed in Chapter 7, if you have only "removed" a computer, you may not "seize" it until you have found property on the hard drive which is encompassed by your property description.

6. There are two important exceptions. First, if during your search you have reason to believe that the evidence you seek in your narrowly drafted requests could not possibly reside on the hard drive, you must stop searching. Fortunately, this exception is more theoretical than actual. Second, as discussed in Chapter 8, federal privacy laws may restrict your ability to search for stored communications and work product or documentary materials contained on a hard drive. Of course, these laws operate regardless of the breadth of your property description.

There is also an important caveat. Your job is not to rummage through subjects' belongings just hoping to find something interesting or incriminating, whether those belongings be private papers or magnetic media. You need to be looking for something, and you must do your best to describe it accurately.

For each item you intend to search and seize, determine whether your description would also require the officer to seize items not justified by probable cause. If it could, then narrow your description until you pass the test. If at some point narrowing the description would cause you to lose relevant evidence, then use the language necessary to seize that evidence, but explain to the magistrate why you have done so, and why it is impossible to narrow the request further.

Remember that you must advise the magistrate of any facts which restrict your search. For example, if an informant who provides the probable cause for your search tells you that the stolen software will only be found on a single floppy diskette with a red label, then you must inform the magistrate of that fact. You may still have probable cause to search the hard drive (i.e., it is likely that the suspect uploaded the contents of the diskette to the hard drive), but you must still tell the magistrate what the informant told you.

Finally, in complex cases, consider serving both the affidavit and the warrant at the scene. Unless there is a pressing need to keep the affidavit secret, you should serve the affidavit along with the warrant.

This advice is controversial, and there will be many times when it is inappropriate, such as when the affidavit reveals the identity, or even the existence, of an informant. However, note that in determining whether a search warrant is insufficiently particular, courts might not consider your affidavit unless it "accompanies the warrant."[7] This can be crucial where your property description is overbroad, but your

---

7. This area is still unsettled. *See United States v. Towne*, 997 F.2d 537 (9th Cir. 1993); *United States v. Dale*, 991 F.2d 819 (D.C. Cir. 1993); *United States v. George*, 975 F.2d 72 (2d Cir. 1992); *United States v. Maxwell*, 920 F.2d 1028 (D.C. Cir. 1990); *United States v. Kow*, 58 F.3d 423 (9th Cir. 1995); *United States v. Hayes*, 794 F.2d 1348 (9th Cir. 1986); *United States v. Wuagneux*, 683 F.2d 1343, 1351 n.6 (11th Cir. 1982); *United States v. Klein*, 565 F.2d 183, 186, n.3 (1st Cir. 1977). These cases all note that your warrant must also explicitly incorporate the affidavit by reference.

Note that a prominent commentator suggests that this rule may not require actual service of the affidavit, but merely proof that the serving officers had the affidavit with them at the scene so that they could refer to it in determining the breadth of the warrant. *See* W. LaFave, *Search and Seizure*, § 4.6, at n.23 (1978); *see Wuagneux, supra*, at n.6 (where affidavit was sealed); *but see Kow, supra; Hayes, supra*, at 1355 ("the purpose of the accompanying affidavit clarifying a warrant is both to limit the officer's discretion *and to inform the person subject to the search what items the officers executing the warrant can seize*") (emphasis added).

affidavit makes clear what you are really looking for and the means by which you intend to separate relevant from irrelevant material.

In most cases, the suspect will know all of the facts without examining the affidavit. It seems unwise to risk suppression of evidence simply to keep the suspect guessing for the brief period of time before the affidavit is available to the public.

9.22–a   Describing software: a difficult problem

Perhaps the most difficult property to describe with particularity is software. Software, in object or source code, is generally unintelligible to the layperson. While it is easy for a police officer to identify a narcotics ledger, it is more difficult to describe software in such a way that a police officer using the description would seize only the media which contain that software.

There are several solutions to this problem. Ideally, you should use as many of those solutions as possible in your property description. If one description does not capture the evidence, perhaps another will. Just be sure to explain to the magistrate your reason for using each description.

1.   List the file names within the software

If the victim used VECTOR.1 as the name for a graphics file contained in the program, which itself contains a hundred file names, then you can search for all files entitled VECTOR.1 on the theory that the thief has not taken the time and effort to change all of the file names.[8] You should attach to your affidavit, and include in your warrant, a list of all file names corresponding to the names used in the victim's software.

2.   Identify the software by certain features of the code itself

What if the thief has altered the software, perhaps by changing the file names? Consider describing the software by certain identifying

---

8. You should state your reasoning to this effect in your affidavit, preferably supported by expert opinion that software thieves sometimes do not have the time or energy to change all of the file names in software they have stolen.

features which you believe will have survived any alteration by the thief. Thus, you might seek to seize "all media containing the phrase "PAS/IEDB," or "Product Administration System/Integrated Engineering Data Base."

A variation on this approach may be useful when you seek evidence that the thief has used parts of the victim's software to develop the thief's software. This use may be inadvertent—in the case of blatant copying, consider listing "bugs" which the thief may have copied wholesale, even while changing the file names and variables to evade detection. Simply include in your property description a list of words, phrases, or bits of code (but not trade secrets) which the victim reasonably believes will still be found in the altered software.

3. Describe the software by its functionality

Another alternative is to describe the software by its function. If the victim's program is a game program simulating the sport of cricket, then search for all game programs simulating cricket. Your affidavit must include evidence suggesting that the only software simulating cricket which is likely to be found at the location to be searched will be the victim's cricket program.

4. Describe the software as "the victim's software," and use an expert to identify that software

Finally, you may describe the victim's software as simply that— the victim's software:

> Any and all media containing part or all of any version (or revision) of the following software, whether in source code or object code: [*listing the programs sought*].

In this case, you are not seeking to seize all cricket programs—you are seeking to seize the victim's cricket.exe program and all portions and revisions of that program.

You must convince the magistrate that a police officer will recognize the described software if it is located on the premises (instead of seizing some other code). You can accomplish this by obtaining an order which allows an expert to assist police in locating and identifying that evidence. This tactic allows the expert to locate property which a typical police officer could not identify.[9]

Experts are particularly useful in information theft cases, where even a description of the functionality of the software (e.g., "computer files detailing the electrical characteristics of component X") would not enable a police officer to identify the software.

Chapter 5 and Appendix B provide sample language allowing an expert to accompany police to identify property. Chapter 5 (at page 212) also discusses some of the pitfalls of using experts employed by the victim to search for stolen property.

9.30   Probable cause

The section of your warrant containing your showing of probable cause is the heart of the affidavit. Here is where you provide the justification for searching computers to find evidence, "removing" computers for further examination, and searching and seizing seemingly innocuous property, such as printers, telephones, modems, copiers, and fax machines.

9.31   Overview

In complex cases, it is often useful to provide the magistrate with an overview of your case at the beginning of your discussion of probable cause. A warrant in a recent case included the following summary:

> This case is about a group of VICTIM employees who used VICTIM's computers on company time without permission

---

9. Courts in California and Texas have approved this procedure. *See Schalk v. State*, 767 S.W. 2d 441 (Tex. Ct. App. 1988); *People v. Superior Court (Moore)*, 104 Cal. App. 3d 1001 (Cal. Ct. App. 1980); *see also United States v. Tamura*, 694 F.2d 591 (9th Cir. 1982). This procedure is no different from allowing police to use a jeweler to assist in recovering a stolen ruby from a pawnshop. Police cannot be expected to separate rubies from sapphires, but a jeweler can be designated to tell officers when they have found the stolen ruby. A thief should not escape detection simply because he or she steals something too difficult for a layperson to identify.

to create a new version of already existing and proprietary software belonging to VICTIM. They then sold that "new" software to UNWITTING COMPANY for two million dollars and pocketed the money. These employees worked in a VICTIM department led by DEFENDANT.

DEFENDANT and several other VICTIM employees accomplished this theft of product, time, and materials by forming a new company, CROOK COMPANY. They transferred the "new" software they had developed on VICTIM's system to that company. CROOK COMPANY used VICTIM employees to create the "new" software, and even sent CROOK COMPANY employees to VICTIM to assist in its development. All of this was accomplished without the knowledge or permission of DEFENDANT's superiors at VICTIM.

CROOK COMPANY sold the "new" software to UNWITTING COMPANY, which was unaware of the true origins of the product. That deception was made easier because the man in charge of the project at UNWITTING COMPANY involving that "new" software, DEFENDANT #2, was a former VICTIM employee and a principal in CROOK COMPANY.

Another use for a summary is to explain the technology involved in the case.

VICTIM makes proprietary VGA chips and associated software. A computer displays pictures on a monitor as a way of communicating information to the user. The part within the computer which displays those images is called a "graphics board." Different boards are capable of displaying images of different quality. Quality is generally defined in terms of the number of colors which may be displayed at a particular resolution.

A "VGA" board is a common video standard for computers. Many companies make such boards, and each board is somewhat different. VICTIM has designed a chip which is used as a very important part of certain VGA boards.

9.32   Expertise

The next portion of your showing of probable cause should set forth your expertise. In order to justify searching and seizing computer evidence, the affiant has to make certain factual assertions; those claims are meaningless unless the affiant is qualified to make them (or relies on an expert).

In addition to law enforcement experience, you should list your training and experience related to computers and high-technology crime, including:

- Length of time on any assignment related to computers or high-technology crime.

- Training courses you have attended.

- Membership in organizations related to high-technology crime investigation.

- Number of high-technology crime investigations in which you participated, and the number of those investigations which involved the type of crime you are currently investigating.

- Your discussions with experts in federal, state, or local law enforcement agencies who have specialized in these cases and have considerable experience in investigating and interacting with persons who have committed the crime at issue (e.g., illegally accessing computers).

- Your experience with computers generally, and with the computers involved in this case.

- Your experience in searching, seizing, preserving, and analyzing computer evidence, including the number of search warrants you have executed which have involved computer evidence.

Consider the following brief statement of expertise:

I am an inspector employed by the _____ department. [*General law enforcement experience omitted*]. Since September 1989, I have been assigned to investigate cases for the High Technology Unit of the _____ department.

I am a member of HTCIA (the High Technology Crime Investigation Association), and have attended meetings where techniques concerning investigation of high-technology crime, including trade secret theft, have been discussed. I have attended over two dozen meetings of the Industrial Security Managers' Group, where I have discussed with security managers employed by some of the largest companies in Silicon Valley their methods of detecting and investigating high-technology crime, including trade secret theft.

I have investigated five trade secret cases and have executed warrants in three of those cases. I am a veteran computer user and own an IBM-compatible computer and an Apple Macintosh computer.

Your statement of expertise in these types of cases can never be too long or too complete.

9.33 Justification for seizing property

In order to obtain permission to seize property, you must provide evidence in your affidavit that:

- certain crimes appear to have been committed;

- *each item* you want to search or seize constitutes evidence of the commission of one or more of those crimes (or is stolen property, or was used to commit a crime); and

- it is reasonable to expect to find *each item* at the premises to be searched.

The next section discuss these requirements in turn.

9.34 Showing that each item may be searched or seized as contraband, stolen property, or as an instrumentality or evidence of a crime

9.34–a   Contraband and stolen property

It is easy to justify seizing computer evidence as contraband or stolen property in the appropriate case. Consider the typical justification for identifying stolen property by checking serial numbers of components matching those listed in the property description:

> MANAGER OF THE VICTIM is a Senior Operations Analyst, Operations & Control Review Group, at VICTIM. He headed an audit team reviewing company records to check for any stolen property. He has informed me that members of the CIM Department checked out many pieces of equipment. The audit team could not find records showing the return of the following pieces of equipment: [*insert list*]. I now ask permission to examine and/or move such [*the same type of property*] as may be found at the scene as necessary to check the serial numbers to determine whether said items belong to VICTIM.

In many cases, you will identify stolen property by the serial number. Consider using the following language in your affidavit and warrant:

> [I request] the authority to view, record, and check with [*victim*], all serial numbers appearing on [*components you expect to find at the scene which match the victim's description of the stolen components*].

A word of caution is in order, however. It is one thing to examine property which appears to be stolen to determine whether the serial numbers on that property match the serial numbers on the stolen property listed in your property description. It is quite another to record the serial number of every component on the premises and "run" those numbers on the hunch that certain components may have been stolen from parties other than your victim.

This problem arises when you are searching a suspected fence's business or residence. In such cases, you often want to do more than merely search for property which you have demonstrated is stolen. You want to check serial numbers on *all* components discovered at the premises because you know that fences typically keep stolen goods at their businesses and residences.

In *Arizona v. Hicks*,[10] the Supreme Court held that moving equipment to examine serial numbers merely because circumstances suggest that the property might be stolen violates the Fourth Amendment. Any movement, no matter how slight (e.g., turning over a chip to examine date codes) constitutes a search. (You may record serial numbers that are in plain sight, however.)

You need concrete evidence that the person holding that property is a fence, and probable cause to believe that the suspect is currently holding stolen property. In cases where you make that showing, include the following language in your property description and your warrant:

> [I request] the authority to view, record, and check with [*victim*] and others, and run an automated record-check of, all serial numbers appearing on [*the type of components you expect to find at the scene*].

9.34–b   *Very few items are instrumentalities*

It may be tempting to state in your affidavit that the suspect's computer is to be seized as an instrumentality of a crime, without further justification. This is a good way to lose your case.

Computers are rarely instrumentalities. A computer does not become an instrumentality if it is used to generate documents containing representations used to defraud others. It does not become an instrumentality if it is used to maintain business records for a criminal

---

10. 480 U.S. 321 (1987).

enterprise (e.g., a prostitution ring). Otherwise, investigators could empty office buildings of every typewriter and file cabinet.

A computer is only an instrumentality of a crime if it is used as an instrument to commit that crime. Although it is impossible to define every case in which a computer may be used as an instrumentality, the most common cases are: (1) those in which the computer is used to break into another computer; and (2) those in which the computer is used to forge documents (e.g., color laser printers being used to forge checks). In such cases, you should state in your warrant that the computer is both an instrumentality, and evidence, of a crime.

In most cases, the computer is relevant only insofar as it contains evidence of the crime. Where a computer is used to generate fraudulent documents, the computer may be searched because it may contain copies of those documents or evidence linking a suspect to those documents. Where a computer is used to maintain business records for a criminal enterprise, the computer is relevant for the same reason. In either case, it is still necessary to lay the groundwork for searching and seizing the computer as evidence of a crime.

9.34–c   Evidence of a crime

When drafting your affidavit, draw two columns on a separate piece of paper. In the left-hand column, list each item you intend to search and/or seize, as in a shopping list. In the right-hand column, list the evidence you need to present in your affidavit to justify that search or seizure. When you have finished drafting your affidavit, check it to make sure that your shopping list is complete and that the affidavit contains the evidence you need to justify your "shopping trip" for each item.

9.34–d   Profiles

In some cases, you need to demonstrate that your suspect fits a particular profile in order to justify seizing seemingly innocuous or irrelevant items. Your suspect may be a pedophile who can be expected to keep pictures of children in his computer. More commonly, your suspect is a "cracker," and you are seeking permission to seize modems, blue boxes, and memory-dial telephones.

Consider how the following profile of a cracker may be used to justify seizing a suspect's computer system, associated peripherals, documentation, slips of paper bearing what appear to be passwords, evidence that the suspect communicates with bulletin boards, telephone access codes and credit card numbers, telephone bills, and documents reflecting orders for merchandise by mail or telephone.

According to EXPERT [*or an affiant possessing the necessary training and experience*], persons who engage in the unauthorized access and use of computer systems (hereinafter referred to as "crackers") usually use their own computer systems to do so. Those computer systems commonly consist of [*insert description—this description should match your property description for computer systems*]. Such systems also commonly include electronic cables linking computer systems to other systems or phone lines.

Crackers usually break into computers to: (1) explore computer systems to learn how they operate and to view information stored on those computer systems; (2) vandalize, or otherwise interfere with the operation of those computers; (3) steal information (including software) located on those computers for their own use; (4) obtain credit information and/or financial records of other individuals or entities; (5) use said information to purchase goods and services; and/or (6) avoid paying the legitimate telephone service or toll charges necessary to access other computers.

INSERT WHERE SUSPECT IS JUST BROWSING:

Although SUSPECT on this particular occasion appears not to be seeking [*credit card information or telephone access codes*], but only to [*vandalize/browse*] VICTIM's computer system, that conduct fits the profile of a cracker. I believe that it is reasonable to assume that SUSPECT is engaging in the other activities associated with crackers, and that evidence of such activities will be found on SUSPECT's computer. Moreover, as will be explained in more detail below, evidence that SUSPECT has invaded other computers and/or gained information commonly stolen from computers (e.g., telephone access card numbers and/or credit card numbers) is evidence that SUSPECT intentionally accessed VICTIM's computer system.

END INSERT

Crackers usually store certain information on their computers. For example, the typical cracker will possess passwords and access codes used to gain entry to other computers. Crackers will also often maintain credit card numbers obtained from intrusions by the cracker, or others, into computer systems containing credit information (such as computers maintained by credit information services). Crackers will also often possess telephone access numbers used to make free phone calls. (Since many of the techniques used to break into computer systems require repeated phone calls, such crackers have an incentive to discover access codes which will allow them to make free phone calls.)

Telephone access codes are like credit card numbers. Phone companies provide such numbers to their subscribers to allow them to place toll calls from any location and have those calls automatically billed to their account. For example, a person charging a phone call to his or her Pacific Telephone credit card number is using a telephone access code. The call then appears on that person's monthly phone bill. (Note that the distinction between credit card numbers and telephone access codes is becoming blurred with the introduction of credit card/telephone access cards by AT&T and others. Such cards allow the user to use one number as both a credit card number and telephone access card number. Thus, I seek both credit card numbers and telephone access codes.)

Many crackers communicate with other similarly inclined individuals electronically, by use of "bulletin boards." A computer bulletin board can be thought of as an electronically generated means of communication between computer users, in which each party to the communication can either send or receive information through their respective computers with the use of a modem. (A modem allows a computer to communicate with another computer over telephone lines.) A person typically operates a bulletin board on one "host" computer. Users of the board call into that computer and leave messages or participate in joint activities on that computer.

There are thousands of bulletin boards across the United States today. The vast majority of bulletin boards are legitimate. However, I am aware that there are many "pirate" bulletin boards used primarily to communicate information on how to illegally access computers and steal information from those computers.

Crackers will commonly use bulletin boards to exchange telephone access codes with similarly inclined individuals. They will also use those boards to exchange information on how to illegally access computers, including the account numbers and passwords for those systems. They will also exchange software used to break into computers (such software seeks to "guess" passwords and access codes by generating numerous letters and numbers). They will also exchange software designed to find, record, or capture telephone access codes. (Such software uses a similar technique to "guess" the access codes.)

Crackers use this information to purchase goods and services (e.g., by using illegally obtained credit information). Many crackers call in those orders to mail order merchandisers, particularly computer stores, to purchase various items. The advantage to such a technique is that the cracker need not present an actual credit card, but only the credit card number.

Thus, the computers used by crackers will often contain such information. Such information found on SUSPECT's computer or premises will be evidence of SUSPECT's intent in accessing VICTIM's computer.

In addition to software used to guess telephone access codes, there are mechanical devices used to circumvent billing systems used by telephone companies. One example is a "blue box." Such devices, and others known by similar names which work in similar ways, send signals through phone lines which "fool" the telephone companies' equipment into allowing the caller to avoid paying for the call.

Crackers often keep documentation of their use of telephone access codes and credit card numbers. Persons illegally accessing computers or computer networks also keep records of account numbers and passwords used to break into those computers. Such documentation may consist of scraps of paper, note pads, or typewritten lists, or may be maintained within the cracker's computer itself. Sometimes crackers will add this information to the computer printouts or computer manuals which set forth procedures used to operate their computer and/or software. Sometimes crackers will add this information to written instructions supplied with the "illicit" software described above. Finally, this information may consist of materials containing instructions on how to unlawfully obtain access codes or access computers.

I need the materials described above in order to identify any access codes, credit card numbers, and computer accounts used by SUSPECT in this case. Telephone bills and credit card receipts maintained by SUSPECT will also provide such information.

You must cover two bases when using a profile. First, you must demonstrate that the profile is valid (i.e., that crackers exist and act in certain ways). If the affiant is not an experienced high-technology crime investigator, then he or she must cite an expert opinion to authenticate the profile.

Second, you must demonstrate that it is reasonable to believe that the suspect fits that profile. Again, you may need an expert opinion on this issue.

9.35 Showing that it is reasonable to expect to find each item at the premises to be searched

In addition to showing that the property to be seized is relevant to your case, you must show that it is reasonable to believe that said property will be found at the premises to be searched. You are seeking permission to search, seize, and where necessary, remove, computers and all of the evidence they contain. Therefore, it is prudent to include some evidence supporting a belief that computers, and computer evidence relevant to your case, will be found at the premises.[11]

Consider using the following justification.

> I know from my training and experience [*or, if you are relying on an expert's expertise, "from discussions with EXPERT"*] that computer systems commonly consist of computer hardware, software, and data, including [*the common description for computer systems set forth earlier*]. More powerful computer systems may include multiple

---

11. Actually, you usually do not have to present such evidence. You are searching for computer evidence which is contraband, stolen property, or evidence of a crime. It is true that if a computer is an instrumentality, you probably have to demonstrate that the suspect is likely to keep a computer at the premises (they are not yet as common as, say, telephones). However, if the computer is stolen, it is likely to be located anywhere the suspect could hide it. The same is true if you are looking for evidence which could be stored on a computer or in documentary form. Thus, there will usually be reason to believe that such evidence is located at any premises under the suspect's control. Nonetheless, it is prudent to include the justification set forth in the text.

computers connected together, including workstations and servers.

Based on my training and expertise, I know that persons who engage in _____ [*this can be a crime, such as drug trafficking, or simply the maintenance of a business*], frequently possess (or have access to) and use computer systems to assist them in their activities, and that those computer systems are often repositories of information relating to those activities.

I believe that any computers and other computer media may be found at the premises listed above.

[*State any additional support for that belief, such as*]:

• I know from my training and experience that computer users commonly keep computer systems, computer hardware, software, and data in their homes.

• I am aware from my training and experience that computer users frequently "backup" copies of software to guard against loss if their computer malfunctions; they keep those backup copies at their residence and business.

• I am aware from my training and experience that software is portable and is often transported to and from residences in automobiles (and is occasionally hidden in automobiles).

• CONFIDENTIAL INFORMANT [*or others*] told me that SUSPECT keeps technical information and personnel, financial, and other business records at [*his/her home or place of business*].

[*Insert specific facts suggesting that certain property listed in your property description may be found on such computers (e.g., a drug dealer would use a computer to keep ledgers, a prostitution ring would use a computer to maintain a database of customers, a cracker would use a computer to store*] *war dialing programs and access codes, and an engineer would use a computer to store stolen trade secrets)*].

Make sure that your affiant either has expertise sufficient to support the justification or has spoken to someone who does. If that experience depends upon the affiant's having consulted a computer literate police officer, say so in the affidavit.

In addition, you may wish to indicate that some of the evidence you are seeking would normally be found within a computer. The Fourth Amendment requires a "reasonable" search; police officers may only search a container for items which they would expect to find within that container.

Although virtually any information may be stored in a computer, it may be prudent to point out to the magistrate that certain property listed in your property description would normally be stored within a computer.

Thus, your warrant might include a description, not just of the information, but also the form in which that information is likely to be found:

> VICTIM's scientific and technical information is contained in drawings, schematics, and software describing the design, architecture, layout, and specification of the chips.

> The drawings and schematics are in document form. The software is on various magnetic and optical media. Some of the software is contained in diskettes; that software may easily be transferred to other magnetic or optical media. There are two types of software at issue here: source code and object code. The source code is extremely valuable because it can be easily copied and altered. That source code (and the object code) is stored on diskettes.[12]

---

12. Be careful to inform the magistrate that software can be stored on a variety of media. The victim may have stored it on one medium; the thief can store it on many media for safekeeping and concealment.

9.36 Justifying removing computer systems, hardware, software, peripherals, and documentation

The passages discussed in the previous sections do more than justify a search of premises for computer evidence—they lay the groundwork for removal of hardware, software, peripherals, and documentation for examination off-site. They provide a reason to believe that computers may contain property mentioned in the warrant (e.g., stolen access codes).

As discussed in Chapter 7, in order to remove items for search off-site, the affidavit must also demonstrate that it would be unreasonable to require the search to take place at the scene. Consider using the following explanation to address this issue (all items in parentheses are to be included in the affidavit).

I know the following facts based on [*affiant's training and experience OR from talking to an expert or computer literate officer*]:

I believe that some of the information sought to be searched/seized may be contained on computers and/or separate (or "loose") "computer media" (e.g., floppy disks, Bernoulli, or other removable storage media, CD-ROM disks, cartridges, or tapes). Searching the subject's computer and separate computer media to the degree necessary to discover all information stored within that computer or media which is relevant to this investigation would be difficult and would risk destruction of evidence. I therefore request permission to remove all computers and computer media for further examination.

It would be difficult to perform a thorough search of the subject's computer at the scene because I may not be familiar with the operating system used on that computer. I may need an expert to perform that search, and I may need different experts depending upon the type of computer found at the premises.

Furthermore, a search performed at the premises could risk destruction of evidence. Persons concerned about detection are able to "rig" their computers in such a way that an otherwise innocuous instruction acts as a signal for the computer to erase data. I may not be able to perform even a cursory search without spending a great deal of time at the scene ensuring that the computer has not been "rigged." Those persons may also employ computer security programs which can only be bypassed, if they can be circumvented at all, by specialists using a sophisticated laboratory.

Computers are capable of storing large amounts of data; a thorough search of a single computer may take days or weeks. It would be impractical to perform such a search at the premises.

CONSIDER INSERTING THIS LANGUAGE WHERE YOU ANTICIPATE SEARCHING A NETWORK:

Searching SUBJECT's facility will be an enormous undertaking. EXPERT and I believe that SUBJECT has [*describe the scope of the SUBJECT's operation*].

A server is used as part of a network and stores information which can be shared by each workstation connected to that network. Each SUBJECT workstation may store from _____ to _____ megabytes of data. The server may store from _____ to _____ megabytes of data. To provide a comparison, the average page of text takes up about 4,000 bytes of data. A megabyte is 1,048,576 bytes of data. A thousand megabytes is roughly the equivalent of 250,000 pages of text.

According to EXPERT, it would take weeks to search each and every file located on all of the magnetic media usually found within a COMPUTER system of the type expected to be located at SUBJECT. SUBJECT's premises would be shut down for that length of time. SUBJECT personnel could not be allowed to use any of their computers during that search because there would be too many ways for them to deliberately or accidentally erase data.

END OF INSERT

It would be difficult to search all loose computer media at the scene. The subject may maintain too many disks to allow a thorough search within a reasonable time. Some removable storage media (such as Bernoulli media) may contain the equivalent of tens of thousands of pages of information. (I cannot exclude even those floppy disks labeled as commercial software, because it is easy for anyone to copy over new information onto those media.)

It is impossible to know how many floppy disks are at the premises until I arrive. In addition, in order to avoid using the subject's computer (which may be rigged) to examine the loose computer media, I would have to bring another computer onto the premises. It is impossible to predict which application programs (as well as other programs, such as drivers) out of the hundreds available have been used by the subject to create files stored on the computer media. Therefore, it is impossible to ensure that any computer brought onto the premises could be used to examine the media. Thus, I request permission to remove the media for further examination.

[Obtaining authority to remove peripherals and documentation for further examination]

As discussed above, I am requesting permission to search and seize computer systems, computer hardware, software, and data located at the premises. I intend to search and seize computer equipment which could be considered to be computer peripherals, including but not limited to display screens (monitors), keyboards, input devices (such as mice and trackballs), printers, tape drives, optical/CD-ROM drives, and modems (used to communicate with other computers), found together or separately from one another.

I need to seize monitors, keyboards, input devices, and printers because they are integral parts of computer systems and are used to completely perform the functions of those computer systems, including the display of data (potential evidence) contained within those systems. In order to ensure accurate retrieval of the evidence contained within the computer, I need to be able to seize and analyze the computer in its current configuration. I need to seize modems because they may contain evidence (in the form of stored phone numbers) of other computers with whom the user(s) of computers found at the premises communicated. *[Insert any additional information justifying seizure of such items in your case (e.g., your suspect is a cracker who uses his or her modem constantly)]*.

I also request permission to seize any documentation or other material describing the operation of any computer, software, and/or computer peripherals found at the premises, including instructions on how to access disks, files, or other material stored within same, including but not limited to computer manuals, printouts, passwords, file name lists, "readme" and/ or "help files." Based on my training and experience *[and conversations with EXPERT]*, I know that such information is usually kept within and around computers and data. That information may be necessary to enable me to operate computers and software searched and/or seized in accordance with the warrant requested by this affidavit. That documentation is also relevant insofar as it may contain information identifying the owner and/or user of that computer, and provide evidence that the owner of the computer knew how to use the computer.

By using this language, you are providing justification for seizing all computers, loose media, peripherals, and documentation *before* you execute your search warrant. (Make sure that you confirm the facts stated above with your expert before signing your affidavit.)

A magistrate who signs such a warrant gives you the authority to search, seize, and, where appropriate, remove those items. This prior judicial approval provides you with a powerful, and probably insurmountable, advantage when the defense brings a motion to suppress.[13]

9.40   Protocols

Protocols are orders which direct or allow officers or third parties to act in certain ways during and after execution of the warrant. A request for authorization of "nighttime service" is an example of a protocol. You should consider using the following protocols when writing search warrants for computer evidence.

9.41   Investigative plans (for when you can't take it with you)

The language allowing removal of computers discussed above works best in cases involving the search of a single personal computer, where you expect to seize the computer and all loose media at the scene. However, complex investigations often involve searches of dozens of computers networked together, and even mainframes.

If you intend to seize an entire network (which may be indicated in a few cases) or a mainframe (rarely a good idea), then you only need to modify your affidavit to describe the added difficulties of searching a network on-site.[14]

---

13. In California and Illinois, you may also be able to justify seizure of computers pursuant to a state forfeiture law. *See* California Penal Code Section 502.01 (limited to computers used to access other computers illegally); Illinois Compiled Statutes, Ch. 720, 5/16D–6 (computers used to commit any felony).

14. You should consider mentioning the effects of seizing an entire network (e.g., possible insolvency of a business) in your affidavit, and justifying that harm based on the need to remove the network. Although this may decrease your chances of getting the magistrate to sign the warrant, it is better to obtain a judicial blessing in advance than be accused of attempting to shut down the subject out of malice. It is also better to avoid surprising your magistrate.

However, you have a problem if you plan to search a network but intend to leave part of that network behind, or perform a lengthy on-site search of that network before seizing it.

As discussed above, you must show that it is reasonable for police to remove property instead of searching it on site. If you perform a substantial search at the site but remove additional material without first searching that material, a court could rule that your removal was illegal on the grounds that you should have searched all of the material at the premises. An investigative plan can be useful because it allows you to explain to the magistrate *before* the warrant is signed why you intend to remove certain items and not others, and to obtain court approval of your actions in advance.

A plan should first explain the procedure you intend to follow, and then discuss your reasons for following that procedure. A typical procedure involves the search of all computer systems and the seizure of any computers (including peripherals) found to contain property described in the warrant. (Depending upon the size of the network, you may remove the server or just workstations.) It also involves the removal of all loose magnetic media (including backup tapes) without prior examination.

In theory, the seizure of computer systems containing property described in the warrant needs no special justification. Each computer is one physical object, and there is no requirement that you make and seize a copy of the magnetic media instead of seizing the computer itself. However, it is nonetheless prudent to obtain judicial authorization first.

Moreover, as explained in Chapter 7, in the extreme case (e.g., seizing a mainframe instead of copying one graphics file), a court could find the execution of the warrant to be so overreaching as to violate the subject's civil rights. A reviewing court is much less likely to find such a violation if the affidavit reviewed by the magistrate disclosed, and sought approval for, the allegedly offensive procedure.

Consider the following justification for seizing computers containing any evidence, as opposed to just downloading copies of the responsive material.

Permission to seize computers and all magnetic or optical media which contain items to be seized, instead of only downloading copies of the specific items set forth in the warrant.

What I intend to do:

As discussed above, I believe that there is probable cause to believe that SUBJECT's computers (as well as computers located at other sites) and SUBJECT's magnetic or optical media contain some of the property to be searched/seized described above. I request permission to seize computer systems and magnetic or optical media found at the scene where those systems and media contain any of that property.

Specifically, I ask permission to employ the following procedure in executing the warrant. I plan to examine each and every computer at SUBJECT (and the other sites) with the assistance of experts designated by this Court. (Those experts are identified below.) If any computer and/or magnetic media appear to contain items to be searched/seized as described above, I will seize the entire computer. If allowed by this Court, I will not pursue an alternative procedure, which would be to examine each and every bit of magnetic media stored within that computer, copy all responsive software and data on the media to other storage media, and leave the original media (and computer) behind.

I will remove "loose" magnetic media, meaning media which are not stored within a computer but are contained in floppy disks, removable media, tapes, or optical media, for later examination off-site.

Why I intend to follow the procedure set forth above:

I am aware that removing computer systems and magnetic media from SUBJECT may inconvenience [*him/her, the company*]. However, I believe that there is no reasonable alternative to the procedure described above.

Searching SUBJECT's facility will be an enormous undertaking. EXPERT and I believe that SUBJECT has [*describe the scope of the SUBJECT's operation*]. A server is used as part of a network and stores information which can be shared by each workstation connected to that network. Each SUBJECT workstation may store from _____ to _____ megabytes of data. The server may store from _____ to _____ megabytes of data. To provide a comparison, the average page of text occupies about 4,000 bytes of data. A megabyte is 1,048,576 bytes of data. A thousand megabytes is roughly the equivalent of 250,000 pages of text.

Isolating the portion(s) of each media containing items to be searched/seized would require the meticulous search of each and every part of each and every magnetic media found at SUBJECT. According to EXPERT, it would take weeks to search each and every file located on all of the magnetic media usually found within a COMPUTER system of the type expected to be located at SUBJECT. Furthermore, according to EXPERT, making copies of just the "responsive" media would take days or weeks because copies would have to be generated a file at a time. SUBJECT's premises would be shut down for that length of time. SUBJECT personnel could not be allowed to use any of their computers during that search because there would be too many ways for them to deliberately or accidentally erase data.

Using the procedure set forth above, the search of each media would take only as long as necessary to determine whether any of the items to be searched/seized were contained on that media.

Moreover, the computer and magnetic or optical media are the best evidence available. Magnetic and optical media are easily erased or destroyed. Leaving magnetic or optical media behind may well result in the loss of those magnetic or optical media as evidence. I believe that it is better to seize the original evidence than to rely solely on copies which have not been authenticated in the presence of counsel representing persons who could face criminal charges based on material found pursuant to this warrant. (This is not to say that such evidence could not be used, as it is clearly admissible, but only that it is better to preserve originals whenever possible.)

While the search and seizure of computers is routine, the removal of loose magnetic media, potentially containing the equivalent of hundreds of thousands of pages of information, requires justification in your affidavit. That justification is particularly important because the defense will be able to show that the officers took the time to search the network. They will argue that if the officers had the time to search the network on-site, then they also had time to search the loose magnetic media.

Consider the following justification for seizing loose magnetic media. The language is a modified version of the language used in the "standard" warrant; the modifications are in *italics*.

> *Although I will be searching computer systems at the premises, it would be too difficult to search immediately all loose computer media found there.* The subject may maintain too many disks to allow a thorough search within a reasonable time. *This is particularly true in this case, where the subject maintains a computer network.*

> *I know from my training and experience that operators of computer networks routinely and frequently generate backups of all data on the system. These backups are stored on magnetic or optical media (including tape, floppy diskettes, CD-ROM disks, optical storage devices, and removable media, such as Bernoulli media).*

> Some optical storage devices and removable media (such as Bernoulli media) may *contain the equivalent of millions of pages of information.* (I cannot exclude even those floppy

disks labeled as commercial software, because it is easy for anyone to copy over new information onto those media.) *It is impossible to know how many tapes, floppy disks, optical storage devices, and/or removable media* are at the premises until I arrive. Thus, I request permission to remove those media for further examination.

In some cases, you may need to follow a more drastic plan: the wholesale seizure of optical storage devices. Many companies use optical storage devices, or "jukeboxes", to store thousands of megabytes of data. You will generally not have time to examine each CD-ROM disk to determine whether the media contains responsive material. If you seize only the loose disks, you may have problems finding a similar "jukebox" to read those disks. If you know that the target uses large quantities of optical media, and you expect to seize all optical storage devices and loose optical media, consider using the following language:

I need to seize without examination optical media, and drives capable of reading same, for two reasons. First, the optical media apparently purchased by SUBJECT hold __ MB *each*. According to EXPERT, to read every file on each disk (SUBJECT apparently possesses approximately __ disks) could take weeks (if they are full; and I will not know whether they are full until they are examined). Second, EXPERT (or victim company) is not sure whether they have equipment capable of reading those disks. If EXPERT does have that equipment, I will return the drive itself (not the disks) immediately.

9.41–a   Investigative plans are not appropriate for every case

You should consider including investigative plans in your warrant when you are searching networks or mainframes in major cases. However, you may elect to forgo using a plan in order to avoid two problems.

First, a magistrate accustomed to "tidy" search warrants may balk at authorizing a particular procedure. Second, once you have obtained permission to use a particular procedure, you are stuck with it—any changes must be authorized by the magistrate before or during the execution of your search warrant.[15]

9.42 Authorizing expert assistance

It is frequently necessary to employ an expert during execution of a search warrant in high-technology crime cases. However, you should obtain specific permission from the court to take an expert to the scene, and justify your request in your affidavit.

A search warrant allows a government agent to search an area in which an individual has an expectation of privacy. It is unclear whether that warrant, absent some authorization, allows the government to compound that violation of privacy by inviting non-sworn personnel (e.g., experts) to the raid. Furthermore, the warrant authorizes a peace officer to search and seize certain property—it does not authorize a non–peace officer to perform those tasks.

Each of these problems can be solved by including a request in the affidavit for an appropriate court order. Your affidavit should request permission for an expert to accompany the officer. Consider using the following language:

> I am not a computer expert.

> INSERT WHERE SEARCHING A NETWORK:

> Although officers familiar with personal computers and related media will be participating in the execution of this warrant, I expect to encounter complex computer systems connected together in a network [*list the type of system you expect to encounter (e.g., minicomputers, mainframes), and list the manufacturers of the computers if you know; if you*

---

15. As a point of interest, magistrates in Holland are required to accompany police officers during service of the warrant and are not allowed to leave until the search is completed. Officers are able to obtain immediate approval for searches of material, and searches become extremely efficient in order to persuade the magistrate not to call a halt to the effort out of exhaustion. *Do not try this procedure in the United States.*

need an expert to search a PC because your affiant is not computer literate, say so]. I am not qualified to search such computer systems and need expert assistance to do so.

END INSERT

EXPERT is a computer expert having substantial experience with [*what you expect to encounter*]. He/she is familiar with both the hardware and software environments which are likely to be encountered in the execution of the search warrant, and with the methods for safely extracting or copying data (evidence) from such systems. He/she has consented to being ordered to assist in this search.

I ask this court to order EXPERT to accompany me and assist in searching any computer systems, computers, hardware, software, or magnetic or optical media found at any of the premises to be searched.[16]

A court order may shield your expert from lawsuits by the defense charging negligence, theft of information, or invasion of privacy. Remember to include the actual court order in your warrant:

This Court hereby authorizes and orders EXPERT to assist police in locating and identifying property identified in this warrant, including but not limited to the items described in paragraphs __ and __ above, and to assist police in searching any computers found at any of the premises.

9.43 Videotaping the premises

A California court recently suggested, without deciding, that videotaping the scene of a search warrant constitutes an unusual invasion

---

16. Language allowing an expert to identify certain property (e.g., trade secrets) which officers would otherwise not recognize is included in Chapter 5, beginning on page 213.

of privacy which must be justified. The court suggested that while the facts of a case might justify entry, preserving the scene on videotape is a further intrusion into the occupants' privacy which must be justified in order for the search to be "reasonable" under the Fourth Amendment.[17]

Never invite the news media!

Allowing the news media to participate in the execution of any search warrant is always a mistake. As noted above, there is no reason to believe that the Fourth Amendment allows persons with no connection to the investigation to invade a suspect's reasonable expectation of privacy in his or her premises. *See Ayeni v. Mottola*, 35 F.3d 680 (2d Cir. 1994) (allowing a lawsuit against a Secret Service agent who invited CBS to enter a residence during execution of a search warrant); *cf. Bills v. Aseltine*, 52 F.3d 596 (6th Cir. 1995).

Moreover, every person who participates in the execution of a search warrant is a witness. If the media photograph the scene, that film or videotape is evidence. If the media successfully resist defense attempts to subpoena that material, the court might dismiss the case.

Although the rationale for distinguishing between photographs and videotape (that tape is a more detailed image than a photograph) is shaky, this decision could prove attractive to courts in other jurisdictions. Thus, just to play it safe, you should consider requesting permission to videotape the premises. Consider using the following justification:

---

17. *See Oziel v. Superior Court*, 223 Cal. App. 3d 1284, 1303 n.11 (Cal. Ct. App. 1990); *see People v. Henderson*, 220 Cal. App. 3d 1632 (Cal. Ct. App. 1990) (videotaped surveillance), citing *Winston v. Lee*, 470 U.S. 753, 759 (1985) (some particularly invasive searches, such as removing bullets from suspects, require extraordinary justification to satisfy the "reasonableness" requirement of the Fourth Amendment).

I seek permission to videotape the execution of this warrant. I expect to examine computers at the scene of the search. Those computers may be operating when I arrive at the premises. The images on the screens of the computers are transient (they disappear when the computer is turned off). I need to be able to videotape any such images because they may be evidence (e.g., incriminating documents being written by the user when the warrant is executed). Furthermore, I want to videotape the examination of those computers to ensure that there is a record of the steps taken during that examination. Should there be a question concerning the procedures employed in obtaining evidence from those computers, the videotape may be useful in documenting what was done.

A simple sentence authorizing videotaping should be included within the warrant.

9.44 Authorization to read stored electronic communications

As discussed in Chapter 8, you need a search warrant to intercept stored communications less than 180 days old. When seeking to intercept stored communications, you must:

- announce your intent to seize electronic communications possibly protected by the ECPA; and

- demonstrate that there is probable cause to believe that those communications are relevant to your investigation.

Consider the following two-pronged justification:

Such information [*your evidence, such as stolen access codes or communications between conspirators*] may be in the form of electronic communications (such as E-mail) residing on any media (e.g., magnetic or optical media). That information may include electronic communications held or maintained in electronic storage by an electronic communication service or remote computing service, as those services are defined within 18 U.S.C. 2703. (These communications are referred to herein as "stored communications.") That federal law, which is part of the Electronic Communications Privacy Act, allows interception of such electronic communications pursuant to a search warrant.

I believe that those electronic communications are reasonably likely to contain evidence of the commission of a felony and I request permission to seize such information. [*Explain reasons supporting your belief.*]

This language exceeds the justification required by Title III because it covers the interception of electronic communications already received by the owner of the computer. However, since a few judges may not be familiar with the distinction between intercepting mail after delivery to the user and intercepting a communication stored by a service provider, it is best to justify both types of seizures.

It is relatively easy to justify seizing communications on the grounds that they are likely to:

- identify members of a conspiracy set forth in the affidavit;

- contain messages relating to the crime under investigation; or

- contain stolen property (e.g., pirated software, stolen access codes).

You should connect your justification for seizing communications to the facts of your case. For example, if you are going to examine all stored communications relating to John Doe, you should inform the magistrate of that fact and explain why your search must be so broad.

In searching for [*your evidence, such as stolen access codes or communications between conspirators*], I will need to read all communications to which John Doe is a party. This is necessary because each such communication may contain [*the evidence*].

In an appropriate case, you should request an order requiring the electronic communication service provider or remote computing service to refrain from disclosing the existence of the warrant to the customer.

Consider using the following language in your affidavit:

> Further, the court is requested to include the following order in the search warrant pursuant to its inherent authority, and as provided for in 18 U.S.C. 2705(b):
>
> "[*Service provider*] shall not notify [*customer*] of the existence of this search warrant."
>
> This order is necessary because disclosure would [*choose at least one*]:
>
> • endanger the life or physical safety of [*an individual*].
>
> • result in flight [*by an individual*] from prosecution.
>
> • result in destruction of, or tampering with, evidence [*specify which evidence*].
>
> • result in intimidation of witnesses [*explain why*].
>
> • seriously jeopardize this investigation [*explain why*].

Remember to include the order in the warrant itself.

Finally, as discussed in Chapter 8, when seizing computers being used to provide electronic communications or remote computing services (e.g., bulletin boards), you should consider requesting judicial authorization to hold the seized material for one or two days before examining it.

If you are seizing both communications and other evidence (e.g., access codes or pirated software), you may choose to draft your warrant to give you permission to examine the media immediately, with an order that you exercise best efforts to avoid reading any communications until an aggrieved party has the opportunity to object. However, it is probably safer simply to forgo examining all evidence for the one or two days required to provide an opportunity for objections.

Although you should draft your own custom order, a typical order might include the following language:

I am aware that seizing stored communications implicates privacy rights which Congress believed important enough to protect under the Electronic Communications Privacy Act (ECPA), specifically, 18 U.S.C. 2703. In executing the warrant requested, it is probable that I will seize such communications, along with other material encompassed in the warrant. I therefore seek this court's permission to hold [*all magnetic or optical media seized/portions of magnetic or optical media seized which appear to contain electronic communications*] for [*one/two*] days before beginning to examine it.

[If you allow yourself to examine some media: "When examining magnetic or optical media, I will exercise my best efforts to avoid reading any such communications."]

This delay is intended to give affected parties a chance to ask this Court to prevent further examination of said materials pending challenges based upon the ECPA. I request court approval for this procedure because I will, by necessity, be seizing magnetic media without examining it first to ensure that it contains only stored communications which are encompassed by the warrant. I seek court approval for this "removal" of items from the premises, and suspension of the search of those items for the [*one/two*] day period required to allow allegedly aggrieved persons to file challenges with this Court.

I therefore request the following order:

In addition to other provisions of this warrant, [*affiant*] is allowed to seize [*all magnetic or optical media/portions of magnetic or optical media which appear to contain electronic communications*]. [*Affiant*] is ordered to hold [*all magnetic or optical media seized/portions of magnetic or optical media which appear to contain electronic communications*] for [*one/two*] days without examining same, pending any requests to this Court by anyone objecting to examination of same by law enforcement, where said objections are based on the Electronic Communications Privacy Act, 18 U.S.C. 2510 *et seq., see* § 2701 *et seq.*

Any such objections must be made in writing within [*one/ two*] days after service of this warrant, with written notice to [*affiant*]. Any such objections shall be made to the undersigned judge, unless that judge is unavailable.

If after [*one/two*] days, no objections are made to this Court, [*affiant*] shall examine the material covered by this order within a reasonable time and shall return any magnetic or optical media which does not contain stored communications (or other property) encompassed by this warrant.

Remember to include the order in your warrant. You should consider placing this order in a prominent place on the warrant, so as to avoid any claim that you were "hiding the ball."

9.45 Navigating the Privacy Protection Act

If you believe that your suspect may qualify as a publisher under the Privacy Protection Act, meet the problem head-on. Explain the purpose of the Act and fit your property requests into applicable exceptions. Consider using the following language:

I am cognizant of the Privacy Protection Act, 42 U.S.C. 2000aa, which is intended to safeguard First Amendment freedoms of legitimate publishers of information to the public. I have drafted this affidavit, and accompanying warrant, to obtain evidence consistent with the requirements of the Act.

[*Insert argument that the materials are not work product and/or documentary materials, based on the fact that they are contraband, fruits of a crime, or property designed or intended for committing a criminal offense. REMEMBER TO NARROW YOUR PROPERTY DESCRIPTION TO ENSURE*

THAT IT COVERS ONLY THOSE MATERIALS WHICH FIT WITHIN THE EXCEPTION.]

The Act prohibits search or seizure of work product and documentary materials, with several exceptions.

[*Insert text pertaining to the particular exception you rely upon to justify using a warrant to seize evidence.*]

Finally, as discussed above, you should consider requesting judicial authorization to hold the seized material for two days before examining it. Although you should draft your own custom order, a typical order might include the following language:

I am aware that seizing arguable work product and/or documentary materials from someone who may be a publisher holding said materials for publication implicates privacy rights which Congress believed important enough to protect under the Privacy Protection Act, 42 U.S.C. 2000aa (PPA).

I believe that any material I seize will not fall within the PPA for the reasons stated above.

[*Or: I believe that it is possible that I may seize some material unrelated to my investigation because that material is commingled on magnetic or optical media with other evidence encompassed in the warrant.*]

In order to further the purposes of the PPA, and to avoid any harm resulting from the mistaken or unavoidable seizure of items protected by the PPA, I request this court's permission to hold [*all materials seized/all magnetic or optical media seized/all materials which may possibly include material held by a publisher for publication*] for two days before beginning to examine said materials.

[If you allow yourself to examine some media: *When examining any materials, including magnetic or optical media, I will exercise my best efforts to avoid reading any material which appears to be held by a publisher for publication.]*

This delay is intended to give affected parties a chance to ask this Court to prevent further examination of said materials pending challenges based upon the PPA. I need court approval for this procedure because I will, by necessity, be seizing materials without examining them first to ensure that they contain material encompassed by the warrant. I seek court approval for this "removal" of items from the premises, and suspension of the search of those items for the two-day period required to allow allegedly aggrieved persons to file challenges with this court.

I therefore request the following order:

In addition to other provisions of this warrant, [*affiant*] is allowed to seize all property encompassed by this warrant, even if that property may be covered by the Privacy Protection Act, 42 U.S.C. 2000aa (PPA).

[*Affiant*] is ordered to hold [*all materials seized, all magnetic or optical media seized, any materials which may include material held by a publisher for publication*] for two days without examining same, pending any requests to this Court by anyone objecting to examination of same by law enforcement, where said objections are based on the Privacy Protection Act.

Any such objections must be made in writing within two days after service of this warrant, with written notice to [*affiant*]. Any such objections shall be made to the undersigned judge, unless that judge is unavailable.

If after two days no objections are made to this Court, [*affiant*] shall examine the material covered by this order within a reasonable time and shall return any materials which are not encompassed by this warrant.

Remember to include the order in your warrant. Again, you should consider placing this order in a prominent place on the warrant, so as to avoid any claim that you were "hiding the ball."

Appendix A-1

Checklist: Initial Investigation for Law Enforcement Investigators

A. Discuss with the victim whether it is willing to assist in a criminal investigation and prosecution. Generally, victims will weigh the extent of the loss, the probability of apprehending the criminal, the cost in employee time of assisting police in an investigation and prosecution, and the affect of publicity of the crime on the victim's stock price and its reputation among customers and vendors. Discuss the following factors with the victim.

1. Advantages to requesting assistance:

   a. The victim may be able to persuade police to serve a search warrant.

   b. Does the victim want to send a message to other potential thieves (employees in particular) that further criminal attacks will not be tolerated?

2. Disadvantages to requesting assistance:

   a. The victim will lose control over the case. The victim should not report a crime unless it is willing to assist in an investigation *and* a prosecution.

   b. The victim will lose employee time (spent educating police, producing documents, and testifying in court) and run up legal fees while the case is pending trial. The victim may also have to pay travel expenses for employees to testify.

c. High-technology crime prosecutions often result in publicity. The possible consequences of publicity include embarrassment over a breach of security, a decline in the price of the victim's stock, or even a full-scale audit by the Department of Defense for firms in sensitive industries.

d. If sensitive information is involved, defense counsel may seek to discover it.

e. Any civil suit that the victim files against defendants will be *stayed* (postponed) until after the criminal case, although a court in a trade secret theft case may award a preliminary injunction.

f. The victim may lose the chance to obtain restitution from a thief eager to avoid criminal prosecution (note that a lawyer may not threaten criminal prosecution to obtain restitution).

B. Consider calling a federal agency.

1. If you are a local agency, consider calling federal authorities when your case involves:

a. crimes solely within federal jurisdiction (e.g., copyright infringement, illegal export).

b. crimes traditionally handled by federal agencies (e.g., theft of classified information, importation of remarked chips).

c. acts by suspects in more than one state, or distribution of stolen property across state lines.

2. If you decide to call federal authorities, call:

    a.   Customs: in cases involving export or import of stolen property, or sale of remarked or counterfeit chips.

    b.   Secret Service: in cases involving financial institutions (including credit bureaus), and, if the FBI declines to assist, computer intrusions generally.

    c.   FBI: in all cases.

C. Decide whether to accept or reject the case.

    1.   Beware of cases where the victim has delayed reporting the crime. Time kills high-technology crime cases. You must decide whether it is still possible to prove that the suspect committed the crime.

        a.   Think about whether the victim is reporting the crime at a late date in order to satisfy an insurance company or to obtain leverage over a competitor in a civil dispute (typically an ex-employee).

        b.   Determine your corporate victim's agenda, and evaluate whether the victim will cooperate in the investigation and prosecution of the case.

    2.   Discuss the grim realities of legal trench warfare, and determine whether your victim is motivated by a momentary desire (anger, fear of further loss), or by something more permanent (a desire to send a message to employees and potential thieves).

D. Initial discussion of the roles of law enforcement and the victim.

    1.   Ensure that law enforcement investigators can communicate directly with a decisionmaker for the corporation.

        a.   In major cases, secure the commitment of the highest ranking local official in a face-to-face

> meeting that the victim will cooperate throughout the investigation and prosecution. Assurances from subordinates are *not* sufficient.
>
> b.   Identify the chain of command in the victim corporation, and secure a direct line of communication to a decisionmaker.

2.   Make sure that the victim understands that it cannot back out after a certain point (typically the service of a search warrant).

E.   Rules of conduct for law enforcement investigators.

1.   Find out who has talked to whom, and what they talked about. Ask for copies of all corporate investigative reports and any other documents generated regarding the case.

2.   Insist on interviewing employees alone. Remember that the corporation may have a legitimate concern when the answers to your questions could reveal sensitive business or technical information.

3.   Insist on being present at all employee interviews. Restrict corporate investigators acting out of your presence to asking questions designed to determine whether an employee is a potential witness.

F.   Five precautions to keep in mind.

1.   Keep your investigation secret. When visiting the company, do not arrive in uniform. Make arrangements with the victim's security department so that you do not have to identify yourself (or sign in at the guard desk) as a law enforcement investigator.

2.   Do not rely on senior management's version of what happened. Talk to the lower-level employees who know how things really work.

3.   Talk to everyone to find out what happened.

4.   Do not leave evidence behind.

5.   Do not dawdle.

Appendix A-2

Checklist: Initial Investigation for Corporate Investigators

A. Has a crime team assembled? If not, gather representatives from:

    1.   security;

    2.   legal;

    3.   human resources; and

    4.   senior management.

B. Determine whether there was a significant loss. (Some of this material is duplicated in checklists for investigating particular crimes.)

    1.   For component thefts:

         a.   calculate the expected net profit that the company would have made but for the theft.

    2.   For computer intrusions, include the amount of time and money required to:

         a.   determine that there was an intrusion;

         b.   monitor the intrusion;

         c.   obtain trap and trace orders and pen registers necessary to locate the intruder; and

        d.   repair damage.

                  Include the salaries of staff members who were required to devote their energies to confronting the intrusion.

3.   For thefts of information, include the amount of lost market share (and profits) which would result if a competitor used that secret to create a competing product faster than would otherwise have been possible.

C. Discuss with the victim whether to report the crime to law enforcement, or, if the crime has already been reported, whether to assist in a criminal investigation and prosecution.

Generally, victims will weigh the extent of the loss, the probability of apprehending the criminal, the cost in employee time of assisting police in an investigation and prosecution, and the affect of publicity of the crime on the victim's stock price and its reputation among customers and vendors.

Discuss the following factors with the victim:

1.   Advantages to reporting:

        a.   The victim may be able to persuade police to serve a search warrant.

        b.   Does the victim want to send a message to other potential thieves (employees in particular) that further criminal attacks will not be tolerated?

2.   Disadvantages to reporting:

        a.   The victim will lose control over the case. The victims should not report a crime unless it is willing to assist in an investigation *and* a prosecution.

    b.   The victim will lose employee time (spent educating police, producing documents, and testifying in court) and run up legal fees while the case is pending trial. The victim may also have to pay travel expenses for employees to testify.

    c.   High-technology crime prosecutions often result in publicity. The possible consequences of publicity include embarrassment over a breach of security, a decline in the price of the victim's stock, or even a full-scale audit by the Department of Defense for firms in sensitive industries.

    d.   If sensitive information is involved, defense counsel may seek to discover it.

    e.   Any civil suit that the victim files against defendants will be *stayed* (postponed) until after the criminal case, although a court in a trade secret theft case may award a preliminary injunction.

    f.   The victim may lose the chance to obtain restitution from a thief eager to avoid criminal prosecution (note that a lawyer may not threaten criminal prosecution to obtain restitution).

D. Choose the correct law enforcement agency.

    1.   Always call your local agency even when you intend to "go federal." They will appreciate getting credit for giving a federal agency a new case.

    2.   Call federal authorities when your case involves:

        a.   crimes solely within federal jurisdiction (e.g., copyright infringement, illegal export).

        b.   crimes traditionally handled by federal agencies (e.g., theft of classified information, importation of remarked chips).

        c.   acts by suspects in more than one state, or distribution of stolen property across state lines.

3.   If you call federal authorities, call:

        a.   Customs: in cases involving export or import of stolen property, or sale of remarked or counterfeit chips.

        b.   Secret Service: in cases involving financial institutions (including credit bureaus), and computer intrusions generally.

        c.   FBI: in all cases.

E. Prepare a presentation for law enforcement.

1.   If your case is important to you, bring someone important. (Limit your party to three people.)

2.   Make sure of your facts before you begin, and remember that everything you say during any contact with law enforcement is "on-the-record."

3.   Present the facts in a clear, organized, and non-technical manner.

4.   Calculate the loss before you make your presentation

5.   Gather and deliver relevant physical evidence (including samples of stolen property) to the meeting.

6.   Bring someone who can explain the law applying to your case.

7.   Describe any investigation conducted before the victim reported the crime.

8.   Emphasize the "real-world" impact of the crime.

9.   Determine whether you are ready to commit the victim to cooperating in the investigation and prosecution of the case.

10.   Discuss what assistance the victim is willing to provide to law enforcement.

F. Initial discussion of the roles of law enforcement and the victim.

1.   Ensure that law enforcement investigators can communicate directly with a decisionmaker for the corporation.

2.   Ensure that the victim understands that it cannot back out after a certain point (typically the service of a search warrant).

G. Rules of conduct for corporate investigators.

1.   Conduct your investigation as if everything that is said and done is "for the record." Act as if you are a police department, because you will be treated like one. Tell employees that their comments will be disclosed to everyone and that they must not guess or speculate.

2.   Avoid writing down information unless it is absolutely necessary to your investigation.

3.   When conducting interviews, only one person should take notes. Synthesize those rough notes into a report that *accurately* and *completely* states the witness's recollection. Have the witness review those notes for accuracy. Destroy any rough notes after including in your report *all* of the information contained in your rough notes. (Certain states may prohibit law enforcement investigators from destroying their notes.)

4.   Record facts, not impressions, of what was said and done.

5.   Do not plan strategy in front of a potential witness.

6.   Everything you tell police will be disclosed to the defense and the press. See Chapter 5 for precautions you should take when investigating information theft cases.

7.   Do not take minutes at meetings of the crime team. Take notes to record facts, not impressions or strategy.

H. Five precautions to keep in mind.

1.   Keep your investigation secret.

2.   Do not rely on senior management's version of what happened. Talk to the lower-level employees who know how things really work.

3.   Talk to everyone to find out what happened.

4.   Do not leave evidence behind.

5.   Do not dawdle.

Appendix A-3

Checklist: Investigation of Component Theft

A. Questions for the victim.

1. What was stolen?

   a. Get a picture or a sample, if necessary.

   b. Identifying characteristics:

      1. Performance-related (e.g., size/capacity)

      2. Manufacturer

      3. Serial numbers

      4. Part numbers

      5. Date codes

   c. Are these components unique in any way?

      Examples include experimental components never released, components custom-made for a particular customer, components individually serialized, and/or components with unique markings (such as date codes assigned to a particular supplier).

   d. What is the value of that property?

      1. Retail and wholesale price

2. Where did the theft occur?

3. When did the theft occur?

4. Who discovered the theft?

5. Is there any indication of illegal entry?

6. Who had access to the stolen property?

7. How was access controlled?

8. When was the theft first reported to management?

9. Has the theft been reported to an insurance company? If not, why not?

    a. Obtain a copy of the report to the insurance company.

10. Has the victim reported the theft to the market (e.g., brokers, suppliers, trade associations, distributors, customers)?

11. Has the victim announced the theft to its own employees?

12. Has the victim offered a reward for the property, either internally or to outside entities?

13. What investigation has been conducted by the victim?

14. Are there any undercover employees working at the company?

15. Does the victim have any leads or theories as to:

    a. the identity of suspect(s)?

    b. the location of property?

16. If the property is located, can we prove that it is the same property as that stolen from the victim? Talk to the people in charge of maintaining and accounting for inventory, and ask for the following records:

a. Records showing that the victim ordered the components from its supplier (assuming that the victim was buying those components, such as chips, to put into its own products). These records may include purchase orders and/or correspondence.

b. Records showing that the victim received components (again assuming that the victim purchased those components elsewhere). These records should include invoices, packing slips, and any internal logs maintained by the victim.

c. Records reflecting storage of those components.

d. Records reflecting use of the parts in production.

e. Records reflecting the number and serial numbers of components manufactured. There should be records indicating how many components were manufactured during a particular period (day, week, month, etc., and the serialization, if any, of each part). Ask for a log of serial numbers for all serialized products.

f. Records reflecting the storage of manufactured components. See paragraph (c) above.

g. Records reflecting sale of components manufactured by the victim.

h. Copies of all documents submitted by the victim to any insurer in support of a claim.

17. How can the victim be sure that the following has not happened?

a. Someone has made a mistake as to quantity in logging the property in or out of the company.

b. Someone has failed to record the sale of the product.

18.   If you find the property, is the victim willing to:

a.   provide funds to purchase that property?

1.   Will the victim's insurance company fund the purchase?

b.   provide a representative to act as an undercover buyer?

B. Initial investigation.

1.   Check building logs and videotape to discover evidence of the theft or access to inventory.

2.   Evaluate which employees had access to the inventory, and concentrate on those employees who have left the company suddenly or have displayed unexplained wealth.

a.   Tap into the rumor mill. Consider interviewing employees, offering a reward, or even inserting undercover agents.

b.   Law enforcement investigators should check with their informants.

3.   Determine whether the victim's records are good enough to prove that the component is missing.

4.   Determine whether the component has unique identifying features.

5.   Get the word out to potential buyers and informants that the stolen component may appear on the market shortly. Consider entering the stolen property into the NCIC system.

C. Where you have located the property or identified a suspect who may be holding that property:

1. If you have identified a suspect, develop probable cause to search the suspect's home or business for the missing property.

2. If you have located the property, check the victim's inventory records to determine whether you can establish probable cause to believe that the identified property matches the missing property.

3. Determine whether the suspect holding what appears to be the victim's property is the thief, a fence, or an innocent third party. This is often done by having an employee of the victim or other person knowledgeable about the stolen components pose as a buyer and ask the following questions.

    a. What is the difference between the suspect's price and the:

        1. retail price?

        2. wholesale price?

    b. How many components are available?

    c. Does the suspect offer a warranty? Is that warranty a manufacturer's warranty, or merely a suspicious guarantee that the store will "make it good"? If the latter, ask why the store does not offer a manufacturer's warranty.

    d. Does the suspect claim to be an authorized dealer? Is that claim true?

    e. What reason does the suspect give for being able to sell the components so cheaply?

    f. Can the suspect get more components than are currently in stock? If so, how many more?

3. Consider surveilling a suspected fence to trace his or her source of supply. During surveillance, place a large order with the fence and watch for a delivery.

4. Consider obtaining an order (or search warrant, where required by state law) allowing installation of a pen register on the fence's telephone. The results may indicate suspicious calls between the fence and a victim employee.

5. Obtain and serve a search warrant to recover stolen property.

6. Establish that the property you have recovered was stolen from the victim.

Appendix A-4

Checklist: Investigation of Computer Intrusion

A. Questions for the victim.

    1.   Who has been notified of the intrusion?

        a.   Is the security division of the local telephone company aware of the intrusion?

        b.   If the intruder is using the Internet, who is the victim's local Internet service provider? Is that provider aware of the intrusion?

    2.   Information about the computer system:

        a.   What type of computer or computer system was accessed without authorization?

        b.   Is the computer used:

            1.   as a PBX?

            2.   for voice mail?

            3.   to store proprietary information?

    3.   Telephone connections:

        a.   Is the computer connected to external phone lines? What are the numbers for each of those lines?

      b.   Who is able to dial in on the line(s) used by the intruder?

          1.   Are those lines reserved for maintenance or other use which is not company-wide?

              If reserved for maintenance, determine whether the intrusion is part of normal maintenance activity.

4.   Computer security measures in place before the intrusion:

      a.   Does the system require a "log-on" identification?

      b.   Does the system require users to enter a password?

          1.   Are there restrictions on the type of password which users may select?

              If the password is reasonably secure (i.e., at least six characters long), it is likely the intruder is a current or former employee, knows an employee, or has obtained the password through "social engineering" of a gullible employee.

      c.   How often is that password changed?

          Knowing the date on which the password was last changed may narrow your field of suspects.

      d.   Does the computer allow different levels of access?

          The level of access gained by the intruder may provide information about the source of your problem, particularly if the intruder is a former employee.

      e.   How does the computer record when a user logs on and off the system?

Make sure that the victim configures the computer to create logs, and stores those logs off the compromised system. If they are stored on the system, they should be encrypted.

f.   Is the computer configured to record the commands typed by the intruder?

Chapter 8 discusses the legality of keystroke monitoring. Discuss this issue with your victim.

5.   Information about the intrusion.

a.   When did the intrusion begin?

b.   How many calls has the intruder made?

A series of attempts repeated every few seconds suggests a war dialer.

c.   Does the intruder always use the same phone line?

This pattern suggests that the intruder knows only that number. If employees know more than one number, your intruder may be a cracker (or a lazy employee).

d.   Did anyone unsuccessfully attempt to access the computer within 30 days before the first intrusion?

Unsuccessful attempts suggest an intruder guessing a password or probing for a security flaw. No prior attempts suggests that the intruder is a current or former employee, or a cracker who obtained the password by social engineering or by intercepting a password sent by an authorized user.

e.   For each access:

1.   What was the date and time of that call?

2.   How long did the call last?

3.   What account(s) was/were accessed?

4.   Who are the authorized users who have access to that account? (Some companies allocate accounts for particular work groups which anyone in that group may access.)

f.   Interviewing the authorized user:

1.   *Warning:* Interviewing a group of employees who share a password may alert any intruder who is a fellow employee to your investigation.

2.   Determine whether the authorized user is your intruder. Does the user have a motive to misuse the computer (e.g., a departing employee stealing proprietary information)?

3.   Ask whether the authorized user disclosed his or her password to anyone, including seemingly authorized users (i.e., social engineering), or displayed the password on scraps of paper taped to the terminal or left in an unlocked drawer.

g.   What is the victim's theory concerning how the intruder was able to access the computer? Consider some of the common security "holes":

1.   *Bad passwords.*

2.   *Electronic mail.* Specifically the *sendmail* program which handles electronic mail in most UNIX systems.

3.   *Telnet.* If crackers have compromised the "calling machine," they can record the

passwords typed in by users using that computer to call the victim's computer, thus intercepting those passwords for their own use.

4. *TFTP and FTP.* Owners may inadvertently place password files in these areas and lose them. Crackers may use the anonymous FTP area to penetrate into "the rest" of the computer. Finally, where the owner has allowed outsiders to place files in the anonymous FTP, crackers and others may store stolen data, illegally copied programs, and pornography.

5. *Network "spoofing."* The victim's computer may have been fooled into believing that it is being "called" by another computer on the network.

h. If you suspect an employee (including a user whose account was penetrated), do you have records documenting which employees were at the victim's facility, and what they were doing?

i. What did the intruder do after gaining access?

1. Are there any new files that were not there before the intruder arrived?

If the victim does not have computer security experts on staff, suggest that it hire a consultant to check for back doors, Trojan Horses, viruses, logic bombs, etc.

B. Gather the following evidence as soon as possible (and after each intrusion).

1. All records of the unauthorized access.

a. Again, make sure that your victim keeps those records in a secure area of the computer, preferably encrypted. Also caution the victim not to use the computer to discuss the intrusion (i.e., by E-mail).

2. All records of system activity on the day (or within a few hours) of the access.

3. Backup tapes of the above.

a. Make an exact copy of that data in the form in which it existed in the computer (i.e., onto a backup tape). Make more than one copy if possible. You should also print out that data to have a hard copy record which you can display at trial.

C. Create evidence of ongoing intrusions.

1. As discussed in Chapter 8, the law usually allows victims to use their computers to track an intruder's activity. Discuss this issue with your victim at the beginning of your investigation. At a minimum, ensure that the computer is configured to "time-stamp" each log-in and log-off for each account.

D. Track damage to the victim.

1. Advise the victim to keep a log of the time employees spend responding to the intrusion. This includes time spent verifying that the intruder did not damage the computer and that the intruder has not left any "trap doors" behind.

E. Track the intruder.

1. Discuss with the victim whether the risk of damage from allowing the intruder to continue his attack on the system is so great that the victim must eject the intruder. Ejecting the intruder will usually end your investigation.

2. If the victim has the capability and inclination to do so, consider creating a "virtual sandbox" inside the victim's computer to contain the intruder.

3. If the intruder is using dial-up lines, obtain a court order allowing a trap and trace. (See below for ideas on what to do when the intruder is using the Internet.) Some states require a search warrant to authorize a trap and trace. The victim usually pays for the installation, and you should discuss this issue with the victim before drafting an order. File the order (or search warrant) under seal.

4. Arrange for the telephone company to install the trap and trace.

5. Assuming that your intruder attacks while your trap and trace is operating, match the calls "trapped" by the trap and trace against the logs of the victim's computer. Look for calls occurring at or about the time of the intrusion. (Remember that the computer's system clock may be any-where from a few seconds to a few minutes "off" from the telephone company computer's system clock.)

6. Continue obtaining trap and trace orders as necessary to trace the intruder to the source of the phone calls.

7. If the intruder is using the Internet, seek assistance from the victim's Internet service provider. It may be able to track the intruder to the computer he is using. Arrange for the victim (or a consultant) to capture and examine the in-truder's data packets for source/destination information.

8. Investigate whether the source of the intrusion as re-ported by the trap and trace or Internet service provider is the actual location of your intruder. Remember that in-truders can route their calls through many different phone

companies before reaching their target. They can also use accounts owned by others.

    a.   If the location returned by your trap and trace is an institution (e.g., a company or a university), contact that institution and seek assistance. If it is a residence, obtain records, such as utility bills, identifying the occupants of that residence. Consider checking whether your local school or police department is familiar with a juvenile living in the residence.

9.   If the intruder is using dial-up lines, after obtaining the requisite order or search warrant, install a pen register on the location identified by your trap and trace. Use the results to:

    a.   Confirm that the intruder is using the telephone number(s) identified by your trap and trace. Remember to account for time zones if your intruder is dialing from out-of-state.

    b.   Determine whether the intruder is using a war dialer (look for dozens or hundreds of calls spaced every few seconds).

    c.   Identify other computers under assault by your intruder (look for numbers listed dozens or hundreds of times).

    d.   Identify the intruder's confederates, caches of stolen data, and pirate bulletin boards.

F. Arrest the intruder.

1.   Prepare a search warrant for the intruder's location. Consult Appendix B (which includes warrants for this purpose) and Chapter 9 for assistance in drafting the warrant.

You may find it easier to draft the warrant if you collect the following information before you begin:

a. Phone numbers for dial-in ports used by the intruder.

b. Passwords to the victim's computer system used by the intruder (make sure that the victim changes those passwords before you file the warrant).

c. The name of the account used by the intruder.

d. Information unique to the victim's computer system which you would expect the suspect to have downloaded to his computer, such as welcoming banners, the name of the victim, and even the name of the victim's computer (if named by its location, such as "Building 4 computer," or by number, such as "Computer X452").

e. Messages or commands sent by the intruder to the victim's computer system.

f. A description of software or data which you believe the intruder stole from the victim's computer system.

2. Consider whether you will be able to prove which occupant of that location is your intruder (e.g., which sibling or employee).

3. When obtaining a description of the residence to include in the search warrant, drive by the residence and look at the telephone line to make sure that it is not connected to an adjacent residence occupied by your intruder.

4. Arrange for a magistrate to sign the warrant.

5. Before serving the warrant, consider:

a. Do you have enough officers to allow the investigating officer to interview the suspect (after providing appropriate *Miranda* warnings)?

b. Are you better off serving the warrant when the suspect is not at home?

If you are planning to "turn" the suspect into an informant, and are going to serve your warrant when he is not at home, determine his where-abouts in advance.

6. During the search, do not ignore the following items which may appear in plain view:

 a. Printouts containing phone numbers, credit card numbers, or any string of numbers which may be access codes. Also look for names of bulletin boards (BBSs) which may reveal data caches.

 b. Pads of paper. In addition to strings of numbers and BBSs, look for passwords.

 c. Evidence identifying the user of the computer (i.e., your intruder). Look for names inside man-uals, or on labels affixed to floppy disks.

 d. Evidence of confederates.

 e. Magazines relating to cracking (e.g., *2600*).

 f. Computer manuals for the computer used by your victim.

7. Subject to *Miranda*, interview the suspect.

 a. Ask him whether the computer you find on the premises is rigged.

 b. If you are going to use your suspect to cooperate in investigating his friends, secure his coopera-tion immediately. A long delay (more than a day) before your "turned" suspect returns "on line" may warn confederates that he is no longer their ally.

Appendix A-5

Checklist: Investigation of Information Theft

A. Screening cases.

   1.   Law enforcement investigators should usually reject cases in which:

        a.   the stolen information is not scientific or technical information;

        b.   the victim has lost information which is something less than its "crown jewels";

        c.   the stolen information is not likely to be discovered in the thief's possession;

        d.   the theft occurred more than six months before the report to law enforcement; *or*

        e.   the thief's conduct is not considered theft within the industry.

   2.   Law enforcement investigators should also be wary of any case in which:

        a.   the suspect is part of a group of employees raided by a competitor; or

        b.   the suspect is a licensee.

3.   Consult with a prosecutor to determine whether the theft can be prosecuted under state and/or federal law.

B. Questions for the victim.

    1.   Background information.

        a.   What is the information?

        b.   How is it used?

        c.   What tangible items contain the information?

    2.   Determine whether the information provided the owner with a competitive advantage.

        a.   Do competitors make similar products which they could improve (or produce at a lower cost) by using the stolen information? Can you quantify that advantage (how much better, how much lower, etc.)?

            You will be stuck with this estimate for the rest of the case. Ask for only the roughest approximation of value, and label it as such in any report that you prepare. Consider asking the victim to consult with several sources from different parts of the company (e.g., marketing and research and development) before estimating value. Be alert to employees expressing dissatisfaction with the technology (e.g., "We may be the only company that uses this process, but Company X's own process is better"). Consider obtaining an opinion from an independent expert.

        b.   If you have a monopoly on this product or service, do you have any reason to believe that others want to enter your market?

In the unusual case where your victim has a monopoly, it may be unwilling to explain for the record why other competitors would (or should) enter that market.

3.   Determine whether the information was not generally known to the public.

a.   Ask the victim to justify its belief that the information is not generally known to the public.

1.   Why do you think that nobody else knows the secret?

2.   How do you know that other competitors do not know that information?

3.   Why isn't the information obvious to all qualified professionals in the field?

4.   Did the victim have to spend an enormous amount of time and effort to develop the information?

5.   Has anyone else attempted to create such information and failed?

Try to steer the victim away from repeating its faith in its security measures to a discussion of what the victim knows about the state of the art in the industry, and why it is confident that other companies do not know the secret information.

b.   Determine the history of the information.

1.   When was the information developed?

2.   Where was it developed, and by whom?

3.   Was there a single inventor, or, as is usually the case, a team of developers?

c.   Explore the possibility that an inventor left the company well before the alleged theft and disseminated the secret throughout the industry (or to the competitor who is a suspect).

    1.   Are all the inventors still with the company?

    2.   Have any of those inventors left the company recently?

    3.   Have any of those inventors joined a competitor?

    These last two questions may identify potential suspects.

d.   Ask whether the victim licensed the information to any person or organization. If so, make sure that the license agreement prohibits disclosure. Law enforcement investigators should reject cases in which the information has been disseminated widely, even under strict licensing agreements.

e.   Investigate whether the information has been published in journals or marketing materials.

    1.   Collect marketing materials (including data sheets and technical "white papers") prepared by the company for any product incorporating the secret.

    2.   Arrange for an expert to perform a literature search for your information. Do not accept assurances that such a search is unnecessary, or that it has already been performed by the victim.

4.   Determine whether the owner took reasonable measures to ensure that information was not disclosed to the public.

a.   Physical security.

1. Are company buildings fenced?

2. Are "no trespassing" signs posted?

3. Are company buildings locked during non-working hours?

4. Are entrances and exits controlled by guards?

    a. Must employees sign in and out of the building?

    b. Must employees wear badges at all times?

    c. May guards search belongings? Do they regularly search belongings? (Many guards are told to search only when they suspect theft.)

    d. Must visitors sign in and out of the building?

    e. Must visitors be escorted at all times?

    f. Are visitors steered away from sensitive areas?

5. Are areas containing sensitive information segregated from the rest of the company (e.g., are there separate rooms for secret documents and laboratories)?

6. Must employees have separate identity devices (e.g., card keys) to enter sensitive areas?

b. Computer security.

1. Does each user have a separate log-on?

2. What password system is used?

    a. Are the passwords assigned by the company or by the user?

    b. Is the password file within the computer protected from outside access?

    c. Are the passwords changed regularly?

    d. Does the company prohibit employees from sharing passwords?

c. Personnel policies regarding secret information

    1. Identification of secret information

        a. Are documents containing secret information marked "proprietary" or "confidential"? ("Proprietary" is used below to refer to both designations.)

        b. Are color-coded covers used to make those distinctions clear to everyone?

        c. Are such documents marked "proprietary" on every page?

        d. Is there a policy governing which employees receive documents marked "proprietary"?

    2. Policies protecting that information

        a. What are the company's procedures governing disclosure of proprietary information?

b.   Has every employee, supplier, and customer furnished with this information signed a non-disclosure agreement?

c.   Is any particular employee responsible for reviewing releases of information to the public (e.g., data sheets, brochures) to ensure that those materials do not disclose trade secrets?

d.   Are employees allowed to take proprietary documents home?

3.   Communication of security policies to employees.

a.   Are employees told that:

1. they have a duty not to disclose company information to competitors or the public?

2. they may not disclose documents marked "confidential" or "proprietary" to the public without approval of senior management or security personnel?

3. they must not take secrets home without permission?

4. they must return company property (including tangible items containing secrets) upon leaving the company?

b.   How are employees told this information?

1. Are they informed of their obligations during orientation interviews?

2. Do they sign employment agreements?

3. Do they sign non-disclosure agreements? Virtually every high-technology company requires new employees to sign non-disclosure agreements. Check to make sure that the employee signed such an agreement, and that the agreement covers the stolen information.

4. When an employee leaves the company, is he or she asked to attend an exit interview where company officials review the employee's obligations with respect to company trade secrets?

5. Are employees frequently provided with memoranda or other materials which discuss security?

6. Are employees shown videos which discuss security?

7. Are there signs posted urging secrecy? (Such signs make impressive courtroom exhibits.)

c.   Possible witnesses for information about communication of company policies to employees include:

1. Personnel department managers who conduct entrance and/or orientation interviews with new employees.

2. Lawyers who conduct exit interviews.

3. Security managers who draft policies on protecting information.

4. MIS managers (managers in charge of computer operations), for issues relating to computer security.

5. Engineers (particularly managers) in the department responsible for the secret information.

6. Managers or employees of departments responsible for marking documents proprietary.

4. Protection of documents ("Document Control").

   a. How do documents get to Document Control?

   b. Who decides whether those documents are marked proprietary?

   c. What records are kept concerning which documents have been marked proprietary, and which have not?

d. What records are kept of which documents have been distributed to which individual?

e. Do employees receiving documents have to sign for them?

f. What records are kept concerning which documents have been returned (e.g., when an employee has left)?

g. Is there any monitoring procedure to ensure that documents are returned after they are superseded by new editions, or when an employee leaves?

h. Is there a policy on deregistration of documents?

C. Identify suspects.

1. Employees with access to the information.

a. Determine which employees had access to the stolen information, and identify any tangible items containing that information. Retrieve all records from Document Control relating to those tangible items to determine which employees received those items.

b. If the victim has identified an employee as a suspect, retrieve that employee's personnel file. Such files often contain performance reviews (and exit interviews) listing the projects in which the employee participated.

1. Make a separate copy of the file before looking at it. If the victim cannot turn that copy over to police for safekeeping out of fear of violating privacy laws, make sure the copy is segregated from the original file in a separate part of the company for safekeeping.

2. Determine whether the employee signed (or refused to sign) an acknowledgment of receipt of proprietary information form.

2. Employees with a motive to steal.

   a. Are other companies raiding the victim for talent?

   b. Has any departing employee who had access to the information refused to disclose his or her new employer?

   c. Look for:

      1. poor performers, who may have moved to another company and used the victim's information to make themselves look like talented engineers; and

      2. disgruntled employees who believe that they can make more money on their own.

   d. Check a suspect's personnel file to determine whether he or she may be angry at the company.

3. Employees who acted unusually before the theft.

   a. Check computer logs for unusual activity by suspects in the month before their departure.

   b. Check building logs for entry into the building during non-working hours.

        c.   Ask security personnel if the suspect's office looked suspiciously "cleaned out" before his or her last day on the job.

        d.   Check phone records for calls to competitors or other suspects.

        e.   Once it is safe to interview employees, ask them whether they noticed anything unusual. For example, employees from other divisions who begin asking technical questions of employees for no reason may be intent on theft.

4.   Employees who acted unusually after the theft.

        a.   Determine whether former employees called current employees with technical questions related to the secret information, or returned to the victim's facilities and examined relevant documents.

5.   Suspicious products.

        a.   The victim should purchase suspicious products through discreet intermediaries, and use reverse engineering to determine whether the competitor developed the product independently.

        b.   When examining software, look for identical code and identical *bugs* (errors). Although an honest competitor might use similar code, it would not copy mistakes.

D. Draft the search warrant.

1.   Use overlapping requests; seek tangible items which can be described easily.

2.   Use broad requests seeking stolen information, and narrow requests seeking tangible items likely to contain that information.

E. Examining the evidence seized during service of the search warrant. You should look for:

1. Evidence demonstrating that documents containing stolen information were possessed by a particular person (e.g., handwritten notations on the victim's documents). Determine whether other documents found close by contain indicia of ownership.

2. Any mention of your victim by the competitor's engineers. Look for material which demonstrates the competitor's unusual knowledge of the victim's technology.

3. Altered copies of your victim's information which can be used to prove that the thief knew the victim's information was secret. A copy of your victim's manual with the logo whited out, or the cover ripped off, is powerful evidence.

4. An exact copy of the information in the thief's handwritten specification.

5. The payoff. Information theft is risky. If you have a suspect, look for a reward, whether it be in the form of cash, a check, a stock option, or a promotion.

Appendix A-6a

Checklist: Tool Kit for Searching, Seizing, and Analyzing Computer Evidence

The items listed below may help you in your search for computer evidence:

1. A real computer tool kit (computer tools such as screwdrivers for opening the case, disconnecting items properly, etc.). You can purchase one of these at a computer supply store. You should also purchase an anti-static bracelet (also known as a grounding strap). Your kit should include a 1/4-inch nut driver (for the computer case) and a Torx (screwdriver); one expert also suggests a 7 mm nut driver (for removing certain circuit boards).

2. Wire cutters, hammer, nail puller, sharp knife. These are used for prying items out of walls, for example.

3. Flashlight

4. Computer cables: parallel, serial, 9 pin, 25 pin, null modem, RS 232, 50-pin flat ribbon (for disk drives). It can be useful to have a spare cable around when you are seizing peripherals or trying to get them to function on-site.

5. Extension cords and power strips. The suspect may have used all of the outlets in the room or office where the computer is stored.

6. Blank disks

a. Purchase both 5 1/4-inch and 3 1/2-inch disks, each in double and high density formats. Buy name-brand diskettes only (such as 3M, Sony, Maxell, Verbatim). Buy pre-formatted disks—they will save you time.

NEVER use the suspect's machine to format a disk.

NEVER bring along disks which have already been used for anything else. If you must bring "used" disks, you must use only those disks which you have personally "wiped" clean with Norton Utilities' WipeInfo or other program. Merely formatting disks does not erase their data.

b. You may also want to use some blank formatted diskettes to insert into diskette drives when you seize the computer.

c. Some disks are available in different colors. For searches where viruses are a concern (i.e., any cracker's computer), you may wish to use color-coded disks, as follows:

1. Green: For factory software for use in analysis

2. Blue: For backup of the suspect's data

3. Red: For destructive programs, such as viruses, found on the suspect's machine

7. Diskette labels, preprinted with the case number and the location of the site to be searched. Use these to label blank floppy disks at the scene. In addition, before arriving at the scene, label any disks you bring with you. Otherwise, you risk confusing your disks with the disks you have seized from the suspect.

8. Write-protect labels (to put over the write-protect tab on 5 1/4-inch disks).

9. Felt marking pens. The more indelible, the better. Do not use ball-point pens to mark disk labels.

10. Color-coded stick-on tags, preferably tags which can be tied onto things (like cables). If they have room to write letters or numbers, so much the better. Avery color-coded file folder labels work well. Wire labels are also useful and can be purchased at electronic supply stores.

11. Package of 1" x 4" self-adhesive labels. Use these to label evidence.

12. Boxes of large and small paper clips

13. Scissors

14. Stapler (with box of staples)

15. Box of rubber bands

16. Cloth gloves (where fingerprints may be important; otherwise, rubber gloves are adequate). You may wish to consider always wearing gloves to avoid depositing body oil on floppy disks.

17. Materials for storing what you will seize

   a.　Large and small boxes. Large boxes can be purchased from moving companies (e.g., Ryder, U-Haul).

   b.　Packing material, such as shredded paper or molded styrofoam, for packing in boxes around seized computer components. (One expert reports that styrofoam balls can "shed" particles which can clog a hard drive. An alternative is to use foam wrapping. Pink or blue foam wrapping should be anti-static.)

   c.　Grocery bags and paper bags (for cables and small components). Avoid using plastic bags because they can store static electricity which can damage electronic components.

18. Tape

   a.　Masking tape (for taping cables to computers, and securing floppy disk drives with a disk inside the drive)

   b.　"Fragile evidence" tape

19. Floppy disk container (can be purchased at computer stores). Purchase 3 1/2-inch containers—you can use shoeboxes to store 5 1/4-inch disks.

20. Sleeves for 5 1/4-inch disks

21. Magnetometer, or less ideally, a compass (for detecting magnetic fields)

22. A computer battery. Batteries run down every few years, and your computer's battery may fail while it is in storage pending trial. If the battery dies, you lose the CMOS information necessary to operate the computer and must spend time and effort finding that information. (As discussed later, you will also obtain CMOS information when you seize a computer.)

23. Graph paper for mapping the search warrant site

24. Tape recorder

25. Camera. You may want a Polaroid in order to make sure you can confirm that your picture is good before you leave the scene, and a 35 mm camera with close-up lens for critical pictures which you expect to admit into evidence. You should also consider purchasing a tripod.

   a.   Film

   b.   Flash attachment, recently tested

26. Camcorder (preferably with clock counter). The Hi-8 camcorders are best.

   a.   Videotape

   b.   Recently tested batteries

27. Standard desk telephone. You can use your telephone to make calls from the scene. Using the suspect's phone erases that phone's "memory" of the last call(s) made by the suspect.

28. Recently tested size AAA, AA, and 9-volt batteries

29. Portable computer system, including portable printer, laser printer labels, and paper. Although such a system is clearly a luxury item,

it can be very useful in logging evidence, or, if the computer has a large hard drive, backing up evidence.

30. Software: The following is a suggested list of software you should consider including in your tool kit. Each software package intended for the IBM PC should be available in both 3 1/2- and 5 1/4-inch versions. You are encouraged to write the author with suggestions for other software for the tool kit; those suggestions will be incorporated in future editions. The author has not used every software package referred to in this chapter.

A word of caution: always used licensed copies of software. It would be embarrassing for an investigator to have to admit in court that he used bootlegged software, in violation of federal law, to search for evidence of a crime.

a. Two copies of the latest version of MS-DOS (and PC-DOS), along with the following older versions (some may be impossible to find):

1. 3.3

2. 4.01

3. 5.0

4. 6.0, 6.1, 6.2

b. The latest Apple operating system boot disk (e.g., System 7.5), as well as Systems 5.0 and 6.0 (for examining older machines)

c. The latest version of Norton Utilities for IBM and Macintosh computers

d. Fastback Plus backup software, version 2.0 (the last version of that product which can be run from a floppy)

e. Software capable of making an image backup. You can choose from SAFEBACK backup software, available to law enforcement investigators from Sydex Corporation (503-683-6033), and CPR Data Recovery Tools, distributed by Tech Assist, Inc. (813-539-7429).

f.   The latest version of Laplink (including cable).

g.   Various versions of "zip" programs, such as PkZip, PkArc, LHArc, GZip, and either Nico Mak Computing's WinZip or Canyon Software's Drag and Zip

h.   Any ASCII editor program

i.   A graphics viewer program

Two viewers now available are VPIC, from VPIC Inc., Box 162857, Altamonte Springs, FL 32716, 407-869-5233, and WinJPG, written by Norman and Ken Yee, 58 Chandler St., Boston, MA 02116, 617-423-2399, nyee@osiris.ee.tufts.edu or kenyee@ksr.com.

j.   You may wish to create a disk with a "clean" operating system (a boot disk) and other utility programs to assist you in securing, examining, and backing up computers found during the execution of a search warrant. You may consider including the following software (for which you must have a license) on that disk:

1.   MS-DOS 5.0 system files (IO.SYS, MS-DOS.SYS, COMMAND.COM, AU-TOEXEC.BAT). You can transfer these files by choosing the "make a disk bootable" option in Norton Utilities. (MS-DOS 5.0 can be used on older machines; you may want a separate disk with the newer MS-DOS 6.22 system files.)

2.   CHKDSK (MS-DOS)

3.   DISKMON (Norton Utilities)

4.   NDD.EXE (Norton Utilities)

5.   SYSINFO.EXE (Norton Utilities)

6.   DISKEDIT.EXE (Norton Utilities)

Appendix A-6b

Checklist: Preparing to Execute a Search Warrant Involving Computer Evidence

A. Determine what computers are at the scene.

1. Check for filings with the state relating to security interests in computer equipment.

2. Consider attempting to trick the target with a survey.

3. Check with the fire marshal for evacuation plans filed by the suspects.

4. If it can be done without tipping your hand, interview the suspect's clients, ex-employees, service vendors, janitors, or landlord.

5. Consider dumpster diving for information (at curbside only).

6. If you can use an infiltrator or informant, ask him or her:

   a. What types of computers are on the premises (mainframe, minicomputers, networks, PCs, dumb terminals, portables)? Depending upon the sophistication of your informant, you may have to settle for information concerning the size of the computers and whether they appear to be connected to one another.

b. What brands of computers are present (IBM, Digital, Apple, etc.)?

c. How many computers are on the premises?

d. What operating systems are being used (e.g., UNIX, VMS, Novell, Windows NT, Windows, OS/2, DOS, Apple System 7.5, etc.).

e. Does the system receive and send electronic mail?

f. Are there any modems on the premises?

g. What programs are run on the computer (e.g., word processing, databases, spreadsheets)?

h. What software is on the shelves? Look for such programs as Symantec's Norton Utilities, Symantec's Disklock, PC Tools, and MS-DOS (note the version).

i. What passwords, if any, must the employees use to access the computer, and where are those passwords stored? Are there any other computer security systems in place, such as SecureID (discussed below), or "destruct" switches or procedures?

j. Are there any scraps of paper on or near the computer which might contain passwords?

k. What kind of backup system does the suspect use, and where are the backup tapes or disks stored? Are they stored off-site?

B. Collect other intelligence about the site.

1. If the site is hostile, determine whether to obtain a court order allowing you to cut telephone service before executing the warrant.

2. If the site is friendly, and your suspect is in charge of the computer or has access to it, make sure that management terminates the suspect's system privileges *and* dial-up access capabilities.

C. Finding a computer expert.

1. Your agency.

    Make sure that your expert understands the principles of searching and seizing computers discussed in Chapter 6. *Computer experience is no substitute for training in how to search and seize computer evidence.* Use trained investigators whenever possible.

2. Federal agencies.

    Most federal agencies have in-house technical experts. A list of such experts is included in Appendices C and D of *Federal Guidelines for Searching and Seizing Computers* (General Litigation Section of the Department of Justice, 1994). The Federal Law Enforcement Training Center (FLETC) in Glynco, Georgia, trains federal agents in computer crime investigation, and is staffed by specialists. The IRS scatters its Seized Computer Evidence Recovery Specialists (SCER) around the country. Almost every IRS District has at least one SCER Specialist, and many have two. The Secret Service also has a few specialists outside of Washington.

3. Other law enforcement agencies.

    Pick the largest agency in your jurisdiction, and ask for assistance.

4. High Technology Crime Investigation Association. (HTCIA).

Most veteran high technology crime investigators belong to the High Technology Crime Investigation Association, with chapters in Southern California, Silicon Valley, Northern California (Sacramento), Texas, Arizona, New Mexico, the Northwest, Chicago, and New York.

5.   SEARCH, Inc.

The Department of Justice, Bureau of Justice Assistance funds SEARCH Group, an organization devoted to assisting the criminal justice community on information technology issues. Part of their support includes training law enforcement agencies in all facets of searching and seizing computers and computer evidence. Their staff experts are knowledgeable and helpful, and may be able to refer you to experts in your area. As of this writing, Mr. Fred Cotton is the resident expert, and can be reached at 916-392-2550.

6.   International Association of Computer Investigative Specialists (IACIS).

This non-governmental organization is based in the Northwest, and offers excellent 72-hour and two-week training courses on searching and seizing computer evidence. Its phone number is 503-668-4071.

7.   Universities.

Consider calling the computer science department of your local university. If they cannot help, ask for names of various professional societies, which in turn may be willing to inform their members that you need assistance.

8.   Victims in earlier cases.

Assuming that you achieved a satisfactory result in their case, former victims may be enthusiastic about helping you investigate your latest case. Remember to perform a records check on any private party who volunteers to assist you.

9. The victim in your present case.

Victims are usually a ready source of technical expertise. However, they are often not the best choice because the defense can accuse law enforcement of employing a biased expert.

10. Volunteers.

Although these people can be very helpful, conduct a background check before accepting their assistance.

D. Plan the raid.

1. Tentatively decide whether you will seize and/or backup computer evidence.

2. Logistics.

   a. Overtime

   b. Replacement officers

   c. Provisions

   d. Equipment needed to process data

   e. Moving company. Look for a company with plenty of insurance, so that it is able to pay for any damage it causes to the computer.

   f. Storage space for seized evidence

3. Prepare your tool kit for the raid (see Appendix A-6a).

Appendix A-6c

Checklist: Serving a Search Warrant Involving Computer Evidence

A. Pre-raid briefing.

    1.   Explain basic evidence-handling techniques.

          a.   Show officers evidence you expect to find (e.g., floppy disks, software manuals, and computer passwords) so that they know what to look for.

    2.   Caution against seizing everything in sight, as such careless gathering may transform a narrowly crafted warrant into a general search forbidden by the Fourth Amendment.

    3.   Tell officers who are computer users that only certain persons are allowed to touch the computers, both before and after those computers have been seized and transported to the police station.

    4.   Test your equipment, such as laptops, camcorders, and tape recorders.

    5.   Make sure you have your tool kit.

B. Secure the scene.

    1.   Remember knock-notice.

2. Move everyone away from computers within 30 seconds of entry.

3. Isolate electricity and telephones (look for modems). Detain all persons until you can confirm that the computer has been isolated from telephone lines.

    a. Determine whether any computers are connected to other computers not on site. If so, determine whether to disconnect those computers.

4. Turn on every monitor at the scene to make sure that nobody has initiated a "destruct" program, such as Norton's WipeInfo.

5. Check for physical traps. Consider walking around the scene with a compass.

C. Search for computer evidence.

1. Look for non-traditional computers, such as wristwatches, telephones, fax machines, copiers, and "personal organizers" (e.g., Casio's Boss, Sharp's Wizard, or the H-P Palmtops).

2. Examine telephones and fax machines for last numbers dialed and last faxes sent and received.

3. In information theft cases, consider obtaining copies from a copier machine for use as forensic evidence.

4. Look for loose magnetic media, particularly backup disks and tapes (including CD-ROMs). Backup media are typically found near the computer. Paperwork may reveal the location of off-site storage facilities.

5. Search for passwords, including passwords written on scraps of paper near computers. Also check the underside of desk calendars.

6. Check the exterior of computers for maintenance tags.

7.   Search for indicia of occupancy at each computer site (each desk, office, etc.).

D. Document the location of computer evidence.

1.   Walk around the site with a camcorder—videotape all monitors displaying any information, and the contents of bookshelves near computers (to record relevant computer manuals).

2.   Draw a diagram, and mark on that diagram the location of evidence discovered at the premises.

3.   Keep a running evidence log.

4.   Use a designated finder to record the location of evidence discovered at the premises.

5.   Label media with the name of the case, an evidence number, and the location where it was found.

E. Decide which hardware to seize.

1.   Can you move the hardware safely? Attempting to move a minicomputer or network is a major problem and should be attempted only when absolutely necessary.

2.   Are you willing to seize a computer if doing so puts your target out of business?

3.   You should generally seize all loose media and documentation after obtaining authorization via a search warrant to do so.

F. Seize computers.

1.   *Refer to Appendix A-6d, which summarizes the three strategies for seizing computers.* When operating a

computer, it is best to record your keystrokes through the use of a camera or dictaphone.

2.   General points to remember when seizing computers:

    a.   Before turning off a computer over five years old, use disk parking software to park the hard drive.

    b.   Label cables, particularly those attached to peripherals.

    c.   Ground yourself before disconnecting cables.

    d.   Cover portions of the computer to protect against tampering.

    e.   Take the computer directly to the lab and ensure that it is stored properly.

3.   If you backup a computer, remember:

    a.   Terminate any programs which are already running.

    b.   Perform a hardware check where it is practical to do so.

    c.   Locate all logical drives and files.

    d.   Label all floppy disks before using them to make backups of the computer system.

    e.   Use all correction and verification options available, and make two backups if time permits.

    f.   Check your backup on your own portable computer, if you have one, before you leave.

4.   Before leaving the scene, try to talk to the owner of the computer about the system. (Remember to give appropriate *Miranda* warnings, and note that asking the suspect about the system can produce incriminating answers.)

Appendix A-6d

Checklist: Implementing Strategies for Searching and Seizing Computer Evidence

IMPORTANT: First, you *must* read Chapter 6 before using this checklist. Second, you are always better off having an expert help you. None of these procedures, including pulling the plug, is without risk. Reading this checklist will not make you an expert—you need to get hands-on training by taking one of the courses mentioned in Chapter 6.

A. Pull the plug.

    1.   Exit all application programs.

        a.   If you are in Windows, exit by typing Alt-F4 until you are at the DOS prompt. (If prompted to "save" a file, select the "cancel" button, and use the "save as" command to save the file to a floppy with a slightly different name.) Remember that Windows allows more than one program to run at a time. You should consider "paging" through the various applications programs running in Windows before exiting the operating system. (Remember to photograph the screen first.)

        b.   If the computer is running DOS, terminate the program running on the screen (probably after examining what the suspect was doing when you arrived). If it is a commercial application, exit it as provided for by that program. If not, first try the Escape ("Esc") key.

1. If this does not work, try pushing the Control ("Ctrl") and Break ("Brk" or "Pause") keys simultaneously. If this does not work, push the Control and "C" keys simultaneously. Also try pressing "Alt-X" and "Ctrl-Q." If you are still unsuccessful, you may have to pull the plug out of the wall (see Step #3 below).

c. If you are dealing with an Apple computer, select SHUTDOWN from the top menu bar.

d. If you have encountered a computer being used as a bulletin board, check whether the menu on the screen provides you with the option of changing the SYSOP log-in password. If so, try to view the old password (which the suspect may have used to protect other programs or files). Then accept the option of choosing a new password. If you are unable to change the password, attempt to exit the bulletin board program normally before proceeding.

Note that federal privacy laws protect bulletin board systems. Read Chapter 8 carefully before searching or seizing a computer which is being used as a BBS.

2. If you are examining a machine over five years old, and have brought disk parking software, place the disk with that software in the floppy drive and run it.

3. Pull the power cord out of the wall (or from the surge suppressor, as the case may be). Do not turn the computer off by using the on/off switch. Place masking or electrical

tape over the power outlet on the computer to remind officers not to use that computer once it has been seized.

4. If the power to the monitor and the computer does not go out, check for external and internal battery units. Do not proceed until you confirm that the computer is powered down.

5. Label each cable entering or exiting the computer.

    a. If a cable is not attached at both ends, label it accordingly. Attach a corresponding label for each port of the computer the cable is plugged into. If a port is unused, label it as such.

    b. After you have labeled all of the cables and ports, take another photograph of the computer. Photograph the front *and* rear of the computer. If the wiring is complex, consider drawing a diagram. The more information you can get, the better—you may not try to set up this computer for analysis until days or weeks after the search, when your memory of the scene will have faded.

    c. Carefully unplug each cable you have labeled. If possible, keep the cable attached to its peripheral. You should consider taking a photograph after the computer has been disassembled.

6. Place a blank, write-protected, bootable diskette in each floppy disk drive, and use masking tape to gently tape it into place. Place a separate piece of tape labelled "EVIDENCE, DO NOT TOUCH," on the front of the case. Tell everyone involved that using the seized computer for any purpose could destroy your case even if no evidence was disturbed.

7. Cover the keyboard with cardboard, and tape that cardboard down with evidence tape.

8.   If you have seized any loose peripherals, label them as not having been connected to anything.

9.   Move the computer.

    a.   For minicomputers and/or workstations, you should use a moving company experienced in transporting computers. In addition, you should look for a company with plenty of insurance, so that it is able to pay for any damage it causes to the computer. (You should contact such a company *before* serving your warrant.)

    b.   Make sure that the movers maintain the computer in the same position that it was in when sitting on the desktop. Keep computers which were on their sides on their sides, and computers which were upended (i.e., in *tower* configurations) in that same position.

    c.   If you are seizing several systems, consider placing each computer in its own padded box; label the box with information about the system and the location from which it was seized. (If you are searching a residence, check the attic, basement, and garage; the suspect may have kept the original packing box for the computer system.)

    d.   Use padding in your vehicle whenever possible. Do NOT leave the computer or any peripheral in the vehicle any longer than absolutely necessary, and never leave it exposed to the sun (heat can destroy magnetic media). Consider not transporting a computer in any vehicle with an operating police radio. Do not place CPUs close to radio units in the trunk of a police car, and avoid transmitting while transporting the computer.

10.   Store the computer in a safe environment.

    a.   Keep the computer away from magnets, speakers (such as those in boom boxes), and radio equipment (e.g., police transmitting equipment, including microwave towers). Keep the computer in a temperature controlled room (i.e., a room with a thermostat, like an office, rather than a warehouse or storage shed). Keep it at least several feet away from heating or cooling ducts. Make sure the room is relatively free from cigarette smoke, dust, and insects. If you are comfortable in the room, the computer will usually be "comfortable" as well.

    b.   Do not place objects on top of the computer (except the monitor). Do not plug in the computer unless it is in use. Do not allow liquids in the room, or at least within three yards of the computer.

    c.   Make sure the room is kept under lock and key at all times.

11.   If you operate that computer again, it is good practice to turn the computer off, either at the surge suppressor or at the on/off switch. Plug in the computer after it has been turned off, and then turn on the computer the way the user would—from the on/off switch or the surge suppressor.

12.   Before leaving the scene, talk to the owner of the computer about the system. Remember to give appropriate *Miranda* warnings, and note that asking the suspect about the computer system can produce incriminating answers. Ask suspects at the scene for "cooperation," namely, passwords and other information about the computer.

B. Hardware check.

You should use an expert to perform a hardware check. Some of the steps listed below are most appropriate when you have reason to believe that the computer owner has rigged the computer or taken other steps to hide data. This checklist assumes that the computer is on when you arrive. If the computer is off, it is usually better to pull the plug and conduct a hardware check back at your lab.

In order to perform a hardware check, you should have a floppy disk loaded with the following programs:

1.   MS-DOS 5.0 system files (IO.SYS, MSDOS.SYS, COM-MAND.COM, AUTOEXEC.BAT, CONFIG.SYS). You can transfer these files by choosing the "make a disk bootable" option in Norton Utilities. If you are searching a newer machine, you should also have MS-DOS 6.22 system files on another disk. As discussed below, you may need different boot disks with different versions of DOS.

2.   CHKDSK (MS-DOS).

3.   The following programs from Norton Utilities:

  a.   NDD.EXE

  b.   DISKMON.EXE

  c.   SYSINFO.EXE

  d.   DISKEDIT.EXE (this is optional)

Write-protect the floppy to ensure that viruses on the computer do not infect your boot disk. Consider booking this disk into evidence. If a suspect claims that you inserted a virus (or planted evidence) while examining the computer, you will have the clean disk available.

Take the following steps after you have exited all application programs, and inserted your floppy drive into the A: drive.

Note: If the suspect was at the keyboard and has left you at the DOS prompt, consider typing F3. Typing F3 results in MS-DOS repeating the command previously typed. You should then type the [up arrow] key. DOS 6.2 includes the DOSKEY program, which, if loaded during boot-up (through inclusion in the AUTOEXEC.BAT file), will reveal previous commands when the up arrow key is typed.

1.   Type A:\COMMAND, and press Enter.

      a.   The computer should check the A:\ drive and report that it is running MS-DOS 5.0 (or MS-DOS 6.22, if you used that version of DOS). If you receive the error message: "Incorrect DOS version," try different versions of DOS until you find one which works.

      b.   If you are still unsuccessful, consider whether to pull the plug, or to continue with this procedure despite the increased risk. (Although the "ver" command will report the version of DOS running on the computer, it is an obvious command to "rig" because the suspect already knows this information, and therefore has no reason to use the command.)

              Note that using your own COMMAND.COM file does not "clear" the computer of other, and equally deadly, traps. Your decision whether to continue will usually depend upon your assessment of the computer owner. Very few computer users who have the sophistication to alter the operating system decide to do so instead of simply encrypting important files. However, some crackers do fall into this category, so beware.

              Watch the hard disk light. If it begins blinking for a prolonged period of time, and the program you are trying to execute appears not to be working, pull the plug out of the wall immediately.

2.   Type A:, and press Enter.

This will put you in the A: drive, and allow you to run the programs on your floppy disk. If it presents an error message instead, give up on the hardware check, and pull the plug as described above.

3.   Type DIR A:, and press Enter.

The computer should display a list of files on your floppy disk. Again, if you receive an error message instead, pull the plug as described above.

4.   Type SYSINFO, and press Enter.

    a.   This will start Norton Utilities' System Information program (SYSINFO.EXE). If the program does not start, or reports errors, proceed to Step #6.

    b.   The first screen presented by SYSINFO will give you a system summary. Record the number of hard disks present, and their size. You might also record the type of BIOS (e.g., Phoenix, Award) and the date. Do not print any information from SYSINFO.

    c.   Page through the program (by selecting the "Next" button) until you reach the CMOS Values screen. Record all of the information displayed on the screen.

    d.   Page through to the Disk Summary screen. This information will usually confirm the number of hard drives installed in the computer.

    e.   Page through to the Disk Characteristics Screen, and record the information under Physical Characteristics.

    f.   Page through to the Partition Tables screen. Check to see whether there is another partition in addition to the DOS partition (labeled BIGDOS). The owner may be running more than one operating system and have partitioned the drive accordingly. You will check any additional partitions back at your lab. More common is to "divide" the drive into one or more logical drives; you will already have discovered such partitions by examining the Disk Summary and Disk Characteristics screens.

g.   If you are familiar with computers, select "View Config.sys" from the menu (you can page through, but you will run benchmarks that will waste your time and might cause problems). *Do not change the CONFIG.SYS file.*

       1.   Examine the CONFIG.SYS file for unusual drivers, such as DoubleSpace (a feature of later versions of DOS which increases the amount of data available on a hard drive by compressing data), Stacker (a different compression program) or security programs (look for lines with words such as "Diskreet" or "Disklock"). Note that you may find drivers for memory management programs (e.g., QEMM, NETROOM, 386MAX); these do not generally pose a concern.

       2.   Finding DoubleSpace or Stacker means that you will need to decompress the data back at your lab in order to read it (typically by configuring your lab machine the same way; note that some versions of Stacker may require a "Stacker card" placed in the computer). You do not need to take any action at the scene.

       3.   If you find a security program, you should attempt to backup all logical drives before pulling the plug. If the computer owner opened the protected logical drive before you arrived, you should be able to backup all of the files in that drive. You may have to perform this backup "manually" because your com-

mercial backup program could fail to recognize the protected drive, or, worse, stop working ("hang") when trying to backup files. If your backup program hangs, you will be forced to reboot, thus "closing" the drive.

5. Exit SYSINFO. You should still be in the A:\ drive.

6. If SYSINFO did not run, check for logical drives the old-fashioned way. Type D:\, and hit Enter, and do the same for all the remaining letters in the alphabet, from E:\ through Z;\. You will see either a corresponding prompt (e.g., "D:\"), or the message "Invalid Drive Specification." The prompt means that data is stored in a logical drive; the error message means that there is not a logical drive with that label.

7. For each logical drive you find, type CHKDSK [that drive]:, and press Enter.

    a. The CHKDSK program returns a description of that logical drive, including the size of the drive, the amount of data in that logical drive, and most important, a list of any problems with that drive (e.g., lost chains, corrupted FAT tables, etc.).

    b. *Do not attempt to fix any problems you find, and do not run CHKDSK/F.* You do not want to alter the contents of the hard drive in any way. You can make changes in the copy of the data you upload to your lab machine. Simply document the problem to avoid accusations later that you damaged the computer.

8. For each logical drive you find, type NDD, and press Enter.

    a. This Norton Utilities program checks the hard disk for various problems. Again, do not fix the problems, but do note them. (You do not have to run the surface disk scan. If you do, and it appears to be taking more than a few minutes, check to make sure that it is configured for "Daily Scan." The "Weekly Scan" takes much longer to complete.)

9.   You have completed the hardware check.

You are now ready to pull the plug, or backup the computer, as you choose.

C. Backing up the computer.

1.   Perform the hardware check procedure described above.

2.   Reboot the computer with a "clean" copy of DOS. (The exception is where you have found a security program which will "close" when the computer is rebooted. In such cases, you must backup immediately using the suspect's operating system.)

3.   Run a "write blocker" program, such as DISKMON.

4.   To reboot, place diskettes with copies of DOS in every diskette drive and turn the computer back on. The computer should boot normally. When the computer requests the date and time, just punch the "Enter" key—do not enter a different date and time. If the computer does not boot normally, you should pull the plug and take the machine to your lab for a more detailed inspection.

If the computer owner is insisting that you backup the computer, demand passwords and other information necessary to reboot the computer with a clean copy of DOS.

5.   If you are backing up onto floppy disks, label those disks in advance with the case name, case number, and, where more than one computer is on site, the type and location

of the computer being backed up. All floppy disks must be new and formatted.

6.   Consider running Norton's UnErase program to restore any "erased" files. You should direct the program to "un-erase" any files you find to a floppy disk. (Type "Alt-F", followed by "T"). Unerasing them to the hard drive will change the suspect's directory and FAT table.

7.   Run backup software. Make sure you are left alone for this step; if you are distracted, you may not notice until you return to the lab that you failed to backup all of the data at the scene. Although usually not practical, it is a good idea to make two complete backups of each machine if time permits.

    a.   Use only those programs which you can run from a floppy disk. If you want to perform a quick file-by-file backup, this probably means using Laplink, or picking up a very old copy of Symantec's Fastback Plus (version 2.0 or earlier). If you want to create a mirror image backup, consider using SAFEBACK or CPR Data Recovery Tools.

    b.   When running a commercial backup program, follow the directions carefully. Pay close attention when setting the parameters for your backup. Use all error correction and verification options available, and, if the program does not do so automatically, instruct it to backup all files, including hidden files.

8.   Check your backup before you leave the scene. If you have a laptop handy, try restoring a file to the hard disk on the laptop. If you are backing up with Laplink, compare some of the files on the host and target computers.

9.   After you finish the backup, put the floppy disks away in a cool, dry, anti-static environment (in anti-static bags, if possible).

D. Searching the computer at the scene.

    1.   If you decided to search the computer because incriminating information was displayed on the monitor when you arrived, photograph that screen immediately. Use the application program to copy the important file to a clean floppy. (Do not save the file to the hard disk—you will obliterate the date and time on which the suspect last saved the program to disk. Worse, if it is a newly created file, the computer may write that data onto a different portion of the hard disk, obliterating evidence in slack space.)

    2.   Print as much of the document or spreadsheet as you can. When examining the document, be very careful not to change any data. When exiting the application program, do not save the current file to disk, but once again, save it to a floppy, and use a different extension for that file.

    3.   Once you have obtained evidence from the program running on the screen, and assuming that you choose to search the computer without backing up, consider first gaining control of the system by rebooting, as discussed above in the section on backing up a computer. Then search the computer using the techniques discussed in the analysis section in Chapter 6. If nothing else, after you have exited the program running on the screen, run a "write blocker" such as Norton Utilities' DISKMON program to make sure that any further examination does not overwrite data on the hard drive.

    4.   If you are searching a network, remind your experts not to overlook data which may be stored in the workstation they are operating. You should usually backup both the server and the workstation.

Appendix A-6e

Checklist: Storing and Analyzing Computer Evidence

IMPORTANT: First, you *must* read Chapter 6 before using this checklist. Second, you are always better off having an expert help you. None of these procedures is without risk. Reading this checklist will not make you an expert—you need to get hands-on training by taking one of the courses mentioned in Chapter 6.

A. Store the computer safely—Dos and Don'ts:

    1.   The computer must be kept:

        a.   Away from magnets, speakers (such as those in boom boxes), and radio equipment (e.g., police transmitting equipment, including microwave towers).

        b.   In a temperature-controlled room (i.e., a room with a thermostat, like an office, rather than a warehouse or storage shed).

        c.   At least several feet away from heating or cooling ducts.

        d.   Free from cigarette smoke, dust, and insects.

    2.   Do not place objects on top of the computer.

    3.   Do not plug in the computer unless it is actually in use.

4. Do not allow any liquids in the room, or at least within three yards of the computer.

5. Keep the room under lock and key at all times.

B. Analyzing seized evidence.

1. Remember the three commandments for analyzing computer evidence.

    a. Do not use the subject's computer for any purpose except transferring the data on that computer to another computer for examination.

    b. The computer you use to examine the suspect's data should either not be used for anything else or have a hard drive partition reserved solely for the suspect's data.

        In the event you must work without a net, you should make two backups of the suspect's hard drive (one of them an image backup if possible) before you begin any analysis not complying with the first two "commandments" stated above.

    c. Perform the analysis yourself, or with assistance—you must participate to make sure that someone less familiar with your case does not miss critical evidence.

2. Open the computer and look for the following items (use an anti-static wrist strap to avoid damaging components).

    a. Look at the hard drive for a paper label with CMOS information on it. Copy that information (such as the drive type) in case you lose your CMOS information before trial.

    b. Make sure that there is only one hard drive.

c.   Examine the circuit boards in the expansion slots of the computer. You may find another hard drive (some drives are in the form of a circuit board—these drives are called "hard cards"), a hardware compression board (e.g., Stacker), or some other device or peripheral. You must use an anti-static bracelet for this task (see below).

3.   When operating the suspect's computer (i.e., to transfer data to a lab machine):

a.   Use an uninterruptible power supply and surge suppressor, particularly if you reside in an area prone to electrical storms or brownouts. At a minimum, use a high-quality surge suppressor.

b.   If you turn off the suspect's computer, wait ten seconds before turning it back on. This allows the voltage in the circuitry to return to zero and the hard drives to power down completely.

c.   It is good practice to make sure that the computer is turned off at the beginning of your examination, either at the surge suppressor or at the on/off switch. Plug in the computer after it has been turned off, and then turn on the computer the way the user would—from the on/off switch or the surge suppressor.

d.   Use an anti-static wrist strap when working inside the case to avoid damaging components.

4.   Transfer the suspect's data to your laboratory machine.

a.   Use a well-known anti-viral program before and after uploading any data.

b.   Run Norton's UnErase from a floppy, and copy any files you find to a floppy.

c. Upload data into a partition (or removable hard drive) which is reserved for that data, and which has been wiped clean.

d. If you use a backup program to upload data, enable all verification options.

e. If you are examining floppy disks:

1. Ensure that all disks are properly labeled and write-protected. If you find an interesting file while searching a floppy, print out a copy immediately.

2. If you find evidence on any floppy disk, consider immediately copying the contents of that floppy to another floppy disk, and storing that second disk in another location.

5. When you can't reboot.

a. Before calling for help:

1. Make sure that you have plugged in the computer and turned on the monitor.

2. Make sure that you are booting from the correct floppy drive with a clean copy of DOS. If the computer has two floppy drives, place clean copies of DOS in each, and close the drive doors before rebooting.

3. If you receive a demand for a password, the suspect is using a power-on password enabled within the CMOS setup. Check any documentation you seized for ways to change this configuration.

4. Another approach is to try to interrupt the boot sequence to access the CMOS

setup utility and disable the password. Many CMOS setup programs allow you to reassign the A:\ drive as the bootup drive. Again, check the computer manual for information on how to access the CMOS during bootup. One common way is to hit the "Esc" key or the "Delete" key while the computer is booting up. (One expert recommends disconnecting the hard drive—a resulting error message may drop you into the CMOS setup.)

b.   Call for help.

1.   Your options may range from getting a simple bit of technical advice from the expert or the computer's manufacturer, to extracting the hard drive for further analysis by specialists in a media recovery lab.

2.   If the media are damaged, trained investigators may consider running media recovery software, such as Norton Utilities' Disk Doctor, *on an extra copy* of the data.

6.   If you want to begin your examination by looking for incriminating file names, consider using the "chkdsk/v" command to obtain a list of the files in the data you uploaded to your lab machine. This command will list every file which DOS finds in a particular logical drive, including hidden files. To copy that list to a floppy, type "chkdsk/v > a:\chklist.txt". This command will create the file chklist.txt on the floppy in A:. To print that list, type "chkdsk/v > prn" (this may take several minutes to print).

7.   If your file has a .zip or .arc extension, you are dealing with a compressed file. Your tool kit should include various versions of the PkZip, PkArc, and LHArc programs.

8.   Use a program such as ZyIndex, Magellan, Norton's FileFind, or other specialized search software to look for key words.

9.   Use a viewer such as XTreeGold for Windows, PC Tools, or even Norton Commander (warning: Norton Commander overwrites data to the hard disk) to examine individual files. Some of these programs can read compressed files.

10.   Depending upon your case, you will want to focus on word processing, spreadsheet, or database files. Run a copy of the application program used by the suspect and examine files with seemingly relevant names.

11.   Organize your search.

    a.   Print a copy of the directory of the hard disk and a directory of files contained within each directory.

    b.   Take notes of where you have been and where you are going. If you find valuable files, consider printing them out *and* making an additional copy onto diskettes.

    c.   Label those diskettes with a distinctive name, such as "[Casename] Hot Files."

Note: Appendix B is on disk.

Appendix C–1

Criminal Law and the Information Age: Protecting Trade Secrets from Disclosure In Criminal Cases

Kenneth Rosenblatt[1]

Our legal system has been struggling to apply traditional principles of criminal law to cases involving "high technology" for over 20 years. Many adaptations are simple translations of previously accepted concepts. Thus, the rules governing admissibility of "computer evidence" fit fairly well within the framework already provided by the authentication, hearsay, and best evidence rules simply by treating magnetic media as a "virtual document." Representations of information contained on magnetic media are generally admissible if a document containing the same information would be admissible.

Similarly, the burgeoning problem of unauthorized access to computer systems spawned laws analogous to traditional crimes. Penal codes now abound with statutes punishing "electronic" trespass, with increased penalties for trespass with intent to commit harm (i.e., theft or vandalism). Such laws are easily adjusted to keep pace with advances in computer technology.[2]

---

1. This article, with a few minor editorial changes, was first printed in *The Computer Lawyer* (Volume 8, No. 1, January 1991) (Prentice Hall Law & Business). The author drafted the text of California Evidence Code Sections 1061, 1062, and 1063 discussed in this article.

2. For example, the California Legislature in 1989 amended Penal Code Section 502 to prohibit the unauthorized introduction of a "computer contaminant" (i.e., virus or worm) into a computer system. *See* Penal Code sections 502(b)(10) and 502(c)(8).

However, the fit between criminal law and high technology has been problematic in other areas. California has just enacted a statute addressing one of the thorniest problems: how to protect confidential information from disclosure during a criminal prosecution without violating the defendant's Sixth Amendment right to a fair trial and the public's First Amendment right to view criminal justice proceedings.

California Evidence Code Sections 1061, 1062, and 1063, effective January 1, 1991, provide prosecutors and victims with new tools to protect trade secrets. Section 1061 provides for protective orders preventing dissemination of secrets incident to discovery. Section 1062 allows closure of criminal proceedings involving trade secrets. Section 1063 provides for sealing of articles containing trade secrets which are filed or offered into evidence.

Background

In the 1970s, states recognized that intellectual property needed special treatment, and began enacting laws declaring that intellectual property was a form of personal property for purposes of statutes punishing theft. *See, e.g.,* California Penal Code Section 499c. However, no provision was made for how such cases were to be presented in court in light of the fragility of intellectual property.

Civil litigants learned early that protective orders were a necessary incident to discovery, and that closed hearings were often required to safeguard trade secrets. Provisions for such orders were soon included in state law and court rules. But legislatures never considered those issues in the context of criminal cases, where the accused enjoys a panoply of constitutional rights unavailable to civil litigants.

For example, defendants in criminal cases are not only allowed discovery of all real evidence involved in the case, but, in California, have also been allowed to shield the identity of their experts from the prosecution until well after most discovery occurs.[3] Furthermore, the Sixth Amendment provides that defendants in criminal cases shall have an open and public trial.

---

3. California's passage of Proposition 115 is expected to prevent this practice.

Defense attorneys are increasingly aware of the potential for frustrating trade secret and other prosecutions involving proprietary information through threats of "constitutionally protected" disclosure. The practice of "greymail," a tactic honed in national security cases where the defense threatens to disclose classified information incident to trial, is alive and well in trade secret prosecutions.

For example, defendants have claimed that the Sixth Amendment allows them to call *any* expert witness in aid of their defense, including competitors of the victim, and that those witnesses can be effective only if they are shown the victim's trade secrets. Defendants have also claimed that the Sixth Amendment allows them to hide the identity of such experts from both the People and the third-party victim.

There are other risks for victims. In addition to the defendant's Sixth Amendment right to an open trial, the Supreme Court has long held that the public itself enjoys a presumption of access to criminal trial and pre-trial proceedings.[4]

This line of cases has two consequences. First, in the rare case where the victim's secret may be disclosed by mere recitation (e.g., the formula for Coca-Cola or the recipe for Mrs. Fields chocolate chip cookies), the prosecution cannot proceed unless there is some mechanism available for closing the courtroom. Second, this First Amendment right may impair the prosecution's ability to present exhibits or other documents under seal.[5]

---

4. *See, e.g., Press-Enterprise v. Superior Court*, 464 U.S. 501 (1984); *Press-Enterprise v. Superior Court*, 478 U.S. 1 (1986) (*Press-Enterprise II*) (preliminary examinations); *Waller v. Georgia*, 467 U.S. 39, 45 (1984) (suppression hearing); *In re Capital Cities*, 913 F.2d 89 (3rd Cir. 1990) (sidebar and chambers conferences); *In re Search Warrant (Gunn I)*, 855 F.2d 569 (8th Cir. 1988); *Certain Interested Individuals v. Pulitzer*, 895 F.2d 460 (8th Cir. 1989) (search warrant affidavits).

5. *See, e.g., In re State-Record, Inc.*, 917 F.2d 124, 127, 128 (4th Cir. 1990); *The Oregonian Publishing Co. v. District Court (Wolsky)*, 1990 WL 192683 (9th Cir. (Or.)) (plea bargain agreements); *Certain Interested Individuals v. Pulitzer, supra.* Note that the public does not have a constitutional right to documents exchanged during discovery. *Seattle Times Co. v. Rhinehart*, 467 U.S. 20 (1984); *but see Public Citizen v. Liggett Group, Inc.*, 858 F.2d 775, 787–88 (1st Cir. 1988) (public may have common law right afforded by local court rule requiring filing of discovery material with the court).

Although Evidence Code Section 1060 provides a "trade secret privilege," the limits of that privilege have so far not been addressed in criminal cases. Indeed, the Comment to that section makes it clear that even the drafters were unsure of its scope.

The poor fit between criminal law and trade secret law has not been evident until recently because victims have reported very few cases to law enforcement. As more victims are turning to law enforcement for assistance, these problems are finally coming into focus. Sections 1061, 1062, and 1063 attempt to resolve these problems by providing a procedure for protecting trade secrets in criminal cases.

Section 1061

Section 1061(b)(1) provides the following procedure for applying for a protective order. The owner of the secret, or the owner's representative (including the People),[6] must apply for a protective order by submitting an affidavit based upon personal knowledge. That affidavit must identify, without revealing, the alleged secret, and present evidence that the secret qualifies for protection under either Penal Code section 499c (which includes only scientific or technical information) or Civil Code section 3426.1. That affidavit is publicly available.

Section 1061(b)(2) allows the defendant to oppose that request by filing a counter-affidavit under seal; that affidavit must be served upon the owner of the secret and all of the parties (including any co-defendants). Sealing is required to allow the defendant to discuss the alleged trade secret material in detail.

---

6. It should be noted that these sections also protect owners of trade secrets who are not victims of the offense. For an example of why such protection is useful, *see Stamicarbon v. American Cyanamid*, 506 F.2d 532 (2nd Cir. 1974). This protection of third parties can create some interesting difficulties where important evidence in the case (e.g., a contract between the defendant and a third party to develop a product based on the victim's secret) is asserted to be a trade secret belonging to both the defendant and a third party. However, note that sections 1060 and 1061 both prohibit protection where that protection would work a fraud or injustice.

Section 1061(b)(3) provides that the movant bears the burden of showing by a preponderance of the evidence that protection is appropriate. The test is whether a trade secret is likely to be disclosed absent a protective order. The court may rule on the request without holding a hearing; any hearing must be *in camera.*

If the court finds that protection is appropriate, it may issue a protective order. That order may include one or more of the following provisions:

- Dissemination of the trade secret may be limited to counsel, their employees, and law enforcement.

- Defendant may view the secret only in the presence of counsel, or at counsel's offices.

- Anyone not otherwise allowed to view the secret must obtain a court order before doing so. That person may be required to sign the protective order and agree to be bound by its terms.[7]

  •• In addition, a party seeking disclosure to an expert must provide the court (but not the People) with the expert's name, employment history, and other relevant information; the court shall evaluate the expert and determine whether allowing that expert to view the information would pose a "discernible risk of disclosure."

  •• Moreover, the court *must* "withhold approval if the expert's economic interests place the expert in a competitive position with the victim, unless no other experts are available."

  •• The identity of that expert may not be disclosed to the owner of the secret or the People until after the termination of the action and only upon good cause to believe that

---

7. The statute also allows the court to require the person to agree to make the owner of the secret a third-party beneficiary of that protective order. In hindsight, prosecutors should not insist upon such a provision because it may raise constitutional problems where a witness is required to testify by compulsion of a subpoena. It should be clear in any event that the owner of the secret has standing to sue a violator of a protective order entered under this section.

a court-appointed expert has disseminated trade secrets. (This latter provision is unfortunate, but the exclusion of competitors as experts makes disclosure much less likely.)

- Other orders "as the court deems necessary to protect the integrity of the trade secret."

See §§ 1061(b)(4)(A)–(D). A ruling granting or denying the request for protection may not be applied as the law of the case, res judicata, or collateral estoppel in the criminal case or in any other action. *See* § 1061(c).

Section 1062

Section 1062 is a narrowly tailored provision allowing closure of criminal proceedings where:

> the proponent of closure has demonstrated a substantial probability that the trade secret would otherwise be disclosed to the public during that proceeding and a substantial probability that the disclosure would cause serious harm to the owner of the secret, and where the court finds that there is no overriding public interest in an open proceeding. No evidence, however, shall be excluded during a criminal proceeding pursuant to this section if it would conceal a fraud, work an injustice, or deprive the People or the defendant of a fair trial."

Section 1062(a).

The first two parts of that test are a fairly straightforward application of the *Press-Enterprise* standards.[8] First and Sixth Amendment concerns demand that closure be allowed only where there is a substantial probability that an open hearing would cause serious harm to the owner of the secret.

---

8. Section 1062(c) satisfies the "narrowly tailored closure" requirement by providing that only that portion of the hearing necessary to protect the secret may be closed.

The third test, requiring the court to find "no overriding public interest in an open proceeding," is less clear. The phrase was suggested by civil liberties organizations, which were concerned that criminal prosecutions could result in the concealment of information vital to the public interest.

Although that language was inspired by a similar phrase employed by the Supreme Court in *Press-Enterprise I, supra,* the Court used it entirely differently in that case. Per *Press-Enterprise,* there is a presumption of open proceedings which may be overcome only "by an overriding interest based on findings that closure is essential to preserve higher values" (such as preserving the trade secret owner's property). *Id.,* 464 U.S. at 510.

Section 1062 appears to allow the public to resist closure by demonstrating an overriding interest in openness after the victim has established its own overriding interest in protecting its intellectual property.

Thus, this test would appear to apply only where the court finds that an otherwise valid trade secret claim is being used to frustrate public scrutiny of an objectionable practice, such as a third party's claim of secrecy preventing the disclosure of a compound used to pollute the environment.[9]

The procedure for obtaining closure is similar to that used to apply for a protective order under section 1061, except that the court must hold an *in camera* hearing to consider evidence bearing on the necessity of closure.[10]

Where a portion of a hearing is closed, a transcript of that hearing,

---

9. The civil liberties organizations may have been contemplating cases where a party seeks to seal a search warrant affidavit describing allegedly criminal activity by claiming that revealing the affidavit would disclose its trade secrets. *See In re Search Warrant (Gunn I),* 855 F.2d 569 (8th Cir. 1988) (the court declined to consider such a claim in ordering disclosure). Note that it would appear that these organizations similarly influenced newly enacted Penal Code section 859.1, which closes trials to protect minors. *See, e.g.,* § 868.7 (closing preliminary hearings).

10. That *in camera* hearing necessarily makes it more difficult for objectors to closure to argue intelligently concerning the need for openness. However, providing the secret to the press is tantamount to disclosure. Requiring the advocate of closure to identify, without revealing, the subject matter of the trade secret should be sufficient. *See In re Iowa Freedom of Information Council,* 724 F.2d 658 (8th Cir. 1983).

redacted to eliminate trade secrets, must be provided to the public as soon as possible.[11]

Defendants may claim that this statute violates their Sixth Amendment right to an open trial. The redaction requirement is not in and of itself a sufficient response because the redacted portion may constitute a substantial portion of the trial. Courts have skirted this issue in the past, and no clear precedent exists.

The only court to confront the issue directly was unable to come to a decision. The court noted that closure might be appropriate in the contempt proceeding before it, but stressed that the only possible penalty in that case was a fine; the court hinted that a possibility of incarceration might preclude closure. *See Stamicarbon v. American Cyanamid*, 506 F.2d 532 (2nd Cir. 1974). A concurrence by Justice Stewart in a later decision suggests some sympathy for that court's dilemma. *See Richmond Newspapers, Inc., v. Virginia*, 448 U.S. 555, 600, n.5 (1980) (Stewart, J., concurring).

However, both decisions appear to have been superseded by the more liberal test propounded in *Press Enterprise I and II*. The Court in *Waller v. Georgia, supra*, applied the *Press-Enterprise* test in weighing the defendant's Sixth Amendment right to a fair trial against the government's interest in closing a proceeding where telephone intercepts would be played in order to protect third parties' right to privacy. Although the Court found that closure was inappropriate in that case, it noted that the right to access in general "may give way in certain cases to other rights or interests, such as the defendant's right to

---

11. This redaction has been held to be sufficient compliance with the public's right to know what happened at a pre-trial hearing. *See United States v. Poindexter*, 732 F.Supp. 165 (D.D.C. 1990). The court in that case held that former President Reagan would testify at trial by means of a pre-trial deposition. The videotape of that deposition would be played at trial after redaction of classified information. The media sought access to the deposition itself. The trial court denied the request on the grounds that national security interests overcame the presumption of openness. The court held that the taping of testimony would inevitably include classified information which could not be avoided without eliminating all questioning. The court also rejected the alternative of allowing the media access, but restricting their right to report what they heard, noting that such a gag order was a practical impossibility (not to mention a prior restraint). Of course, the redacted portion in that case would never be introduced as evidence at trial.

a fair trial *or the government's interest in inhibiting disclosure of sensitive information.* Such circumstances will be rare, however." *Waller*, at 45 (emphasis added).

At least one court has held that the closure of a *small* portion of a trial to preserve classified information is acceptable, and that the presence of a jury does not eliminate the basis for closure. *See United States v. Pelton*, 696 F.Supp. 156 (D. Mary. 1986) (noting that the Classified Information Protection Act suggests that the court instruct the jury not to reveal such information).

Although no court has yet applied the *Press-Enterprise* test to a request to close the courtroom to protect trade secrets, it appears that the Supreme Court would allow closure because to deny it would discourage prosecutions involving sensitive technical information. This logic has been applied to uphold closure on a case-by-case basis where necessary to protect witnesses from psychological harm, even though such closure seals the core of the trial from public view. *See Globe Newspapers Co. v. Superior Court*, 457 U.S. 596 (1982), *see e.g.*, California Penal Code section 868.7, *Eversole v. Superior Court*, 148 Cal. App. 3d 188 (1983). The reasoning behind such protection—that it is necessary in order to encourage victims to come forward and initiate prosecutions—also applies to owners of trade secrets in technical cases.

Section 1063

The cases following *Press-Enterprise* make it clear that most court proceedings are open to the public. A corollary to that rule is that this openness requires affording the public (and the media) access to documents filed as part of those proceedings. Although this rule does not extend to documents exchanged during discovery,[12] it clearly applies to documents admitted into evidence.

Although the Uniform Trade Secret Act provides for sealing in civil cases, there was no statutory procedure for sealing such documents in criminal cases before § 1063. Section 1063 requires the

---

12. *See Seattle Times Co. v. Rhinehart*, 467 U.S. 20 (1984).

prosecution to provide in advance of each criminal proceeding a list of articles it intends to introduce under seal during that proceeding. That list is available to the public.

Section 1063 provides a two-part procedure for resolving disputes over sealing. The court first holds a hearing on the People's request to seal, and hears objections to sealing in open court. The court then conducts an *in camera* hearing (excluding both the public and the media) to consider those objections in light of "appropriate constitutional standards." This phrase glosses over some disagreement over the extent to which the *Press Enterprise* presumption of openness applies to the standard for sealing certain documents. The various groups involved in hammering out this section agreed to defer that issue to a later date.

For any documents not included in the People's list, section 1063 allows the People, the defendant, or the owner of the secret to request sealing at the time the article is made a part of the court record. Such a request to seal must be made part of the written public record, and objectors are given an additional two days to object to sealing.

Conclusion

Cases involving proprietary information often result in a collision between the rights of the defendant and the rights of the owner of the trade secret. Although courts must still address issues arising out of that conflict, these new statutes may provide ground rules for handling such cases.

Appendix C–2

Sample Protective Order for Information Theft Cases

_____.

Attorneys for the State.

_____ COURT OF _____, COUNTY OF _____
STATE OF _____

No. _____

	Plaintiff,	PROTECTIVE
STATE		ORDER
v.		
DEFENDANT		
		Date:
	Defendant.	Dept:
_____/		

Upon application of the People of the State of _____, [and (*victim*)], it appearing that the above-entitled action may involve trade secrets, and good cause appearing;

IT IS HEREBY ORDERED that:

1. For purposes of this Order, a "trade secret" is any information found by this Court to qualify as a trade secret under the civil or criminal law of this State. The designation of information as a trade secret in this proceeding is solely for purposes of this protective order. This Court's decision to designate, or not to designate, information as a trade secret shall not be construed to mean that the information is or is not a trade secret as defined by [*applicable trade secret statute, both civil and criminal*]. Such a decision shall not prejudice either the People or the defendant in this case in any way.

This Court has [*or: the parties have*] designated the following information to be a trade secret: _____.

2. For purposes of this Order, an "article" is any tangible item containing a trade secret.

This Court has [*or: the parties have*] designated the following items to be articles: _____.

3. The People or the defense [*or: any party*] may ask this Court to designate other information as a trade secret. Any individual or entity claiming to be the owner of information may also request designation of that information as a trade secret. This request may be made at any time and in any form.

[*(An option)*: Information contained within articles produced in discovery may be designated "a trade secret" by the labeling of such materials as "confidential." Those materials shall be deemed to be articles containing a trade secret unless any party objects thereto and files an affidavit based upon personal knowledge contesting that designation during the pendency of this action.]

In determining whether information shall be designated as a trade secret, this Court may consider any testimony provided during any part of this proceeding, and any affidavit based on personal knowledge filed with this Court. This Court may also take testimony *in camera* in aid of its decision. A request for designation of information as a trade secret shall not be construed to mean that the People or the defense asserts that the particular information is a trade secret as defined under [*civil and criminal trade secret statutes*]. A decision or failure by the People or defense to request that information be designated as "a trade secret" shall not be construed as a concession that the information is not a trade secret under [*civil and criminal trade secret statutes*].

4. Any trade secret or article encompassed by this Order which has been produced in discovery by the People, or any other individual or entity, shall be used solely for the purposes of this criminal proceeding and for no other purpose.

5. No trade secret and/or article shall be made available to anyone other than a "qualified person." As used in this Order, "qualified persons" means counsel for the People and counsel for defendant(s) (including associate attorneys, paralegals, stenographic and clerical employees assisting such counsel, and law enforcement agencies), the defendant(s) (subject to paragraph 6 below), and retained experts as selected and approved pursuant to paragraphs 7 and 8 below.

Such persons shall read this Order, agree in writing to be bound by its terms, and agree to: (a) maintain trade secrets and articles in confidence; (b) refrain from using, disclosing, transmitting, or revealing same to anyone other than a qualified person; and (c) refrain from using same except in connection with the trial or preparation for trial of this proceeding.

Neither a trade secret nor any article shall be filed, or caused to be filed, with any Court or otherwise made part of the public record without prior approval of this Court. Counsel shall retain the originals of all written agreements signed by persons to whom any trade secret or articles are provided, subject to paragraph 8 below.

6. All trade secrets, articles, and notes or other records regarding same, shall be maintained in the custody of counsel of record for the parties, with the exception that the People may allow other law enforcement agencies to retain custody. No partial or complete copies of a trade secret shall be retained by anyone else, including defendant(s), at any location other than an office of counsel for the defense or the People, with the exception of experts retained by either party.

Subject to paragraphs 7 and 8 below, such experts may retain articles on a temporary basis for purposes of study, analysis, and preparation of this case. A person with custody of a trade secret shall maintain it in a manner that limits access to qualified persons only.

7. An expert retained by the People may become a qualified person under this Order upon consent of [victim] by signing a copy of the agreement attached hereto and incorporated by reference herein as Exhibit A to this Order. If the People seek to retain an expert without consent of [victim], that expert must be approved by this Court pursuant to the provisions of paragraph 8 below.

8. If an attorney for defendant(s) desires to give, show, make available, or communicate trade secrets and/or articles to any expert, the attorney must first identify that expert to the Court. That identification shall include the name and resume of the proposed expert. That resume shall include the expert's name, address, and employment history.

This Court shall examine the expert *in camera* to determine whether his or her character, credibility, and motivation make the expert suitable to receive a trade secret. This Court shall not approve any expert whose economic circumstances place him or her in direct or indirect competition with the alleged victim in this case, [victim].

Neither [victim] nor the People shall be present at the examination. A court reporter shall report the examination and prepare a record of the proceedings. That record shall be sealed, and is not to be unsealed absent an order of this Court, a higher court of this State, or a federal court. If the expert is deemed unsuitable, that expert shall not receive any trade secrets or articles.

Should this Court be satisfied that the proposed expert is suitable, that person shall be deemed a "qualified person" for purposes of receiving articles and trade secrets for temporary study, analysis, and preparation of testimony upon signing a copy of the agreement attached hereto and incorporated by reference herein as Exhibit B to this Order. Counsel for defendants shall file the original signed agreement with the Court before disclosing any trade secrets or articles to that expert. The agreement filed with the Court shall be sealed and unopened absent an order by this Court, a higher court of this State, or a federal court. Counsel for defendants shall retain signed copies of that oath in their offices.

9. Upon Court approval, counsel for the defense or the People may show trade secrets and articles to percipient witnesses to determine whether they are familiar with, or have observed, said information and articles. Such percipient witnesses must sign a copy of the agreement attached hereto and incorporated as Exhibit C to this Order before receiving or viewing any trade secrets or articles. Percipient witnesses are not qualified persons under this Order and are not allowed to retain any trade secrets or articles.

10. Upon final termination of this prosecution, the parties, and each qualified person (including experts) shall assemble and return to [*victim*] all trade secrets and articles, except that any documents or copies which contain or constitute an attorney's work product may be destroyed rather than returned.

11. Should any trade secrets and/or articles be disclosed, through inadvertence or otherwise, to individuals or entities not entitled to receive same, then the defense and the People shall use their best efforts to bind them to the terms of this Order. The defense and the People are required, as to each individual or entity, to: (i) promptly inform them of all the provisions of this Order; (ii) immediately identify them to the Court, the People, and [*victim*]; and (iii) promptly request them to sign an agreement agreeing to be bound by the terms of this

Order. Such a signed agreement shall be filed with the Court and served on [*victim*].

12. This Court may amend this Order at any time to afford additional protection to the trade secrets in this action.

IT IS SO ORDERED.
[DATE].

_____

Judge of the _____ Court

Exhibit A (*without the caption*):

1. I understand that as part of being retained by the [*State*] as an expert in this case, I am being shown information which has been deemed confidential in this case, and that I have certain obligations imposed upon me by the Court in this case with regard to that confidential information.

2. I have been shown a copy of the protective order signed by Judge _____ on _____ [*date*] protecting confidential information, and articles containing same, in this action. I understand that the protective order and this agreement allow me to receive and use the confidential information only for the purpose of discussing those documents with qualified persons as defined under that protective order. I understand that the protective order prohibits me from disclosing, revealing, or transmitting this information to any person other than a qualified person. I agree to view and/or inspect this information only in the presence of one of the following persons: counsel for the People, counsel for defendants, associate attorneys, paralegals, investigators, and/or law enforcement officials.

3. I agree to abide by all of the provisions of the protective order entered by the Court in this action.

Dated:_____

_____
Witness

Comments generally

Exhibit B, omitted here, is the same as Exhibit A, except that the word "defendant" is substituted for "State." Exhibit C, also omitted, is the same as Exhibit A, but does not include the recitation that the witness has been retained as an expert.

The protective order assumes that the parties have stipulated to the protection of certain information, and documents or magnetic media containing that information, or that a Court has made such designations after the parties could not agree. The order governs what can be done with protected information and articles. It also sets forth procedures for designating additional information.

Protective orders should be tailored to the needs of each case. This sample order assumes a very cautious victim or an untrustworthy defense team. In many cases, counsel can remove some of the more aggressive provisions, such as the *in camera* examination of defense experts.

Comments concerning certain paragraphs

1.   This paragraph aims to protect both sides against adverse claims in a civil case that failure to obtain protection in one case waives it in the other.

3.   Allowing the owner or any party to designate documents as containing trade secrets can be very useful where your victim is required to produce thousands of pages of documents as part of discovery. Rather than filing a motion for each document, the victim merely designates material as a trade secret and places the onus on the defense to challenge that designation. (Most civil firms already have stamps labelled "confidential," which is why that phrase is used instead of "trade secret".)

It may be possible to force this option on reluctant defendants by arguing that requiring the victim to file a motion for each article produced violates its Fourth Amendment guarantee against unreasonable searches. *See, e.g., Millaud v. Superior Court* 182 Cal. App. 3d 471

(Cal. App. 1986); *Pacific Lighting and Leasing Co. v. Superior Court* 60 Cal. App. 3d 552 (Cal. App. 1976).

4. This provision draws upon the inherent power of the court to control discovery. For third-party victims, you will once again rely upon the victim's constitutional guarantee against unreasonable searches.

5. The prohibition against filing items with the Court is designed to prevent defense counsel from filing a protected document in the public domain. The particular danger is that the defendants, ostensibly protecting the document, file it under seal. Defendants later move to unseal that document, claiming that the prosecution or the victim are unable to show that it should remain sealed from public view.

7. Victims may occasionally demand that the State sign on to the protective order. If your victim demands this provision, there is little harm in including it. You may want to include it anyway so as to vitiate a defense claim that the protective order is not evenhanded.

8. The concern here is that the defendant may hire an expert who works for the victim's competitor. There are many civil cases upholding restrictions on hiring experts who may compete with the victim.

Appendix D

Introduction to Computers and the High-Technology Industry

1.00   Introduction

Because high-technology crimes involve computer technology, you need to have some knowledge about how computers work in order to understand certain high-technology crimes, and to comprehend what victims and witnesses tell you during an investigation.

There are plenty of lavishly illustrated books available which describe how computers work in great detail, and this chapter is no substitute for them.[1] Indeed, this chapter is *very* simplistic. However, this tutorial is different from those books in that it seeks to relate computer technology to the crimes you will investigate. For example, you need to know more than the difference between *source code* and *object code*—you need to know why thieves prefer *source code.*

This chapter also includes a list of the major companies in the high-technology industry, and the products they produce. You can use this information to better understand the high-technology industry and to convince victims that you "know the territory."

Important terms are printed in *italics* the first time they appear.

1.10   How a computer works

---

1. One such book is White, Ron, *How Computers Work* (New York: Ziff-Davis, 1993), available in many bookstores and computer stores, and from the publisher directly at 800–688–0448, ext. 8367.

You have used computers for years. An automatic teller machine (ATM) is merely part of large computer network; so is a terminal accessing criminal history information.

This tutorial will focus on the average computer used in almost every business in America: the *personal computer* (the *PC*). Personal computers are also called *microcomputers*. Larger computers come in several sizes, including *minicomputers, mainframe computers*, and *supercomputers*, and will be discussed later in this chapter.

1.11 The parts of the computer you see on your desk

The typical computer system consists of a large box (or *case)* containing various electronic components, a monitor, a keyboard, a mouse, a printer, and a modem. The case and its contents are commonly referred to as "the computer."

A *monitor* is like a television screen; it allows you to see what you type on the *keyboard*. The computer can display results on the *monitor*; it can also print out those results on the *printer*. A *mouse* is a pointing device; it is used to point at objects or text on the screen.

A *modem* is a box which allows your computer to communicate with other computers over a telephone line. Items connected to the computer are often referred to as *peripherals*.

1.12 What you cannot see the computer do

We first consider what the computer does with information you type on the keyboard. (Entry of information is also referred to as *input*.)

Everything inputted into the computer is converted into groups of 0's and 1's. You can also think of these as "on" (1) and "off" (0).

A single 0 or 1 is called a *bit*. A group of eight 0's and 1's is called a *byte*. (01000101 is a byte.) A group of bytes is called a *word*.

The 0's and 1's which instruct the computer to do something are called *software*. A collection of instructions is called a *program*. (Think of a recipe for baking a cake. An instruction to add a cup of flour is software, and the list of instructions for baking the cake is a program.) When you instruct the computer to add 1+1, the instruction to add the two numbers is software; the numbers themselves, including the result ("2"), are *data*.

1.13 The hardware inside the case

Hardware is any physical item which sends, receives, manipulates, or stores 0's and 1's. Hardware is tangible—you can see it and touch it. When you open the case of a computer, what you see inside is hardware. The most important hardware is the *central processor unit*, or *CPU*. The CPU is a *microprocessor*, which is a type of *integrated circuit*.

An integrated circuit, also called a *chip*, is a small piece of silicon the size of a fingertip which can manipulate and store millions of 0's and 1's. The amazing thing about computers is that while the case takes up several square feet of space, most of the work is done by a piece of silicon the size of your thumbnail. Chips are described in more detail in Chapter 3. For the moment, note that the small size of chips makes them a tempting target for thieves.

1.13–a Memory

The microprocessor needs to store information it is not currently working with for later use. Such information is stored in *memory*. A certain amount of memory is built into the microprocessor. However, computers also include additional memory in the form of *memory chips*.

Memory chips are specially designed to store millions of 0's and 1's in a very compact space. The microprocessor sends instructions which store and retrieve 0's and 1's into and out of memory as needed.

Most of the information stored in memory is stored in *RAM* (*random access memory*). The contents of that memory change frequently while the computer is in use.

Some memory in the computer is *ROM* (*read-only memory*). The user typically cannot change the contents of ROM short of removing the ROM chip and using special equipment to reprogram it. (Thieves commit cellular phone fraud by reprogramming the ROM chips in cellular telephones to change the billing information transmitted by those telephones). ROM chips are used primarily to store instructions executed by the computer when you turn it on.

Most RAM is *volatile*, meaning that turning off the computer eliminates all instructions and information stored in memory. This means that turning off a computer during a search will erase evidence of what the computer owner was working on at the time you entered the premises. (As discussed in Chapter 6, a copy of that information may be stored on the hard drive.) In contrast, ROM is *non-volatile*.

1.13–b   Circuit boards

The microprocessor, memory chips, and other electronic components of the computer are embedded in *circuit boards*. The circuit boards are connected to each other by connectors and wires. The circuit board containing the CPU (the microprocessor) is a major component of the computer and is frequently referred to as the *motherboard*.

Other circuit boards used in computers have special names. For example, a user may change how information is displayed on his monitor (e.g., changing from *monochrome*—black and white—to color) by adding a different *graphics board* (which will include special integrated circuits designed for that task). Those extra circuit boards are commonly referred to as *cards* (e.g., a *graphics card*, or a *sound card*).

1.13–c   Storage media

1.13–c(1)   Hard drives

Memory chips are not the only means available to store instructions and data. Virtually all computers come equipped with a *hard disk*. A hard disk, also called a *hard drive*, is a storage device that stores data on a platter within the device. The drive resembles an oversize hockey puck.

Hard disks store anywhere from millions to billions of 0's and 1's—far more than can be stored on a memory chip. The data on a hard disk does not disappear when the power is turned off, although the data can be erased and overwritten by the user. Every few years or so, a small fraction of hard disks suffer a major loss of memory (and have to be replaced) as a result of a *hard disk crash.*

The ever-present risk of such a crash persuades careful users to *backup* their programs by copying them to *floppy diskettes* (also called *floppy disks), magnetic tapes*, and *removable media drives.*

1.13–c(2)   Floppy drives

A floppy disk is a small version of a hard disk platter. When you slide this disk into a slot in the computer, the computer is able to access the 0's and 1's on the disk. The slot is part of a box called a *floppy disk drive.* (Do not be confused—although the floppy disk is separate from the floppy disk drive, the hard disk and hard disk drive are combined into one sealed unit.)

You use floppy disks to *upload* and *download* information. A computer user *uploads* information by copying information from the floppy disk to the hard disk ("up" into the computer), and *downloads* by copying information from the hard disk to the floppy disk ("down" to the floppy disk).

When the computer receives information from the floppy disk in the floppy drive, it is *reading* from the disk (also called reading from the drive). When the computer downloads information to the floppy disk, it is *writing* to the disk/drive.

The terms "upload" and "download" are also commonly used to describe the transmission of information between the user's computer and another computer. To "upload" is to transfer from the user's computer; to "download" is to receive from another computer.

A floppy disk fits in a shirt pocket. The implications for theft of information are obvious; a thief can download several hundred pages of information and take it away in his or her pocket. Perhaps equally important, thieves can store stolen information in very small places away from their computers.

1.13–c(3)   Magnetic tape

Computer users soon find floppy disks to be an awkward way of storing large amounts of data. Backing up a 200 MB drive can take 50 or more floppy disks. Users turn to *tape backup* systems, which store data on tapes that look like cassette tapes but are smaller and thicker. A typical tape used with PCs can hold several hundred megabytes.

1.13–c(4)   Removable media drives

Another storage alternative is the *removable media drive*. These drives allow removable "hard disks" to be placed into a drive attached to the computer. The removable media (which range in size from as big as a VCR tape to as small as a box of matches) typically store over 100 MB of information.

The advantage of removable media over tape is that the media can be read from the removable drive (as if the drive were an extra hard drive). To read files stored on tape, the user must first copy (*restore*) the files from the tape back to the hard drive installed in the computer, a relatively slow process.

1.13–c(5)   CD-ROMs

A more recent advance in storage technology is the *CD-ROM (compact disc read only memory)*. A laser creates a CD-ROM by etching a pattern onto a platter—the platter is then used as a master to press individual CDs in a process similar to the method used to create compact discs. (Indeed, the latest generation of CD-ROM drives can read CD-ROMs *and* play compact discs.)

The most recent development is the introduction of relatively inexpensive *CD-R drives (CD-recordable)*, which allow users to record their own CDs that can be read in a standard CD-ROM drive. This means that users are able to backup their data onto CD-ROMs capable of storing over 650 MB.

1.13–c(6)   Magnetic and optical media

Hard disks, floppy disks, magnetic tape, and removable media are all *magnetic media* because they store 0's and 1's by magnetizing certain portions of the disk or tape. You will use the term *magnetic media* in search warrants to ensure that you are authorized to seize computer evidence at the scene.

CD-ROMs are not magnetic media, but *optical media*. This difference is relevant for our purposes only insofar as investigators should ask permission to seize "magnetic *and* optical media" when requesting a search warrant.

Thus, when you search for computer evidence, you are mostly searching for computers (which contain data stored on hard drives), floppy disks, tape cassettes, removable media drives (and removable media), and CD-ROMs.

1.14   How the computer operates

Assume that you want the computer to add 1+2, then add 3+4, and finally add the results of both calculations together. The microprocessor causes various 0's and 1's to be manipulated (also called *executing* the instructions), and adds 1+2. The microprocessor sends the result (3) in 0's and 1's to memory, where it is stored on a memory chip.

How does a computer "send" data? The pathways used to transmit 0's and 1's throughout the computer are called *buses*. Thus, in the example above, the microprocessor sends the result to memory along a *bus*.

The microprocessor then executes the instruction to add 3+4. It sends the result (7) along the bus to memory, where it is stored in a separate place in memory. The microprocessor then retrieves both results out of memory and adds them together. It then stores the final result back into memory.

The microprocessor now has the result in RAM. Depending on what you instructed it to do, the microprocessor will do any of the following, either alone or in combination:

- display the result on the monitor;

- print the result on a printer;

- send that result to another computer along a modem;

- store that result on your hard disk for permanent storage; and

- copy that information onto a floppy disk inserted into the floppy disk drive.

1.15   Software: how we "tell" the computer what to do

We now look at how what you input into a computer causes the microprocessor to manipulate 0's and 1's to accomplish various tasks. The basic set of instructions which operates the hardware is called an *operating system*. Each type of computer has its own *operating system software*. Think of the operating system as a set of programs which acts as a traffic cop, making sure that the computer is able to execute instructions efficiently.

Among other things, the operating system allows the user to give instructions to the computer with simple commands. For example, the command *"mem"* in one operating system will instruct the computer to report on the computer's usage of RAM.

For PCs made by IBM (*IBM personal computers, or IBM PCs*) and machines which can run the same software as IBM PCs (known as *IBM compatibles*), the most common operating system is called *DOS*. DOS and other operating systems are discussed in more detail below. For purposes of this tutorial, IBM and IBM-compatible computers are identical and will be referred to as IBM compatibles.

Although DOS commands are useful, its one-word commands are insufficient for performing word processing, data manipulation, and other tasks. When you use a computer to perform such tasks, you use an *application program*.

Examples of such programs are *word processors* (used to create documents), *databases* (used to organize large amounts of information, such as a list of employees for payroll), *spreadsheets* (used to manipulate financial information), *graphics programs* (used to translate information into pictures), *communications programs* (used to communicate with other computers), and computer games.

These programs provide you with an *interface* (or means of communication and translation) between English language or keyboard commands and the 0's and 1's of the computer. Thus, when you *interface* with the computer, you are usually communicating with the computer by way of an application program.

Both operating systems and applications programs are written by *programmers*. Writing large programs in 0's and 1's is inefficient, so most programs are written in *higher-level languages*. Those languages are composed of English-like words and phrases which serve as instructions. Examples of such languages include *BASIC, COBOL, FORTRAN, PASCAL, ASSEMBLY,* and *C.* Programs written in these languages are referred to as *source code.*

1.15–a   Source code and object code

Before executing the program, the source code must be converted to 0's and 1's (*machine language,* commonly referred to as *object code*) by programs known as *compilers* and *assemblers.* On large computers, programs are often *compiled* by the computer moments before the computer executes the instructions in the program. Most programs sold to *end users* (the person who will actually use the program, i.e., you) have already been compiled into object code.

You must know the difference between object code (0's and 1's) and source code (English-like words and phrases) because programs are a prime target for theft.

Source code is far more valuable than object code because it can be modified to suit the needs of the thief. For example, a program which helps race car designers can be modified to assist sports car designers. As an added bonus, while modifying that code to suit his or her special needs, a crooked programmer with sufficient time and skill can make it appear as if the programmer wrote the program without ever possessing the stolen source code.

Object code cannot be easily modified. Thus, unauthorized copying of object code can often be detected because the 0's and 1's in the original and copy of the stolen software will match.

Why not just translate stolen object code into source code? While compilers can readily translate source code into object code, it is very difficult, and sometimes impossible, to *disassemble* (translate) object code back into usable source code.

1.15–b   Software piracy

Application programs are kept on a hard disk or on floppy disks. Users generally buy application programs on floppy disks and copy them onto their hard disk. Many software companies now offer programs on CD-ROMs.

As you can see when operating a computer, there is no limit to how many copies you can make from a single floppy disk. The practice of making copies of a program and using or distributing those copies without permission is called *software piracy*.

1.15–c   Organization of programs under DOS

In order to use application programs, users must have some way of organizing them on the floppy disk or hard disk so that they can retrieve them when needed. Operating systems such as DOS store programs, and data generated by those programs, in *files*. You can name those files using almost any combination of eight letters and numbers, followed by a "." and three more characters. (Some operating systems do not have this eight-character limit.)

The DOS file system is similar to a filing cabinet. DOS stores your files in *directories*, which can be thought of as the drawers of the cabinet. Each directory may include *subdirectories*, which are similar to the individual file folders kept within each drawer. The user creates those directories and subdirectories, and each user creates his or her own system for managing files.

Although the "file cabinet" analogy is helpful, it is not exact. DOS organizes directories and subdirectories in an upside-down tree-like configuration. There is one *root directory* for each *logical drive*. (A *logical drive* is typically a single hard disk, although, as discussed below, users may divide a single hard disk into multiple logical drives.)

The root directory is the "file cabinet" containing all the other directories and subdirectories. The user will normally create other directories "underneath" the root directory containing other applications programs, which, if displayed graphically, would look like an upside down tree, with directories spreading from the root directory.

The root directory usually includes some of the files containing software needed to run the computer. It is normally the *C:* directory, which is the directory reserved for the first (and usually only) hard disk. (Many computers have two floppy disk drives, labelled *A:* and *B:*—computers with only one floppy drive use the A: label for that drive.)

When you start up your computer (called *booting* the computer), the first thing you usually see on your monitor after the computer finishes its initial setup activity is "C:". This is called *the prompt* (also called *the C prompt*). (DOS users can modify the C prompt to look different; the letter C will usually remain in the prompt. The most common prompt is "C:\>".)

Other operating systems substitute pictures or other representations in place of the prompt to make the computer easier to use. These systems are called *"GUIs,"* (pronounced "gooeys") for *graphical user interface*. The most popular GUI program is Microsoft's *Windows*. (Apple Computer popularized the use of GUIs, and computer users still argue over whether Microsoft's Windows is a worthy contender to Apple's operating system.)

The C prompt in DOS tells you that the system is working and that you are in a directory of your first (and usually only) hard disk. (Many IBM compatibles with larger hard disks actually divide, or *partition* their hard disk into two or more logical drives: C, D, etc. Do not be surprised if you find such an arrangement.)

The computer now awaits a command. The most common command tells the computer to *run*, or execute, a file, which means that the computer begins reading and executing instructions from the program in that file. The user will usually run an application program.

Although this tutorial is too short to include instructions on how to operate a computer, you should at least be aware of one DOS command at the outset: *format*.

As discussed above, data stored on hard disks and floppy diskettes is permanent unless accidentally damaged or deliberately removed. You may erase information in a file by commanding the computer to *erase* or *delete* that file. You may erase all of the information on a hard disk or floppy diskette by commanding the computer to *format* that disk. That command erases the directory structure of all files on the disk and prepares the disk for new data.

Knowing the format command is important because a suspect caught at a computer can immediately erase incriminating information by inputting the format command (e.g, "format c:"). Thus, securing the area around the computer to be searched or seized is essential.

1.16   Big computers: from minicomputers to supercomputers

Large companies cannot perform all of their tasks on PCs. Instead, they use computers with more power and storage capacity, ranging from minicomputers (typically about the size of a steamer trunk), mainframe computers (larger; some occupy a room; others are the size of a refrigerator), to supercomputers (about the same size as mainframes, and even more expensive). As technology improves, these computers keep shrinking, so it can be difficult to estimate the capacity of a computer by its size. Many minicomputers are the same size as personal computers.

The good news is that as computing power increases, many large (meaning more powerful) computers will look and act similar to PCs. The bad news is that this day has not quite arrived, and dealing with crimes against larger computers is difficult. However, there is one consolation: you will never have to actually operate a computer larger than a PC because you will not be competent to do so. You will need a computer expert to perform the work under your supervision.

Therefore, we spare just a few words to explain those features of larger computers which you will encounter in your search for evidence of invasion or theft. We ignore supercomputers because they are rare outside government installations and certain universities.

The first difference between PCs and large computers is where they are housed. PCs are generally used in a typical office environment, while mainframe computers are usually housed in special environments called *computer centers, data centers*, or *the glass house.*

Larger computers and their peripherals tend to be vulnerable to impure air (smoke in particular) and heat. Thus, computer centers are well air-conditioned, and precautions are taken to keep airborne dust and other particles away from the computer. Indeed, the threat of fire requires special protective measures.

One such measure used in many computer centers is *halon gas*, which is released when sensors detect a fire. Some centers allow employees to release the gas if a fire is detected, giving you just one more thing to worry about when executing a search warrant.

The largest computers also require a large and uninterruptible power supply, and a sizable array of cables. Thus, many computer centers have raised floors with removable panels under which cables and other electrical equipment are housed. Consider looking under these panels when searching a computer center.

Large computers use certain memory storage devices which are not used with PCs. Large computers often use *reels* of *magnetic tape*, as well as *tape cartridges*, to store information. The reels are about a foot in diameter and are kept in a plastic *hub* for ease in handling. The cartridges are about four by six inches, are self-contained, and are typically stored in high-density free-standing racks.

While floppy disks are inserted into a disk drive, reels are *mounted* on *tape drives*. Each tape has several feet of *leader* which does not store information and can be touched without destroying data. Cartridges are mounted in tape changers. Like hard disks and floppy diskettes, the memory in tapes and cartridges is permanent unless destroyed or erased.

Large computers also use large hard disks called *disk packs,* which can store very large quantities of information. Think of a disk pack as a stack of about a dozen extra large phonograph records encased in plastic. Again, this memory is permanent, but more fragile than the floppy and hard disks on PCs. These packs are bulky but portable. Their drives are typically boxes the size of a small washing machine; the packs are mounted on an opening at the top, much like a record placed on a turntable.

Finally, while you would use a keyboard to communicate with your PC, large computers are operated at a *console* by a specially trained employee called an *operator*. These consoles feature a keyboard, a monitor, and a printer. The monitor and printer provide the operator with a record of the computer's status and operation.

1.20   Networks

Companies cannot afford to give every employee a mainframe or minicomputer, and making every employee stand in line to use one is inefficient. Providing each employee with his or her own independent PC is also ineffective because many engineers need greater computing power; many financial managers need to share a common pool of information. The solution is to connect tens, hundreds, or even thousands of computers together into a *network*. With the network, each user is connected with other users and can share information and computing power.

Networks come in all shapes and sizes. One method is to provide employees with *dumb terminals* which all *access* (communicate with) the company mainframe. Dumb terminals consist of a monitor and keyboard without a CPU; the user uses the monitor and keyboard to communicate with the mainframe.

Some dumb terminals feature disk drives allowing the user to upload to, and download from, the mainframe. This extra feature allows an employee, among other things, to steal information from the mainframe by using any terminal located within the company.

Many companies do not use dumb terminals. Instead, they simply provide each employee with his own PC, which is connected to the network along with the mainframe or minicomputer. (Many of these computers are more like minicomputers than PCs—an example is the engineering *workstation*). Again, this provides the thief with numerous opportunities to steal information from the mainframe.

Many companies attach their computers to telephone lines, allowing *remote access* by an authorized employee working at home. As discussed in Chapter 4, remote access also allows an intruder to access the system by telephone.

Some networks are international. The Internet system, for example, connects thousands of universities, government agencies, and businesses across the United States. Other networks are local, meaning that they reside within a particular company or division of a company. Such networks are called *local area networks*, or *LANs*.

Some of these networks are nationwide, connecting branches of the same company in different states. A network spanning more than one location, say across town or between cities, is called a *wide area network*, or *WAN*.

Networks allow all employees to share computer power, share information, and send *electronic mail* (*E-mail*). Networks within a company can be connected to larger networks (such as the Internet).

Many LANs are composed entirely of PCs. One or more PCs are usually designated to contain files used by all of the participants in the network, and are called *file servers*. A file server is generally a more powerful PC with a larger hard disk. When searching a network, you will concentrate on the file servers.

1.30   Some of the major players and their products

You will have difficulty investigating high-technology crime, much less avoiding embarrassment, unless you know some basic facts about the high-technology industry. The following is a brief run-down on the major players, and their products, which define the industry.

The list is organized by product. Included is some information to accurately define what product has been stolen, and the significance of the theft. A brief acquaintance with the terms and concepts used in the industry will go a long way in establishing rapport with your victim and witnesses. You can refine your understanding of these terms by regularly reading several computer magazines, such as *PC Magazine* or *BYTE*.

1.31   Minicomputers and mainframes

IBM (International Business Machines, aka "Big Blue") is still the largest and most prestigious computer maker in the world. IBM is the biggest player in the mainframe market and is also well known for its minicomputers.

DEC (Digital Equipment Corporation) makes the VAX family of computers, noted for their ability to connect with computers made by many other manufacturers.

Amdahl is an important player in the mainframe market.

1.32   Personal computers

Again, IBM is an important player, but no longer the dominant force that it once was.

The industry is fragmented into hundreds of companies that make *IBM compatibles*, which run the software available for IBM's machines. Some of the larger companies in this arena are Compaq,

Hewlett-Packard (H-P), Digital, Dell, Gateway 2000, Acer, Zeos, Zenith, and Packard-Bell.

Apple Computer makes the Macintosh and Power PC line of computers. The Macintosh line is famous for its ease of use and graphics capabilities. The PowerPC line is discussed below.

1.33   Different classes of personal computers

Personal computers are generally classified by the strength of their microprocessors. That strength is commonly measured by the number of bits the chip processes simultaneously (8, 16, 32, or 64 bit presently) and the speed at which the chip operates (*clock speed*).

The first personal computers widely used in business were called just that: personal computers (PCs). They were built around a microprocessor manufactured by Intel Corporation called the Intel 8088 microprocessor. Such machines were also called "8088 computers." These chips processed 8 bits at a time and ran at 4.77 MHz.

IBM then introduced a model called the PC/XT (the "XT"), also built around an 8088 chip. Similar computers used a faster Intel chip, called the 8086.

Later came the PC/AT computer (the "AT"). AT-class computers were built around the Intel 80286 microprocessor. The 80286 was much faster than either the 8088 or 8086. AT computers were also different from PC or XT computers because the buses in the computer could carry more data simultaneously. The AT computer had a 16-bit bus, rather than an 8-bit bus (think of a 16-lane freeway versus an 8-lane freeway). This allowed for better performance. The 80286 allowed the AT to utilize more memory.

The next step was Intel's introduction of the 80386 microprocessor. Computers equipped with the 80386 were called "386's." Intel offered the 386 in speeds ranging from 16 to 33 MHz. Advanced Micro Devices (AMD), an Intel competitor, introduced a 40MHz model.

Some computers used the 80386SX chip instead of the 80386. The 80386SX was a less expensive chip, but did not perform quite as impressively as the 80386.

The 80386 chip was better than the 80286 because the 386 had a 32-bit bus, and additional modes of operation allowed much better utilization of large amounts of RAM. This generally meant that computers using the 80386 could run more sophisticated software than those using the 80286 chip.

Intel later introduced the 80486 ("486"), which is expected to remain the standard "entry-level" microprocessor until 1996. For our purposes, the 80486 is much the same as the 80386, but faster.

Finally, Intel introduced the Pentium (they decided not to call it the 80586 because of the risk that they could not prevent others from using the same name). The Pentium has a 64-bit bus and is about 80% faster than the 80486. Other companies, such as Advanced Micro Devices and NexGen, manufacture chips designed to emulate the 80486 and the Pentium.

Just when you thought you had the hang of it, along comes Apple Computer with a different classification. Apple's machines do not use Intel microprocessors. Rather, they incorporate microprocessors made by IBM and Motorola Corporation. Moreover, the machines are not known by the Motorola chip numbers.

Apple has introduced many versions of its Macintosh, each built around one of the Motorola 68000 series of microprocessors (the 68000, 68010, 68020, 68030, and 68040). Its latest line is built around the PowerPC, which is a chip developed by IBM, Motorola, and Apple. The PowerPC is intended to challenge Intel's dominance in integrated circuits.

The computer industry has also devoted considerable attention to creating portable computers (also called *laptops*). While most desktop computers weigh anywhere from 20 to 60 pounds, computer companies are now making lightweight "notebook" and "laptop" computers weighing from 3 to 6 pounds.

1.34 Components

1.34–a Microprocessors

As you might have guessed, the main name for chips is Intel, which created the 8086, 80286, 80386, 80486, and the Pentium.

1.34–b   Memory chips

Virtually all memory chips are made in Japan and Korea. Major foreign manufacturers include: Hitachi, Matsushita, Mitsubishi, Toshiba, Panasonic, Sanyo, Samsung (Korea), and Siemens (West Germany). American producers include Texas Instruments, Micron, Cypress Semiconductor, and IBM (mostly for its own use). As discussed in Chapter 3, these chips are commodities and, along with the latest microprocessors, are the most commonly stolen computer component in the world.

1.34–c   Specialized chips

Many American and foreign producers make chips for specific applications (computer modules in automobile engines, appliances, etc.), and there is not enough space here to list them all. Among the scores of companies are AMD, Harris, and National Semiconductor. Intel and Motorola are also active in this field.

1.34–d   Disk drives

Many different vendors make hard disk drives. Some of the most prominent are Seagate, Maxtor, Western Digital, Conner, and Quantum. Sony and Teac specialize in producing floppy disk drives.

1.34–e   Keyboards

Most computer makers manufacture their own, or they buy from tiny companies. Some prominent names include Lexmark, Keytronics, and Northgate.

1.34–f   Mice

As discussed above, a mouse is an input device. Leading "mice" manufacturers include Microsoft (the largest software company in the world) and Logitech. Some manufacturers have developed alternatives to mice, including a *trackball*, which looks like a small pool ball sunk halfway into a keyboard.

1.34–g   Monitors

Some of the largest monitor manufacturers are: NEC, Sony, Nanao, MAG, Samsung, and Panasonic. While on the subject of monitors, we pause for a word about *graphics standards*. Unlike commercially available color televisions, computers are capable of displaying video images in a variety of resolutions.

The industry has agreed on a number of standards which will be used by software written for IBM-compatible computers. Although you need not memorize these, be aware of the following standards, listed in ascending order of desirability: monochrome, Hercules, CGA, EGA, VGA, and SVGA.

VGA and SVGA display images in color, with SVGA offering the greatest resolution. In order to display graphics images, the user must buy (either included with the computer, or separately) a *graphics card*. Leading card manufacturers include ATI, Diamond, Number Nine, Matrox, and Orchid.

1.34–h   Printers

The highest performance printers are *laser printers*. These use laser technology to produce a typewritten page. Hewlett-Packard leads the field in laser printers, followed by Epson, Lexmark, Brother, and Okidata. Other types of printers include dot matrix (about to disappear), daisy-wheel (obsolete), and ink-jet (a printer offering laser printer quality for a rock-bottom price).

1.34–i   Modems

Modems communicate with other computers. The leaders in modems include U.S. Robotics, Supra, and Hayes, which pioneered the field (thus the phrase *"Hayes compatible"*). At least a dozen other companies make modems, all of which conform to the standard used by Hayes. Modems are classified by how many bits per second they can send and receive. This number, also properly referred to as *BPS*, and occasionally as the *baud rate*, is usually 2400, 4800, 9600, 14400 (14.4K), or 28800 (28.8K).

1.35 Software

1.35–a Operating systems

Although DOS is still the most popular operating system for IBM compatibles, Microsoft's Windows is the standard for the majority of serious computer users. Microsoft's newest version of Windows, Windows '95, was released in 1995.

DOS will probably lose its dominant role in 1996. In addition to using a graphical user interface which makes Windows easier to understand than DOS, Windows allows users to *multitask* (i.e., to run more than one program at a time). The popularity of Windows has made Microsoft the dominant software company in the world.

Different flavors of DOS exist, such as Microsoft's MS-DOS, IBM's PC-DOS, and Novell's DR-DOS, but they are virtually indistinguishable and are referred to collectively as DOS. At this writing, the most recent version of MS-DOS is version 6.22. Some older machines are running MS-DOS 5.0.

IBM champions an operating system called OS/2, which is similar to Microsoft's Windows. IBM recently released a version of OS/2 called "Warp," which constitutes the first serious challenge to Microsoft's Windows.

Apple Computer uses its own "System" operating system in its computers. These operating systems are updated often. (At this writing, the most current system is System 7.5.)

Minicomputers and mainframes use different operating systems. Digital Equipment Corporation's (DEC) computers (the VAX line of computers) use Digital's proprietary VMS system. The most popular operating system for minicomputers and workstations is UNIX, which also comes in several flavors (e.g., AT&T UNIX, Berkeley UNIX, IBM's "AIX," SCO's UNIX, Sun Microsystems' Solaris). Mainframes use various operating systems which are unique to their manufacturers.

1.35–b Application programs

Utilities are programs designed to make it easier to use your computer. You will use certain utilities, such as Norton Utilities, to view files residing on a computer which you have seized. You will also use certain programs to "backup" data from such a computer.

Computer assisted design, computer assisted manufacturing (CAD/CAM) programs such as AutoCAD allow engineers and other users to create and manipulate complex drawings on the screen and are used to design a wide range of products.

Word processing programs allow you to create documents. The leading players are WordPerfect Corporation's Word Perfect, Microsoft's Word, and Lotus Corporation's Word Pro.

Graphics programs are part of the "desktop publishing" segment of the industry. Desktop publishing allows you to create newsletters, charts, posters, and even slide shows and transparencies. Among the many products in this field, you may run across Adobe Systems' Pagemaker, Quark's QuarkXpress, Software Publishing's Harvard Graphics, Adobe's Illustrator, and Microsoft's PowerPoint.

Database programs store information. Leading products include Borland Corporation's DBASE IV, Microsoft's Access, Borland Corporation's Paradox, and Claris's Filemaker Pro.

Spreadsheet programs allow you to manipulate numbers (such as financial information). The leading programs include Lotus Corporation's Lotus 1-2-3, Microsoft's Excel, and Borland's Quattro Pro.

Communication programs allow you to use your computer to communicate with other computers. Leading programs include Procomm Plus and DCA's Crosstalk.

1.40   Quantities and measures

1.41   Size

Engineers like to throw numbers around. Some of those numbers are useful to know because they describe quantities or classes of components.

Hard disks are referred to by their storage capacity. A *megabyte* (*MB*) is 1,048,576 bytes (often rounded off to one million bytes). A *gigabyte* is 1024 megabytes (often rounded off to one thousand megabytes). Common hard disk sizes are 540 MB and one to two megabytes.

Floppy diskettes are referred to by their physical dimension and storage capacity. Diskettes for personal computers are sold (with minor exceptions you do not care about) in two physical sizes: 3 1/2 inches and 5 1/4 inches. These figures refer to the diameter of the floppy disk. Both sizes are commonly used in IBM-compatibles. The 5 1/4-inch disks are somewhat flexible; 3 1/2-inch disks are smaller and rigid. Floppy diskette drives are built to accept either 5 1/4-inch or 3 1/2-inch disks, but not both. The 5 1/4-inch disk is virtually obsolete.

The 3 1/2-inch disk used to come in two capacities: double density (720K) and high density (1.44 MB). Now the 1.44 MB size is standard. Note that the high-density disks are labeled as 2 MB. The reason for the discrepancy is that while the disk can theoretically store 2 MB, DOS formats it in such a way as to only accept 1.44 MB (this increases its reliability).

1.42 Time

Marking time in the computer industry has spawned a new vocabulary:

* Millisecond: one thousandth of a second.

* Microsecond: one millionth of a second.

* Nanosecond: one billionth of a second.

Engineers also refer to megahertz (MHz), usually when talking about the clock speed of a chip. (Note that this gauge is becoming less meaningful because of changes in chip design.)

MHz is the unit of measurement used for the speed of the chip. The same microprocessor can be designed to run at different MHz within the limit of the chip. Thus, manufacturers are selling 486 chips running at speeds of 25MHz, 33MHz, 50MHz, 66MHz, and, as of this writing, 100 MHz. Pentium chips are selling in 60 MHz, 90 MHz, 120, 133 MHz, and 150 MHz (announced) versions.

The higher the MHz, the higher the price for the microprocessor. Trade secrets relating to higher MHz microprocessors may have value; the converse may be true for lower MHz.

Bibliography

In addition to his own experience, the author relied on the books, studies, and articles listed below and on unpublished materials distributed at various high-technology crime seminars.

Arkin, Stanley S., et al., *Prevention and Prosecution of Computer and High Technology Crime* (New York: Matthew Bender, 1988).

Cheswick, William R., and Bellovin, Steven M., *Firewalls and Internet Security: Repelling the Wily Hacker* (Reading, Massachusetts: Addison-Wesley, 1994)

Coleman, Jerry P., *Free Computers for DA's: Hitting the "Hackers" Where it Hurts*, Prosecutor's Brief (Summer 1989).

Cook, William J., *Federal Guidelines for Prosecuting Thefts of Trade Secrets* (Chicago: United States Attorney's Office, Northern District of Illinois, 1991).

Cook, William J., *Federal Law and the Interstate Transfer of Stolen Computer Data: Riggs and Brown*, The Computer Law and Security Report (March/April 1992).

Cook, William J., *Paying the Bill for Hostile Technology: PBX Fraud in 1991*, (Chicago: United States Attorney's Office, Northern District of Illinois, 1991).

Cook, William J., *The Benefits of Involving Law Enforcement in Trade Secret Theft Cases*, Licensing Law and Business Report (January/February 1992).

Department of Justice, *Basic Considerations in Investigating and Proving Computer-Related Federal Crimes* (Washington, D.C., 1988).

Department of Justice, *Expert Witness Manual* (Washington, D.C., 1980).

Department of Justice, General Litigation Section, *Federal Guidelines for Searching and Seizing Computers* (Washington, D.C., 1994).

Fiatal, Robert A., *The Electronic Communications Privacy Act: Addressing Today's Technology*, The Prosecutor (Summer 1988).

Fishman, Clifford S., *Wiretapping and Eavesdropping* (New York: Clark Boardman Callaghan, 1994).

Hayes, Dennis, *Behind the Silicon Curtain: The Seductions of Work in a Lonely Era* (Boston: South End Press, 1989).

Lederman, Eli, *Criminal Liability for Breach of Confidential Commercial Information*, 38 Emory Law Journal 921 (1989).

Milgrim, Roger M., *Milgrim on Trade Secrets* (New York: Matthew Bender, 1995) (Volume 12B of "Business Organizations" by the same publisher).

Mock, Lois, and Rosenblum, Dennis, *A Study of Trade Secret Theft in High Technology Industries*, prepared for the National Institute of Justice (Washington, D.C.: Department of Justice, 1988).

Parker, Donn, et al., *Computer Crime: Criminal Justice Resource Manual*, 2d ed. (Washington, D.C.: Department of Justice, 1989).

Pooley, James H.A., *The Executive's Guide to Protecting Proprietary Business Information and Trade Secrets* (Chicago: Probus, 1987).

Rosenblatt, Kenneth S., *Tips on Investigating and Prosecuting Thefts of Trade Secrets*, Prosecutor's Brief (Summer 1989).

Rosenblatt, Kenneth S., *Deterring Computer Crime*, Technology Review (February/March 1990).

Rosenblatt, Kenneth S., *Criminal Law and the Information Age: Protecting Trade Secrets from Disclosure in Criminal Cases*, The Computer Lawyer (January 1991).

Sauls, John Gales, *Computer Searches and Seizures: Challenges for Investigators*, FBI Law Enforcement Bulletin (June 1993).

Sterling, Bruce, *The Hacker Crackdown* (New York: Bantam, 1992).

Stoll, Clifford, *The Cuckoo's Egg: Tracking a Spy Through the Maze of Computer Espionage* (New York: Doubleday, 1989).

Vance, John R., *Almost Everything You Wanted to Know About Cellular and Cordless Telephones, Tone, Voice and Digital Pagers and Pen Registers*, Prosecutor's Brief (November, 1992).

Table of Cases

Index